TILL MY TALE IS TOLD

TILL MY TALE IS TOLD

WOMEN'S MEMOIRS OF THE GULAG

EDITED BY
SIMEON VILENSKY

TRANSLATED BY
JOHN CROWFOOT, MARJORIE FARQUHARSON,
CATRIONA KELLY, SALLY LAIRD,
AND CATHY PORTER

ENGLISH EDITION PREPARED BY
SIMEON VILENSKY, JOHN CROWFOOT, AND
ZAYARA VESYOLAYA

A *Virago* Book

Published by Virago press 1999

Copyright © Indiana University Press 1999

Abridged from <u>Dodnes' tiagoteet:Zapiski vashei sovremennitsy</u>, compiled by
Simeon Vilensky (Moscow: Sovetskii pisatel', 1989)
© Sovetskii pisatel' 1989

A CIP catalogue record for this book is available from the British Library

ISBN 1 86049 509 5

Printed and bound in Great Britain by
Clays Ltd, St Ives plc

Virago Press
A Division of
Little, Brown and Company (UK)
Brettenham House
Lancaster Place
London WC2E 7EN

I write in the name of the living,

That they, in turn, may not stand

In a silent, submissive crowd

By the dark gates of some camp.

—Yelena Vladimirova, "Kolyma"

People today will tell me:

all that was over and done with long ago,

so there is little point in recalling it.

I know very well that the tale of these events

has indeed been long buried and forgotten.

Yet why, then, do they sometimes still rise

so vividly before our eyes?

Is it not because there was

something else in this tragic past,

apart from the tale,

that lies far from forgotten but,

to this day, continues to loom over our lives?

—Mikhail Saltykov-Shchedrin, "Bygone Poshekhonie"

CONTENTS ━━━━━━━━━━━━

PREFACE ▬▬▬▬▬▬▬▬▬▬
TO THE RUSSIAN EDITION

The women whose memoirs are included in this book (with the exception of Veronica Znamenskaya) were imprisoned, sent to labor camps, or exiled sometime during the Soviet era. After the Twentieth Congress of the Communist Party in 1956, they were declared innocent of the crimes for which they had been sentenced and were rehabilitated. Almost all of the selections, most of which are excerpts from longer memoirs, had not been published previously. The manuscripts were given to me with the consent of their authors, or, in the case of posthumous publication, with the consent of those to whom the authors had entrusted them. I myself was among such custodians.

A word of explanation is necessary with regard to the writings published here posthumously. Uncertain how long they would live, the authors often gave their unfinished manuscripts to friends or relatives for safekeeping. Later, some of the authors expanded and edited their texts, and the revised manuscripts were also handed on, either to their previous custodians or to new keepers. Some were retyped, either in part or in full. Except during the brief Thaw under Khrushchev, works that depicted aspects of life that would not pass the censorship were officially classified by the punitive organs as "slandering the Soviet system," with drastic consequences for those found in possession of them. In such situations the proscribed works suffered various fates. Some of them came to exist in many variants in almost folkloric fashion. For this reason there may well be discrepancies between the texts published here and those in the possession of others.

Almost all of the authors of the memoirs included in this book were arrested in the 1930s. They write about themselves, but they have much more to say about the fates of their comrades in the prisons and the camps. And it is this compassion, in resistance to a heartless and dehumanizing system, that gives their writings an undeniable moral force.

"It seemed as if the monstrous Stalinist regime had given birth to a new type of human being," writes Vera Shulz in her memoirs, "a submissive, inert creature, mute and devoid of initiative. So it is important that our contemporaries hear the voices of the surviving representatives of another generation of women, born at the beginning of the century, who through the nightmare of false accusation, torture, humiliation, hunger, and unspeakable deprivation, bring to us the ideals of true humanity."

Unfortunately, it was impossible to publish the memoirs in their entirety: in a single book there would have been room for the full-length texts of only two or three unknown authors. But there are many such unknown authors, and one of my aims in planning this book was that publication of fragments from their larger texts would draw attention to their writings. In deciding which passages to include, I have been guided largely by my own experience of Stalin's prisons and camps. Each memoir is prefaced by a note about its author, usually written by a close friend who did not share this fate. Their reminiscences further expand the horizons of this book.

A quarter of a century ago I first attempted to publish an anthology that included writings by people who had been repressed. In 1963 a collection entitled *For the Sake of Life on Earth* was published by a press in Magadan. At the last minute, an order came to exclude works by authors who were "not officially resident in Kolyma," which meant, among others, those whose remains repose in the camp graveyards of that vast region. The editor of the volume, Nikolai Kozlov, then secretary of the Magadan branch of the Writers' Union, suffered a nervous breakdown. He was brought to Moscow to be treated for his "manic struggle for justice."

The authors represented here embrace almost the entire Gulag Archipelago. The works were written long ago, free of internal censorship and without any hope of prompt publication. From the unlocked cells of the socialist wing in Butyrki Prison, where Socialist Revolutionaries, Anarchists, and Mensheviks were held in 1922, through peasant victims of dekulakization, to Bolshevik Party activists, themselves despatched in the late 1930s to Kolyma where they perished—each has its own history and prehistory.

The memoirs describe the endless procession of those designated "enemies of the people" and "socially dangerous" elements by the Soviet regime and condemned to imprisonment, labor camps, and exile. Many of these memoirs were begun, and some were even completed, in secrecy, behind barbed wire. The price for them was life itself.

SIMEON VILENSKY
MOSCOW, 1989

PREFACE ━━━━━━━━━━━━━
TO THE ENGLISH EDITION

When this collection was published in Moscow in 1989, it was received as a revelation by a great many of its readers. At that time few in our country had read books that told the truth about Soviet totalitarianism and the Gulag.

As a former prisoner in a labor camp in Kolyma and also as the one responsible for the publication of this book, I can appreciate how much harder it must be for people raised in quite different political and social conditions to comprehend, let alone have a feeling for, the surrealistic reality of that period. In the West there is a much clearer conception of Nazi Germany's totalitarian system.

During the Second World War, Adolf Hitler established his "New Order" in the many European countries he occupied. In 1945 Allied soldiers liberated the surviving inmates of the Nazi concentration camps. After the war, at the Nuremberg Trials, German fascism and its ideology were condemned for "crimes against humanity." In the West many books have since been published presenting documentary evidence and investigations of this tragic twelve-year period in the history of the twentieth century.

The Soviet totalitarian regime existed for more than seventy years. It was neither overthrown nor formally brought to justice. Unlike the Nazis, not one of the Bolshevik leaders was ever tried and punished. Whereas the Nazi elite was expelled from German public life, the Soviet elite transformed its appearance and remained in power. Moreover, many sections of Russian society today are nostalgic for the Communist past.

Infused with a mixture of hatred and intolerance, Communism, in pursuit of its ends, managed to exploit everything that humanity holds dear, including the teachings of Christianity. For instance, the declaration in the so-called "Moral Code of the Builders of Communism" that "Each man is another's friend, comrade, and brother" is consonant with the Christian exhortation: "Love one's neighbor as one's self." In practice, however, Soviet people were encouraged to denounce one another to the authorities.

The number who regularly informed on their "comrades" and "brothers" remains a secret to this day, but there are grounds to believe that the total reached into the hundreds of thousands.

The Soviet state was a monopoly that controlled all aspects of production, research, science, and culture. People who worked for the state were paid minimal wages. This allowed the regime to allot vast resources to preparations for war and significant sums for free education. Yet tens of thousands of people with higher educations soon found themselves working at unskilled labor in the camps. Wielding spades and picks alongside students torn from their studies were the professors who had been lecturing to them not long before. Both students and professors were convicted on fabricated charges of "anti-state" activities. Indiscriminate and arbitrary arrests kept Soviet citizens in a state of constant fear and maintained a steady supply of slave laborers, half starved and deprived of all rights. Whenever the Gulag needed more hands, new arrests were carried out.

The picture that this book paints will not seem so extraordinary, however, if we remember the criminal mentality of the Bolshevik leaders and their underlings, including those who investigated political cases. Women who were arrested first had to pass through prisons where they were intimidated, deprived of sleep, and, in some cases, subjected to torture by their interrogators; then they were sent to the camps, where they were tormented and robbed by the criminal inmates.

Three years after Stalin's death, Khrushchev delivered his famous "secret" speech at the Twentieth Congress of the Communist Party, and the rehabilitation of those who had been wrongly convicted began. At the same time, however, documentary evidence of the crimes committed by the regime was being secretly destroyed. Relatives of the tens of thousands who had been shot were falsely informed that those euphemistically condemned to "ten years without right of correspondence" had died in the camps from a variety of diseases.

Thus, victims of the Bolshevik regime were rehabilitated by those who themselves fully deserved to be placed in the dock at a public trial like the ones held at Nuremberg. Over forty million wrecked lives can be laid at their door, and the evil they brought on Russia and the world is impossible to define. Yet, even in those dark years, no amount of camouflage could conceal the true nature of the Soviet totalitarian regime from the eyes of perceptive citizens of "the most progressive government in the world." According to a common anecdote of the time, in the year 2000 an encyclopedia would carry the following entry under the letter H: "Hitler, a petty tyrant of the Stalin period."

In that diabolical and phantasmagoric existence, where everything was treacherously unstable and where words themselves existed quite apart from their meanings, another reality suddenly began to shine through—a world of openness, kindness, and honor. These qualities, it turned out, had not passed out of existence after the Bolsheviks seized power but, rather, remained innate to certain individuals from different generations and different parts of society. Such people include the authors whose memoirs are gathered in this book.

Before bringing his people to the Promised Land, Moses led them through the wilderness for forty years, until a new generation of free men and women had grown to maturity. The peoples of the Soviet Union were imprisoned in their own land. They were not given forty years or a spiritually regenerating path through the wilderness. But not everything is so hopeless. And that is the message of our book.

SIMEON VILENSKY
MOSCOW, 1998

TILL MY TALE IS TOLD

OLGA ADAMOVA-SLIOZBERG

ONE

Olga Adamova-Sliozberg

My Journey

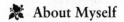 **About Myself**

I was born in 1902 in Samara on the Volga. My parents were highly skilled tailors, among the best in the city; they made clothes for the governor's wife and the local gentry. So we were quite well off, and I was sent to a private school.

I attended the gymnasium set up and financed by Nina Khardina. Her father, the barrister Khardin, had gone down in history as the man for whom Lenin worked as an assistant during his years of exile in Samara. Lenin was a frequent visitor at Khardin's house and was on friendly terms with his daughter Nina. When Nina's father died, she received a considerable inheritance, which she used to build and run a gymnasium for girls.

After the 1917 Revolution, I went to Moscow to study at the university. In 1928 I married a senior lecturer at Moscow University, Judel Zakheim. He was an exceptionally able and erudite biologist who taught the history of natural science. Just recently, in 1987, someone gave me a snapshot of him, taken with a group of students in 1934. On it was an inscription, faded now after half a century: "Our beloved teacher." He was remembered long afterward by all his students.

I was blessed with a wonderful family, a husband I loved dearly, two children ages four and six, and work that I found interesting. All this was shattered by our arrest in 1936 on a completely incomprehensible charge. In 1956 we were rehabilitated "for lack of corpus delicti"—posthumously, alas, in the case of my husband.

I am now eighty-six years old. Thanks to the determination of my parents and my brother and sisters, my children were not handed over, like so many, to children's homes, but grew up healthy and were properly educated. I have a loving family and spend my days surrounded by my children, grandchildren, and great grandchildren, sixteen in all; thanks to them, I never lack for anything. Yet it grieves me still that what should have been the best years of my life were spent in prison and camps, and that my husband perished at the age of thirty-seven.

Sometimes I wonder what, after all, the most significant thing in my life has been. Before my arrest, I led a very ordinary life, typical of a professional Soviet woman who didn't belong to the Party. I worked hard but took no particular part in politics or public affairs. My real interests lay with home and family.

Then suddenly my life was torn apart, and with my arrest came a passionate desire to fight against the injustice that had destroyed everything dear to me. I decided that I had to survive, so that I could share with others all that I had learned behind the barbed wire.

Hence these memoirs, begun all those years ago in 1946, several times buried in bottles underground, then dug up again and continued during the long "period of stagnation" under Brezhnev, when there seemed no hope at all that they would ever be published.

Now that the truth is known about the "enemies of the people," there is growing public sympathy and interest in our fate, and I am glad that I too have played a part in uncovering this chapter of our history.

Writing these notes is the best thing I have done in my life.

1988

OLGA ADAMOVA-SLIOZBERG DIED IN 1992. —SV

A Chip of Wood

In 1935 I hired a nanny to take care of the children. She was a hardworking woman, scrupulously tidy, about thirty years old and deeply reserved.

Marusya and I lived side by side for a whole year. I was satisfied with her work, and she with her employment, but I knew absolutely nothing about her life.

One lunchtime a letter came for her. Marusya read it, and a change came over her face. She excused herself, saying that she had a very bad headache and had to lie down. Sensing that some misfortune had befallen her, I sent the children out for a walk and, alone with Marusya, tried to find out what had happened.

At first Marusya refused to answer and lay with her face to the wall, but then she sat up on the bed and shouted in a hoarse, bitter voice:

"You want to know what's happened to me?! All right, then, I'll tell you; only don't you be angry. You keep saying what a good life we have these days. Well, I used to have a husband no worse than yours, and three children, the best in the world. I built up our home by the sweat of my brow, tended the animals, worked day and night. My husband could turn his hand to anything—bootmaking, tailoring; we lived in plenty. We had a woman who worked for us, and what's wrong with that? It wasn't a crime! Look at you, you have hired help and so did I; I had an old woman stay in the house to help my mother while I was out there breaking my back in the fields.

"Then in 1930 I went to stay at my sister's in Moscow and that's when my whole family was arrested for being "kulaks"—"dekulakized" they call it; my husband was sent to the camps, Mother and the children to Siberia. Mother wrote to me saying get yourself a corner in Moscow somehow, maybe you can help us out, there's no work to be had here at all, it's such a worry, I'm stuck here in this earth dugout with the children.

"So ever since then I've been working in people's houses and sending Mother and the children everything I earn—and now look what they've written . . ."

She handed me the letter. It was from a neighbor: "There's been no news of your old man for three months now; we heard he was digging a canal. Your children were living with their granny; they kept getting sick, the dugout's damp and there wasn't much to eat, but they were managing. Your Mishka was friendly with my boy Lenka, he was a good lad. But then they all came down with the scarlet fever—mine were all sick with it, too—and they barely pulled through, but God's gathered all yours to Him. Your mother's beside herself, won't eat or sleep, just keeps moaning and groaning, I'm afraid she's not long for this world either."

"Is that what you call justice? They ruined us, drove us from our homes . . . And now all my poor little creatures are dead, my own flesh and blood . . ."

That evening I waited impatiently for my husband to get home. He was a senior lecturer at the university, a biologist; I thought he was the wisest and cleverest man in the world.

I felt as if a terrible weight were crushing my heart. The clear, happy, comprehensible world I knew had started to waver before my eyes. What had Marusya or her children done wrong? Could our entire life—so irreproachable, clean, hardworking—be founded on the suffering and blood of innocent people?

My husband came home, pleasantly excited as always after his lecture, content at the thought of a day's work done and a well-earned rest at home with his dear ones. The children rushed to scramble on top of him. There was nothing I loved better than to watch them squealing with joy as they mounted this attack on their father's broad back. But today, catching Marusya's black look, I called my husband into another room and in great agitation told him everything. He looked very sober.

"You know, you can't make a revolution wearing white gloves. The destruction of the kulaks has been a hard and bloody process, but it had to be done. Marusya's tragedy may look straightforward to you, but things aren't as simple as they seem. Why did her husband get sent to the camps? It's hard to believe he was totally innocent. People don't get sent to camp for nothing. I wonder if we shouldn't get rid of Marusya; there's always been something fishy about her . . . Well, I don't insist," he added, seeing my expression. "I don't insist; maybe she's a perfectly decent woman, maybe there was some mistake in this particular case. But if you chop down trees, you know, the chips are bound to fly."

That was the first time I had heard this phrase, so consoling to those who remained unscathed, so bitter to all those who fell under the axe.

My husband then spoke at length about the historical necessity of collectivizing of the villages, of restructuring rural life, and about the enormous things that had already been achieved before our very eyes, and the inevitable sacrifices that had to be made . . .

I believed him. For me, too, all the horrors of that time were taking place a thousand miles away. I was living in peace among my family; my world seemed unshakable. And anyway, I was used to believing my husband; he was so honest and wise.

So Marusya continued looking after my children and going about her household tasks; but now and then, peeling potatoes or darning a stocking, she would pause, motionless, and stare at the wall, and her hands would drop into her lap, and a worm of doubt would steal into my heart.

But I was quick to reassure myself: if you chop down trees, the chips are bound to fly . . .

My Journey to Calvary Begins

One ordinary Saturday I returned home from work full of thoughts about how I would spend Sunday, how delighted my little girl would be with the doll I'd brought her, what a thrill my son would get from seeing the elephant tomorrow at the zoo.

I always claimed that, unlike other mothers, I had no illusions about my children and saw all their faults. But it wasn't true. In my heart of hearts, I knew that mine were the cleverest, the most beautiful, the most charming children in the whole world.

I opened the door and was taken aback by the smell of boots and tobacco.

Marusya was sitting there telling the children a story in the midst of utter chaos. Heaps of books and manuscripts were scattered about the floor. Cupboards had been flung open, clothes hastily stuffed back; underwear protruded from half-open drawers. I had no idea what had happened, but my heart froze in a dreadful premonition of misfortune. Shielding the children, Marusya got up and said in a strange, quiet voice, "It's all right, keep calm!"

"Where's my husband? What's happened?"

"Don't you understand? They've taken him."

No, it was impossible; it couldn't happen to me, to him! Of course there had been rumors (just rumors—it was only the beginning of 1936) that something was going on, that there had been arrests . . . But surely all this applied to other people; it couldn't happen to us.

"He sat there all pale, said to give you his watch and to tell you everything would be sorted out and you shouldn't worry. He told the children he was going away on business."

"Of course it'll all be sorted out! You know what an honest person he is, Marusya, what a good man!"

Marusya smiled bitterly and looked at me.

"Oh, dear, you and your education! They never come back, the ones who end up there."

But I believed in the justice of our courts. My husband would come back, and this alien smell and topsy-turvy apartment would be no more than a dreadful memory.

After that a strange period began. The children knew nothing. I would play with them, and it seemed as if nothing had happened and that I'd simply had a bad dream. When I went out on some errand or walked to work, I would look at people as if through glass; an invisible barrier separated me from them. They were normal, and I was already somehow different. Friends and acquaintances spoke to me in a special tone of voice; they were clearly afraid of me. People would cross the road to avoid me. Others became especially attentive, but this was heroic on their part, and both they and I knew it.

One old man, a member of the Party since 1908, came to visit me one day and said, "Put your affairs in order; you may be arrested as well. And remember, answer their questions, but don't say anything you needn't; every unnecessary word will lead to endless further questions."

"But my husband's innocent! Why are you telling me all this—you, a Bolshevik! So you don't believe in justice either?"

He looked at me and said, "Remember what I've told you."

I felt it beneath my dignity to listen to his advice and tried to go on living as if nothing had happened.

It so happened that a conference of star workers from the brush and bristle industry was taking place at the time in Belorussia, and since I worked in this area of manufacture, I too attended. Indeed, strange though it seems, I was appointed conference secretary. When we gathered in Vitebsk from all over the Soviet Union, it proved to be the first time that those working in the industry had met since the Revolution. From the presentations at the conference we learned, among other things, that in Tashkent they had just invented a machine that had already been in use for ten years in Belorussia; that technology used to brilliant effect in Ust-Sysolsk in the Urals was still unheard of in Minsk.

I threw myself into the work and for the time being forgot that when I went back to Moscow, I would return to the same empty apartment, the same endless queues to hand in parcels at the prison . . .

I was arrested the day after I returned.

It seems absurd when I remember it now, but my first thought was: I've got all the materials from the conference, but they're all in draft form, and the whole lot will go to waste; no one else will be able to sort out my notes.

So while they carried out a four-hour search of the apartment, I busied myself putting all the conference papers in order. I was totally unable to grasp the fact that my life was over. I wrote and cut out and pasted and felt as I did so that nothing had happened; I would finish my work and hand it in, and my boss, the People's Commissar, would say, "Well done; you didn't lose your head, you realized it was all a misunderstanding!" I don't know myself what on earth I was thinking of; but whether from sheer force of habit or because I was too shocked to understand what was happening, I worked flat out for four hours, conscientiously and productively, for all the world as if I were sitting in my own office at the ministry.

At last, when the search was completed, the investigator in charge took pity on me.

"You'd better say goodbye to your children," he said.

Say goodbye to the children . . . Yes . . . I was leaving them. Perhaps for a long time . . .

No, it was impossible . . .

I went into the children's room. My son was sitting up in bed.

"I've got to go away on a business trip, darling; you stay here with Marusya and be a good boy."

His lips twisted in a pout.

"It's funny; Daddy went off on business, and now you're going. What happens if Marusya suddenly goes off too—who's going to look after us?"

I kissed his skinny little leg.

My little girl was snuffling sweetly, her nose buried in her pillow. I adjusted her blanket. She muttered something in her sleep.

For the first time in my life, I understood what it meant to stifle tears. I was choking, but to this day I remember with pride that I managed to hide my grief from my son.

We left the building, and the door closed behind us. We got into a car. And with that, my life, my ordinary human life, came to an end. Now and then, from force of habit, something would flash through my mind. There was something I'd left unfinished, something I had to put right. I'd meant to seal that window, there was a draft, and my son would catch cold. No, that wasn't it. Something important. Mother! I'd hidden from her the threat that hung over me, reassured her with invented news about my husband. Now she was going to find out.

I hadn't given her a hug when we last parted, and I'd kept postponing talking to her. I'd wanted somehow to prepare her. No, but that wasn't the main thing, either. I'd wanted to go and see Stalin, get a personal interview with him, explain that my husband was innocent. No, that wasn't it—there was something else I hadn't done, something else . . .

The Lubyanka

My cell in the Inner Prison at the Lubyanka was not unlike a room in a hotel. There was a polished parquet floor and a large window, now boarded up. Five beds were occupied; the sixth was free. A slop bucket stood in the corner. A small hatch and a peephole had been cut into the door.

I was brought in at night, when everyone else in the cell was asleep. I was shown my bed, but it seemed as unthinkable to lie down on it as to fall asleep on top of a hot stove. I longed to talk to my neighbors and learn what lay in store for me. I had not yet learned to wait and endure in silence. No one paid the slightest attention to me; they all turned their faces to the wall, away from the light burning on the ceiling, and continued sleeping. I sat on the bed, and the night dragged on, and I felt as if my heart would break in two . . .

There were only two hours to go till reveille, but I will never forget them.

At last, at six o'clock, there was a knock on the door: time to get up.

I jumped up, certain that I would be summoned today, that everything would be cleared up. I would prove that I and my husband were innocent; I could surely convince them . . .

The first law of prison life, which I was soon forced to learn, is that patience is everything. Once I had grasped this (the first two or three days I kept expecting to be summoned at any moment, but in fact it took five days), I began to look around me and get to know my neighbors. Zhenya Bykhovskaya immediately attracted my attention with her foreign dress, black with red trim.

"Now there's a genuine spy," I thought, seeing the foreign-looking sponge she washed with and the lacy underwear she wore. Zhenya had a nervous tic, which spoiled her appearance.

"So they've caught you," I thought. "I've no reason to despair; my case will be sorted out in due course, but your face gives you away immediately—you can't stop grimacing."

As I later found out, Zhenya had worked undercover in Fascist Germany and had left because of some serious illness; she kept having fainting fits, and it had become too dangerous to stay. Once she had lost consciousness in the street when she was carrying Party documents. She was rescued by a Communist doctor to whom she was taken quite by chance. She was brought back to the USSR in 1934 and arrested in 1936. One of the main reasons for her arrest was that she had too easily evaded the Gestapo, especially during the fainting episode. Obviously she must have had Gestapo connections.

I began to feel more at ease about my own case when I compared myself with the "real" criminals. Set beside them, I thought, I was so clearly innocent that a mere child, let alone the wise and experienced investigator who would deal with my case, would surely be able to see the difference.

My neighbor on my right, Alexandra Mikhailovna Rozhkova, was a sweet-looking woman of about thirty-five. She had already been sentenced to five years' imprisonment and had so far served three in the camps, but now she had been summoned for further investigation in a new case concerning her husband, a Trotskyist who had allegedly been involved in the murder of Sergei Kirov, the Leningrad Party boss, in December 1934.

Every morning Alexandra Mikhailovna carefully washed and dried her white collar and sewed it back on her blouse, expecting to be summoned at any moment for questioning.

She told me various stories about the camp, where she had been able to work as a doctor and so had lived not too badly, and in passing she mentioned her son, who was the same age as mine.

"What! You've a son out there? And you haven't seen him for three years?" And here she was fussing over her collar and asking me what was on in the Moscow theaters!

I was horrified. Stupidly and cruelly, I said, "You can't love your son as much as I do mine. I just couldn't survive without mine three whole years."

She looked at me coldly.

"You'll survive ten if need be. And you'll fuss about your food, and your clothes, and you'll fight for one of the bowls in the wash house and a cozy corner in the barracks. Just you remember: everyone suffers the same. Last night you were moaning away and tossing and turning so that none of us could sleep, and Sonya over there [Sonya's bed was opposite mine] had been up ten nights in a row with the interrogator; that was the first night she'd been allowed to rest. And you woke me up, too. I couldn't go to sleep again for thinking of my son—my son that I don't love, according to you, as much as you love yours. I had a terrible night."

She taught me a good lesson. I never again forgot that the agony is the same for everyone when your very flesh is torn apart.

Sonya, who according to Alexandra Mikhailovna had not slept for ten nights, was a twenty-seven-year-old brunette from Riga. Fate had taken her from Latvia to Berlin, where she had married a man named Olberg, a Trotskyist who also came from Riga. She divorced him in 1932 and came to Moscow with her new husband, a Soviet citizen.

When she was still in Berlin she and her then-husband Olberg had set up a "Russian circle" to teach Russian to German engineers who were planning to work in Moscow. Around one hundred people attended at one time or another. They were for the most part unemployed and pro-Soviet; many dreamt of Russia as the Promised Land. There may have been spies and terrorists among them, but Sonya was the last person to know about that. Nevertheless, she became the main witness in the affair. For three months now she had been summoned every night, interrogated until five in the morning, then given just one hour to rest; during the day she was not allowed to lie down.

Sonya struck me as a weak-willed woman without character. The interrogators quickly brought her around with simple bits of sophistry which seemed to her irrefutable. This is roughly how the interrogations would go:

"Was Olberg a Trotskyist?"

"Yes."

"Did he conduct discussions in his 'circle'?"

"Yes, to give the students practice speaking Russian."

"Being a Trotskyist, he could not help but discuss events from a Trotskyist perspective?"

"Yes."

"Are Trotskyists terrorists?"

"I don't know."

The interrogator would bang his fist on the table.

"So you defend Trotskyists, do you! You're a Trotskyist yourself! Do you know what I'm going to do with you? You'll be overjoyed when they finally shoot you! We're arresting your husband" (he meant her second husband, whom she adored). "I think you'd better remember that you were once a member of the Komsomol and cooperate with us. So, I repeat: Are Trotskyists terrorists?"

"Yes."

Then Sonya would be brought face to face with the various German defendants: she would be taken to the investigator's office, where some crazed-looking Karl or Friedrich would be sitting, utterly bewildered. He would plead with her: "Frau Olberg, please confirm that I went to your Russian circle only to learn the language!"

The investigator would ask, "Do you confirm that Karl [or whatever his name was] was a member of Olberg's circle?"

"Yes," Sonya would answer, and Karl would sign "Yes."

This brought the meeting to an end, whereupon Karl, reassured, would go to his cell, not realizing that he had just signed his own death sentence.

Sonya always returned tear-stained to our cell.

"That's the seventieth person I've given false testimony about, but there's nothing I could do."

Zhenya Goltsman was thirty-eight years old. She had joined the Party during the first days of the Revolution.

Her husband, the writer Ivan Filipchenko, had been brought up by Maria Ulyanova, Lenin's sister, and was thoroughly at home in Lenin's family. He shared their dislike of Stalin. This was the cause of endless quarrels and disputes between him and Zhenya, which sent Zhenya into despair; for if there were two men in the world she loved more than her own life, they were her husband, who had made a revolutionary of her and whom she regarded as the most upright Communist and the most talented writer, and Stalin, whom she simply worshiped.

After Filipchenko was arrested, Zhenya remained at liberty for a while and was merely summoned from time to time for questioning. But once she had been arrested she was interrogated daily. She would return somber-faced and not say anything to anyone. Once my cellmates were instructing me how to behave under interrogation; they told me it was better to say very little, otherwise you were liable to get confused and might be unable to extricate yourself, and they advised me to check that the interrogator had written down what I'd actually said, for otherwise I might find myself signing something completely different. Zhenya interrupted them sharply: "Remember, it's your duty as a Soviet citizen to help unmask the conspirators.

Sometimes things that seem insignificant can give the investigators a vital clue. You should tell them everything you know."

But one day Zhenya returned from the interrogation in tears, her face covered in red blotches, and demanded paper to write to Stalin. Unable to restrain herself any longer, she confided in me what had been happening to her. Zhenya, consistent with her advice to me, considered it her duty to the Party not to hide anything from the investigator. Consequently she had passed on everything Filipchenko had said about Stalin. The investigator seized on Zhenya's words, appealed to her Party conscience to tell him more, and, having wrung from her everything he wanted, proceeded to summarize her evidence in a final statement, from which it emerged that Filipchenko had planned to kill Stalin.

This final statement Zhenya refused to sign. Yes, Filipchenko believed that the country would begin to breathe again only when Stalin was dead, and had said he wished the country rid of him, but he certainly had no intention of committing a terrorist act.

Since Zhenya had signed all her previous statements about Filipchenko, the investigator switched tactics and started swearing at her and even beating her. Zhenya was deeply shaken and from then on spent her days writing letters to Stalin.

Of course Filipchenko was already doomed, irrespective of whether Zhenya signed the final statement or not, but she was tormented by the thought that he would be shown her testimony, and that he would die believing that she had betrayed him. So she insisted that she could not sign this last statement, even though she had willingly signed all the previous ones. At this point they started interrogating her at night, refusing to let her sleep during the day, and putting her in the punishment cells.

Then suddenly she was left in peace. A few days later, someone tapped through the wall that Filipchenko had been shot and had wanted his comrades to know that he had died a true Communist. Zhenya was devastated by the news. She was tortured above all by the fact that he had left her no farewell message—which meant that he knew she had testified against him.

The fifth inhabitant of the cell was Zina Stanitsyna, a girl of twenty-eight. Before her arrest, she had lived in Gorky and taught mathematics at one of the city's institutes.

I asked her what she had been charged with, and she replied that she had deserved to be arrested.

"What did you do?" I asked, astonished.

"I failed to see what one of our teachers was up to. He lived in Moscow and came to Gorky once a week to give a lecture on dialectical materialism.

He was very open with me and said lots of critical things about the current state of affairs, but I took this to be a sign of great intelligence on his part and concern about the Motherland. He used to spend the night in the student hostel, but he kept his things at my apartment and would entertain his friends there. I was surprised at how heavy his suitcases were. He said they were full of books, but after his arrest it turned out that he was a Trotskyist, and the suitcases had been full of Trotskyist literature. The friends that came to see him were fellow oppositionists. So I discovered that all this time my apartment had been a secret meeting place for members of the opposition."

I listened to Zina with respect. She was clearly a woman of principle, quite without self-pity. But I was horrified by the conclusion to her story.

"I decided to suffer the punishment I deserved and remove any stain from my conscience. I remembered that a certain professor (I don't recall his name) gave lectures to the mathematics teachers at our institute. Once, when he was proving a theorem, the electricity suddenly failed. There were no lamps or candles. I split my ruler and lit a splinter from it, as peasants do. The professor finished his lecture by the light of the splinter and at the end remarked, "Life has gotten better, life has gotten jollier (obviously he was poking fun at Stalin*), God be praised, we've reached the age of the splinter!""

"And you went and told all this to the investigator?"

"Of course!"

"But didn't you feel bad when the professor was arrested?"

"Later, when I was made to meet him face to face, I did feel a bit uncomfortable."

"Did he plead guilty?"

"At first he denied it, then he said he'd completely forgotten the incident and hadn't attached any significance to it at the time."

"But you've ruined someone's life for a complete trifle!"

"There are no trifles in politics. Like you, I failed to understand at first all the criminal significance of his remark, but later I realized."

Our conversation was interrupted by Alexandra Rozhkova. Wise from her experience in camp, she said, "Once you've cast suspicion on someone, there'll be no problem uncovering more serious failings later on. Show me a person, and I'll show you the law to fix him."

I had no desire to talk further to Zina, but a tiny crack had already appeared in my determination to help the investigators and be as open with them as possible.

---

* A reference to Stalin's famous remark in 1935, "Life has become better, life has become more joyous."

The Investigation

After everything I'd seen and heard, I was no longer quite so confident of my ability to prove that I and my husband were innocent. But I still considered myself quite different from my cellmates, all of whom had gotten involved in politics in one way or another.

I wasn't a Party member, and neither was my husband; his real passion in life was science. Maybe there had been some kind of plot, but why should I be answerable for it?

I would picture the investigator, a clever, subtle man like Porfiry in *Crime and Punishment*, and, putting myself in his position, felt sure that he would understand in an instant what kind of person he was dealing with.

At last I was summoned.

My investigator turned out to be a wretched little creature no older than twenty-five. A couple of fishing rods stood in the corner of his cramped little office; obviously he went fishing when he'd finished his night's work.

After the first interrogation, he wrote, "I admit that my husband was a Trotskyist and that we held Trotskyist gatherings."

I wrote, "No."

So we sat through the entire night. In a bored voice, the investigator would say "Think it over; confess." Then he'd look at his watch, and after ten minutes he'd ask the question again and repeat, "Think it over"—and again look at his watch.

While I was thinking he would stand up and walk around the office, and occasionally going up to the fishing rods to make some adjustment.

Three hours went by in this fashion. Then he started asking other questions: "What have you heard about the death of Alliluyeva?* What did she die of?"

I replied calmly and confidently that she had died of appendicitis; I'd read about it in *Pravda*.

The investigator banged the table with his fist. "You're lying! You heard something completely different! I've got witnesses!"

Suddenly I remembered with horror that a couple of months ago I'd been invited to the home of an Old Bolshevik named Tronin, a man I respected enormously. One of the guests, Rozovsky, had related how Alliluyeva had shot herself after Stalin had crudely shut her up in front of guests when she had tried to speak up for Bukharin. This Rozovsky had been arrested before I had, we assumed for embezzlement or some such thing. Under interrogation, he might well have repeated what he'd said about Alliluyeva in my presence.

---

* Stalin's wife, Nadezhda Alliluyeva, shot herself 9 November 1932.

I was overcome with fear. Tronin and his family would be arrested for spreading anti-Soviet rumors. "Show me a person, and I'll show you the law to fix him."

"I read in *Pravda* that she died of appendicitis," I repeated. But I was shaking with fear, for it was true that Rozovsky had talked of Alliluyeva's suicide.

Finally the investigator said, "Think it over in your cell. Remember, your only chance to see your children again is to come clean. Obstinate denials will only get you classified as a hardened political enemy."

I returned to my cell at half past five in the morning. Judging from what I told them, Alexandra Rozhkova and Sonya said I would most likely be classified a petty criminal and given three to five years. Zhenya thought I'd be released. While they argued about it, I understood for the first time that I might actually be convicted and lose my children.

Two weeks later, I was summoned again. Everything was the same as before, right down to the investigator fiddling with his fishing rods, and the whole thing got on my nerves. But there was no discussion of Rozovsky, and I realized that Rozovsky had said nothing about me.

After another two months I was summoned a third time, and the investigator showed me a deposition in my husband's handwriting, in which, in answer to the question, Are you a Trotskyist? he had replied, "Yes."

"That's impossible!" I cried. "It's not true!"

"Of course it's true, but he certainly made us suffer while we wrung it out of him!"

At this my interrogator gave a crooked smile, and it dawned on me that my husband must have been tortured to have signed such a thing. I shuddered, but at the same time felt proud for him that he had said nothing about me, no matter what agonies they'd put him through.

Once more I was made to sit there six hours. This time the interrogator shouted, called me a political prostitute, assured me that I'd never see my children again and that they'd be put in a children's home. This was what I feared more than anything, because, they changed the children's names in those homes, and afterward it was impossible to find them. At least that was what they said in our cell. I think these rumors were spread by the investigators themselves to frighten us even more.

Once more I was taken back to my cell and waited, but I received no further summons. The investigation was over. I had been "unmasked."

A Mother's Gift

A mother and daughter were put in our cell together. This was apparently a unique case, since relatives were routinely separated. The daughter was forty years old, the mother seventy-five; a neat, thrifty old lady, very religious, she was the granddaughter of one of the Decembrists exiled to Siberia.

She looked around attentively and resignedly spread her hands.

"Well, now, we might as well drink some tea and have a few rusks! I toasted some on the radiator." The rusks, well toasted, were neatly cut up with a piece of thread (there are never any knives in prison, after all) and sprinkled with salt.

Her daughter Tamara was a doctor. In her every gesture you sensed that she belonged to the same breed as her mother; outwardly she was always calm and neat. Her self-control was sorely needed: she had been charged under Article 58:8 with the most serious crime, terrorism. The interrogator had sworn that he would wring a confession from her, and he'd employed his entire arsenal of weapons to that end. Tamara was beaten and put for five to eight days at a time in a freezing cell for "rudeness" and refusing to confess. She was summoned every night and forbidden to sleep during the day. Sometimes poor Tamara would return at eight in the morning, sit with her back to the door, and attempt to sleep sitting up. Then there would be a shout: "No sleeping!" This torture went on for days on end. Her mother and all the rest of us tried to screen her, but we were told to move away.

No sooner had the signal to go to bed been given and Tamara had lain down than the keys would clank in the lock and the guard would shout, "Interrogation!"

For all her self-control, a change would come over Tamara's face, and tears would well in her eyes. But her mother made the sign of the cross over her and whispered: "Be strong!"

Tamara's case turned out badly, although she hadn't signed a single statement. There had been too much testimony against her. It was senseless; it had been beaten out of the witnesses who gave it, but it was enough to secure her fifteen years' imprisonment.

For some reason, though, they decided to let her mother go. No one knew why, but one day the senior guard in charge of our floor came into the cell and ordered the old lady to gather her things. We guessed that she was being released, as indeed turned out to be the case. The dear old lady gave away all her possessions—someone got a comb, someone a toothbrush, someone a pair of warm socks. She saved all the best things for her daughter, then made the sign of the cross over her and said, "I bless you and give you permission, if things get very bad, to take your own life. Don't torment yourself. I will bear the burden of your sin before God!" Tamara kissed her hand and wept. But as her mother gave her final blessing, her face was so radiant and so beautiful, it was as if she were giving her daughter the gift of life itself.

Butyrki Prison in 1936

Four months after my arrival in the Lubyanka, the peephole in the door opened one evening and the guard said, "Sliozberg, pack your things."

Zhenya Goltsman came up to me.

"See, I was right. You're going to be released. I'm so happy for you. Don't forget the rest of us who are stuck in here."

We exchanged kisses. Zhenya was a very good person; she was genuinely glad to think I was being freed. The others couldn't help being a little envious. I know this from my own experience: you can be happy for friends when they are lucky, but at the same time your heart somehow aches all the more for yourself.

Alexandra Rozhkova was convinced that I was not going to be released, but simply taken to another cell. Sonya said nothing.

We bade each other farewell and I left the cell. I was escorted into the yard and put in a "Black Crow." This was a closed green van for transporting prisoners. Inside it was divided into individual compartments, each so cramped that tall people had to sit hugging their knees. In 1937 these vehicles became so widespread that a class of seven-year-olds was reported unanimously to have answered "green" when asked the color of a crow.

So there I was, shoved into one of these compartments. I had no idea where I was being driven. Somewhere inside me still glimmered the foolish hope that I would be taken home and released. The "Crow" came to a stop. We had entered the yard of Butyrki Prison.

It was a luminous August night. In the first courtyard of the prison stood several large lindens whose leaves glinted in the moonlight. I had not seen a single tree for four whole months; now my heart contracted so painfully that I almost fainted. I was led into a second yard, this one bare and gloomy, and thence to the prison building. My file was handed over in a sealed packet, my details noted, and I was led to my cell.

The cell was huge. The arched walls were dripping; on either side, leaving only a narrow passage between them, were low continuous bed boards packed with bodies. Assorted rags were drying on lines overhead. The air was thick with the foul smoke of strong cheap tobacco, and loud with arguments, shouts, and sobs.

Dismayed, I stood there with my suitcase and bundle. A pregnant woman came up to me; she had been put in charge of the cell. "Don't worry," she said. "Almost everyone here's a political like you. I'm a weaver from the Trekhgorka factory, Katya Nikolaeva. You'll have to sleep somewhere near the slop bucket; that's the rule for all the new people."

A huge wooden bucket stood in the corner, and there was a free space on the bed boards nearby. I was about to settle myself there when I noticed two free spaces in the opposite corner by the window, on either side of a woman with long black braids who was lying fast asleep.

"Maybe I could go next to the window?" I asked Katya.

Katya hesitated.

"Well, do as you like, but you won't have the best of neighbors."

I went over to the window and lay down.

My neighbor, Anya, was evidently glad of my company. A large kettle full of hot water had just been brought in; I had sugar and biscuits and invited her to join me. Then I started asking her about our cellmates. She had something bad to say about each of them. As far as she was concerned, the cell was a den of criminals. Suddenly I noticed Zhenya Bykhovskaya sitting on the bed boards opposite. In the four months that we had spent together at the Lubyanka, I had grown very fond of her, and had quite forgotten my original conviction that she was a spy.

"Do you know that woman over there?" I asked my new acquaintance.

"Oh, she's a spy of the lowest sort; I'd like to kill her with my own hands."

After that I went up to Zhenya. Being nearsighted, she hadn't noticed me before, but when she recognized me, she covered me with kisses and made room for me next to her. Silently I moved my things from the other side of the room. Anya watched me malevolently; once more she was left with three sleeping spaces to herself.

Curious, I asked Zhenya who on earth she was.

"She's the former wife of the well-known philosopher K—. He left her and has been living in Leningrad for the last few years. Out of revenge she denounced him to the secret police, saying that he was a secret Trotskyist and double-dealer. So they put him in prison, but then arrested her as well for not having informed on him earlier. Now she spends all her time writing statements denouncing everyone in the cell, so no one talks to her. If you've been transferred here, it means your case has been concluded. It's a shame; I thought they'd let you go. Now you'll just have to wait for your sentence. I can't hope for anything less than ten years. But your case is simpler; you probably will get away with five."

When Zhenya invited me to come and lie next to her, her neighbor, Motya, greeted me warmly. She nudged her own neighbors, Nina and Valya, coaxing them: "Never mind; 'cramped but cheerful,' as the saying goes. We've got to make room for good friends."

Thanks to Motya's efforts, a gap about eighteen inches wide was created, and I squeezed in. There was room enough to lie down, but one thing bothered me: we were lying face to face like sardines, and Motya's cheeks were covered in horrid black patches and blotches. Zhenya assured me that she wasn't infectious, but I couldn't help trying to protect my face with my handkerchief.

"Don't you worry," Motya said, "it's only frostbite."

Motya was dreadfully upset by these patches. She would spend hours massaging her cheeks, as Nina had taught her, and kept asking if the patches were getting any fainter—there was no mirror, of course.

Motya knew how to read, but, as she put it, she hadn't had much practice. In fact she felt sorry for me, reading away for days on end.

"You should take a rest," she said, and was amazed when I assured her that for me reading was the best way of resting.

Motya, when she wasn't busy with her disfigured cheeks, simply lay with her eyes closed and listened to Nina and Valya chatting. Both of them were pretty and young, not more than thirty years old. Nina was the wife of a senior military man; Valya's husband was a regional Party secretary. They had become great friends and loved to talk about the good old days before their arrest, quite forgetting anything that might have darkened the horizon then. They assumed that Motya was fast asleep while they talked, when in fact she was listening eagerly and from time to time, turning to me, would relay some item of news in a whisper: "Valya used to have a maid! She had her mother-in-law at home, but they still kept a maid."

"Well, she was out at work, and there was the child to look after."

"But he was eight years old! And they had the old lady at home as well."

Once Valya related a funny story about some bigwig who had come to see them uninvited. She had gone and hid in the nursery while her husband locked himself in his study and took a nap. The guest was left to drink tea with Valya's mother-in-law. Afterward he went out on the balcony to have a smoke, whereupon the husband emerged from his study, remarking loudly, "So the old windbag's gone!" Motya chuckled at this story along with the others, then whispered to me with a sly twinkle in her eyes, "See, they had four whole rooms."

"How come four? A nursery, a study, their living room—that makes three."

"No, you see the mother-in-law had her own room. She was telling Nina . . . And Nina, you know, had three fur coats—a sealskin, a white one, and the one she's got here, a Boston coat with a fox fur collar. Nina had a lover!"

"How do you know?"

"She was telling Valya. Once she was on her own at the seaside, left her husband behind, and this lover turns up. 'I missed you,' he says; 'the city's empty without you!' But then the husband shows up as well, so the lover has to jump in his car in the middle of the night and beat it. You'd have thought one man was enough, let alone two, but there you are; they know how to live it up, the bosses!"

"Why do you call them all bosses? Was I a 'boss' then too?"

"No, your husband was a teacher. That's honest work. But their old men were bosses."

Motya hated the "bosses," and for good reason. She was twelve years old when her peaceful childhood was shattered. She had been brought up in a village near Tarusa, 350 kilometers from Moscow; childhood to her meant hunting for mushrooms and berries, whole days splashing with her friends in the Oka River, nighttime excursions, and of course her grandmother, who was the best singer and storyteller in the village. She was a good pupil and loved school; her teacher called her Little Edison.

"I was so smart at arithmetic—anything that needed brains or nimble fingers. I could mend the electric stove or change a fuse. I got water piped from the stream into our schoolyard. Our teacher loved me."

All this came to an end in 1929, when Motya's parents were dispossessed as "kulaks" and exiled to the Northern Urals with their three children, Motya being the oldest. It was September. They were driven into the forest, unloaded, and told to build themselves houses. Sleet was falling; the old women wailed, and the children wept. Somehow or other they made themselves earthen dugouts and cobbled together stoves. There were no livestock, and nothing to feed the children. The middle daughter in the family died the first year. Motya's father and mother went to work felling trees, and Motya was left to run the household.

"It was so dreary," she said. "The summers were rainy and didn't last long; the winters were fierce, and there was no school. Mother and Father worked from dawn to dusk, and I had to look after my little brother, stoke the stove, and melt the snow to make water; it was all damp and dirty and smoky in the hut. There weren't many other kids around, and anyway everyone was out working the whole day long. It got dark early, and there was no kerosene. I used to sit there with a lighted splinter or a wick lamp, and my little brother kept catching cold and falling sick."

Motya lived like that until 1935. She passed seventeen years of age but was refused an internal passport on the grounds that she was the daughter of kulaks. Things were bad at home: her father wandered around like a thundercloud; her mother and brother were constantly ill. Motya started working with her father felling timber, while her mother stayed at home with her brother. Then in 1935, after Kirov was murdered, the father got filthy drunk one day and suddenly burst out, "It'd be a good thing if they slaughtered the lot of them; ordinary folk have suffered enough!"

Naturally her father was arrested. Meanwhile her mother kept coughing and coughing, and finally last winter both she and Motya's brother died.

"I felt so miserable and so fed up, I decided to run away and go back to my granny in the village. I had no passport and no money, but by early spring 1936 I'd got myself ready. I made myself two pairs of boots, baked some rusks, and set off on foot."

Over the next three months, Motya covered almost two thousand kilometers on foot. She slept in villages or sometimes in haystacks. Early on in her journey, she spent a night out in the forest, fell deeply asleep, and awoke to find her cheeks frozen by the early morning frost. One pair of boots fell to pieces straight away; after that, she walked barefoot wherever possible. In some villages people fed her out of Christian charity; in others she worked to earn her crusts. And finally she reached home. Her grandmother, overcome with fear and joy, wept buckets, fed her non-stop, smothered her with affection, rubbed her feet with warm lard, took her to sleep in her own bed, and was frightened to let her out of the house. But they found her out anyway. She had lived at her grandmother's only a week when they came and arrested her.

"Still, I'm not sorry I ran away. In camp there's plenty of company; you even get to watch movies sometimes, and at least you're safe from anything worse!"

Thus I began my time in cell No. 105, awaiting my sentence. I spent three months there altogether.

Of the hundred-odd women in our cell, there was one old lady who had been an SR, two Georgian Mensheviks, and two Trotskyists. All of them had been languishing in prison and exile for eight to fifteen years. Now they had been brought for reinvestigation from the OGPU prisons for political prisoners. These people had already defined their relation to the government and especially to OGPU: they saw them unequivocally as the enemy, their opponent in political struggle. For the Trotskyists, the main enemy was Stalin, whom they sardonically called "Daddy." They mocked us by asking why "Daddy" didn't come to our aid, since we supposedly loved him so much.

The SR and the Mensheviks hated Lenin most of all. He had destroyed democracy, they said, and paved the way for every lawless abuse. They almost rejoiced to see all their direst predictions come true.

Psychologically it was easier for them: everything was quite straightforward and made perfect sense. It was also easier in that they had gotten used to prison and were well accustomed to its awful routines. All their ties with the outside world had been severed; they had no children, no parents, and their husbands had either perished long since or, like them, were wandering from prison to prison.

They discussed every city in terms of its prison:

"Did you like Oryol?"

"You must be joking! Stone floors and exercise yards with huge high fences!"

"What about Samara?"

"The place isn't bad, but they only give you fifteen minutes in the wash-house."

They were experts on all the rules, knew how to stand up for their rights, and the prison authorities were rather afraid of them. These prisoners immediately got themselves put on special diets and were sent to the hospital right away if they needed it.

They discussed politics as if everything were perfectly obvious: the revolution had died ten years ago (fifteen, according to the Mensheviks and the SR lady), the country was heading for collapse, and the sooner it happened, the better.

They greeted each new batch of arrested Communists with ill-concealed joy: people who had condemned their views and actions now had to share the same fate along with everyone else.

I looked at these women and prayed that I would never become like them. I feared above all that I too might cease to remember anything but prison life or to hope for anything beyond a political prison with a decent library and a proper exercise yard.

At first I tried not to believe all the sad tales I was told. For if everyone was as innocent as I was, it meant that the newspapers were nothing but lies, and the speeches our leaders made were lies, and the trials and sentences were all lies, too. No, it was impossible! Somewhere, in solitary confinement blocks or in the men's cells, were those wretched conspirators who had so confused things that you could no longer tell who was innocent and who was guilty. Yet in each individual case it was impossible not to believe what people were saying. I could not but believe one old lady, Sofya Solomonovna Pinson, when she talked about her face-to-face meeting with Muratov, a lecturer at the university who knew my husband and me:

"I demanded to be allowed to see him. I was taken into the investigator's office, and there sat a gray old man with shifty eyes. Only when he started speaking did I realize it was Muratov [He was no older than thirty-three then.] I pleaded with him: 'Andrei Alexeevich, tell them it's not true, I've never belonged to any terrorist organization.' And suddenly, can you imagine, he says, 'Ah, Sofya Solomonovna, there's no use denying it! I've already confessed that you and I planned to murder Kaganovich.* I advise you to own up as well.' Can you imagine? I planned to murder someone like Kaganovich! When I couldn't even strangle a chicken!"

The most unhappy people in prison were the Communists. They kept assuring everyone that there had been a counterrevolutionary plot, and that if mistakes had occurred in liquidating the conspirators—well, when you chop down trees, the chips are bound to fly. They would say that you had to amputate the gangrenous part from the live body in order to save the organism as a whole.

If you asked them why the interrogators beat people up and forced them to give false testimony, they would simply say, "It has to be done," to which there was no possible rejoinder.

All of them were convinced that Stalin had no idea what was going on in the prisons, and they were constantly writing him letters.

They would accuse themselves of a criminal lack of vigilance. It was very hard for them. Hardest of all was the fact that, while they stubbornly defended the justice and good sense of the authorities' actions, they themselves were gradually losing faith.

Yet they had devoted their entire lives to the Party. They had been its children and foot soldiers.

And now I'll try to describe what I myself felt. My feelings were significant precisely because they were shared by so many others who, like me, had ended up behind barbed wire quite out of the blue.

My husband had always reproached me for failing to read the newspapers thoroughly and for taking so little interest in politics. I frequently used to grumble: our apartment was too small, we didn't have this or that, foreign things were good and ours were useless.

Only now, when absolutely everything was conspiring to make me hate life in our country, when the greatest injustice had been perpetrated against me—only now did I appreciate how well I had lived before. How good it had felt to work, and to know that what I was doing was right and necessary. How good it had been to bring up my children in the sure belief that every opportunity would be open to them. How confidently I had walked the earth and felt it to be my home. And if I sometimes got cross and complained that our home was messy or shabby it was precisely because it was my home and I wanted it to be beautiful.

---

* Lazar Kaganovich (1893–1991) was a member of Stalin's Politburo and a close ally.

Now everything around me conspired to fill me with hatred. I searched in vain for anything that might contradict the overwhelming conclusion: that those responsible for ruining our lives, for refusing to seek the truth and forcing us instead to lie, were Party members. And for this monstrous work, they were still being amply rewarded.

Once when we were out taking exercise, an ordinary convict who had been cleaning the yard came up to me and whispered, "Yagoda's been arrested, Yezhov's taken his place."*

I took this news back to the cell, and what hopes the fall of Stalin's secret police chief aroused! We were all convinced that we would be set free.

But time went by, and people started getting even harsher sentences. Those who had got five years under Yagoda started being given ten or twelve years under Yezhov. There were even rumors of twenty-five-year sentences.

One morning the door of the cell opened, and a young woman was brought in. Her name was Lira. She walked in boldly, glanced sharply around, and headed straight for Anya.

Someone warned her away, but Lira said confidently, "I've taken a fancy to her."

For the next three days, Lira and Anya never stopped chatting. Lira had brought some tasty things to eat and generously shared them with Anya. They laughed and whispered together, thick as thieves. Anya was transformed: at last she had found someone who really valued her.

But after three days, Lira suddenly gathered up her things and moved to a free place not far from me and Zhenya.

She stood on her bed, beautiful, shapely, provocative, and in a ringing voice shouted to Anya across the entire cell: "I'd like you to know that I spent three days with you just to find out what filthy lies you wrote about K—, who had the misfortune to be your husband. You denounced him out of jealousy, and you were dead right, he betrayed you—betrayed you with me! How he loved me! I'll never regret I met him, even though I'm in prison because of him."

Anya threw herself at Lira like a cat, but someone pulled her back and she choked, unable to utter a word.

Lira meanwhile stood with arms akimbo and even did a little dance. "Oh, and he's not sorry he left you, either! Better to die in prison than live with a bitch like you! But he adored me, and we had three whole years of happiness."

---

* Nikolai Yezhov replaced Genrikh Yagoda as head of the secret police in September 1936.

Anya was so shattered that she had to be taken to hospital. Three days later she returned, even more morose than before, and from then on she blocked her ears and lay with her eyes closed.

It was the evening of 6 November 1936.

More and more new prisoners were being brought into our already over-crowded cell. They lay on the tables, on the floor under the bed boards, and in the passage between them.

Almost all of them had the same thing to say: "I'm here by accident. I was arrested by mistake, and they should soon let me go."

One woman came in with an enormous belly; she was probably nine months pregnant. Some of the women squeezed up to make room for her to lie down; someone lent her a scarf, another a coat to try to make her a bit more comfortable. At around midnight she began to groan and bite her hands. She had gone into labor and was taken off to the hospital.

Then at two in the morning the door opened, and with great commotion, a woman of about thirty-five came in, wearing a low-cut flimsy pink dress and a flower of some kind in her hair.

She kept sobbing and couldn't stop talking. Gradually we gathered that her first husband had been a Trotskyist, but he had disappeared nine years ago, leaving her a son, Lyovochka. The boy was lame and sickly. She had waited for her husband for nine years and was afraid to marry anyone else for fear he'd be unkind to Lyovochka.

But finally she had made up her mind to marry again. On 5 November she had moved in with her new husband, and the following day she was arrested right there at her wedding table.

She related all this in floods of tears and kept crying, "Lyovochka, my Lyovochka!"

We were upset enough as it was by the thought of tomorrow's holiday—7 November, the anniversary of the Revolution—by the constant arrival of new prisoners, and by the sight of a woman going into labor right there in our cell. And now here was this arrested bride in a pink dress with flowers in her hair.

Suddenly, in one corner of the cell, a woman went into hysterics and started wailing, "Yura, my Yura!"

Then everyone got going:

"My little Irochka!"

"My darling Misha!"

Half the cell was in hysterics. I buried my face in my hankie and felt an almost overwhelming desire to join in and shout, "My Shurik, my little Ellochka!" But I bit my hands till they bled, stopped up my ears, and closed my eyes. Next to me lay Zhenya Bykhovskaya, and we squeezed up together for comfort.

The door flew open, and there were shouts from the guards. Women, struggling hysterically, were dragged out and thrown into the punishment cells, put in empty cells, or carted off to the hospital. Two hours later, all was quiet again.

That was how the holiday began on 7 November 1936.

And on 12 November I received a summons to the military tribunal of the Supreme Court. Everyone was astonished, since my case had seemed so trivial.

I realized how serious my position was by the expressions on the faces of the most experienced prisoners. There was a woman in our cell named Sonya Ashkenazy, a Trotskyist. I have said nothing of her because she always kept silent herself. Sonya was dying of consumption and took great pains not to infect her cellmates; she ate from her own dish, coughed into a little container, and always lay with her face turned to the wall. Out of the blue Sonya came up to me, looked at me with her beautiful eyes, and kissed me on the lips. I realized that in Sonya's view it no longer mattered if I got infected, for nothing could matter to me now. As if in a dream, I gathered up my things and left the cell. I was taken to the Pugachov tower (where Ye-melian Pugachov* was supposed to have been imprisoned two hundred years before) and handed the indictment.

My trial was to be held three days later, on 15 November.

The Trial

The indictment had been clumsily put together. It said that the same Muratov, whom my husband and I had known at the university, had told a certain Morenko that he had enlisted me in a terrorist organization whose purpose was to murder Kaganovich, and that I might have overheard a conversation between Muratov and my husband on 5 December 1935.

All this was complete fantasy and totally vague, but on this basis I was charged under Article 58:8–17—in other words, with terrorism, the minimum sentence for which was eight years and the maximum capital punishment. This was all explained to me by the man—a colonel of some sort—who handed me the indictment. It had been signed by Vyshinsky, the

---

* Cossack leader of a rebellion against the empress Catherine the Great; he was executed in 1775.

Procurator General of the USSR, and ended with the words "Stubbornly refused to cooperate with the investigation and would not admit to anything."

I thought that I would meet my husband in court. He too must be awaiting trial and suffering just as I was.

And as always, I thought of the children. Now was the moment of truth; now I would learn if I was ever to see them again.

I sat for three days in that round tower and formed in my heart a new determination to fight. I was even pleased that I was to be tried in a proper court, rather than in absentia by the usual anonymous three-person tribunal or "troika." I kept rehearsing the evidence of my innocence and the patent falsity and nonsense of the charges against me.

On 15 November I was taken by "Black Crow" to the Lubyanka. There I was made to wait in the hairdresser's room, where there was a table with a mirror and an armchair. I was the only prisoner there, and for the first time in seven months I saw myself in the mirror. I was pleased with what I saw: my face was very thin, but my eyes flashed with determination. I was convinced that I was about to see my husband, and I wanted to cheer him by my appearance.

I had to wait a fair time, about two hours. Somewhere a clock struck twelve. Lunch was brought in. Every detail is engraved in my memory: I recall that I was given pea soup with a chunk of meat in it and some sort of meat with buckwheat porridge. This wasn't prisoners' fare; it had probably been brought from the staff canteen. Before I had time even to finish my soup, they came for me and led me into the courtroom.

There were no other defendants. Investigators in uniform sat in the seats reserved for the public. On a raised platform stood a long table covered with red cloth. To the right of the table was the defendants' bench, behind a barrier of light polished wood.

I sat down on the bench. Behind me stood two guards with rifles, and the head of the Butyrki Prison, Popov, a tall, thin man with a huge mustache that stuck out in all directions.

Directly opposite the bench was a great round clock; the hands pointed to 12:45.

"The court is in session; please stand."

I jumped up. A dozen judges came in. The presiding judge was Vasily Ulrich. I looked at these men in their uniforms and medals. Most of them were elderly; several could have been my father. A tall man with gray hair, wearing numerous decorations, began to read out the indictment. I already knew the whole thing by heart, so I simply looked at the judges and thought,

"Surely these people, Bolsheviks, men that I'm used to treating with great respect, men that I'd rush to and trust to protect me if I were in danger—surely they can't have me convicted?"

The chairman asked whether I had anything to say. I stepped forward: "Yes, I do."

If I do say so myself, I made a first-rate speech. It was unnecessary and impossible, I said, to prove my innocence; it was up to them to prove my guilt. My accuser, so the investigator had said, was himself a Trotskyist bandit, while my character was unstained; why should they believe him and not me? Muratov alleged that he had proposed that we murder Kaganovich, and I had supposedly agreed! What evidence could I produce against such wild allegations?

And what kind of formulation was this: "Sliozberg may have overheard a conversation." Perhaps she might have, but in fact she didn't. Can you have a person put to death for the fact that he or she "might have heard"? I finished by asking the judges, when they came to decide my fate, to bear in mind that I had two small children.

At a certain point I realized that no one was listening to me.

"The judges will now withdraw to confer."

The judges withdrew. Through the open doorway I saw that the table in the other room was set with glasses and dishes of fruit.

The clock struck one.

Five minutes later the judges returned, and the chairman read out, "sentenced to eight years' strict regime incarceration in prison and a further four years' deprivation of rights."

I felt as if I'd been scalded with boiling water. I turned and saw Popov standing with his arms idiotically outstretched as if he was about to embrace me (later I learned that many women fainted at this point, and it was his job to catch them). I did not faint, but pushed Popov aside and ran into the corridor as if to escape. All of a sudden the words registered: "incarceration in prison." I didn't even know there were such sentences. I stopped and turned to Popov, who was following on my heels. "I think I heard the words 'incarceration in prison.' You mean to say I'm to spend eight years in prison?"

"Yes, that's the sentence."

"Oh why did I humiliate myself and tell them about my children!" I burst out.

"You did well to mention them; they were going to give you five years' deprivation of rights, but now it's been reduced to four."

I was led into a large hall where some ten convicted prisoners were already sitting. Among them were Zhenya Goltsman and Zhenya Bykhovskaya. Both had received ten-year prison sentences, Bykhovskaya in solitary confinement.

We sat in silence, crushed. None of us wept.

On that day around one hundred women were condemned. The court was in session for sixteen hours, an average of ten minutes for each person.

I had used up fifteen minutes with my speech—which meant that someone else had been dealt with in only five.

Solovki

After the trial we were taken into a large cell with a few hastily constructed bed boards—it looked as if it had once housed some kind of club. Here we spent two days.

I immediately rejected any possibility of seeing my children, knowing that a visit to this place would mark them for the rest of their lives. I hadn't yet decided whether I had the strength to see my mother and father, but the authorities decided the question for me: there was no suggestion of a visit; instead, we were loaded onto a train and sent north to Solovki. The journey took four days. With me in the compartment was the writer Vilensky-Sibiryakov. He was suffering from a serious stomach ulcer, but was keen to talk to me because his wife, Marfa, had been with me in cell 105. I tried to recall every detail about her, and he listened eagerly. This was the last scrap of news that he would ever have about the wife with whom he'd lived for thirty years. They had served a term of exile together in Siberia before the revolution; that was when he had adopted the pseudonym Sibiryakov. He died in Solovki. Later I would meet his daughter in one of the camps in Kolyma.

We then crossed the White Sea to the Solovetsky archipelago by steamer. The steamer was called the *SLON*, from the Russian acronym for "Solovki special camps." "Slon" means "elephant" in Russian, and everyone said this kindly animal would bring us good luck. Alas, all the Solovki prisoners traveled on the *SLON*, and it hadn't yet brought them much by way of luck!

Prison cells had not yet been built at the former monastery on Solovki, although there had been a camp there since 1923. So we were temporarily put in one big room, the former refectory. There were huge stoves which covered half the wall and made the room very warm. The windows were large, and the floors were made from long, good-quality planks. The walls were whitewashed, and there were wooden folding beds with backs to lean on during the day. We were served a reasonable dinner.

We were visited several times by the prison governor, Monakhov, a big man with a good-natured face. He was clearly very curious about us.

"What on earth did you do to get such sentences?" he asked one day.

"Anyway, you're all stuck here for the next eight or ten years," he said the next time. "So sort yourselves out as you like in groups of four or five."

This was quite extraordinary: no one had ever done this before—on the contrary, if any two prisoners got friendly, they were routinely separated. Everyone became quite agitated, for choosing companions for the next eight years was easier said than done.

I was quite clear who I didn't want to be with. The person closest to me was Zhenya Bykhovskaya, but we were not allowed to be together, for she had been sentenced to solitary confinement.

Zhenya sat in a corner, already detached from the rest of us; she had nothing to say to us now that we were full of plans for our communal life. My heart contracted with pity for her, but I had to look after my own life. I walked past her without looking and went up to the other Zhenya—Zhenya Goltsman, who was sitting next to a pretty young girl, the stepdaughter of Professor Dmitriev.

I knew her already; her name was Lida. Zhenya and I decided to have her in our cell so that we could help her with her studies. Zina Stanitsyna then asked to join us, and that made up our foursome.

Zhenya set only one condition: we were not to break the prison rules and tap messages from cell to cell. Zhenya was a Communist, and no matter where she was, she was determined to obey Soviet law. The rest of us agreed.

Once in our cell, we set up a regular routine. We got up at eight and did exercises in front of the open window. Then we had breakfast and sat down to our studies: for two hours a day, Zhenya taught us English, then we had two hours of mathematics with Zina. I taught French to Zhenya for an hour and spent an hour on Russian with Lida. Then I read French literature, for the library contained some 250 volumes in French.

Zhenya read Lenin and Marx, Zina busied herself with vector analysis, and Lida toiled over her lessons in mathematics, Russian, and English. Zhenya kept a stern eye on us to make sure we all read *Pravda* from cover to cover. On no account would she let me get away with skimming through the newspaper instead of reading it properly.

We spent an hour each day walking in the little garden, which was overgrown with grass and lilac. Then at eight in the evening we undressed again, did our exercises, and had some tea.

We never lay down or slept during the day to make sure that we would be tired enough to sleep at night.

Monakhov often looked in on us, and he probably watched us through the peephole too. Once, coming in and seeing that we were reading an article in English, he said, "What good progress you've made! I can't seem to get the hang of it myself, though I've had a go three times."

Zhenya joked back: "Join our little circle, then, and we'll teach you properly."

He waved his hand dismissively. "No thanks; life's short enough as it is."

His was indeed short, poor fellow. In late 1937 he was arrested for having been too liberal. Later I heard he had died in the transit camp in Vladivostok.

The nights were very hard. Tired out at the end of the day, I would fall fast asleep, only to start awake two hours later as if from a stab in the heart. I was unable to fall asleep again, and the hours before we got up were an indescribable torture. I would lie quietly, my eyes closed, and force myself not to remember. At the slightest failure of will, they'd come swimming before my eyes—the faces of my children, my husband, my mother . . . But I mustn't let them, I mustn't, or I'd start screaming out loud.

In those long nights I learned that it is indeed possible to control your thoughts, to cease to remember, or regret, or tear yourself apart with guilt— on your own account, or your husband's, or your mother's, or because you insulted someone or didn't love them enough or failed to show compassion. It is possible to stop feeling. But it is terribly hard.

Once we were visited by the assistant doctor. Behind him, as always, stood an escort (the doctor was a prisoner). Giving Lida her eyedrops, he whispered, "Sonya Ashkenazy has died. They found her this morning."

I remembered her beautiful eyes and the way she had kissed me before my trial.

Thus we spent an entire year. But in the autumn of 1937, they suddenly stopped giving us books from the library. After several months without books, we were given a new catalogue, containing a list of high school textbooks but no foreign or scholarly publications. We were allowed one book each per week. We wept as if we'd been given an extra sentence, and tried to guess the reason for it. Zhenya reckoned that prisoners had been using the books to send messages to one another, and it was therefore our own fault.

What made it especially unbearable was that the pages of our favorite books were being handed out as toilet paper. Once I was given a half-page of Heine, another time a leaf from Tolstoy's *Cossacks*.

At the same time they stopped giving us newspapers. It was then that I quarreled with Zhenya for the first time.

We were visited by Vinogradov, the senior guard. He was a member of the Komsomol and not a terribly bright lad, but we loved him all the same. Clearly emulating Monakhov, he made efforts to instruct us. If we complained of the cold, he'd say, "They will turn the heat on. Soviet prisons are there to educate, not to punish." Or he'd drop in to give us a sort of Party bulletin on the achievements of Stakhanovite workers, and conclude reproachfully, "See how the Soviet people have been toiling away, while all you could do was make mischief and land in prison."

Lately there had been no sign of Monakhov, and it had been a good two months since Vinogradov had called in. And when he came this time, he was quite different from his old self.

"Stand up!"

We stood.

"Any complaints?"

"None."

He turned to go. At this point I asked him why we weren't getting newspapers any more.

"That's orders."

"But you said yourself—Soviet prisons are there to educate. How can we get educated without newspapers?"

Vinogradov couldn't think what to say. But suddenly Zhenya came to his aid. In her best pedagogical tone she announced, "It's the politically illiterate who need educating; people such as ourselves must be answerable for their own actions."

Vinogradov brightened up and nodded vigorously. "Absolutely, absolutely!" He shut the door behind him to escape further discussion.

I flew at Zhenya: "How dare you barge in like that?"

She was put out.

"Well, it was obvious he didn't know what to say."

Now we had time on our hands. We fashioned a set of chess pieces out of bread and started to play. For three days we enjoyed the game, but on the fourth day Vinogradov appeared, swept away our chess pieces, and said, "Not allowed."

"And why might that be?" I asked Zhenya. "Just to torment us, perhaps?"

"I beg you not to say things that border on anti-Soviet slander. If chess is forbidden, it must mean someone's been smuggling political documents into the chess pieces."

I dismissively waved her away.

For two days now we had not been taken out for exercise, and when at last we were let out for a walk, we gasped. Our sweet little garden had been carved up into separate yards enclosed by high walls. There was not a blade of grass or a bush to be seen.

One day we were doing our exercises in our long prison pants and home-made bras when the door opened and an entire commission marched in. We must have looked pitiful in our grayish calico bloomers reaching down to the knees and our bras sewn from foot rags. Since our window was open and the door now stood wide, there was a freezing draft, and we were soon blue with cold.

Leading the commission was a colonel in a gray astrakhan hat and an overcoat with a matching astrakhan collar. He had a well-fed ruddy face and smelled of wine and hair cream. Behind him stood four soldiers, with Vinogradov bringing up the rear.

"What's all this?" the colonel asked Vinogradov, gesturing squeamishly at us. "What's going on here? Is this a prison or a health resort? Health resorts are the place for sport; prison's a place for punishment. I want this stopped immediately!"

We made a move to get dressed.

"Stand still! Why aren't the beds made to regulations? Why is the window open? This is a prison cell, not a gym!"

There was a book lying on the table—Yelizarova's memoirs of Lenin.

Suddenly I said, "Lenin used to do exercises for two hours a day when he was imprisoned under the tsars. That was a prison, too, after all."

"Be quiet!" the colonel shouted, then turned and went out.

Everyone left, and the door was locked once more. Five minutes later Vinogradov came back, informed us that exercises were forbidden, then seized Yelizarova's memoirs and left.

At one point we acquired from the library a copy of Barbusse's book about Stalin. There was a big portrait of Stalin in it, and Lida for some reason started gushing about how handsome he was.

"Do you think he is too?" she asked me.

All my accumulated rage came bursting out: "No, I don't like faces with low foreheads."

Zhenya drew herself up: "I consider that to be a political statement."

The atmosphere in the cell became so charged that I was quite glad when, a week later, Vinogradov ordered me to pack my belongings.

I said goodbye to everyone. Zhenya kissed me and said, "I think they're going to review your case. Yours was so trivial! I wish you luck!"

Alas, what an optimist she was.

I was taken to a cell inhabited by four other women. As we introduced ourselves, I learned that all of them had been sentenced to three years in camp under Article 58:10 (agitation). Now their terms were up, and they were convinced that their transfer from camp to prison meant they would shortly be sent back to the mainland and released.

But they were very worried at being detained so long, and tried to reassure themselves that it was just because it was winter and the White Sea crossing was closed.

Then they asked me about myself and were horrified to learn that I was a terrorist and had been sentenced to eight years in prison.

When I tried to explain that everyone nowadays was either a terrorist or a spy and was given a sentence of eight to ten years, they obviously didn't believe me. Three years ago you really had to have done something to earn such a sentence.

This conversation took place on my first evening in the cell, and the following day I noticed that all of them looked a bit embarrassed. They were whispering among themselves and evidently wanted to say something. Finally Nema Rabinovich, the eldest of them, spoke up: "Our sentences are already over, and we're about to resume our lives as free people. In any case we ended up here only by chance, and the charges against us were trivial, whereas your case is completely different. I'm sure you won't take offense if for the brief period that we have to share this cell we avoid associating with you."

Now, this was one for the books! I could never have imagined such a thing.

Thus began our life in that small cell, with five of us crammed into about fifteen square meters. While they all huddled together in one corner, I sat alone in another. I think it was even worse for them than it was for me, for they must have felt terribly ashamed. Yet I envied them dreadfully. They talked to one another, had a laugh now and then, asked each other riddles, and ate their meals together.

I sat there alone, with neither books nor paper; all I could do was mentally compose poems and smoke cigarette after cigarette. Five days passed in this fashion. Finally I was given a book to read (the other women were given four books and could swap them among themselves). I rationed myself, reading only thirty pages a day, which for me was barely a mouthful, and looked longingly at the books they left unread, preferring to talk to one another about their future.

Another three days went by. Suddenly the senior guard entered and asked Nema Rabinovich to come with him, leaving her belongings behind. Everyone decided this meant she would be released. Fifteen minutes passed. The senior guard returned to summon Masha Yarovaya, while Nema reappeared looking white as a sheet. Masha went out. Nema still said nothing. Finally she spoke: "They've extended my sentence to ten years. I've still got seven years to go." Then she sat down on her bed and began to chain-smoke.

The door opened, and Masha ran in sobbing. She threw herself on her bed. "They've slapped on an extra seven years! It's God's punishment for what we've done to poor Olga. For the past week my heart's been torn in two just looking at her! They've slapped on another seven years, seven years, seven years!"

The two others were summoned in turn and likewise came back weeping and lamenting. It was terrible to see all their hopes and dreams crushed. Nema and Masha had been bursting to see the children they'd left behind in the homes of strangers. Nyura Ivanova had been planning to settle down with one of the convicts from their camp who was due to be freed in the spring. She'd been going to wait for him and had made all sorts of plans for helping him in the meantime by sending him parcels.

Shura Alexeeva was expected any day by her mother, who had barely managed to survive this long. Shura was her one and only daughter. Every week her mother wrote, "Only twelve weeks to go, only eleven, only ten; I'm waiting, waiting, waiting!"

Several hours went by. Then the hot water was brought in. I had a few fruit drops, and went over to their corner: "Let's make up! Be my guests." I put the fruit drops on the table.

"I'm not angry with you, how could you have known? But I'm the one in danger now: you've got ten years, and I've only got eight."

What reserves of vitality human beings have! In the evening all five of us sat on Masha Yarovaya's bed, and I told them the story of *In the Abyss* by the French novelist Georges Honnet. This was one of the novels that I'd taken out of the prison library to practice my French, and it was an extremely stirring tale. These novels had stood me in very good stead: I would retell them with minor variations to my fellow prisoners and became known in prison and in the camps as an excellent storyteller.

In the spring of 1938 we found out that the women's prison on Solovki was being disbanded, and all the inmates were to be transferred to the mainland. My one and a half years at Solovki had come to an end. What lay in store for me now? In June 1938 we were transported south and eastward to Kazan, on the Volga.

Kazan Prison

The regime at Kazan Prison was designed to crush us completely, both physically and psychologically.

Reveille was at six in the morning. At five past six the guard would march into the cell to fold back our beds and screw them to the wall. If our beds weren't yet made, he would threaten to put everyone in the punishment cell; terrified, we would rush to get ready.

By seven minutes past six the beds were screwed to the wall, and there we were in an empty cell with a stone floor, stone walls, and a bare twenty-watt bulb in the ceiling. A sloping screen covered the outside window, with a wire mesh on top. Some indirect light entered the cell, but we couldn't see the sky. Six little benches, forty centimeters long, were screwed to the wall; there was a table, half a meter long and thirty centimeters wide, also screwed to the wall, and a slop bucket in the corner.

It was difficult to walk around in the cell. We were given rough men's boots, size 44, and as soon as they went clump-clump on the floor, there'd be a hiss from the warder: "Do you want to get put in the punishment cell?"

We could talk only in whispers; a word spoken out loud would earn you a spell in the punishment cell.

The day was broken up into segments: the morning trip to the toilet and slopping out; breakfast, dinner, supper; fifteen minutes' exercise; the evening trip to the toilet and slopping out; bed.

We were forbidden needle and thread, and no games were allowed. You would be put in the punishment cell for making chessmen from bread.

Once a week we were allowed one book each.

I can't imagine now how we could have read in that semi-darkness. Katya Toive actually went blind.

Books were our only diversion, our only happiness, bread and water for our brains, which were otherwise shriveling and suffocating for lack of nourishment.

That was when I understood what a really good book was: a book that would make you feel human again when you'd read it! For so long now it had been drilled into our heads that we weren't human, that we were the dregs, garbage; this was the message hammered home not just by the prison officers, whom we despised, but by the newspapers, which we still hadn't learned to disbelieve, and by the people running the Party and the country; it was hammered home so hard that we ourselves had started feeling that we must be guilty of something.

But here were Tolstoy and Dostoyevsky speaking to me, and in my human essence I felt myself their equal.

My perception as a reader became extremely acute. I felt that I understood not only what a writer was saying but what he needed to say, and why he had chosen precisely this form rather than some other to convey his thoughts.

There was a rule that had been honored from time immemorial: politicals had to be given textbooks. But we were given ABCs and elementary arithmetic books. Our degrees and qualifications greatly irritated the prison authorities.

So we would sit on our prison stools, forty centimeters wide and screwed to the wall, sit and endlessly think. But what to think about? It was hard to find a single theme that wouldn't break one's heart.

Daydream? But what about? My sentence—eight years—seemed endless. Only some general political change could bring about a review. But so powerful was our hypnosis that for a very long time, even there in that burial chamber, alone with my thoughts, I could not bring myself to hope, let's say, that Stalin would die or be overthrown. In my mind that would mean the death of the Revolution itself.

Only in the very depths of my soul, where thoughts can wander without yet becoming words, did some feeling of protest begin to form.

If he was infallible, a genius, it meant that I and hundreds of thousands of people were condemned to sit in these vile cells, and thousands of people, instead of doing normal useful work, were obliged to spend days on end looking through a peephole and making sure that we found not a moment's relief from the grief that was choking us.

Remember? That was out of the question. You would go mad. The merest shadow of a recollection was to be banished immediately, the brain switched straightaway to mechanical exercises: counting, reciting poetry, forming words from the letters of longer words. But sometimes memories would overwhelm you, and your will would cave in. And then it was terrible.

The walls of Kazan Prison were one and a half meters thick, but sometimes we would hear the great horns of the Volga steamers. And I had been brought up on the Volga! The very sound rocked my heart: immediately I would picture the great wide river, the steamers, my youth . . .

I would try not to hear and not to believe that right now, as I sat in this stone vault, life all around was going on much as before.

Fortunately, my memories of freedom and of our former life became less and less frequent. I sought instead to create a kind of shadow life out of my prison existence.

Zina Stanitsyna, my cellmate from Solovki, had ended up in the same cell as me here, too. She taught us all algebra and geometry and gave us problems to solve, and in this way we somehow passed the time.

I would give whispered accounts of various French novels.

It was hardest of all for Olga Ivanovna Nikitina, an elderly textile-worker. She had worked at the loom for thirty-five years and, like all weavers, was almost deaf. She couldn't hear our whispers, and it was forbidden to talk out loud. Her eyesight was too poor to read in the prison darkness.

Olga Ivanovna was a long-standing member of the Party, one of the workers from the textile mills in Ivanovo who had fought at the front with Furmanov in the Civil War. She had been sentenced to ten years for having stood up at a meeting and asked, with characteristic forthrightness, "You claim all these people are traitors, but was Lenin blind? Couldn't he see what sort of people surrounded him?"

Now she sat and whispered to herself for days on end—always trying to prove that she had done right by speaking out.

Olga Ivanovna had a daughter "outside," fifteen-year-old Natasha. The silly girl had no idea that letters to prison were censored. She wrote to her mother that she wanted to continue her studies and to join the Komsomol, and in order to get herself accepted she was hiding the fact that her mother was in prison. "I always write that you've died; otherwise they won't take me. You can't get by in life unless you deceive 'them.'"

Her mother had no way of warning her that her letters were read by a censor, and could only reply, "You should be honest, as your mother always was before the Motherland; you should always write the truth."

But Natasha wrote back, "You were always honest, and you ended up behind bars, while people with fewer principles are doing nicely for themselves and are staying out of prison." And she continued to write letters which made poor Olga Ivanovna tear her heart out with worry over her daughter.

The slightest reminder of life outside was painful.

Once I happened to notice our guard taking home a parcel of children's toys. It seemed unbelievable to me: in half an hour he would see his children!

From time to time, roughly every ten days, five or so women guards would march into our cell, strip us naked, and carry out a search. They searched our hair, our mouths, and even . . . Their dirty hands groped all over our bodies, our underwear was thrown on the filthy floor, and when we complained, the prison director would answer, "If you've had your head cut off, you can't go weeping for your hair."

What could they possibly find? A fragment of a letter which, according to the prison rules, should have been handed back to the authorities the day after it was received; a photograph of a mother or child that had been hidden away somewhere; a chess piece fashioned out of bread—to have any of these things on your person was considered a crime which warranted the most severe punishment. The authorities of course knew perfectly well that we couldn't be in possession of anything really criminal, and the searches were carried out solely to frighten and humiliate us.

So the six of us would sit there on our stools, sunk in torpor, while time seemed to stand still and weighed like stone on our hearts.

Then something happened to shake me out of this oppressive lethargy. Maria Danielyan, one of my cellmates, used to tell me about the Baku underground in the early years of the Revolution. I envied her for having lived such a full life at a time when I was vegetating amid mundane everyday concerns. I looked up to Maria, and although we never talked about the repressions of the 1930s for fear of being overheard, I desperately wanted to know how she explained and made sense of what seemed to me inexplicable. Maria, after all, was a historian by profession.

One day Maria said, "If I ever get out of here I'll start my life all over again as if none of this had happened. I'll never tell anyone what I've been through, and I'll try to forget all about it myself."

I was indignant.

"That would be downright hypocrisy. We never used to imagine that there was this dark underside to our everyday life, but it was there all the time. It was there while we were still free and believed in justice. Those terrible interrogations, those cellars in the OGPU prisons where people were beaten up and forced to sign false statements—they were there all along. How can I go and forget about all that if it's still going on when I happen to be released? I don't want to forget, I want to understand."

It was dangerous to talk at any length on this theme. Maria stopped talking to me and declared that I was sliding into outright opposition. And I understood that she had simply forbidden herself to think. Instead, she wrote constantly to Stalin, assuring him that she had never criticized the decisions and actions of the Party.

But I didn't want to stop thinking.

This voluntary enslavement, the enslavement of one's own thoughts, filled me with profound revulsion. I was determined to go on thinking, to remember everything, and to survive to tell others what I had seen. I would bear witness!

This decision gave new purpose to my life. I entered into every story my comrades told me and tried to recall every detail of what I saw around me.

My life had acquired meaning.

Liza

It was Saturday, the day we were allowed to write to our families. The day before, we'd been given our letters from home—so commonplace and predictable, yet so warm and dear and vital to us. The children are fine, good, beautiful; you be brave; look after yourself; we need you. Although I knew perfectly well that no one would write to say the children were ill or that Mother couldn't sleep at night and was dying of grief, I felt reassured. I drank in every stroke of my mother's dear, painstaking handwriting, kissed my son's printed letters and the outline of my little daughter's hand traced in ink—that hand that had once been so tiny but was now as big as my palm.

We lived with these letters a single night—the next day we would have to hand them back. Even the photos would be taken away, so we had to imprint them on our hearts. There were Mama, Papa, and the children. My little girl had had her head shaved bare, and it was winter now, so she must have been ill—maybe with scarlet fever? Or diphtheria? I had no idea; all I knew was that last week she was alive and had had her hand traced in ink. And that I was lucky—my children were living with my parents, who loved and cared for them, and every two weeks I would get letters that warmed my heart and restored my will to live.

Liza, my neighbor in the cell, had had no letters for two months now. She had two little daughters "outside," ages six and twelve. The eldest, Zoya, used to write to her conscientiously, telling her that her younger sister, Lyalya, had been naughty and torn her new dress, that she had her hair in braids now and they were already twenty centimeters long. And she had sent a snapshot: two little girls, very smart, their hair smoothly combed and parted at the side. Amazingly, Liza had managed to hide this photo during searches. This was a serious crime for which she might have been put in the punishment cell, and Liza worried so much about it she'd decided she'd better hand it in lest she have a heart attack from anxiety.

Liza was a bit of a hypochondriac, always fretting about her health. She was a solid, rather unattractive woman. She told us that she was a good singer, but unfortunately we had to take her word for it, since we were allowed to do no more than whisper. Liza loved boasting how she had been a great success with men, but I found it hard to believe, looking at her plain face and strong, crude figure. In general I didn't get on particularly well with Liza—she talked too much about the food and clothes and furniture she used to have.

But the previous day, when the letters were being handed out and Liza once again got nothing, she had wept long and hard, and that night she told me her story in a whisper.

"All of you come from good backgrounds, but I had a miserable childhood. My mother and us two sisters used to go from house to house singing—we were beggars. We never had a father; it was mother's boss that got her in the family way. Me and my sister were born when she worked as a cook for some official." Liza was ashamed of this and had never mentioned it before. I realized then why she disliked our stories about childhood so much—the music lessons we had, the wonderful Christmas trees, how my father used to spoil me, and so on.

"We would have been all right, only mother drank. Mind you, she had a wonderful voice, like the opera singer Nezhdanova's; she'd get drunk and start singing and have a good cry. She sang beautifully, and she was always kind to us, but she used to drink out of grief. I always envied children who were brought to school by their mothers, and if I happened to see children with their daddies, all clean and smart and nicely dressed, I felt like slinging a lump of mud at them.

"We lived in one corner of a basement. Then came the Revolution, when I was fourteen. Some people came to see us and said we were being moved from the basement to an apartment on the second floor. A rich family had lived there, but they'd escaped abroad, leaving everything behind, and we were given their apartment along with all their furniture and belongings. There was a grand piano and fine clothes and lovely crockery. Mother got us all dressed up and dressed herself up, too.

"Three rooms they gave us; we lived in just the one, because it was so cold, but we looked after the other rooms and kept them nicely dusted. Then it got warmer, and we started using all the rooms. Mother was put in charge of the entire building, and me and my sister worked in a factory. We were very popular there because we were always singing—at work and at special gatherings in the evening. We were very well turned out, because the rich family had left a sewing machine and lots of dresses, and Mother spent the whole time sewing and altering. She even stopped drinking, except now and then when friends came around. Our house became a kind of club; all our comrades would come over, and we'd have something nice to eat— mother used to work as a cook, of course—and drink just a glass of vodka each and sing endless songs.

"Then mother died of consumption. But at least she'd had a happy last few years. And me and my sister got married. I married the chairman of the factory management committee, and she married the foreman. They were Party people, so we joined the Party too. We lived very well. The saddest moment was when Lenin died. That was when I joined the Party, in honor of him—I was one of the so-called "Lenin recruits." My husband made me study hard like Lenin had commanded.

"I had my two little girls and dressed them up like dolls. My eldest started learning the piano. She was doing fine and loved to sing as well. She had a fine little voice, clear as a bell. Sometimes we'd have a children's morning at the factory, and our little girl would stand up there and sing in her silk dress with her Young Pioneer's tie, and my husband would say to me, 'There's not a girl in the world sings better than our Zoya. She's going to be an Artist of the People when she grows up.' Then I'd recall how we'd tramped from door to door, and I loved our Soviet government so much I would have given my life for it.

"In those days Zinoviev was the Party boss in Leningrad, and my husband had great respect for him. We'd voted for him. Then we were told he'd betrayed Lenin, we were very upset and couldn't understand it at all. So Kirov took over. I liked Kirov, too; he came to our factory, and I organized a party for him and sang.

"Then we were arrested. They said my husband was a Zinovievite because he'd voted for Zinoviev. I'd voted for him, too, because I thought he was on Lenin's side. If I'd known he'd betrayed Lenin, I would have throttled him with my own hands."

Liza cried the whole night. It was the first time she had told me all this, and I was ashamed of myself for having thought her a bit vulgar and stupid with her constant talk of fine clothes and furniture.

That Saturday afternoon we'd been given our ration of paper to write letters. Liza wrote home, too, telling her daughters to take care of their health and study hard.

Suddenly the hatch was opened, and a letter was handed in for Liza. But it was not the usual kind of letter at all.

"Dear Mama," wrote Zoya, "I'm fifteen years old now and I'm planning to join the Komsomol. I have to know whether you're guilty or not. I keep thinking, how could you have betrayed our Soviet system? After all, we were doing so well, and you and Papa were both workers. I remember how well we lived. You used to make us silk dresses and buy us sweets. Did you really go and get money from 'them'? You'd have done better to let us go around in cotton frocks. But maybe you're not guilty after all? In that case I won't join the Komsomol, and I'll never forgive them on your account. But if you're guilty, I won't write to you anymore, because I love our Soviet government and I hate its enemies, including you if you are one. Tell me the truth, Mama. I'd rather you weren't guilty, I wouldn't join the Komsomol then. Your unhappy daughter Zoya."

Liza froze.

She had already used up three of the four pages allotted for writing letters. She sat as if turned to stone. Then on the fourth page she wrote in big letters: "You're right, Zoya. I'm guilty. Join the Komsomol. This is the last time I'm going to write to you. I wish you happiness, you and Lyalya. Mother."

She held out Zoya's letter and her answer for me to read, then banged her head on the table, choking with sobs.

"Better she should hate me. How's she going to live without the Komsomol, a complete outsider? She'd come to hate the Soviet system. Better she should hate me."

She sent off the letter, handed in the photograph, and from that day on she never said a word about her daughters and never received a single letter from them.

Suzdal

Ten months in Kazan Prison had turned all of us, and especially me, into semi-cripples. We were dying of scurvy and utterly demoralized. I virtually never awoke without a headache. All it took was for the door to open unexpectedly or a book to fall on the floor for me to suffer an acute attack of migraine.

Meanwhile Kolyma needed workers, and a decision had already been made to transfer us to a camp there. But beforehand we were to be given a rest in slightly better conditions.

We knew nothing of all this, so we were desperately worried when on 10 May 1939 we were packed into vans and loaded onto a train.

I lay on my berth in the sleeping compartment with a dreadful headache and constant nausea brought on by the slightest jolt.

Around me everyone was talking excitedly, trying to catch up on everything that had happened in the past year.

As if through a fog, I saw Zhenya Goltsman sitting by me. She was changing the wet rags on my forehead. I took her hand and pressed it, and she pressed mine in turn. That's how we made up from our quarrel. Zhenya sat with me the whole night, and from time to time I felt her cool hand touch my burning forehead. Later the train stood for a long time in a siding, and I simply lay there, racked by pain.

The following day we arrived at Vladimir Prison, and there too I saw and felt nothing apart from this nauseating headache. I remember being in some vehicle, an open truck that was transporting us the forty miles to Suzdal. To this day I have no idea why they decided to take us in an open vehicle in broad daylight down the crowded streets of Vladimir, rather than loading us into a truck and covering us like goods with tarpaulins, as they did with other prisoners. The most astonishing thing was that one of the tires went flat in the middle of a busy main road. While the driver was changing it, a crowd of people gathered to stare at us in horror. I remember the face of an old Jew. He had raised both hands and was praying loudly for us in Hebrew, and the tears flowed constantly down his cheeks and his long gray beard. Probably some member of his own family was in prison. Seeing his face contorted with horror, I glanced at my fellow prisoners. We were indeed a dreadful sight to behold: in our prison uniforms, brown with gray stripes, with our gray-green faces, dull eyes, and surrounded by frightened guards who kept trying to disperse the crowd.

In Suzdal we were struck by the wooden houses and churches. It seemed strange to get out and walk along unpaved roads, strange that the floors in the reception area of the prison were made of wood, not stone, and were newly washed. The place smelled of freshly baked bread, manure, hay, and other good things.

But the greatest surprise awaited us on the way to the washhouse, where we were taken as soon as we arrived. It stood in the middle of a flowering cherry orchard! And for three years we hadn't seen trees, the sky, the moon, or rain! We had taken our exercise in walled-in prison yards paved with asphalt, and been made to look at the ground as we walked. We had been constantly submerged in the revolting smells of prison: disinfectant, slop buckets, boots, cheap tobacco, and the flesh of ill and unwashed bodies. And suddenly here we were amid a cherry orchard in full bloom!

The moon was up, and all the leaves were glimmering; bedecked with flowers, the trees whispered in the breeze.

We were seized with excitement. We breathed in the smell of the earth, the flowers, the trees, surreptitiously snapped off a twig to chew. The bitter-sweet taste of cherry wood pierced our hearts. We longed to fling ourselves on the earth and drink in its aromatic freshness with our entire bodies!

We lined up to wash. Being ill, I was allowed to go last so that I could spend as long as possible in that marvelous garden.

We were taken back to the prison at dawn. It took another hour to sort us all into cells.

My cellmate turned out to be Lida Dmitrieva, with whom I'd already shared a cell in Solovki.

Our prison cell was housed in a wooden building, and before the Revolution had been a monk's cell. It was furnished with wooden bedsteads, their mattresses stuffed with sweet-smelling hay, with a wooden table and two stools in the center. None of the furniture was screwed to the floor, and the cell felt much like an ordinary room. The most wonderful thing of all was the window. Only the lower half was boarded up; through the top half you could see churches, a bare springtime wood, the silhouettes of crows and jackdaws flitting over the trees, and even an apple tree in blossom!

And above all this spread the pale gold morning sky with its rosy clouds. The sky! If people weren't used to seeing it every hour and day of their lives, they would be astonished at the sight and would travel halfway around the world to marvel at it, as landlocked people travel to see the sea. I couldn't get my fill of it, and sat for hours at the window.

Four days after we arrived, I was awakened at night by the chop, chop of an axe outside the window. Lida had awakened, too.

Surely they weren't chopping down our orchard?

Alas, it was all too possible. At Solovki they had cut down all the trees in the exercise yards, plowed up all the grass, and dug up every last plant and shrub. It had pained us dreadfully then, too, but now, after three years in prison, we had felt the cherry orchard such a miracle of beauty—as indeed it was!

The orchard was visible from our exercise yard, and we would glance at it as we walked to and fro and dream of Saturday, washday, when we would be able to enjoy its wonderful fragrance again.

And now they were chopping down all the cherry trees. All night we listened, and with every ringing blow we felt as if our own bodies were being hacked to pieces.

Perhaps tomorrow they would board up the window and we would once again be deprived of sky?

Lida and I wept all night. In the morning we stepped out fearfully for our exercise—and saw our cherry orchard, rustling in the breeze, marvelous, untouched.

We were wrong. They had simply been repairing the fence.

From our two-month stay in Suzdal, I kept above all the memory of golden sunsets and of our sweet-smelling cherry orchard.

Human beings need both so much and so little!

So much—because we need beauty, it seems, as well as bread. And yet so little, because it sufficed for us to be able to see the sky through our window and to walk once a week through our orchard. I have known many fine things in my life, heard Chaliapin sing and Rachmaninoff play, seen beautiful paintings and read wonderful books—but the sky in Suzdal and the flowering cherry orchard remain with me as the strongest aesthetic experience of my life.

In Transit

Our two months in Suzdal were up, and on 10 July 1939 we awoke to the realization that something unusual was happening. There was noisy commotion in the corridors; one by one the cells were being unlocked. We heard shouts of command and—much more surprising—the babble of prisoners' voices. At last it was our turn.

"Pack up your things."

And half an hour later:

"Leave the cell."

We were led into the yard, where thirty or forty women were already milling about. Once again I was struck by the greenish pallor of people's faces and the odd expression they wore. Several of the women had had their heads shaved bare. Among those I already knew were Maria Danielyan, Nina Verestova, and Liza Tsvetkova—the Liza who had stopped writing to her daughter. Zhenya Goltsman was nowhere to be seen. I asked Nina what had become of her, and she told me that Zhenya had died. Happily, this turned out to be untrue.

Olga Ivanovna Nikitina was not among the prisoners. She was lying paralyzed in the prison hospital.

A voice rang out:

"Which of you is Olga Sliozberg?"

I called back, and a young woman named Olga Radovich came up to me. She was twenty-eight years old, well turned out, with golden braids pinned in a crown on her head and a little white collar on her prison dress. Prison had dimmed but not entirely suppressed her natural Ukrainian rosiness.

"I've been wanting for ages to share a cell with you," Olga said. "I've heard all about you, and I'm sure we've got lots of interests in common."

I had heard about Olga, too: she was an art historian by profession and enjoyed giving literary readings and reciting poetry. We did indeed have lots of interests in common, but in fact we never got on particularly well: Olga was surprised that I tormented myself seeking reasons for what had happened to us. To her it was obvious that we had simply fallen into the hands of bandits; all we could do was somehow struggle through and survive these terrible years.

Once our names had been called several times and everyone was checked we were put under escort, loaded into covered trucks, and taken back to Vladimir. For the last time we glanced at our cherry orchard, the belltower, the silhouette of the monastery. A new and unknown life awaited us.

We spent the night in Vladimir, and the next day we were loaded into converted freight cars heated by a small stove and began our journey to the East.

There were around seventy women in our wagon. We never stopped talking—after three or four years of isolation in prison, it was intoxicating to meet so many people at once. Here at last we could talk at the tops of our voices, shout and sing. If you stood on the bed boards, you could look out through the narrow slit of a window.

It was on this journey that I at last heard Liza sing. She really did have an extraordinary voice. She sang effortlessly; the music seemed to pour out of her. Sometimes she sang romances by Glinka or Tchaikovsky, and then her style seemed a bit crude and amateurish. But when she sang Russian folk songs—"Far, Far beyond the Volga," "The Steppe Is All Around," "Oh My Garden, My Garden"—her performance was the best I have ever heard.

Among our fellow prisoners in the wagon was a Tatar from Kazan, Askhab. She was an uneducated woman, semi-literate, a mother of six. I have no idea why she had been imprisoned; she never spoke about it. Askhab immediately got down to business: she unraveled threads of wool from an old blanket, found herself two sticks for needles, and started knitting a sweater. I asked her who she was knitting it for.

"Are you stupid or what? When we get to camp, I'll swap it for bread or sugar." I hadn't known you could swap things for bread and sugar. Askhab could obviously teach me a thing or two.

But businesslike Askhab could also sing. When the rest of us had fallen quiet, her high, tender voice could be heard singing Tatar songs so full of charm and sorrow that you wanted to weep.

There were many good storytellers among us. Galya Ivanova knew many of Pushkin's narrative poems by heart; she could recite the whole of "Eugene Onegin," Griboyedov's "Woe from Wit," and "Lieutenant Schmidt" by Pasternak.

Olga Radovich recited wonderfully, and Natasha Onufrieva remembered perfectly the entire text of Dostoyevsky's *The Idiot*. It took her three days to relate it.

One day, I remember, somebody was "reading" "Woe from Wit" to us. At one of the stations, the officer in charge of the escort guard came up to our wagon with three soldiers. They had obviously been listening outside for some time before they abruptly threw open the door and demanded that we hand over the book. We told them there was no book, whereupon the officer smiled sarcastically and said, "I heard you myself, you were reading it out loud." They started to search; the entire wagon was turned upside down—but of course no book was found.

No one in the wagon talked about politics or about their "cases." We were all happy just to have escaped prison and to be on our way to the camps.

One evening during one long stretch of the journey, the jolting of the train cause the bolt to slip, and the door of the wagon slid wide open. It was sunset. The boundless steppe all about us was in full bloom, and the breath of it, laden with grass and flowers, entered our stuffy, fetid, overcrowded wagon in great scented waves. Our hearts stood still. Suddenly a hysterical voice rang out: "Guard, guard, come and close the door!" The train was moving, and no one heard. Then came other voices: "We must call the guard or they'll think we did it on purpose and meant to escape!"

None of us wanted to escape. What could I, for example, have done with freedom and no passport? I had no more ambitious dream than to be once more in our apartment on Petrovka Street in Moscow. But there I'd be arrested the day after I arrived, and sent back to prison with an extra sentence slapped on.

So we stood in silence and stared at the "freedom" that lay right there at our feet.

In Sverdlovsk or Irkutsk, I don't remember which, the train stopped for a day, and we were taken to a "disinfection station." We undressed and handed over our clothes for treatment and were about to go upstairs to the washroom when we realized that the staircase was lined from top to bottom with guards. Blushing, we hung our heads and huddled together. Then I looked up, and my eyes met those of the officer in charge. He gave me a sullen look. "Come on, come on!" he shouted. "Get a move on!"

I suddenly felt relieved, and the situation even seemed quite comic.

"To hell with them," I thought. "They're no more men to me than Vaska the bull who frightened me when I was a child." Staring brazenly at the guards, I was the first to mount the stairs. The others followed.

So we braved the double line of guards. We subsequently learned that they'd already put four groups of women from our prison train through the same ordeal.

There was a wall-length mirror on the landing upstairs. It had been three years since we'd last seen ourselves, and being women, after all, we all rushed to have a look in the mirror. I stood in the crowd and stared, unable to figure out which of the women was me.

Suddenly I recognized my mother's tired, mournful eyes, her graying hair, the familiar melancholy set of her mouth . . .

It was me. I stood there gaping, unable to believe that I was no longer a young woman whom strangers in the street would call "miss," but this sad, middle-aged woman who looked at least fifty years old.

"Come on, come on!" shouted the guards. "Your group has twenty minutes to wash!"

We rushed into the washroom, grabbed bowls, surreptitiously washed out our scraps of underwear, and joined in the usual scramble of prisoners on these long journeys.

But for a long time afterward, I kept thinking of that gray-haired woman who had stared at me from the mirror with her sad, weary face, trying to get used to the idea that this was me.

Our train journey lasted thirty-four days. There was one period when we were given very little water: there were no vessels to store it in, and the periods between stops were very long. I didn't suffer too badly from thirst, but one of the women in our wagon, a doctor by the name of Zavalishina, was a diabetic. She was literally dying of thirst. We gave her double and triple rations, but they seemed no more than a drop to her.

I used to save half a glass from my ration to wash with. Once, noticing me cleaning my teeth and washing my face, she reproached me: "How cruel to use water for washing when other people are dying of thirst!" I was terribly upset, and to this day it tears my heart to remember the look in her eyes.

She died on the thirtieth day of the journey.

Kolyma

After four years in prison, where the main punishment had been to deprive us of dignity by giving us no work, we found ourselves at the camp in Magadan, on the Sea of Okhotsk. You could immediately tell us apart from the old camp hands by our pale faces, frightened looks, and complete lack of alertness. For the first three days we did no work but had a good rest and talked from dawn to dusk about the advantages of camp over prison life.

The camp population (around a thousand women) seemed to us enormous: so many people, so many conversations to have, so many potential friends!

Then there was nature. Within the compound, which was fenced with barbed wire, we could walk around freely, gaze at the sky and the faraway hills, go up to the stunted trees and stroke them with our hands. We breathed the moist sea air, felt the August drizzle on our faces, sat on the damp grass and let the earth run through our fingers. For four years we had lived without all this and discovered in doing so that it was essential to our being: without it you ceased to feel like a normal person.

And finally there was work. We had dreamt of work and spoken of it with such fervent longing that the old camp hands, who hated their enforced hard labor, must have doubted our sincerity.

On our third day in camp, we were told that those who felt strong enough could go out to work the next morning (the maximum period of rest was a week).

There was great excitement, as on the eve of a major holiday. Eighteen prisoners, including me, decided that we would go. We longed to get out of the compound, to walk down a road, to be in unbounded space, to see the forest, the sea.

The man organizing the prisoners into work groups the following morning told us to choose a leader. I was appointed, and immediately surveyed my brigade with proprietary interest. It was made up almost entirely of gray-haired intellectuals; among us were two professors, a writer, two pianists, a ballerina, and half a dozen Party workers. We were all city people. After four years of enforced idleness our muscles had atrophied. But all of us dreamt of proving by our labor how "honest" and "Soviet" we were.

We were led out of the compound, and found ourselves walking through a vast building site where a new town was being constructed. In the wasteland on the edge of the town, the roof was being put on a new hospital. Cheerful, ruddy-faced girls were cleaning the windows and chatting and flirting with the guards.

A fine Kolyma drizzle was falling, but we felt quite cheerful, almost like free citizens.

Kolmogorsky, the foreman, came up to us. He was a well-built man of about forty, who looked to us a bit of a dandy with his tall hat of gray astrakhan, his shining boots, and his padded work jacket tightly fastened with a wide belt at the waist. Smiling politely, he turned to me and explained our job:

"You're going to dig a ditch. It's already been started and it's now one meter deep. You've got to get it down to three meters. The work norm for each person is to dig out nine cubic meters of soil a day. You don't have to work yourself; the norm doesn't apply to the brigade leader. In summertime the work day is fifteen hours. You have one hour's break for dinner. Work begins at six in the morning and ends at nine in the evening. Dinner will be brought to you at one P.M."

Then he handed out some heavy, rusty spades, and we set to work. We had no idea how much nine cubic meters was, and only the vaguest sense of what a fifteen-hour day would mean. We were full of enthusiasm.

I positioned my workers three meters apart, found a place for myself, and we started work. I announced that there would a ten-minute smoke break every hour when I gave the signal.

It was drizzling. The soil was clay. We discovered that it was very difficult to get our spades in at all; we could get only a bit of wet clay on the very tip. The clay was incredibly heavy and had the infuriating habit of sliding off as we slowly lifted each spadeful to the edge of the ditch: we hadn't the strength to toss it up in a single jerk. I didn't have a watch, but I was sure that we had been at work for ages already, and I was totally exhausted.

"Smoke break!"

"But we've hardly worked twenty minutes," my stalwart team protested.

Maybe, but I had no more strength left, and neither did anyone else. We laid down our spades and seated ourselves on the handles.

"End of break!" I commanded, and we started digging again.

By dinnertime we had probably had about thirty breaks, and it became harder and harder each time to give the order to resume work.

Dinner was brought and seemed luxurious by our standards: fresh fish soup, pieces of fried Siberian salmon, and even some fruit drink. Tired though we were, we ate with appetite, but the signal to resume work came in no time at all.

The day seemed interminable. Kolmogorsky dropped by to see us. I tried to gather from his expression whether we had done much, but it was impossible to judge.

During one of the breaks, some of the girls from the floor- and window-cleaning brigade came up to us and laughed.

"Kolmogorsky's done you a nice turn, hasn't he?" said one. "Lovely work!"

"What about you, do you manage to do the norm?" I asked.

"Us? We can do three times the norm and sit twiddling our fingers. But we're used to it; we've all been in the camps five, seven years."

I looked at her with respect.

"And what sort of person is Kolmogorsky?"

"He's finishing his sentence, been in the camps since 1930. He's a Cossack, quite a smart fellow. He's got himself set up very nicely, thank you, with more girls than he knows what to do with."

We continued digging. The signal to stop took forever to come, and I lost track of the number of breaks. The return journey seemed unbelievably long.

On that first day, instead of going straight to eat, we went back to our barracks first to wash before supper—only to find that we had no strength to return to the canteen. We collapsed on our beds, fell instantly asleep, and minutes later, so it seemed, heard the bell for reveille. After this we always made sure to go to supper straight from work, filthy and smeared with clay as we were, and dragged ourselves back to the barracks only afterward.

We dug for three days and realized with alarm that the ditch didn't seem to be progressing at all, let alone at the rate of nine cubic meters per person per day.

At the end of the third day, Kolmogorsky came up and measured what we'd done. Then he smiled ironically and invited me into his office. I went in. His table was luxuriously set, with a tablecloth of fresh sacking, a bottle of ethyl alcohol, a tin of condensed milk, some salted salmon, spring onions, and some lard. It was a feast from a fairytale. I was invited to sit down. Kolmogorsky offered me some neat alcohol and told me I couldn't refuse or I'd lose his "protection."

I valiantly swallowed the stuff; it was the first time in my life that I'd drunk it. It was disgusting, but I realized that it was essential to get on good terms with Kolmogorsky.

The spirits made me weak at the knees, but my head remained clear.

"Well, it's a bad business, very bad. You've done just three percent of the norm. I suppose your ladies have been carrying on in the bushes with the men?"

"What do you mean? All our women are conscientious workers; they've been trying their hardest! But the work's very difficult for us; we're city women, and we're not as young as we were, and we've been four years in prison. Give us some other type of work—washing floors and windows; then we'll be able to show you what good workers we are."

"Come off it! If you'd done even half the norm, it would be different. But three percent! Confess now: aren't your ladies running after the men?"

"No, of course not! Can't you see what kind of people they are? They're all trying as hard as they can. They're all former Party members, after all."

Suddenly the mask of the kind interlocutor dropped from Kolmogorsky's face.

"Oh yes, former members of the Party, are they? Now, if you'd been prostitutes, I'd have been happy to let you wash windows and do three times the norm. When those Party members in 1929 decided to punish me for being a 'kulak,' threw me and my six children out of our home, I said to them, 'What've the children ever done?' and they told me, 'That's Soviet law.' So there you are; you can stick to your Soviet law and dig nine cubic meters of mud a day!" He laughed. "Keep to the letter of the law! But hold on, little lady! I could switch you to being brigade leader of the girls in the house. You weren't a Party member, were you? You're a very attractive lady, I'd be happy to do you a favor."

"I'm afraid you're mistaken. I was a member of the Party, too," I said, and left.

It was the first time in my life that I'd made myself out to be someone I wasn't.

Galya

I subsequently was transferred to Elgen, the women's camp some 500 kilometers northwest and inland from Magadan. There I worked felling timber. For a time my partner was Galya Prozorovskaya. She was stronger and more skillful than me, but she got steadily weaker, and we began finishing our joint norm (eight cubic meters a day between the two of us) later and later in the evening.

I was always the first to give in. "Let's chuck it in, Galya; we'll make it up tomorrow. I can't go on any longer."

Scared, Galya would answer, "What about the norm? Are we going to make do with 400 grams a day?"

Those who fulfilled the norm got 600 grams of bread a day; those who failed got only 400. Those 200 grams made all the difference. On 400 grams of bread a day, you simply couldn't survive working in temperatures of -50 degrees centigrade.

"I know, I know! Well, let's make one last effort." So we would set to work on our stack, with me unscrupulously "stuffing" the stack with snow and brushwood. Galya would beg me, "Please don't! What if they catch us. I'd be so ashamed."

By hook or by crook, we put our eight cubic meters together, by which time it was already dark and we still had to walk the three miles home. The frost paralyzed our backs, faces, and hands. It took the greatest effort of will to walk for an hour and a half or two hours home along the deserted forest road, when each foot seemed to weigh a ton, when your knees shook from weakness and hunger, when the scarf covering your face had turned into a shield of ice, and it was difficult even to breathe.

But at the far end were our warm barracks, a bowl of hot if watery soup, 200 grams of heavy, damp, tasty—so tasty!—bread, and our bed boards to rest on, and the blazing stove. So on we went.

But every day we left our patch of forest later than the day before, and the journey home each day took longer because the trees to be felled were that much farther from the barracks.

One evening Galya and I were walking home, barely dragging one foot after the other. It was very cold. The moon was shining and illuminated our snowy path.

We were already close to the camp when Galya suddenly fell flat on her back. She lay there motionless.

"Galya, Galya!" I shook her.

There was no answer. She lay lifeless on the snow. There was not a hope of my lifting her; I hadn't the strength. I pulled her hand from her sleeve to check her pulse—and felt nothing. If she had died, she'd be picked up later—and I should leave straightaway or I'd freeze to death myself. But what if she was alive? Within an hour she'd turn into a lump of ice. Either way, there was nothing I could do.

I took a few decisive steps away, then turned back.

"Galya, Galya!"

No answer.

"Galya, dear! Galya!"

No answer. Then suddenly I heard the squeak of a sledge in the snow and the clip-clop of horses on the road running parallel to our path, about 200 meters away. I ran, tottering in the snow, shouting, stumbling on tree stumps, falling, out of breath from running and yelling in the freezing air.

At last there he was, a peasant with a sledgeload of manure.

"Comrade, in God's name, save us; there's a woman freezing to death down there!"

He was extremely grumpy—for he too was frozen stiff, worn out and dreaming of a warm stove and dishwater soup and his evening's ration of 200 grams of bread.

I begged him, wept, clung to his jacket. Swearing, he turned back to our road, and together we hoisted Galya onto the frozen dung.

Fifteen minutes later, we were back at our barracks and sitting by the stove. At my request, the cook poured our savior a bowl of soup. He turned out to be a singer from Leningrad. We talked about music and the theater while Galya, revived, lay on her bunk and let the tears flow endlessly down her cheeks.

Bread

Once a month, the prisoners who'd managed to fulfill the norm logging were given an extra kilogram of bread.

We dreamed endlessly of this bread. Usually I managed to earn it, but one month things didn't work out, and I failed to fulfill my monthly norm.

For some time I'd felt a premonition of something unpleasant. On the eve of our free day, returning from work, we rushed to look at the lists. My name was nowhere to be seen.

My day off was spoiled. True, my neighbor gave me a chunk of her bread, but this was nothing compared to a kilogram.

When I returned from work the following day, the prisoner who was our barrack orderly greeted me with a cry: "Run and see what's under your pillow!"

My heart leaped: perhaps I'd got my bread ration after all!

I ran to my bed and threw off the pillow. Under it lay three letters from home, three whole letters! It was six months since I'd received anything at all.

My first reaction on seeing them was acute disappointment.

And then—horror.

What had become of me if a piece of bread was worth more to me now than letters from my mother, my father, my children!

I opened the envelopes. Photos tumbled out. My daughter looked up at me with her gray eyes. My son was frowning, deep in thought.

I forgot all about the bread and wept.

Basya

Basya was nineteen years old, and had been sentenced to five years in corrective labor camps for Zionism.

She had been arrested together with her fiancé, a twenty-year-old student named Osip. Basya had classically angelic looks. She was petite, with golden curls, blue eyes, bright rosy cheeks, and lips like cherries. But her appearance could hardly have been more deceptive. Basya was no angel but a young woman of very strong character. And what a voice she had: unbelievably shrill and piercing. She wanted to have a say in everything, always insisted on the truth, and if she was in the barracks, you were certain to hear every word.

One morning when the jobs were being distributed, the work assigner came up to Basya and said, "You're on floor-washing today."

Washing floors was considered privileged work: women's work, done inside where it was warm, not like loading firewood onto oxen or hacking away at the soil. Basya readily agreed, but when we got back from work that day, we found her weeping bitterly and recounting in her shrill voice how the camp director had treated her to some sausage and lard, but then he'd started pestering her, so that she'd ended up slapping him with a wet rag, and he'd gotten mad at her and said, "Tomorrow you'll be hauling logs with the oxen."

Basya was terrified of these animals and could never get them to obey her. They were used to rough voices swearing at them. Basya would run around them, call them "disgusting beasts," and weep—whereupon they would lie down and pay no more attention to her than to a fly. Two or three days would pass, and then she'd be summoned again by the director to wash floors, only to end up once again with the oxen. Finally, the director got fed up with all this and decided to take stronger measures. "I'm getting no work out of you," he said on one of his checkups. "You mess around all day, no one else can use the oxen, and by the end of the day nothing's been carted at all. Tomorrow you're going to be paired with Prokhorov to haul logs."

Prokhorov was one of the few men in our camp. He repaired harnesses and tools and carted the heaviest logs. He was a man of about fifty, terrible to look at, huge, with shoulders as broad and square as a chest of drawers, and arms that reached almost to his knees. When he was arrested as a "kulak" he had killed three men. He had the foulest mouth of anyone we knew, and Basya was absolutely terrified of him. She kept sobbing and saying that she wouldn't go with Prokhorov; it would be better to end up in the punishment cell. Suddenly Prokhorov came into the barracks.

"What are you howling about?" he asked Basya. "Scared of Prokhorov, are you? It's the bosses you should worry about, not me! I won't do you any harm." He turned and went out.

Basya was puzzled but relieved, and the next day she went to work with Prokhorov and a pair of oxen. From that day on, a strange friendship developed between the huge, gorilla-like Prokhorov and angelic Basya. He fed her well and did all her work for her. Basya put on weight and told everyone what a good fellow Prokhorov was.

Once Prokhorov told a story that set the whole barracks to laughing. Basya kept stamping her foot at him and shouting, "Shut up! Shut up!" but Prokhorov took no notice and went on with his tale:

"I was loading up the carts when all of a sudden I look up and I'll be damned if I can see Basya anywhere. So I search for her high and low, and at last I find her standing behind a tree, crying her eyes out because her fingers have frozen and she can't do up her trousers! So I do up her trousers for her right and proper, and fasten her belt and set fire to an armful of hay—'There you are, my darling,' I say, 'get your fingers warm.' And I sat her down on the logs and got her home safe and sound. That's Prokhorov for you!"

Basya worked with Prokhorov for two years, and he guarded her like the most devoted watchdog.

Gold

It was haymaking time. On our way to the fields, we had stopped to have a rest and cooked some gruel. Afterward I went to wash the dishes in the stream. I had scooped up some water and sand to wash a basin, and when I poured out the water, I noticed two tiny grains of gold at the bottom. "Gold! Gold!" I shouted. All the women crowded round me to look, and Prokhorov, who was our foreman, came up. "Gold my foot! That's just fool's gold," he said authoritatively, and quickly rinsed the basin out. Our excitement over, we went back to our work and forgot about the gold.

We walked on. Prokhorov was in front, leading the horse. I found myself walking alongside him. After a long silence he said, "What an idiot you are. All that education and you're still an idiot. What do you need gold for? Here we are making hay, and we're not so badly off. But if they find gold here do you realize how many people are going to end up cripples? Haven't you seen how they work down in the gold mines? Where's your old man been work-ing? You don't know? I wouldn't be surprised if he's lying buried at the bottom of a mine shaft. A man can do one season on that job and he's finished. What an idiot you are!"

"So it was gold after all?"

"What else? Of course it was gold."

Mirage

Many prisoners asked for their cases to be reviewed, sent appeals to the Procurator General of the USSR and wrote letters to Stalin.

I never wrote myself, not our of pride but because I was convinced that nothing would ever come of it.

But my mother lived on the hope that she could get me released. For four years after I was arrested, she "petitioned" on my behalf, setting off every day as if to work. She went the rounds of all the authorities, right up to the Procurator General and the offices of the Soviet "president," Kalinin him-self. There wasn't an office in the land that she hadn't been to; she'd been everywhere, stood in endless lines, begged for my case to be reviewed, wept and tried to touch people's hearts with pity—for her daughter, a mother of two, who'd been sent to prison for no reason at all.

And finally—wonders will never cease!—she did succeed in getting a review.

Whether because the original indictment had been cobbled together so carelessly, or because there had been some temporary letup in the repres-sions, on 3 June 1940 I was acquitted of preparing a terrorist act against Kaganovich.

That summer we were working on Bird Island, as we called the place where two mountain rivers met. Our brigade leader was a good man, a Siberian named Sasha who'd been arrested as a "kulak." On the banks of the river, several large stacks of timber had been left from previous years and never officially counted, so we were always able to top up our own work with the results of someone else's labor. There was no need to over-work; our productivity was always high, and we always got fed the top rations. Moreover, the men—most of them Siberians, victims of "deku-lakization" like Sasha—had made rafts to go fishing, and they would treat us to the fish they'd caught. There were lots of birds' nests, too, and we often found ducks' eggs. It was the easiest summer of my whole time in camp or prison.

One morning the manager of the camp stores came out from Elgen and brought us the mail. There was a telegram for me. "On 3 June 1940 you

were fully rehabilitated by a Decree of the USSR Supreme Court. So happy."
It was signed by my whole family.

I went mad! I walked about in a daze, as if drunk, already in my mind's
eye hugging my children, my mother and father, telling them everything I'd
been through. I pictured my homecoming down to the last detail, from the
moment I arrived at the station to the blessed finale when I'd lay my head in
my mother's lap and at last have a good long cry.

But time passed, and I got no official word of the appeal. Winter set in.

Our life on Bird Island vanished like a dream. We were set to work
digging trenches. The cold was ferocious, with temperatures of -50.

One day we were digging our trench when the brigade leader, Anya
Orlova, came up to me and stood for a long time in silence. Then she said,
"Be brave, Olga!" and handed me a telegram. It read: "The Procurator
General of the USSR contested the Supreme Court's decision; on the second
appeal you were sentenced to 8 years' deprivation of liberty for failing to
denounce your husband (Article 58:12). Bear up. Mama."

Without a word, I showed the telegram to my comrades. They read it.
No one spoke.

Anya looked at me compassionately.

"Why don't you go back to the barracks and lie down."

"I don't want to."

At that moment it seemed unthinkable to go sit by myself in the barrack.

That night, burying myself under the covers, I kept repeating like an
incantation: "I will survive. Just three years and four months to go. I will
survive. Just forty months. I'll survive, I promise you, Mama. Hold on and
wait for me, Mama. I will survive."

Then the letters started coming. Mother told me the whole story, how
she'd gone from pillar to post, how everyone had tried to talk her out of it
and even threatened her with banishment from Moscow, but she'd paid no
attention, she just wanted the truth. How on the day the appeal was heard,
she'd sat in the street from early morning till five in the afternoon, waiting in
the rain outside the courthouse.

She wrote that all this time she'd concealed from the children the fact
that I'd been arrested, telling them that I'd had to go away on business, but
now she had told them everything. After all, my son was ten already, and my
little girl eight and they could understand everything.

A Goner

The winter of 1943 was very hard. Our bread ration was reduced from
600 to 500 grams. Apart from bread, all we got was soup made from dirty

outer cabbage leaves and herring heads (and in a half-liter scoop all you got was two or three cabbage leaves and one head), three tablespoons of sticky gruel with half a teaspoon of vegetable oil, and for supper a fish tail the size of a finger. Meanwhile we were working ten hours a day in temperatures of minus fifty degrees. So people started gradually giving out.

At first I worked with Galya Prozorovskaya, but after she collapsed in the forest, she was transferred to a workshop where she patched prisoners' clothes.

After that my workmate was Raya Ginzburg. We worked happily together, although the two of us could barely walk—she was covered in boils, and my feet seemed to weigh a ton; my knees buckled under me as if they were made of cotton wool. We dragged on till March, when the order came for a group to be transferred to work at the farm and greenhouses at the central camp in Elgen. They were starting their springtime work there and needed people to clear the land of snow and prepare seedlings in the greenhouses. Our brigade leader naturally tried to get the weakest members of our brigade transferred. Raya was among those chosen to go, and I was left on my own.

It was considered great good fortune, of course, to be relieved of logging work, and conditions in Elgen were certainly easier: you worked not out in the forest but in the relatively civilized agricultural center. From time to time you could get out of the cold, and at least once a month you could buy yourself a loaf of bread for fifty rubles (roughly our monthly earnings). Yet Raya was terribly reluctant to go without me. We had grown very fond of each other and knew that if we parted, we might never meet again: the twenty-odd kilometers separating us would be as insuperable as the distance from Moscow to New York in ordinary life.

Raya got ready for her journey and bequeathed to me her meager possessions: I stuffed the remnants of hay from her mattress in mine, and that made my nights a bit more comfortable; she also left me her wicklamp (they had electricity at Elgen) and her knife: she was bound to be searched and would have to throw away the knife anyway.

Previously I had been considered strong, and plenty of people had wanted to pair up with me for work, but now virtually all my friends had been transferred elsewhere, others had remained in pairs, and those who had been left on their own were mostly younger and stronger than me and paired up with one another. I realized then for the first time that I too was almost a "goner," and that no one was very keen to work with me.

I wasn't offended. I myself was afraid to team up with the weakest people: a pair, after all, had to fulfil the norm for two—eight cubic meters of wood, and with a weak partner I would be obliged to take on five or six cubic meters myself, which would obviously be beyond my strength. I decided to work on my own. I already had the knack: I would use a short, one-meter, two-handed saw to fell a larch tree at the root, saw it up into three-meter logs, and put together a four cubic meter stack. It was possible to use a two-handed saw on my own because at that temperature the blade cut through the trunk as smoothly as if it were running in the narrow groove of a lathe.

Somehow I fulfilled the norm and managed to get my "first category" rations (500 grams of bread). But I felt miserable working all day in the forest alone. Miserable and afraid, because I have a very poor sense of direction. I would finish work after almost everyone else had left, and I was always afraid that I'd lose my way. To get lost meant certain death. The days dragged, and it seemed that winter would never end. But six weeks later, a further group was summoned to work at the farm, and this time I was among them.

We walked from early morning until night to cover the twenty kilometers to the farm, and I doubted that I would ever get there: I had no strength left in my legs at all.

We arrived late in the evening, and Raya was the first to greet me. She had boiled some water and gotten me some rusks, and had gathered a whole bundle of hay for a mattress. And she had saved me a place on the bed boards next to her. What a difference such friendship made! We talked for hours. Raya had had the good luck to be sent to a course on vegetable gardening and had done very well. She was more or less guaranteed work at the farm. This seemed to us salvation: the work was all in one place and much lighter than lumber work. In the summer you could always eat some of the vegetables on the quiet, and in the winter you worked in the greenhouses.

Raya had already talked about me to Onishchenko, the farm manager—told him how hard-working and strong and skillful I was. She was sure I would be able to stay and work there, too. I had my doubts, knowing how weak I had become. I could barely move my cotton wool legs. But I hoped nonetheless to be able to rest a little and recover some of my strength, and prayed that I would be allowed to stay more permanently.

The following day we began work, clearing the farm compound of snow. We carted the snow away on sleds, harnessing ourselves to them in pairs, like horses.

Several times I noticed Raya glance at me with alarm. She was trying to pull even harder, for I could barely move.

"I'm making things difficult for you," I said. "I've grown so weak."

"Not at all, only try to look a bit more lively; otherwise Onishchenko will notice. He doesn't like people to 'give out' on him."

Onishchenko stood at the gates of the farm compound, and every time we dragged past with our sledgeful of snow, he observed us carefully to see how we were working. He had to select his permanent workers from among us, and he was giving us all a good looking over. Every time we passed him, Raya would throw me a worried glance and beg me to cheer up: "You look so miserable; couldn't you try and liven up just for a few meters? Please try and smile!"

I could imagine just what I looked like: my neck and chin stuck out, my whole body craning forward, while my cursed legs refused to move and merely dragged along behind me. And I was supposed to smile! The best I could do was bare my teeth in an idiotic corpse-like grin.

No, there was no deceiving Onishchenko. He got rid of me. After we'd cleared the snow, all the unwanted workers were removed from the farm and sent back to work in the forest.

Once again I said goodbye to Raya.

Altunin

I wish I could remember the first name of a remarkable man whose surname was Altunin. He came from somewhere in the Voronezh region. I believe he was originally a tanner, who prepared raw hides. Later he became a Party worker. He was a handsome man of about forty, a classic Russian with a reddish beard. He had obviously once been very strong, broad-shouldered and thickset. In '38 and '39 he had worked down in the mines in Kolyma, and there he had started to "give out." He had grown terribly feeble and used to cough his lungs out. But he had wonderfully skillful hands, and was given work as a toolmaker in a women's construction brigade in Magadan.

One day he told me his story.

"As soon as it all started in 1937," he began, "first this comrade was an enemy, then that one—and we began by expelling them from the Party and ended up killing them, our own comrades. I used to pretend to be ill.

"That way I could get out of going to Party meetings and having to put up my hand to say 'yes, I agree.' But then I realized something had to be done. We couldn't go on like this: we were killing the Party, killing good, honorable people. I couldn't believe they were all traitors—people I knew well.

"So one evening I sat down and wrote what I thought. I sent one copy to my local Party organization, one to Stalin himself, and one to the Party's Central Control Commission. I wrote that we were killing the Revolution. Maybe all this wrecking and sabotage was just local, in which case it wasn't a total catastrophe, but if it was going on all over Russia, we were dealing with a counterrevolution.

"I poured my whole heart into this letter. I showed it to my wife and she said, 'This is suicide; you'll be in prison the day they see it.' But I said, 'Let them put me in prison. Better to be behind bars than to raise your hand and say "yes" to having your comrades killed.'

"Well, it turned out just as she said. I sent off my letter, and three days later I was in prison. I got the treatment, then a ten-year sentence and off to Kolyma."

"Didn't you ever regret what you'd done?" I asked.

"Well, there was one time I regretted it. There was a terrible frost, and we'd been sent to root out stumps in the forest. All we had were some rusty axes—no picks, no crowbars. We really suffered over those stumps. We just about managed to get four of them up, and then we decided—to hell with it; we made a nice campfire and burned the stumps. In the evening the foreman turned up, and we hadn't done a thing.

"We went straight from the forest to the punishment cell. The cell was three square meters, and there was no glass in the window. And no stove. I started running. I ran round and round in that cage, and suddenly I felt really sorry for myself: other people ended up in there for nothing, whereas I knew just what I was doing when I put myself inside. And what was the point of writing what I wrote? Everything had gone on just as before. Maybe Solts [an Old Bolshevik in charge of the Control Commission] felt a bit ashamed, but old Mustache—what did he care? There was no getting through to him. And right now, I thought, I could be sitting at home with my wife and kids in a warm room with the samovar purring. But the moment that thought entered my mind, I started beating my head against the wall to banish it forever. So I spent the whole night running to and fro in my cage and cursing myself for even once having regrets for my nice cozy life."

Altunin worked with us for one winter. In the spring of 1940 he died in the camp hospital of tuberculosis.

Polina Gertsenberg

For a while my neighbor on the bed boards was a doctor, Polina Gertsenberg, a Jewish woman from Poland and a member of the Sejm, the Polish parliament.

Doctors had the right to get other prisoners released from work on grounds of illness. People would give a great deal for the chance to rest from their heavy labor and some of the doctors, succumbing to bribes, did rather comfortably for themselves. But Polina starved along with the rest of us, and was reluctant even to prescribe herself the fish oil that she got for the most emaciated prisoners.

One day, to the great consternation of the authorities, an order arrived to fly six prisoners back to the mainland. All were former members of the Polish Sejm, and among them was Polina.

The Chief Procurator of Dalstroi, the Far Eastern construction organization that controlled Kolyma, came up to Elgen from Magadan to attend to the matter. His first order was to make sure that Polina was properly dressed. She was summoned to the camp store, where the camp director ceremonially presented her with a silk dress, suede shoes, and a sealskin coat. He was astonished when Polina declared that she would make the journey in the same clothes that she had been wearing for the past two years. Protest and cajole as they might, the authorities were unable to persuade her to take off her quilted trousers or her patched felt boots. Nor could they force her to change.

So in the end she went in the same old clothes to have her farewell talk with the procurator. Pretending not to notice her attire, he informed her that a treaty had been signed with Poland, and concluded with the words: "Our countries are now fighting against a common enemy—German fascism. I hope that on your return to Poland you won't spread any slanderous rumors about the Soviet Union."

"I can give you my word," Polina replied, "that I will spread no such rumors. On the contrary, when victory is achieved, I shall tell the truth, the whole truth, and nothing but the truth in parliament, in the press, and everywhere I go."

There was nothing the authorities could object to in that. Polina left to the accompaniment of their scowls and our envious and admiring glances.

Release

Nadya Fyodorovich was due to be released in 1941. She had been arrested in 1936 and sentenced to five years.

She had left behind a nine-year-old son, a proud, nervous boy. Boris had lived at first with his grandmother, but after she died in 1938, he had drifted from relation to relation. Everyone found him a burden and, after keeping him a short time, would try to dump him on some other aunt or uncle.

Nadya counted the days until her release and longed to be able to bring her son home again.

For the day of Nadya's release, 25 June 1941, we prepared an entire trousseau: someone gave her a skirt, someone else a nightdress or a scarf.

Nadya was the first among us to finish her sentence. We had no idea that the war had begun—we never set eyes on a newspaper. Yet there was a distinct sense of alarm in the air. Nadya was nervous, both preparing herself for freedom and doubting that it would ever come.

25 June came and went. Another agonizing month went by. At last Nadya was summoned to see the camp director.

In the morning, as usual, we set off for work. Nadya remained in the barracks. Before we left, I went up to her: "Maybe this is the last time we'll see each other, and this agonizing wait really will be over for you."

"I don't know," said Nadya. "I have a strange feeling about all this."

We returned that evening to find Nadya sitting smoking by the stove.

The prisoner on duty in our barrack warned us in a whisper: "Don't say anything; she's gone crazy. They're not letting her out."

Nadya had been made to sign an order committing her to camp "until release by special order."

All this time her son had believed that his mother would be let out on 25 June. She had kept begging him not to quarrel with his relatives, to be patient just a little longer. She couldn't bear to think how he would react to her letter telling him that their reunion had been indefinitely postponed.

In fact, her son never received the letter. The censors would on no account allow a prisoner to let the outside world know that her term had ended but that she was being kept "until released by special order."

Nadya waited for her son's answer, but none came. At last, in the winter of 1942, she received a letter from a stranger. He had picked Borya up at some remote station in Siberia near Irkutsk, and found that the boy was suffering from pneumonia. He had taken him in and nursed him till he was better. He reproached Nadya for having forgotten about her son as soon as she was released; she was a bad mother; she had probably gone and gotten married and was doing nicely for herself while her fourteen-year-old son, hitching a free ride on the train all the way from Ryazan to Irkutsk, was dying of hunger.

We knew by then that the war had begun and that many of our letters were not getting through. Nadya rushed to the camp director and wrote a letter to the procurator, begging them to let her son and this stranger know that she had served her sentence but was still in prison. But they refused.

So she never found out what became of her son. Meanwhile, as it turned out later, her son, now a homeless orphan, joined a gang and eventually, in 1947, himself turned up in the Kolyma camps with a five-year sentence on some criminal charge.

A number of other women finished their sentences soon after Nadya, but all of those convicted of serious political crimes were kept in camp until "release by special order." Soon there was a whole group of "over-term prisoners." There was, it is true, a kind of comfort in numbers; other prisoners, more or less prepared for the worst, reacted less tragically to their fate than Nadya. But there were several instances of suicide. People were unable to bear the thought that the release they had longed for, counting the weeks and days, might be indefinitely postponed.

Conditions in camp became harder and harder—constant tormenting hunger, harsh discipline, absolute dejection. It was in these circumstances, on 27 April 1944, that my sentence came to an end. If I was to believe my family's letters, the Supreme Court had changed the charge against me from Article 58:8 (terrorism) to 58:12 (failure to denounce). This was the least serious political offense, and those charged with it were being released on time. But for four years I had received no official word that the charge had been changed, and therefore had no idea whether there really had been some decree to this effect, or whether my mother had been deceived and everything had remained as before.

The winter of 1943–44 was the hardest of all for me. Unable to concentrate on anything else, I was obsessed with trying to guess whether I would be released or not. I would walk back from work thinking, If I get back to the barracks before five, I will be released; if I'm any later, I won't be. If it's a hundred steps from here to that pine tree, I'll be released; if it's more I won't be . . .

At last, on 1 April 1944, I received a summons and was told that on 6 August 1940, the charge against me had been changed to Article 58:12 (failure to denounce).

"Freedom" became a reality.

I lived those last weeks in a fog, afraid even to think of release, and not knowing what to hope for. I was told that in any case I would not be allowed to go back to my family.

I dreamt of going back to "my" room, locking the door (I would definitely lock the door), lying on my bed, and reading by normal electric light.

I dreamt of eating my fill. Of never again going to work in the forest in the terrifying cold of Kolyma, but getting a job in a warm, cozy office. I dreamt of no longer being subjected to searches, scoldings, curses, no longer living side by side with prostitutes and thieves; I imagined spending summer Sundays walking the entire day. I would walk as far as I wanted, and no one would forbid me, no one would yell: "Stand to attention! A step right or left and I shoot!"

I was released exactly on time, on 27 April 1944. Out of our whole group, I was the only one to be freed. The rest were detained until 1947. My mother's endless petitions had saved three years of my life.

Everyone considered me lucky. But I kept weeping. How could I live alone, without the comrades that I'd grown so close to in camp?

I immediately petitioned to be allowed to go back to the "mainland," but was told that I would be restricted forever to Kolyma.

Forever . . . How many times was I forced to sign that promise, "forever!"

Forever on Kolyma, eternally in Karaganda, forbidden for all time to go to Moscow . . .

This eternity turned out in the end to be no more than twelve years, until the 20th Party Congress. But how long those twelve years seemed to last!

Nikolai Adamov

By 1944 I knew that the sentence given my husband—ten years without right of correspondence—was a code for execution. I was a widow.

And then I found a friend, a support in life, and I married him. His name was Nikolai Vasilievich Adamov. Nikolai was a miner's son from the Donbass in southern Russia and Ukraine, the eldest of four children. At the age of thirteen he had gone to work in a candy factory. In 1918, when he was sixteen, the Whites took control of the Donbass. The miners, to prevent their getting coal, flooded the mine where Nikolai's father worked. His father was captured and hanged by the Whites. Nikolai was now the main breadwinner and head of the household. He was reluctant to leave his mother and sisters, but the need to fight, the desire to avenge his father, proved stronger. He left home to join the Red Army, and fought with them for the entire Civil War.

In 1927 he graduated from a veterinary institute. He was drafted into the army once again and became a political commissar in the Special Far East Regiment. In 1935 he was arrested for voicing anti-Stalin opinions. The investigator asked him about his wife. Realizing that they were after her as well, Nikolai said that he wanted to give important evidence to a representative of the NKVD. Left alone with the NKVD man, Nikolai said, "Bear in mind that if my wife is arrested, I'll give evidence to ensure that you get an even worse sentence than mine." His wife was left unscathed, but got so scared that she decided to renounce Nikolai herself.

Nikolai was sentenced to five years, and in the spring of 1937 he was brought to Magadan. Soon afterward Colonel Garanin, whose very name filled prisoners with horror, began his reign of terror there. He was responsible for getting a great many prisoners an extra ten-year sentence "for sabotage," and he had shot people in the camps with his own hand.

At that time the worst place of all was the so-called "Serpantinka," the special punishment camp where Nikolai ended up.

The barracks in the Serpantinka were so overcrowded that prisoners took turns sitting on the floor while everyone else remained standing. In the mornings the door would open, and the names of ten or twelve prisoners would be called. No one would answer. The first people that came to hand were then dragged out and shot. Once Nikolai was among the dozen seized, although a totally different group of people had been named. They were pushed into the back of a van and driven off. All the guards were drunk. There was a heap of sacks in the corner of the van, and Nikolai crawled under them. The van stopped, the prisoners were led out, and after a few moments shots were heard. The guards returned alone and drove back to the camp. In the evening Nikolai succeeded in crawling out from under the sacks and joined a group of prisoners sawing firewood.

One day the door opened and Nikolai's name was called. He naturally refused to answer. The guards left, then returned and asked again which of the prisoners was Adamov the vet. The pigs apparently were ailing. "Ah, well," said Nikolai, "in that case—I'm Adamov." He was taken to the pigsties, where the pigs were on their last legs, half buried in filth. He washed them down, cleared away the manure, rubbed their legs with iodine—and the pigs survived.

The authorities set store by his evident "qualifications," and he became firmly established at the piggery. At that point Garanin disappeared, the surviving prisoners were transferred to ordinary camps, and those who had finished their sentences were released, among them Nikolai.

After his release, Nikolai started work at a warehouse in Yagodnoye, and later became its director. And that was where we met, for I started work there too when my term ended.

NKVD men frequently came to the warehouse, and I was terrified of them. I felt they could rearrest me at any moment for no reason. I tried to answer all their questions as quickly as possible and to be polite to them. Nikolai watched me ironically. "What are you so scared of? To hell with them. They're used to getting sozzled on free booze, but they won't get any from me."

I lived with Nikolai for two years in Kolyma. I loved his courage and independent spirit.

In 1946, thanks to the constant efforts of my family, I was allowed to leave. It was hard to part with Nikolai, but my maternal feelings won out. As we parted, he told me, "Wait for me, I'll come and find you." I didn't believe him, but he was true to his word.

Home

The journey home took an entire month: six days on a steamer from Magadan to Soviet Harbor, nineteen in a train to Moscow, and we had had to wait five days in the Bay of Nakhodka while our special train was filling up.

I stared eagerly at people who had spent all those years "on the other side" and survived the war knowing nothing of the camps. People seemed coarsened and exhausted. I was astonished to hear women in a queue for hot water cursing and shouting, "Are you a human being or a policeman?"

In my time (before 1936) no one ever swore at the police; "Our police are there to protect us" was the slogan in those days.

Once a stranger came up to me on a platform, gestured vaguely toward the East, asked me, "Are you from there?" and handed me a packet of tea. I don't know what it was that he had glimpsed in my face.

I wired home from all the main stations on the way, but in the end no one was there to meet me: on the last day, somewhere near Ryazhsk, our train went onto a siding and stood there for eighteen hours. Then we were taken around the circular railway line to Moscow's Riga Station, and it was only on the morning of 6 August that we at last arrived.

I was so agitated by that time that I was unable to find my way home. A man offered to escort me for 200 rubles, and after a half-hour tramride I was home.

Only an elderly relative was there at the flat to greet me. Mother and Father were at the dacha; my brother and sister had been waiting at the station for two whole days to meet me and were probably still there.

Fifteen minutes later, my brother's wife appeared, and within an hour all the rest of the family had assembled.

My sister told me that she and my brother had met endless trains and gone up to all the exhausted old women they saw, thinking they were me. I threw away my camp dress, and my sister-in-law gave me her navy blue suit and yellow knitted top.

We set off for the dacha. On the platform at our station, the children had already spent three days waiting for all the local trains. My sister told me that my daughter was wearing a light blue dress, and my son was in a yellow shirt. The train pulled in. My eyes searched frantically up and down the platform; there were lots of people, but I couldn't make out my own children. In the distance a boy and girl were running toward us, but I couldn't tell whether they were mine. When the train stopped, a tall girl, almost a young woman (she was fifteen years old), rushed up to me and cried out in a strained, unnatural voice: "Mama! Mama! Mama!"

Then I heard my sister say to my son, "Come on, Shurik."

And a young man came up to me, tall and awkward, his voice still breaking. His eyes were both mine and his father's. And he pursed his lips just as his father had done when he was anxious.

We entered the garden gate. There on the terrace sat Mother in her armchair. Behind her stood my older sister, a doctor, with a syringe at the ready (they were afraid my mother's heart would give out when she saw me).

It was Mother who had changed the most. From a sturdy sixty-year-old woman who could wash piles of laundry and polish the floors better than any machine, she had become an old, old lady, unable to rise from her chair.

"It's you, it's you," said Mama, and the tears ran from her eyes. "My God, I've lived to see you! It's you!"

I ran up, fell to my knees, and buried my face in her hands.

"Mama!"

Father was nearby, at one of the sanatoriums in Bolshevo. He had gone blind in one eye, and a cataract was forming in the other. Before operating, the doctors had decided to give him some general medical treatment.

The following day I set off with the children to the sanatorium. I sat down with my son on a bench in the garden and sent my daughter to fetch her grandfather, so that she could prepare him a little. A few minutes later, my father's tall figure appeared. He was almost running, holding his arms out like a blind man and crying, "Where, where?"

I ran up and hugged him, and we both burst into tears. I heard people nearby speculate that I must be his daughter just back from the front . . .

That evening, when we were all sitting at the table, I asked: "Is it true that Stalin's ill?"

Nobody knew, but my son answered in a voice laden with meaning: "I don't know whether he's ill or not, but if he were ill and I had to give my life's blood and die for him, I'd gladly do it."

I realized this was meant as a lesson and warning to me, and bit my tongue. I still remember my son's words. Later I was relating how a young man had been standing at the door of the wagon in our train with his jacket thrown over his shoulders, and the wind had whipped the jacket off. He had jumped out to rescue it, and the train had left him behind. My son remarked that he had probably had his Komsomol card in his jacket pocket. "I would have done just the same if I'd been him."

On another occasion I asked him, "Shurik, do you remember anything of our former life?"

"No," he said sharply. "Nothing. I've never thought about it."

But then, a fortnight or so later, he suddenly said, "Mama, did you put on that navy blue skirt and yellow top on purpose?"

"No, why?"

"Because that was what you were wearing when you left, and I was convinced that one day the door would open, and in you'd come wearing just that, a navy blue skirt and a yellow top. And so you did."

Only then did I recall what I'd been wearing when I was arrested. And he had remembered all this time. Which meant, of course, that he had never stopped thinking.

I knew without doubt that when two weeks were up, I would be obliged to find a place to live where I would be allowed a residence permit 200 to 250 kilometers from Moscow. But everything seemed so tranquil and serene; we were at our dacha, with just the family and no strangers around, and no one paid any attention to us . . .

Several times I tried to tear myself away. On one occasion I even traveled as far as Gus-Khrustalny, rented a room there, and got a residence permit. I started looking for work, but it wasn't easy.

"Go to Moscow," my landlord suggested. "The minute anyone asks your whereabouts, I'll send you a telegram. That's what lots of people do."

I paid him for three months in advance and went back to Moscow to be with my family.

My mother behaved like a little child. She cried every time I left and said, "Why do you have to go? No one will find out that you're here. And if they do, we'll say that you came back to see your ailing mama."

Amazingly enough, I lived on Petrovka Street in the heart of Moscow for three years, and no one informed on me, although dozens of people knew that I was there. Throughout those three years I lived in constant fear. I fretted terribly: at the dacha I was relatively safe, but here at home in Moscow, where lots of people knew me, there was bound to be talk. Someone would surely guess that I was staying there without a residence permit, and then the police would come and drag me off, and once again I'd be condemned to solitude and exile. The slightest noise or an unexpected phone call in the night would have me jumping out of bed and hiding behind the cupboard. Each night I swore I'd leave the next day, but in the morning there I was again at my mother's bedside, assuring her there was no need to fear: "Don't worry, mama darling; I'm not going to leave you. Of course I'll stay here!"

My relationship with my daughter was perfectly happy and simple. We shared a bed, and at night she would snuggle up to me with her tender young body, half child, half woman. I would breathe in the scent of her hair and lips and feel as if we had never been parted. She believed that a girl should tell her mother absolutely everything, and before long I had heard all the secrets, joys, and fears of her teenage life.

But things were more complicated with my son. I was afraid to tell him anything of what I had learned "on the other side." No doubt I could have convinced him that there was a great deal wrong with our country, that Stalin, his idol, was actually far from perfect, but my son was only seventeen. I was afraid to be completely frank with him. But little by little I won him over. He would scrutinize me carefully, and after about three months he declared, "I like you, Mama!"

"What do you like about me, son?"

"You're not a bit like Aunt Sonya."

Sonya was a distant relative of ours, whose husband, once a very important man, had been arrested. Sonya was forced to leave her apartment in the House on the Embankment,* but for some reason she was never exiled.

She used to make the rounds of friends and relatives, lived on handouts, begged and wept and constantly bemoaned her lost grandeur. Shurik couldn't stand her ingratiating tone, her sensational stories and pitiful attempts to restore her fading beauty with a kind of violet-colored face powder. She had been abroad in her time and would whisper about how wonderful life was there, and how awful everything was at home.

My son's instincts were right. How I loved Moscow—though I lived there as if on a volcano! How I longed to be part of the life that excluded me, and how I hated, how violently I loathed, all those who had tied the hands and stifled the voice of our people!

This was how I lived for three years. Then in 1949 it was announced that Moscow was to undergo a "cleanup" in honor of Stalin's seventieth birthday. I knew several other people who were in the same position as I was, "illegals" living in Moscow. We all went into a spin. Some left immediately (though it made no difference; they were arrested just the same in the country), and there were two cases of suicide—and that was only in our small circle. Two of my Kolyma comrades, Lipa Kaplan and Olga Radovich, took their own lives.

It was obvious I had to leave and become a homeless stray again. I decided to go to Ryazhsk, where I knew an old lady, a retired teacher. I bought a ticket for 30 August, but on the 29th, as I was sitting at my mother's bedside peacefully reading her a book, two young men wearing light well-cut suits came in and asked me to go with them.

---

* A vast apartment complex on the Moscow River near the Kremlin built to accommodate the Soviet elite in the early 1930s.

My mother's face contorted in horror.

"She doesn't live here; she was just visiting. I'm ill, I'm about to die, she was just on a visit, she . . ."

Mother was having a heart attack. She was gasping for breath, but between gasps she gripped my hand and continued her hopeless fibs.

I tore my hand away and stood up.

Father came in. He had only recently had the cataract removed and could barely see. I saw his poor eyes fill with tears.

"Comrades, let me explain, she just came here to visit her mother . . ."

They didn't pause to listen.

I never saw my mother or father again. Both of them died soon after my second arrest.

"Pack your things; we don't need to tell you what to take."

I went to the cupboard, then stopped. "Why should I bother to take anything with me? The children can make better use of my things than I," I thought. "Obviously I won't survive this time; how could I possibly stand it all over again?"

In the end I took nothing except a towel, my toothbrush, and a pack of cigarettes.

1949: Butyrki, Cell No. 105

I had been arrested as a "second-timer," and no new charges were brought against me. The sentence was decided in advance: I would be exiled. But before that, prisoners in my position were kept in prison for half a year. When the investigative stage was over, I was transferred from the MGB Moscow Region Prison at the Malaya Lubyanka to Butyrki.

After my time in the Kolyma camps, exile did not seem to me too dreadful a prospect. I pictured myself working, reading, and perhaps making a few friends; I would make a home of sorts for myself. I had grown weary in Moscow after three years' constant fear of being arrested at any moment.

Meanwhile, however, I had not been officially sentenced, and four months had already gone by. I knew perfectly well that some second-timers got sent back to the camps. Horror at that prospect would have finished me off had I not firmly resolved that I would commit suicide rather than go back to the camps. The thought that there was at least that way out consoled me a little.

By an odd coincidence, I landed up in cell no. 105 in Butyrki, exactly where I'd been put in 1936. Over the last thirteen years, conditions had changed dramatically. In 1936 the cell had been dirty, with lines of ragged washing hung overhead. The prisoners wept at night, shouted, chatted, walked around, slept in rows on bed boards. By 1949 a regime of perfect orderliness had been imposed: the floor and walls were so clean they shone, and we slept on separate beds with mattresses. On the wall hung a board showing Butyrki's place in the socialist competition with other similar establishments. I was appalled. Prison was no longer a kind of natural catastrophe, a bolt from the blue as it had been in 1937; it was an established mode of existence, a well-regulated system designed to last for years.

The prisoners likewise differed markedly from those I remembered from my previous stint.

In 1936 the overwhelming majority of the prisoners had been Party members or members' wives; now only some ten percent belonged to that category. Many of the women had been arrested because of their alleged connections with Germans (the "Under-the-Fritzes," as they were called), and there were a number of semi-literate peasants, members of some religious organization who even had their own pretender to the throne, a certain Mikhail who in terms of age could not possibly have been the real Grand Duke Mikhail Romanov.

There were also a great many Latvian and Estonian women, who kept aloof from the rest of us. And there was a group of Party members who, all things considered, were probably supposed to have been imprisoned in 1937, but by chance were spared. They were united in their conviction that the arrests of 1937 had been perfectly just. Proof of this, in their opinion, was the fact that they themselves had committed no crime and had been left untouched.

Most terrible to see were the "children."

In 1937, when their parents were arrested, they had been six to eight years old. Now they were between eighteen and twenty. They had been imprisoned solely for being the children of their parents. Only yesterday they had been students, members of the Komsomol.

At first I couldn't imagine what these young girls were doing there. When I realized, I pictured my own daughter lying on these prison beds, frightened and bewildered. It was even worse to imagine my son, the mortal sorrow in his eyes when he realized the truth.

I kept asking everyone whether by any chance they'd come across a tall, slim girl called Ella, and several told me they thought they had.

I met the daughters of well-known Bolsheviks like Kosior and Rakovsky, of the writer Artyom Vesyoly, of Nikolai Bukharin's brother, and of many high-up figures in State Security itself.

I looked with aching pity at my companions in misfortune, knowing that they were condemned to follow the same road to Calvary that I had already traveled. They kept presenting proof of their innocence, hoping they could somehow "sort things out," but I knew they were doomed.

A skinny girl with braids and legs as thin as sticks was put in our cell. She looked to be about sixteen or seventeen. The girl glanced around and headed toward me. I quickly turned away; my nerves couldn't take it. I couldn't bear to look into her childish eyes and see the tears flowing down her cheeks. The whole day I tried to avoid her, but in the evening I discovered that she had got the bed next to mine. She lay there puffing ineptly at a cigarette and weeping. Her skinny shoulders shook like a little bird's. I learned that her name was Valya and that today was her twentieth birthday. Her story was very simple.

"I was seven years old when my father was arrested. Mama was in such despair that my aunt and I had to stand guard over her to keep her from throwing herself out the window. She kept saying what a good man papa was and what torture he was going through, and how awful it was to be alive in such times. Then Mama herself was arrested. My aunt took me in. I was supposed to tell everyone that my mother and father were dead. Probably my aunt put the fear of death in me, I don't remember, but I was somehow given to understand that if anyone found out my papa and mama were in prison, something terrible would happen. I always wanted to be at the top of the class and the best-behaved so I could "show them," though what it was I had to show them I didn't know. I graduated from school and went to college. And then I fell in love. His parents had been "repressed" as well, and he'd hidden it from everybody too, but we were open with one another. Everything that had seemed to me a source of shame became in his eyes a virtue. And now it's all over, it's all over!"

My God, how sorry I felt for Valya! How sorry I felt for all those girls who could no longer believe in justice or see the slightest glimmer of light in the abyss that some incomprehensibly evil force had hurled them into.

Gradually my bed became a kind of club for the girls. I was terrified that I'd earn myself a term in the camps instead of exile, but I couldn't help it; I had to try and comfort these girls. Mentally I would scold myself and swear that I would try to be more restrained, only to find myself once again saying things to one of the girls that would guarantee me ten years in the camps if the investigator ever got wind of them.

"You silly girls," I'd say. "You think your life's over, and you're only twenty. But in five years' time 'he' won't be there anymore and you'll still be only twenty-five, and your whole life will still be in front of you."

The girls responded in chorus: "You're absurdly optimistic. Can't you see that the problem isn't just this one person? Even if he disappears, all his henchmen will still be there. Do you think that you're going to be able to elect a new government?"

"It's so contrary to nature, it simply can't go on for much longer!" I said.

I loved these girls whose shining eyes would soon take on the dull, despairing look of prison. And in loving them, my heart was filled with pain, for as I looked at them I saw my own daughter, who perhaps at this very minute was languishing on some prison bed, full of fear and bewilderment, and seeking in the eyes of some older woman the comfort and support she needed. With all the force of my maternal love, I tried to instill in these girls some courage and faith in life and in human beings.

I was told the story of a certain boy, the son of a Bolshevik who had been executed. The boy had been recruited by State Security. He made numerous acquaintances among children whose parents, like his, had been "repressed," and he reported back every word of dissatisfaction they uttered, every puzzled question they raised. As a result of his denunciations, many of his friends were arrested.

I had known the mother of this boy in Kolyma. She was a lovely person, completely honest and a very good friend. She had talked a lot about her only son, his exceptional kindness, brilliance, honesty. And here he was playing this dreadful role.

Eagerly I questioned my girls: what did they think of this boy? They were strangely indulgent. The general opinion was that he was a nice boy but a "starry-eyed ninny."

In my young companions' vocabulary, this meant a naive kid who believed every slogan he heard and every word he read in the papers.

So he was a starry-eyed ninny. But my son, in that case, was a ninny too. I was afraid to disillusion him. Yet at the same time I feared that his youthful ardor and integrity could lead him down the very path that this other boy had taken . . .

Believe it or not, these four months in Butyrki in 1949 have remained in my memory as a bright interlude. I felt so needed. The girls clung to me like a brood of chicks to an old mother hen. I tried in the way I behaved to show them that even someone who has gone through Kolyma camps can remain a human being. I brought them a little light in that darkness.

The Journey to Karaganda

In mid-December 1949, I was sent on the long journey to exile in Kazakhstan. We were taken in a Stolypin wagon as far as Kuibyshev (the new name, since 1935, for Samara), where we were kept in appalling conditions in the transit prison. Our cell, which was meant to hold two hundred people, was a hastily converted stable. The powerful odor of horse manure combined with the stench of the slop bucket and the huge, densely packed mass of unwashed and ailing bodies combined to create an unbearable atmosphere.

When we first arrived, there were two hundred of us, and we occupied all the two-level bed boards in the cell. But then more and more prisoners were brought in. Women lay in the passageway, under the bed boards, on top of the table and underneath it. The stench left us choking for breath. There were no books to be had, no medicine of any kind. Quarrels flared up, and prisoners became hysterical.

"When are we going to get out of here?" we kept asking the senior guard, but he simply shrugged and answered ingenuously, "What can I do? All the prisons and camps are full to bursting; no one's willing to take you. Whose fault is it that there's such a horde of you?"

Whose fault indeed?

When finally we were summoned to resume our journey, we were naturally overjoyed. "It may be worse, but at least it'll be different," said our Ukrainian prisoners, quoting a national proverb. We heartily agreed . . .

But the real horror was still to come. In the early dusk of that January day, we were driven to the distant siding where our train stood and loaded into the wagon. The temperature was minus thirty degrees. It was five o'clock in the evening and already getting dark. As I scrambled up the ladder after the other women and climbed into the wagon, it at first appeared to be pitch dark. It was icy cold inside. As we got used to the darkness, we realized there were numerous cracks and chinks, through which we caught a glimpse of the gray winter evening. There was a small stove in the wagon, but we had neither firewood nor matches. The two-by-two beds were covered in a layer of ice.

I was warmly dressed, and my family had given me a quilt; others, too, had warm things and began undoing their bundles and wrapping themselves up in whatever came to hand. But next to me was a young girl whom I had already noticed in the truck as we were being driven from the prison.

She had a sweet face, her glance was bold, and I guessed her age to be twenty-three or twenty-four. She was dressed in a cotton summer dress and a padded prison jacket, with thin stockings that had been darned and re-darned. I invited her to join me under my quilt, and we introduced ourselves. Her name was Olya Kosenko. She snuggled up to me but continued to shiver, unable to get warm.

"Why are you dressed like that, Olya? Why don't you have anything warm?"

"That beast of an investigator decided to punish me for being cheeky, and he wouldn't let me have any parcels from home. So I'm in the same clothes I've been wearing ever since I was arrested in the summer. They gave me this jacket and a pair of boots to wear for the journey, and that's it."

We sat for several hours in this dark icy wagon. At last we heard some movement. The bolts in the neighboring wagons clanked open, and there were footsteps on the roof. At last our door was opened, too, and in came the guards and an electrician. We were given a single electric bulb. Then they threw us an armful of wood and some matches, left us, and bolted the door. Our ration of wood was meager, and we had no idea when we would be given a fresh supply, but we lit the stove nevertheless and warmed ourselves a little.

The journey to Karaganda took sixteen days. At first we were desperately cold, but one day our train came to a halt next to a goods train loaded with coal. Suddenly our guard, a Ukrainian who sometimes enjoyed a brief chat in Ukrainian with Olya, opened the door, handed Olya a bucket—she'd been appointed "wagon leader"—and told her, "Collect as much coal as you can."

Olya jumped out of the wagon and managed to collect a good two dozen buckets of coal. Then the wagon door was closed again, but we all felt more cheerful. We noticed that women from several of the other wagons had been collecting coal as well.

I remembered what Tolstoy had written: Russian laws are tolerable only because everybody breaks them; if no one broke them, they would be unbearable.

If we had not had the guard's blessing to steal from the coal wagon, I doubt we would ever have made it to our destination alive, with no more fuel than our ration of an armful a day.

I made a bed for myself and Olya, and we chatted the whole day long, snuggled up to one another.

Olya had been given a terrible sentence: twenty years. The investigator, she claimed, had fixed it on purpose: Olya's fearlessness, her refusal to submit to him, her argumentativeness and harsh, sometimes coarse words had infuriated him.

Olya had been very unlucky with the investigation of her case. She had been arrested in 1947 with a group of philology students at Kiev University.

Her investigator had longed to win his own laurels like the heroic NKVD men of 1937, and he'd dreamt up a story about some great terrorist conspiracy aimed at wresting the Ukraine from the USSR. Olya, he decided, was just the person to give him the evidence he needed. He made up and forced her to sign monstrous statements incriminating dozens of her friends.

He even thought up a link with the Gestapo, which had allegedly re-cruited a whole group of young Ukrainians during the war. (Fifteen-year-old Olya had in fact behaved heroically at the time: in order not to get sent to Germany, she had deliberately infected herself with trachoma, knowing that the Germans would take only healthy people.)

The investigator counted on being able to break the will of this skinny twenty-three-year-old girl with a mixture of threats, beatings, stints in the punishment cell, week-long interrogations with a succession of investiga-tors, promises to release her if she complied, and refusal meanwhile to let her have parcels from home. But he was unable to get anything out of her. Infuriated, he promised, "I'll get the harshest twenty-year sentence slapped on you." And he was as good as his word.

But one day, after Olya had already been sentenced, the investigator called her in and asked her, "Well, have you shed your tears of remorse for being so stubborn?" And when Olya replied that she had not wept and had no intention of weeping, he laughed and told her, "Let's bet on whether you'll weep or not! Your nice little fiancé has been arrested, and I've made sure he'll be given to me to deal with."

This time he won, and Olya felt terrible. Her fiancé came from her native village and was not even acquainted with any of the accused. He had come to Kiev solely to deliver parcels to the prison and inquire about Olya—and thus to his cost made himself known to the authorities.

During this exhausting period of investigation, which lasted eight months, Olya was supported by her cellmate, an elderly woman named Maria Gertsevna who took a motherly interest in her. Olya often spoke of this lady; "I've been so lucky," she'd say. "First I had her to help me keep my spirits up, and now I've met you." Poor little thing, she was still able to talk of "luck"! But there was another side to our friendship which caused me much sorrow. This intelligent, bold, generous-hearted girl was an anti-Sem-ite. She would relate endless stories about how the Jews were able to set themselves up nicely, about the Jewish manager of their local shop who had got cushy jobs for his entire family, about the Jewish investigator who had dealt with her friend in the prison in Kiev and what a scoundrel he was, and so on.

When I pointed out that her own investigator was a Ukrainian, and they didn't come much worse than that, she replied, "You just don't know what those Jews are like, Olga Lvovna. There aren't so many in Moscow, but in Kiev there's no getting away from them."

I could easily have put a stop to these painful conversations by telling her that I myself was Jewish. But then the foolish girl would have felt that she couldn't stay with me. She would have frozen and starved without the food and the quilt that my Jewish relatives had sent to me. So I put up with her talk as far as Karaganda.

On the sixteenth day of the journey, the guard entered and called our several names. "Pack your things; we'll be arriving in two hours."

There were only five of us lucky ones being sent into exile. The rest, all with long sentences of ten to twenty years, were going on to Novorudnya, where they would be kept under the harshest regime and sent to work down in the mines. We started to gather up our possessions. Olya looked at me with her eyes full of tears.

"So I'll be left on my own again!" We sat down in the corner on our bunk.

"Olechka," I said, "I have something to say to you. You've given me a great deal of pain these last sixteen days, because, you see, I'm Jewish." Olya gasped and covered her face with her hands. Through her fingers I could see that her cheeks, ears, and neck were aflame.

"Yes, Olya, it's been very hard to listen to your talk, because I've grown very fond of you. Since you've been in the prisons, Olya, you've met two women who've acted like a mother to you, me and Maria Gertsevna. Why did you never once mention to me that she was Jewish? Why didn't you draw the same kind of illogical conclusion from her as you drew from your encounters with Jewish scoundrels: 'All Jews are kind-hearted, friendly, and loving.' That would be just as untrue and unfair as what you actually said: 'All Jews are sly; they're all just out for themselves,' and so on, but at least it would be consistent. In return for all the pain you've given me, I want your promise that you will never be so unfair again, and that when you speak of Jews, you will remember not only that shop manager who found jobs for his whole family, but me and Maria Gertsevna, too."

Olya was silent. Our train pulled into the station and I got up. Olya flung her arms round my neck, in a flood of tears.

"What a lesson you've taught me! Forgive me! I promise I'll never forget what you said!"

I never met Olya again. I heard later that she died in Novorudnya. If this is untrue and you happen to read these lines, Olya, do let me know!

In Exile

My journey into exile in Kazakhstan took place in the winter of 1949–50. In April 1950 my husband, Nikolai Adamov, came to find me in Karaganda. But a year later, on 29 April 1951, he was rearrested, and I relived the whole nightmare of the months that followed the arrest of my first husband—the difference being that in 1936 I had hoped for justice from the Soviet courts, while this time I knew perfectly well what awaited Nikolai. I should add that whereas my first husband and I had been arrested for no reason at all, under Stalin's laws Nikolai was undoubtedly guilty of "agitation" (Article 58:10).

Nikolai was an old Communist and an avowed enemy of Stalin. He considered it his duty to fight against him and gathered together a group of young people, to whom he explained that Stalin had destroyed the Party, that in 1937 he had drowned every thinking person in a sea of blood, and that he was responsible for the huge loss of life at the beginning of the war.

He condemned Stalin for having concluded a shameful treaty with Hitler, for destroying the entire command of the Red Army, and for executing Blucher, Marshal Tukhachevsky, Uborevich, and hundreds of others.

During the two years that we spent together in Karaganda, Nikolai was living on the edge, but he felt inspired and full of hope, and whenever I pleaded with him to be careful, he would say that he wanted to die fighting, not as a lowly slave. During the investigation, he tried to win over the investigator, who was terrified that he himself might come to be regarded as an enemy of the people. The case was quickly concluded, and Nikolai was given his ten years.

Thus began another terrible period in my life: endless queues to make inquiries and hand in parcels at the investigation prison, and nothing to return to but an empty, devastated house.

The Doctors' Plot

Rumors about the arrest of a group of doctors began reaching Karaganda in 1952.

Natasha Vakula, secretary to the manager who ran our sewing workshop, told us that a parcel from America addressed to someone named Rabinovich had been opened before her very eyes at the post office. The parcel contained cotton wool which was riddled with thousands of typhus-bearing lice.

On another occasion, a seamstress stood up at one of our general meetings and told us how she remembered from childhood that some Jews had killed a Christian baby and used his blood to make matzos. Her story was greeted with embarrassed silence. "No need to talk about things that can't be proved," someone eventually said, and that ended our discussion of the matzo incident.

But it was clear that a pogrom was brewing.

At the time I was working in a mass-produced clothing factory. I was appointed to deal with workers' wages (I was, after all, an economist by training), and this meant spending time in the workshop office. I was the only Jew there, and the only person in exile. The minute I came in, all the lively chatter in the office would cease, and all eyes would turn on me as if I were one of the murderous doctors in person and a regular eater of matzos boiled in blood.

One night an article, "The Murderers in White Coats," was read on the radio, and I had the "pleasure" of hearing it.

The next day I went to work as if to my execution. I sat down at my desk and began turning my mechanical calculator and clicking away at my abacus. The bookkeeper, Maria Nikitichna Puzikova, arrived a little late that morning. As the wife of a member of the Party Regional Committee and hostess to the elite of Karaganda, she enjoyed the highest status among us.

That morning she came in positively beaming.

"Heavens," she said, "what dreadful goings-on! What a criminal lack of vigilance! Imagine allowing all those Jews into the Kremlin and entrusting the health of our leaders to them. Sergei and I were awake the whole night after we heard that article from *Pravda*, 'The Murderers in White Coats,' read out on the radio."

Maria Nikitichna fluttered out of the office and a minute later returned with a newspaper in her hands.

"Why don't you read the article out loud to us, Olga? You do read so well."

"I assume you've had enough basic schooling to read it yourself, Maria Nikitichna," I replied. "I don't have the time." So I lived in an atmosphere of hostile curiosity and constant baiting. Our director, Anisya Vasilievna, was a good person. She had progressed from being a semi-literate peasant girl and servant to being promoted off the factory floor and becoming a member of the Party, one of the most decorated women in Karaganda. She had a naturally inquisitive mind and adored Stalin, to whom she felt she owed her happy life and career, but at the same time she was obviously curious to know what kind of people we exiles were.

She enjoyed talking to me, but checked up on every word I said. On one occasion I told her that Marx was a Jew. Soon afterward a big article on Marx appeared in *Pravda* in connection with some anniversary, and there it was stated that Marx was a German.

"There you are, Olga," Anisya Vasilievna reproached me. "I believe what you tell me, you being an educated person, and now it turns out you've not been telling the truth."

"Who would you sooner believe?" I asked. "*Pravda* or Lenin?"

"Well, of course I believe Lenin absolutely."

I went to the Red Corner at the workshop and found a volume of Lenin containing his article on Marx, which stated clearly that Marx was a German Jew.

On another occasion Anisya said, "Tell me, now, what was it those Jewish doctors were after? Didn't they appreciate how well they lived in the USSR? Why did they want to go killing our leaders?"

I couldn't think what to say. "They must have been out of their minds," I offered. "There's no other explanation."

Stalin's Death

A meeting was being held in the director's office. Apart from me, there were no other exiles present. Suddenly a woman from the workshop burst into the office without knocking: "Anisya Vasilievna . . ."

"Why have you come in without permission? Please leave."

"But Anisya Vasilievna . . ."

"I've told you, we're busy."

"Stalin's dying."

It was as if a bomb had exploded. Anisya Vasilievna cried out and slumped sideways, suddenly taken ill.

I felt as if all eyes had turned on me. Terrified that my expression would give me away, I covered my face with my hands. I was trembling. I told myself, "It's now or never. Everything's got to change. Now or never. What if some Malenkov or Beria or Monster or Devil takes over this colossus and decides to prop it up with yet more millions of bodies? It'll keep going another twenty years then, enough for my lifetime. It's now or never!"

I realized that they were talking about me.

"What a hypocrite! She pretends to cry, but when she uncovers her face, she's completely dry-eyed."

Now that the end was in sight, I kept thinking, they'll grab me and finish me off.

Everyone put on mourning rosettes.

I kept torturing myself: should I put one on or not?

Anna Petrovna, our Party Organizer, summoned me and pinned a rosette to me. "You have to wear it," she said.

After that I was afraid to take it off and wore it longer than anyone else, until Anna Petrovna herself came up one day and removed it.

We all listened to the funeral service. Beria spoke: "We know what has to be done."

He knew, all right.

Malenkov said, "May our enemies, whether inside the country or outside it, remember that we will not lower our guard." I did remember.

And now it seems to me that things were never so hard as in that year of Stalin's death when, ever so slowly, we caught the first occasional signs of movement and a faint glimmer of light.

On 4 April 1953, I was enjoying the sun outside on my lunch break when suddenly one of our exiles, the seamstress Ida Markovna, rushed out of the workshop and threw her arms around my neck. Choking with emotion, she told me that there had just been a radio broadcast saying that the whole doctors' plot had been fabricated by Riumin and his accomplices. Our happiness knew no bounds. What a joyful moment that was! We wept, daydreaming that our shameful sentences would also be repealed, and that we'd be allowed to go home to our children.

As I went back into the office, I heard Puzikova declare, "Of course the Americans have so much money they can buy whoever they need!"

Lightning flashed through my brain. "I'll show you, you bitch!" I thought.

I went straight to the director's office and said loudly, "Come out here, Anisya Vasilievna." This was a gross and unheard-of violation of the office hierarchy.

"What are you saying, Olga?"

"Just what you heard. Come out here with Anna Petrovna." They came out.

"Maria Puzikova implied just one moment ago that the Supreme Court of the USSR had been bribed by the Americans. I spent eight years in prison for failing to denounce my husband, and I don't want another sentence on account of Puzikova. Her words fit precisely under the terms of Article 58:10—discrediting a Soviet court. This is normally punishable by ten years' imprisonment. Everyone here heard her words and can confirm what I've just said. I won't go to the MGB, but I'm reporting this before witnesses. It's up to you to go to the MGB yourselves."

They all stood rooted to the spot.

"Maria, how could you have said such a thing?" Anisya Vasilievna exclaimed.

"I don't know, I don't know; I wasn't thinking!" Maria burst into sobs and rushed home.

Of course, Puzikova's unfortunate remarks had no legal consequences; all that happened was that her husband, a member of the Regional Party Committee, beat her up, so badly that she was unable to come to work for four days and on the fifth appeared covered in bruises, which she attempted to conceal with powder.

All the same, I couldn't resist going up to Anisya Vasilievna: "Anisya Vasilievna, let me ask you, as a member of the Party, what made Riumin and his accomplices slander all those innocent people and bring shame on the country with that idiotic trial? Did Riumin not appreciate his life under the Soviet system? What could have made him commit such a crime?"

Rehabilitation

Slowly, slowly the sky began to clear after Stalin's death. It was a year before they started repealing sentences of "eternal exile" and giving people back their passports, containing, to be sure, a note of their conviction and a ban on their living in thirty-nine cities. For some reason I was one of the last to be released from exile. All my friends had already left, and the time dragged unbelievably slowly. I would go to bed at eight in the evening, as soon as I got back from work, then wake at three, read, fret, and worry until morning came.

At last, at the end of 1954, I was released from exile and was able to travel the fifty miles to Djezkazgan, where Nikolai was in the camp at Kengir.

I had heard rumors that there had been disturbances in this camp, that the prisoners had refused to go to work, demanding that their cases be reviewed, that Georgy Malenkov* should come and visit them personally, and that the camp regime should be reformed.

Knowing Nikolai, I had no doubt that he was behind all this.

On arriving in Djezkazgan, I learned that all these protests were over, and big changes had been made in the rules. Prisoners were now allowed to see their relatives for a whole week, and special quarters had been set aside for this purpose, with two entrances—one for the prisoners that led out from the compound, and one for the visitors that led in from outside. There had been nothing like it in the camps before.

I entered a cramped little room containing a bed, a table, and two chairs, and sat down with a pounding heart.

The door opened, and Nikolai came in.

I barely recognized him. In the last three years he had become an old man, eaten up by tuberculosis. He could barely walk or speak. I spent a week with him.

It was one of the hardest weeks in the whole of my terrible life.

One day one of the men in charge of the camp came in and said they

---

* Stalin's heir apparent.

could release Adamov on grounds of health if I signed a statement to the effect that I would take care of him and that I would make no further claims.

I of course agreed to sign, and together we returned to Karaganda. Nikolai died soon after his release.

I went to Moscow to petition for my rehabilitation.

By that time a few people were already being rehabilitated, but the process was dreadfully slow. In order to apply, you had to produce certificates from every place where you'd been registered as living since your release from camp, but I no longer remembered where and how many times I'd been registered. You were asked to provide references from your place of work, but employers weren't very inclined to give them; indeed, they had probably been instructed not to do so. But finally I put in my application. My case fell to one Ivanov, a procurator with eyes the color of pewter. Whenever I got to see him, after standing five or six hours in line, he would intone in his wooden voice, "Your case will be dealt with in due course. You have not yet reached the head of the line."

On one occasion he opened a cupboard and showed me a whole library of files. "This is the professors' case that you and your husband were involved in. You can see that there were more than a hundred people involved in the case, and we have to go through them all individually."

"But how many of the people involved are still alive?"

This brought him up short. "A few of them . . ."

"Well, perhaps it would be a good idea to start with the ones who are still with us; otherwise I'm afraid that none of us will survive long enough to reach the head of the line."

So the process dragged on until the Twentieth Party Congress in February 1956. After the Congress, at the beginning of March, I found out that my case had been transferred to a different procurator. I was asked briefly to describe my case. I wrote, "I've been awaiting trial for twenty years. Will I see justice before I die?"

Together with my sister-in-law, who accompanied me everywhere, I was invited in to see the procurator. We were greeted by a cheerful fellow of about thirty-five, a military man, to judge by his appearance. I handed him my application.

My sister-in-law, who hadn't previously seen what I'd written, was horrified and started apologizing.

"Please excuse her; she's become so nervy."

He smiled broadly. "You have a right to be; it's understandable. But things will move more quickly now. It shouldn't take more than a month."

"But I'm going to be expelled from Moscow. The police came around yesterday and ordered me to leave within twenty-four hours."

"Hide from the police, then. It'll all be over soon. Can you find somewhere else to live for a while?"

"I could stay at my sister's."

"Give me her phone number, and I'll call you there."

On 8 March the phone rang, and I heard the procurator's cheerful voice: "Here's a present for you for International Women's Day. Your case has been dealt with, and you will receive your rehabilitation certificate in the office of the Supreme Court. They will let you know the day. Congratulations."

When I arrived on the appointed day to fetch my certificate, I found around twenty people in the reception room, most of them women of around fifty or older. There was one old woman, a Ukrainian, who looked half-mad. She kept muttering to herself. A man about forty was sitting by the window and smoking.

Each of us was called in turn. People would come out of the office and remain waiting for something else. When my name and my husband's were called, the man sitting in the window gave a start. I went into the office and was handed my certificate of rehabilitation. I was told that I should wait in the reception room, where we would receive documents entitling us to passports and compensation.

The certificate announced that my case had been reviewed by a Plenum of the Supreme Court on 24 May 1956 and closed for lack of evidence.

I had been arrested on 27 April 1936. So I had paid for this mistake with twenty years and forty-one days of my life.

When I returned to the reception room, the man who had been sitting by the window came up to me. "Did your husband teach the history of natural science at Moscow University?"

"Yes, he taught there in 1936."

"I was a student of his. What a fine teacher he was!"

We both fell silent. A soldier came out and began handing out the certificates needed for our passports and money.

I was apparently entitled to two months' pay for myself and my husband and a further 11 rubles 50 kopeks (in new money) for the 115 rubles that had been in my husband's possession at the time of his death.

When she was handed her certificates, the old Ukrainian woman started yelling: "I don't need your money for my son's blood; keep it yourself!" She tore up the certificates and threw them on the floor.

The soldier who had been handing out the certificates came up to her: "Calm down, citizen," he began.

But the old woman started shouting again and choked in a paroxysm of rage.

Everyone was silent, overwhelmed. Here and there I heard stifled sobs and tears.

I went back to my apartment, from which no policeman could evict me now. There was no one home, and finally I was able to weep freely.

To weep for my husband, who perished in the cellars of the Lubyanka when he was thirty-seven years old, at the height of his powers and talent; for my children, who grew up orphans, stigmatized as the children of enemies of the people; for my parents, who died of grief; for Nikolai, who was tortured in the camps; and for all my friends who never lived to be rehabilitated but lie beneath the frozen earth of Kolyma.

Translation by Sally Laird

YELENA VLADIMIROVA

Yelena Vladimirova ──────

From "Kolyma: A Narrative Poem"

🌺 About the Author

Yelena Lvovna Vladimirova was born on 20 September 1902 in Petersburg, into a family with strong nautical traditions. Her father was a naval officer, and her mother was related to Admiral Butakov, a well-known commander of the Russian fleet. Lena was educated at the Smolny Institute for Well-Born Daughters. Not long before the Revolution, she became involved with a left-wing youth group. In October 1917 she and her father had a violent quarrel inspired by their political differences, and she left home.

In 1919 she joined the Komsomol. After fighting against the anti-Soviet Basmachi groups in Turkestan (Central Asia), she helped organize famine relief in the Volga region. In 1921 she was sent to Petrograd University by the Komsomol. There she met and married Leonid Syrkin, one of the organizers of the Komsomol in Petrograd. From 1925 Vladimirova worked as a journalist for various newspapers and magazines, including Leningradskaya Pravda, *the Army paper* Krasnaya Gazeta, *and the women's magazine* Rabotnitsa.

In 1937 she and Syrkin moved to the Urals, to Chelyabinsk, where he was sent to edit the regional paper. That same year, however, he was arrested and shot; Vladimirova, as the wife of "an enemy of the people," was dispatched to Kolyma.

In 1944, she was working at a hospital serving many of the area's camps. Some of the former Party and Komsomol members there set up an underground group, and she wrote its manifesto: "Stalin's So-Called Socialism in the Light of Leninism." An agent provocateur denounced them, and they were all arrested. Three, including Yelena, were sentenced to be shot. But later this was commuted to hard labor.

Vladimirova spent more than eighteen years in camps and in prison. Her only daughter, Zhenya Syrkina, to whom many of her poems were dedicated, was killed in 1942 during the Second World War, at the Battle of Stalingrad.

YURY LYUBA

From the memoirs of Valery Ladeishchikov

31 December 1944. I am in a small courtroom. They read out the verdict: "Magadan Military Tribunal . . . sentences Yelena Lvovna Vladimirova, Yevgeniya Alexandrovna Kostyuk, and Valery Alexandrovich Ladeishchikov to be shot. The other defendants are to serve sentences of seven to ten years in the camps."

In Magadan Prison we found ourselves in neighboring cells on death row. We tapped messages through the walls to keep each other's spirits up: "Don't lose heart!"

My position was more complicated: it was the second time I'd been sentenced to death. The main charge against us was anti-Stalinist agitation based on Leninist principles. Officially this was called "counterrevolutionary propaganda." We spent three months on death row, then all our sentences were commuted to fifteen years' hard labor.

In mid-April 1945 we were taken from the transit prison. However, the truck went only as far as Nizhny Butugychag, and from there we walked, uphill all the way. In the upper part of the valley there was no bush, or grass or reindeer moss, only rocks and snow. The narrow camp was strung out across the ridge and into the next valley. The geologists who first mapped these desolate regions had given them romantic place names: now there was the Don Jose valley, the "Carmen" ore enrichment plant, and the "Bacchante" labor camp [mining and prospecting for uranium].

Only occasionally did Yelena Vladimirova come over from the Bacchante with her theater team. Conditions in Butugychag were dreadful; I doubt there are worse anywhere in the world. But Yelena Lvovna bravely endured all misfortunes, and knew how to cheer up others. And her poetry expresses this courageous endurance.

About Lena Vladimirova

I did not meet Yelena Vladimirova in Kolyma. She was in Magadan, and I was in various camps in the Elgen district. But I'd heard of her, because her poems had been passed on by word of mouth. I can remember some of them as well as if I'd written them myself; she expressed all the pain of our lives. This is one that I remember (I may have a word wrong here and there):

We grow fewer and weaker, my friends,
There are more farewells with each day . . .
We cannot tell what tomorrow may hold—
We don't know what will happen today.

We live in hard, in frightening times,
Uncertainty followed by lies;
How we long to believe we are not alone,
To hear a cry from the dark, "We're alive!"

As before, we hold true to the banners we love;
The skies may be clouded, but still
We measure our joy, now a thing of the past,
By what suits the commonweal;

Though my path be hopeless, though it be soaked in blood—
Yet I shall not cease my cries:
Summoning my last drops of strength, I'll shout,
"Comrade! We're alive, we're alive!"

In 1944, a rumor suddenly spread that Lena had been condemned to death.

Even in our woeful existence, the news came as a bitter blow. Many years passed. I finished my sentence and was even allowed back to Moscow. Then I was arrested a second time and exiled to Karaganda "for life."

In 1954 I was again permitted to move around freely. By then many cases were under review, and some prisoners had already been released. One day I met Gerta Norten, a wonderful Finnish painter, who had just been let out of the camps. She and I became friends, and she told me a lot about her life.

Unexpectedly she mentioned Lena Vladimirova. Only then did I learn that Lena's death sentence had been commuted to fifteen years in the camps. After 1953, Lena had made many applications for her case to be reviewed, Gerta told me, but none of them had been answered. I immediately wrote a letter to Lena in her camp, and told her what a blow her arrest in 1944 had been for me and my friends; I said how we'd loved her poems and how much they'd meant to us, and how happy I was that she was still alive. I ended my letter with a line from her poem: "Comrade! We're alive, we're alive!"

Thus began a long correspondence. In 1955 I was planning to make the lengthy trip back to Moscow, and I let Lena know. She sent me a copy of one of her requests for a sentence review and the receipt for a registered letter that she'd sent to Olga Shatunovskaya. Shatunovskaya, like Lena and me, had served her sentence in Kolyma; one of the first former camp inmates to be rehabilitated, she was now working in the Central Committee as a member of its Commission for Party Regulation.

When I reached Moscow, I went straight to Shatunovskaya with Lena's petition and the receipt for the letter, sent six months earlier. In the commission's mail room, Shatunovskaya found out that the letter had arrived, but had never been passed on to her. Several other appeals, it turned out, had been similarly sabotaged by Stalinists in the office. Shatunovskaya personally took on all these cases, and in less than a month Lena was rehabilitated.

On her way back to Leningrad, she passed through Moscow and stopped to see me. During that week we became as close as two sisters. We spent all the time together and also typed up a copy of "Kolyma," her narrative poem.

That was the only time we ever met, I'm sorry to say, though we continued writing to each other long afterward. Lena died in 1962.

OLGA ADAMOVA-SLIOZBERG

To My Friends

Since we've gotten onto the subject, I'd better tell you how I wrote my Northern Tale [the poem "Kolyma"]. It's a story in itself.

When my death sentence was commuted to hard labor, I was sent off to a barren place in the mountains, a narrow valley shut in on all sides by volcanic hills. It was all so bleak and hopeless that I wondered how to use what remained of my life and strength. My capacity for intellectual work, I now realize, was extraordinary. I could do whatever I liked in my head, no matter what the conditions. I decided I would write a story about my experiences. Well, I couldn't "write," of course. I started making it up in my head. But I couldn't count on surviving for long myself so somehow I had to preserve what I was "writing." An impossible idea came to me—but it's often the impossible ideas that work. I had to find a young woman who would agree to learn and memorize every word by heart. I found her, and we set to work.

When we came back from felling trees, we would sit down somewhere outdoors and pretend to be chatting. In fact, we were working. If anyone had overheard a single word, both of us would have been finished.

But then we were separated. I was sent away from Kolyma, and for over a year work stopped. Then I pulled myself together again, and pretty soon I had finished. I resorted to paper only when I needed to firmly memorize the latest sections by writing down the first letters of each line (after that I threw the paper away). The finished poem ended up a substantial piece: around four thousand lines. But now, I realized, I wasn't happy with much of it. Revise that kind of thing in your head?! I doubted that it was possible. But I set to work, and I did it. It was even harder than the "writing." But possible. The human mind is very adaptable! Now I had to get my tale in verse out of my head and record it. I decided to write it out on cigarette papers and bury them. This work, I now realize, was in vain, because (a beginner's mistake) I put the papers in a tin box. It probably has rusted and rotted away by now—not that it matters anymore.

I remember how I wrote down the poem. Most important was to do it openly, in full view of everyone, without trying to hide anything, right under the guards' noses. I would take my needle and a bit of mending, a stump of pencil and a scrap of paper. Then I usually sat next to a puddle, a bucket, or a jug—so that I could drop the paper into the water if need be, and get no more than a spell in the punishment block. I remember sitting by our "club" one day. It was early spring, I was writing away, and just behind me was a large pool of melted snow. Suddenly the duty guard started running toward me. "Keep calm!" I said to myself. "Don't move an inch until you have to!" But my heart was going at full speed (you can imagine!). Then I noticed: he was staring at something above my head. It had nothing to do with me. Someone had committed the frightful offense of hanging their wash out on the club roof. Anyone who knows the risk I was taking, when I'd already been sentenced to death once, will understand how I felt.

Finally, I got it all written down. There were about twenty lines to each cigarette paper, about two hundred papers in all. I carried the lot in a little gauze bag around my neck, taking care that they didn't get too crumpled before I had a chance to hide them in my tin box.

A friend would keep a lookout for me, a true friend who shared the risk I was taking. She didn't hold any of the same beliefs, but not once in all those years did she abuse my trust.

Now I have written down my story again from memory, and have sent it to the place where we Communists are supposed to communicate our thoughts and experiences. [Vladimirova sent "Kolyma" to the 20th Congress of the Soviet Communist Party in 1956.]

That's it, in a nutshell.

LENA, 1956

The March to Work
[Extract from "Kolyma"]

. . . Around was quiet
Such as one finds in death alone,
The quiet of grief, of drifting sleep,
Of polar ice . . . Not noticing
How slow his fellows set out for work,
Because he was so sunk in thought,
Matvei went with them through the gates.
But then, astonished, he swung around:
How could he be hearing such a sound?
It was squealing, tuneless, wild,
The tinny sound of lid on lid,
How could a band be playing here?
Propping his crutch up in the snow,
Stiffened with cold under his rags,
A lad in a jacket, missing one leg,
Was banging the tight skin of a drum;
Beside him stood a clarinetist,
As yellow and bony as a corpse;
On he played, raising his clarinet
Like the black beak of a giant bird.
Two trumpeters were next; their lips,
Already blue and decomposed,
Were clamped to their trumpets' shining brass,
Which was all aglow in the fierce cold.
They seemed a company of ghosts
Abroad in the frozen early mist,
Filling the world from end to end
With unutterable delirium.
The band did all it could to play
Though muffled by the vicious cold;
The snaredrums beat relentlessly,
The kettledrums were rattling.
Flying in the face of the sad crowd
Of those who wanted sleep and bread,
The triumphal march blared to the sky
With a relentless impudence.
It chased after the human flood
That trickled slowly through the gates,
Flogging the backs that bowed before it,
Lashing them with its strident toots.
It rose to the sky, came rushing back;

Its cadences went tearing off
To the empty hills, like ancient kings
Cold had petrified; struck deaf and dumb,
They turned their indifferent eyes away.
Homeless, unheard by anyone,
The music buzzed like a giant fly
In the valley's gleaming sugarbowl.
No one was stirred to answer it,
And its travesty of freedom was spurned
By lifeless nature, on one side,
On the other, by people half-alive . . .
The march dragged on . . . Up on the hills
The first brigades had shrunk to specks,
While others were still left in the yard
Winding out through the gates and past the fence.

Translation by Catriona Kelly

BERTHA BABINA-NEVSKAYA
AND HER HUSBAND, BORIS NEVSKY

THREE

Bertha Babina-Nevskaya ────
My First Prison, February 1922

🌺 **About the Author**

Bertha Alexandrovna Nevskaya was born in 1886. Her father was an engineer. She was educated at a gymnasium (classical high school) in Petersburg, and since women could not then go to university, she attended the Women's Higher Courses there.

While still at school, she was attracted to the revolutionary movement. In 1907, at the age of 21, she joined the Socialist Revolutionaries (SRs) and carried out propaganda work for the party.* One of the sailors from the mutinous battleship Potyomkin *was imprisoned in the city's Peter and Paul Fortress, and Bertha, masquerading as his "fiancée," brought him food and wrote letters for him. Later, she married fellow SR Vladimir Golovin, and they went to live in Italy. After her husband's premature death, Bertha and their son Vsevolod (who would die at the front in 1942, fighting the Germans) returned to Russia.*

In 1913 she married again. Her second husband, Boris Babin, was another active SR and they had one son, Igor. Bertha and Boris shared all subsequent ordeals until Boris died in 1945 in Kolyma. "We experienced all the joys and sorrows of life," wrote Bertha Alexandrovna. "For almost a quarter of a century we faced errors and achievements, difficult ordeals and frequent separations. Then that life was ended abruptly by those who also once shared the same great dream. They destroyed its living soul and then perished at the hands of their own Party."

---

* The Socialist Revolutionary Party was founded abroad by émigrés in 1902. In addition to political agitation, the SRs organized a terrorist Fighting Detachment.

After the February 1917 Revolution the Socialist Revolutionary Party split, and Bertha and her husband Boris sided with the more radical Left SRs. * *In later years, however, Bertha would condemn the Left SRs for their extremism in 1918. More than once she said that they were responsible for breaking with the Bolsheviks and thus bringing to an end the first post-October socialist coalition government.*

In 1922 she and many others from both factions of the SR party were arrested. After being imprisoned and tried in Moscow, she was sent into internal exile until the late 1920s. Thereafter she was often arrested and exiled. In between she worked at various journals and as a translator, since she knew French, Italian, and German. In 1937 Bertha was arrested yet again. The next 17 years she spent in Kolyma. After her release in 1954, she lived for four years in Ukhta, in the northern Komi Republic, before returning to Moscow.

In Moscow her small room was always filled with friends and visitors. She became the heart and soul of the "Kolyma fellowship" of former political prisoners, retaining a great love of life and a now rare loyalty to the ideals of her youth. One year, on 7 November (the anniversary of the 1917 October Revolution), I dropped by with a red ribbon pinned to my jacket. "How lovely!" exclaimed Bertha Alexandrovna, and she began searching for a similar decoration for herself. Shamefacedly, I admitted that I was wearing red quite by chance: I had hastily borrowed my daughter's jacket after she returned from a Komsomol gathering.

Bertha Alexandrovna's life was long and difficult, but indisputably happy. Over 90 when she died, she retained to the end all the qualities that had made her a charming woman, and the dignity that helps us to face the perversities of life and the inevitability of death. Only during her last months in the hospital, where she died on 17 February 1983, did she finally stop working.

An hour before her death, she suddenly sat up in bed. The nurse attempted to restrain her.

"No, I must go," Bertha Alexandrovna said. "The guards are waiting to escort me."

NATALYA PIRUMOVA

---

* The Left SRs opposed the Brest-Litovsk treaty with the Germans in March 1918. They left the government and renewed a campaign of assassination.

It is easier to see home and family ruined, than to
tolerate the destruction of our castles in the air.
　　　　　　　—Charles Dickens

That morning we had only just finished drinking our tea when the chief
guard entered the cell with a long list in his hands. One after another, he
read out our names, adding in each case, "Pack your things!"

Barely had he left, and the key ceased rattling in the lock, when a joyful
clamor broke out: "We're going to Butyrki, to Butyrki!" An onlooker might
have assumed we were being released or invited to attend some celebration.
He would not have been far wrong. For Butyrki was very different from the
Lubyanka. Those already with experience of imprisonment under the new
regime told us that we would find our husbands and relatives there. Moreover, there were various privileges in Butyrki (walks in the exercise yard,
visits) that were unthinkable in the Cheka's prison. Joyfully excited, we
began to gather our modest belongings.

The other women in the cell were also content. "We're finally rid of
those socialists!" they sighed with relief. "At least there'll be some quiet
now."

Indeed, we had raised objections on the slightest pretext. We demanded
extra trips to the bathhouse, more exercise time, visits—things we knew
were quite out of the question. Each day we summoned the prison director
to our cell, insisting on our immediate transfer to Butyrki. This, of course,
was not for him to decide, but for the investigators working on our case.
Our behavior constantly upset the fearfully submissive petty embezzlers and
black marketeers who shared our cell: they always tried not to attract attention and kept as far apart from us as possible.

Our bedding was taken away, and we settled down on our bundles. The
hours dragged slowly by, and hardly anyone touched the porridge and thin
soup we were given at lunchtime. Only toward evening were we summoned
from our cell. In the courtyard stood a prison truck. At that time it was still
the unmistakable "Black Crow": fifteen years later, in 1937, such vehicles
were brightly painted, labeled "Meat," "Milk," or "Dried Fruits," and were
suffocatingly cramped inside. But in 1922 it was a black vehicle rather like
a cat basket, with a tiny barred window at the rear and two long benches
inside. The interior was almost pitch black. Yet as soon as we clambered in,
we were greeted by joyful exclamations. Seated inside were men and several
women from other cells. Wives were reunited with husbands, sisters with
brothers. For the first time in almost three weeks, I heard my husband Boris's voice. We had been parted for such a long time, it seemed!

Yet our life together had begun with a longer separation. Boris was imprisoned for six months and then sent into exile, and so he was not present

when our son Igor was born. But that was all under the Tsar. For the time being we continued to measure our lives by other standards, and what lay ahead was still "shrouded in mist."

There was no end to the stories we had to tell and the questions we wanted to ask. The guards rode up front and did not interfere. Suddenly a young voice rang out above our muffled conversations: "Comrades! They are now going to put us in quarantine, which could last 10 days. Don't consent to this. Demand an immediate medical examination and transfer to the socialist block!" "Most certainly! You're quite right!" came the reply from all sides.

The vehicle passed through the prison gates.

It was totally dark in the courtyard when we were led into a large, almost empty room and locked in. "This is the 'railway station'," explained the experienced among us, for the most part young Menshevik supporters of Julius Martov. From this reception area, prisoners were then allocated to blocks. By that time we were thoroughly tired, cold, and hungry. But all was forgotten in the joy of seeing our loved ones again. One and a half hours passed before the block guard came to visit us.

"Comrades," he said (yes, we were once respectfully addressed in such places!), "you must spend some days in quarantine. It won't be for long. A doctor will examine you, and then all who are fit will be sent to their cells. This is for your own good, so as not to bring any dangerous diseases into the prison." It must be admitted, there was a certain logic to what he said. Typhus was still very widespread, and there were a great many other epidemics. But we were young and felt fine. The idea of quarantine did not appeal to us at all.

"We won't go, we won't go!" everyone shouted in chorus. "If we must have a medical examination, we have a doctor of our own. Call in Doctor Donskoi!"

Dmitry Donskoi had been an SR long before the Revolution and was a member of the party's central committee. He and other Right SRs would shortly be put on trial, and they had already been in prison for some time.

An excellent doctor, he was fanatically devoted to his profession. Later exiled to Narym in central Siberia, Donskoi remained there to the end of his days. The vast northern expanses had hardly known what medical care was until then. Thanks to his efforts, an excellent hospital was built in the nearby town of Parabel; he personally supervised its construction. He organized and taught a series of courses for medical personnel, and he trained many skilled nurses. Even the local women overcame their prejudices against the Russian "shamans" and often came to give birth in his hospital. In 1937, seeing what was coming, he committed suicide.

So in February 1922, sitting in the "station" at Butyrki, we demanded that Donskoi examine us without delay.

"I cannot make that decision myself," said the block commandant finally. "I shall call in the prison director."

About an hour later, the director appeared. Dmitry Popov was such a striking figure that he deserves a few words.

Tall, broad-shouldered, and then about forty years old, he had fought in the Civil War and belonged to the pre-Revolutionary cohort of Bolsheviks. At that time he was quite well disposed to all imprisoned socialists, especially the Left SRs. He was also attracted to my friend Sonya Bogoyavlenskaya, or so my prison companions later assured me. Sonya was a plain redhead but exceptionally charming, intelligent, cheerful, and sharp-witted. Popov even permitted her to keep a little dog in her cell! When we needed petty favors, therefore, Sonya was usually entrusted to negotiate. Popov had a respect bordering on reverence for Boris Kamkov, an imprisoned leader of the Left SRs (I shall describe him a little later), and even tried to discuss politics and philosophy with him.

And where are you now, Sonya, my darling? You died many years ago, of course, at best in some camp hospital. We last saw each other in autumn 1936. She was visiting Moscow from Turukhansk, where she lived in exile with her husband, Misha Samokhvalov. (Misha, a Left SR, fought in the Red Army during the Civil War and would later die in the accursed gold mines of Kolyma.)

The fate of the director of Butyrki was as tragic as that of most Old Bolsheviks. When the clamp-down began in the early 1930s, Popov was one of those entrusted to carry it out. He unswervingly followed orders until 1937 when he became a captive in his own prison, and was then "dispensed with" by Stalin's executioners.

"Comrades," said Popov as he entered, "please be reasonable: it's night, and Dr. Donskoi is already asleep. Why can't you wait, at least until tomorrow morning?"

"Wake him up!" cried the young. "Doctors are used to being woken at all hours!"

After lengthy wrangling, agreement was reached, and soon Donskoi was brought to us.

It was the first time I had ever seen him, and for some reason he reminded me strongly of the water sprite in old German ballads. He had long straight fair hair, and a long pointed beard and mustaches, and he wore a fur coat so long it reached the ground. This water spirit, however, gave us a welcoming smile and was in a very jolly mood. The medical examination took no time.

"They're all fit and healthy!" he declared.

The guards led us out. It was probably around 2 A.M., and an impenetrable wintry darkness filled the courtyard.

Doors were noisily unlocked, we climbed stairs, another door opened. . . . Suddenly, after the dark, the cold, and hours of waiting, I was dazzled by a bright electric light and deafened by a loud and well-trained choir: "We are the blacksmiths," they sang, "and our spirit is young. We are forging the keys to happiness." A crowd of men and women rushed to greet us, and I was passed from one embrace to another. Blinded and deafened, I did not recognize any of them. Later I found out that many old comrades were there: from the Petersburg underground, from my student years, and from many different towns and cities where we had lived during our wanderings. We were in the "socialist block." Members of various left-wing parties were held there, and some had already been in prison for several years. The only absent socialists were the "deviationists" of the ruling Bolshevik Party, although several had already been imprisoned by then (followers of either Shlyapnikov or Safronov, I don't remember which). The "socialist block" was locked from the outside, but inside everything was run by the prisoners themselves.

After this uproarious welcome, they took us to the "club." The table was laid with vast copper kettles of boiling water and small teapots containing a strong brew. Every conceivable kind of food that our comrades possessed in those spartan years, from their rations or parcels, was laid out. Around a table in one of the corridors, the Council of Elders was seated in grand session. Most of its members were leading Right SRs (among them Gots, Timofeev, Gendelman, and our old friend Gelfgot); others came from the Menshevik Central Committee. Later we would jokingly refer to the council as the "shadow cabinet." They were busy allocating cells to the new arrivals: husband and wife were given their own cell, while the single shared with others. The decisions were based on a definite "table of ranks"; i.e., they depended on the position that individuals had formerly occupied in their party. The brighter and warmer cells were nicknamed "Arbat" or "Zamoskvoreche," after Moscow's better residential areas. Others were more crowded and poorly lit. Boris and I did not care where they put us. We simply wanted to be alone and rest after all the excitement of the day. Our cell was rather a long way from Butyrki's desirable "Arbat"—I had the reputation of having been overly friendly with the Bolsheviks for a time. It was also quite cold. The prison's central heating system was not working, and we did not yet have a stove.

Once we were finally on our own, we could not control our laughter anymore. "Does this remind you of anything?" Boris asked.

"It's all like some theatrical performance," I replied. "I constantly have the feeling that we are on stage and taking part in some extraordinary play. They can't really keep us locked up here! Whatever for!?"

The next morning I was laid low by an acute migraine, something from which I have suffered almost since childhood. Only one thing helped: to lie still without speaking and not to touch a drop of water; otherwise I would begin to feel nauseated.

Boris sat next to me. He went out a few times, came back, and tried to talk. I did not react and could understand nothing. By evening, however, the headache was completely gone. After drinking a cup of water and eating a piece of bread, I got up.

At that moment someone knocked at the door. Boris went out and returned with two comrades.

"Look who's come to see you," he said. "Do you recognize them?"

One I knew very well. Volodya Trutovsky and I had worked together in the party underground. Then we had collaborated on our beloved Petersburg newspaper. A semi-legal publication, each issue appeared under a different title, and it was closed down before the First World War. It was there I acquired my training as a journalist. I was a proofreader for the paper and published my first review there, of a collection of poems by workers. After the Revolution, Volodya was the People's Commissar (or perhaps a deputy people's commissar) for Public Services [in the short-lived coalition government]. Now here he was, standing in front of me and smiling, the same as ever.

Tall, thin, and dark, he had a typically handsome Ukrainian face with shining merry black eyes, a curly head of hair, and a little dark mustache. His companion was known to me only from photographs, publications, and endless stories. Shaking my hand, he introduced himself: "Kamkov."

A tall man or at least above average height and solidly built, he had large dark eyes which radiated intelligence and vivacity. His hair was thick and wavy but I think it was his eyebrows that caught one's attention: they were wide and black, and with his equally black and brilliant eyes created a distinct impression. He was wearing the very simple uniform of that time: a loose collarless peasant shirt without a belt, made of coarse, rough sailcloth. I remembered a photograph of him in an elegant black suit and tie, standing on the steps of the Bolshoi Theater, where the Fifth Congress of Soviets was then taking place.

He looked just as good in his current dress. There was a certain negligent grace and elegance in his movements. He always wore an irreproachably clean gray shirt, and his gait, slightly rolling, hands in pockets, recalled a sailor on land. (He was then not yet 40. The leaders of our Revolution had to be 10 years older!)

We exchanged greetings and went to see where they were living. Unlike the Right SRs, all the members of the Left SR Central Committee shared a single large room. As long as we were together in prison, they observed this tradition. Later, during periods of exile in Chelyabinsk and Voronezh, I saw that they not only treated everyone as equals, but also maintained genuinely communist relations among themselves. Comrades who were exiled with Kamkov to Tver confirmed these observations. Anyone who had shared the same political convictions would find a joyful welcome in Kamkov's house. If they were young and "unimportant," it made no difference: he took an interest in them all, and provided practical help. The same was true of the famous trio of Left SR leaders, Maria Spiridonova, Ilya Mayorov, and Alexandra Izmailovich, in their various places of exile during the 1920s and 1930s; it was also true of Irina Kakhovskaya. All the above-mentioned comrades were earning quite well by then, but they lived very modestly and spent the minimum on themselves. If friends were less fortunate, however, or had a large family to bring up, they never wanted for anything. Kamkov and his comrades set an example of real communism, in both their attitudes and their everyday behavior.

But I have digressed. I would like to return to that first night in Butyrki Prison.

Our fellow prisoners showed us their "club," the kind of thing the Bolsheviks later set up everywhere. There were chess and checkers, and recent newspapers and periodicals: even the weekly *Socialist Herald* was there, although it was published abroad by the Mensheviks and always gave a very sardonic account of events in Soviet Russia. At that time the prison library contained a wide choice of reading matter. By a long-established pre-Revolutionary tradition, prisoners left their books behind on release (apart, that is, from those they would need for their work). People could quietly read and study in the club; many did so. Almost every week there were talks, and representatives of the different political groups held discussions that went on for hours. Sometimes debates became so heated that you forgot the participants were prisoners and expected them to immediately go out and put their ideas into practice.

I can clearly remember one such impassioned discussion. If a real socialism, embodying the ideals of truth, justice, and liberty, was ever to be established in Russia, argued one of the Right SRs, it would not happen for at
least another 200 years! Kamkov spoke for the opposing view. The Revolution was by no means over. In a number of other countries, he argued, the
Revolution would yet take place as a result of the postwar depression and
events in the Soviet Union. By the mid-20th century the socialist system
would triumph in Europe.

Within fifteen years both debaters had fallen victim to Stalinist "socialism." Meanwhile the rise of fascism in several European countries would
lead, after the bloody Spanish tragedy, to the horrors of the Second World
War. Yet could we possibly have imagined anything of the kind? We were
convinced that, in the end, the differences between us and "them" [the Bol-
sheviks] would not hinder the building of a new world. Although we would
always have to argue, and argue stubbornly, they would release us from
prison and we would build the new world together! We did not take what
was happening to us seriously: it seemed more of a fairground staging of the
French Revolution—without the guillotine, of course. Wasn't it Marx who
said that history repeats itself, first as tragedy and then as farce? No one,
including the various shades of Marxists, suspected what an enormous guillotine awaited us all in the not so distant future.

Every morning, in the meantime, on the noisy iron landing of one of the
staircases running through Butyrki Prison, handsome "Georges" Kachorovsky led our physical exercise classes.

An excellent singer and musician, he organized an amateur prison or-
chestra of various string instruments. He managed to start regular singing classes as well, putting together a wonderful choir of male and female
voices. Georges trained the soloists himself. Some of them were really rather
good, and their performances gave us all great pleasure.

Kachorovsky was a student when the First World War began. Drafted
into the army, and an officer when the Revolution broke out, he was swept
up by events and sided with the most popular party of the day, the Socialist Revolutionaries. After the party split, he remained with the Right SRs:
he had given them his allegiance and remained loyal to his choice (I doubt
that he understood the different political nuances and tendencies). He also
shared their fate. In 1923, while serving a three-year sentence on Solovki,
an island concentration camp in the White Sea, he fell victim to the tragic
events there. For refusing to cut short their exercise period, his wife, Lida
Kotova, her brother Vanya, Natasha Bauer, Georges, and three other comrades were shot dead by guards on the camp watchtower. This was part of

a general "tightening up," intended to bring the period of liberalism in the prisons to an end.

However, foreign socialist parties heard of the events and protested. The Soviet government was still trying to remain on good terms with them, and set up an investigation. Someone was dismissed and a few scapegoats were punished. The British Labour Party, then in power, sent a delegation to Moscow, which expressed a desire to visit Solovki. It was impossible to reach such places in winter, they were told, since no ships could cross the frozen sea and airplanes did not fly there then. Members of the delegation expressed astonishment that a socialist state could detain socialists, albeit of a different persuasion, in places that were inaccessible for most of the year.

Following this, the inmates of the camp were moved to other prisons, to Suzdal (like Solovki, a former monastery) and to Verkhneuralsk Prison. They found conditions no better there. The rules were just as arbitrary, and protests, hunger strikes, spells in the punishment block, and even severe beatings followed.

Fifty years have passed, and the Solovetsky Islands are one of the places where our grandchildren spend their summer holidays. They go on organized trips, or on their own, and sail across the White Sea to these islands of banishment and death. The landscape in the Far North is picturesque and beautiful in its own restrained way. The flowers bloom, birds sing, vacationers catch fish, and even the most indifferent are entranced by the poetry of the sunlit "white nights." The graves have been leveled, the monastery walls keep their silence, and few remember what happened here. Youth is a thoughtless and carefree time. Blessed ignorance!

But in early 1922, our "socialist block" led an existence of anecdotal originality. On our third day there, I was shuddering from the cold and damp. As Boris tried to warm our cell with an iron stove given by our comrades, someone knocked at the door. A handsome and elegant young man, dressed like a prisoner, entered, and after clicking his heels, he introduced himself as Duke So-and-So. Unfortunately, I do not remember the name, though it was one of the most imposingly aristocratic surnames in Tsarist Russia. I was dumbstruck by this unexpected intrusion.

"Do not be surprised, Madame, this is no charade," said our guest, lightly rolling his r's: "I came to ask if there was anything that you needed. Can I be of service in any way?"

We later learned that he was a former Guards officer, and by no means the only one of his kind in Butyrki. Imprisoned as "White" officers, they were free to move between the blocks and any other prison buildings, some-thing denied to us socialists. So the management commission of our block entrusted them with various tasks, and they would sometimes also serve the individual cells. In return they were given extra food from our slightly bet-ter prison rations.

I admitted that I got very cold in the cell.

"Oh, that's easy!" smiled the former guardsman. "By evening you will have an excellent little stove."

"How can you manage that?" I asked in surprise.

"Very simple: I shall make one for you, out of bricks. Yes indeed, we have learned to do a great many new things! A la guerre comme à la guerre!"

"Merci, monsieur," I mumbled, not knowing what to say.

"Not at all! I'm honored to help such a young lady. Especially since we're here to serve the socialists."

The last remark rang quite ironically from his lips. Nevertheless, by evening our cell was indeed heated by a marvelous little stove, and our friends came by to warm themselves at its enchanting heat. Throughout our stay in Butyrki, the duke cared for us unstintingly, helping in every conceiv-able way. We became friendly and sometimes even talked about French po-etry, which this scion of the old Russian ruling class knew extremely well. I saw no point in discussing politics. Sooner or later, I probably would have tested his reaction to the Decembrists. But our acquaintance did not last long. Soon the "socialist block" was disbanded.

I was not then very interested in the details of our daily existence, I must admit, and so have only vague recollections. Still, I can recall a few more peculiar features of our life in Butyrki. The first few days were taken up with visits. Among those we went to see was the Right SR Arkady Altov-sky. Today he is an old man of almost 90, as meek and timid as a lamb. An underground member of the party and a participant in the 1905 Revolu-tion, he emigrated to escape arrest and graduated with distinction from the electro-technical institute in Grenoble. In 1917 he returned to Russia, and from 1919 onward he was always in and out of prison. After surviving about twenty years in Stalin's camps, he worked in the northern Russian town of Ukhta, where he had served his sentence. Then he was rehabili-tated, and he is now a pensioner in Moscow. In 1922 I did not know him. I wanted to see his wife, Nina Averkieva. We had been imprisoned at the Lubyanka together and then both been taken to Butyrki.

Entering their cell, I froze in astonishment. When I had visited several other long-term inmates, I was no longer quite so amazed. We had all read of the various indulgences that the (alas!) much more naive tsarist government had permitted its Decembrist opponents. Something similar took place here, in that brief idyllic period from 1920 to 1922.

On the wall hung a carpet, and a small rug lay in front of the bed. The bed was covered by their own blanket and several brightly covered cushions. For eyes already tired of the prison's gray monotony, this created an inexpressibly vivid impression.

A still more exotic sight, however, was the host of this unusual abode. Altovsky was a handsome brown-haired man, and wore a red shirt that went well with his dark-skinned face and little black beard. He sat on the bed, picking out a tune on the guitar, and did not even get up when I entered. Yet it was Nina who most amazed me. She was lounging on the cushions in her own colorful dressing gown. Formerly plain and frowning, with a gray little face and two pigtails trailing forlornly down her back, she had bloomed overnight and become unrecognizably attractive. This was a quite different woman. Her cheeks had a high color, her eyes sparkled, and her hair fanned out over the cushion. I realized that my presence was superfluous. After wishing the happy couple every joy, I quickly left.

Nina Averkieva is long gone. She was the daughter of old revolutionary intelligentsia parents from Saratov. At one time our brothers studied together at the Petersburg Polytechnic Institute. Both were arrested in 1914, with several other comrades, after the First World War had begun. In a little over a month, they were released from prison. A search warrant for my room had also been issued. They did not find any compromising material, of course, but they were especially thorough and even made me undo the diaper of my newborn son, Igor. Now, when the occasion arises, he sometimes asserts that he was also "searched by the Tsarist gendarmes." After returning in 1955 from Kolyma, I went to Ukhta, where Igor was serving a second camp sentence, despite being innocent of any crime. There I met Arkady Altovsky, who was then still chief engineer of the local power station.

The cell of our old friends Alexander Gelfgot and his wife Yelena Tumpovskaya (born Armand) had a simpler and more modest appearance. As a member of the SR Central Committee, Gelfgot lived in a cell near the "Arbat." It was warm, there were many books lying around, and they also had some things from home. If I am not mistaken, they even had their own kettle, which as soon as we appeared, they quickly brought to the boil, using a little iron stove.

With our tea we were treated to a most refined prison delicacy—uncooked cranberries sprinkled with sugar. But the most pleasant things in the cell were Yelena's kindly eyes and smile. A quiet, wise woman, she had already borne a great deal in a life of sorrow. Like the rest of us, she would spend 18 years in the camps after 1937, dying in 1966. She came from the family of a well-known Petersburg doctor. A widower, he raised four daughters, three of whom then took part in the revolutionary movement. Yelena was the second oldest and became attached to the SRs' Fighting Detachment.* A military tribunal sentenced her to be executed, and for some time she sat on "death row." Then, however, the death penalty was commuted to a life sentence of hard labor. She managed to escape from Siberia, and soon the Revolution began.

Yelena and I were bound by a common fate, first as members of the SR party, and then by our years of wandering and suffering in the Civil War, which we spent in southern Russia (Rostov, Krasnodar), where the White general Denikin was in control. Our elder sons were contemporaries and friends. As the wife and loyal helper of Alexander Gelfgot, Yelena was frequently imprisoned in our own Soviet period. Now we had met in Butyrki.

Gelfgot, a brilliant redhead with a Mephistophelean beard and a constant joke on his lips, acted as though he had forgotten our long and sharp disputes when I had "deviated." That was a thing of the past now, and there was no point in going back to it.

The men started a game of chess, and Yelena and I began quietly to remember the children we had left behind in the world outside. The children of revolutionaries, on this we were fully agreed, were the most unfortunate children in the world! Yet we could not begin to imagine then what they would have to endure because of us.

Translation by John Crowfoot

---

* The Detachment was responsible for the assassination of over one hundred leading Tsarist officials between 1901 and 1908.

NADEZHDA GRANKINA

FOUR

Nadezhda Grankina ——————————

Notes by Your Contemporary

🏵 **About the Author**

Nadezhda Vasilievna Grankina was born in St. Petersburg in 1904. Her father was a priest, and after his first wife died, he did not have the right, under canon law, to remarry; thus the two children he had by his second wife were considered illegitimate. His second wife's brother, a deacon at the church in Tsarskoe Selo (where the Tsar had his summer palace), took the children in and brought them up as his own. So it was only when she entered the gymnasium that Nadya discovered she was illegitimate: many parents would not let their daughters be friends with her, and this wounded her deeply.

Soon after the October Revolution, Nadezhda applied to join the Communist youth organization. "Why do you want to be in the Komsomol?" they asked. "Because the Communists are the heirs of Christ," she replied, "and in the name of Christ I want to help the Communists." Naturally her application was turned down.

In 1919 her mother took her south, away from the starvation in Petrograd (as St. Petersburg was then known), to Yelizavetgrad in the Ukraine. There Nadezhda worked as a ward orderly in a hospital. She again applied to join the Komsomol, and this time she was accepted. Soon afterward, however, during one of the frequent membership purges, she was expelled for being the daughter of a priest. She was not yet 18 when she met and married Yevgeny Grankin, a Red Army commander who had sustained serious wounds in the Civil War. He soon was expelled from the Party for being a follower of Leon Trotsky.

In 1930 the Grankins and their eight-year-old daughter came back to Leningrad (as Petrograd was now called) and moved into the cramped flat of Nadezhda's mother. Yevgeny's health deteriorated. He was completely incapable of working, but his pension was insufficient, so Nadezhda had to earn enough for the two of them. To add to all this, their daughter contracted poliomyelitis and was crippled for life.

Yevgeny Grankin was first arrested in 1931, but he managed to prove that because of illness he had been unable to maintain any ties with his former comrades. While his case was being investigated, Nadezhda was called in for interrogation. She thought that she should tell the whole truth and informed the investigator that she had read Trotsky's Letters. *Later she paid dearly for this candor.*

Yevgeny was released, but a year later he was rearrested and sentenced to exile. Nadezhda was given permission to visit her husband and was told that he was in Samara, on the Volga. But he was not there, it turned out, and she was sent on to Orenburg, where her passport was taken away from her. Meanwhile, Yevgeny had been in a prison hospital in Leningrad the whole time. Penniless, with nowhere to live and an invalid daughter on her hands, Nadezhda was trapped in exile. Fortunately, by the autumn of 1933 her husband was rehabilitated, and Nadezhda returned to Leningrad.

In 1936 Yevgeny was arrested yet again, and a year later he died in Belgorod prison in southwest Russia. Nadezhda was picked up soon afterward and sentenced to ten years' imprisonment. She too was held in Belgorod at first, and then, by stages, moved north (through Kursk, Kazan, and Suzdal) and east to Kolyma.

Their sick daughter was taken in by Nadezhda's mother. In 1942, both grandmother and daughter died of starvation during the siege of Leningrad.

In 1947 Nadezhda Grankina was released. From 1956 until her death in 1983, she lived in Leningrad. Her memoirs fill a voluminous manuscript running to five hundred pages, written over many years: Nadezhda wanted to reproduce with the utmost exactitude the experiences she had undergone.

ELGA SILINA

Kursk

What you suffer is not as important as what you
learn from the experience.

It is difficult to describe such things, and I do not even know if I shall succeed. But let me try.

From March 1938 they began to convoy people out of the prisons to the labor camps where they had been assigned. For some reason I was moved only in July, after spending eight months in prison in Belgorod. In those years it was quite common for prisoners to be led through the streets on foot. And it was on foot that we left, accompanied by a crowd of idle on-lookers, and by weeping women who could make out their loved ones in the convoy. They threw their husbands cigarettes and bread, begging the guards to hand them food, and calling out words of farewell. Some held up children so that their fathers could get a glimpse of them and say goodbye from a distance. The children were crying. We were loaded onto a prison train—into "Stolypin" wagons—and taken north to Kursk.

The prison conditions there were even harsher than in Belgorod. Up to a hundred people at a time, and more, were crammed into one small cell with a single tiny window just under the ceiling. By the left-hand wall, close to the window, were four beds pushed together, across which ten people could lie. On the only other bed, by the right-hand wall close to the door, lay a young woman with a year-old child. On the other hand, the food was better than in Belgorod, the toilet bucket stood inside the cell, and the guards paid less attention to us.

I was chosen to be cell leader, and took on this bothersome task so that time would pass more quickly and there would be no opportunity to think. It was my duty to keep order in the cell. Today I cannot imagine how I managed, given the extraordinary assortment of people under my care. I remember when our pregnant woman was due to have her baby. She had already been in prison for eight months and had left five other children behind at home. In our cramped conditions we tried as best we could to protect her. One morning she began to moan a bit, then lay down on her back, pulled up her knees, and pushed as hard as she could. "She's having it! She's having it!" the women next to her screamed. I flew to the door and began hammering on it with my fist. There was no response. The baby shot out onto the knees of the women who were sitting on the floor and began to cry, flailing thin arms and legs. The woman who caught it gnawed through the umbilical cord, tore the white scarf from her head, ripped off a strip with her teeth, and bound up the navel. Everyone in the cell was on their feet and screaming as though all one hundred women had gone into labor the minute they saw the woman give birth. I grabbed the wooden lid off the toilet bucket and banged it on the door. At last the guard appeared, and the woman and her son were taken off to the medical section.

I used to give out the food, and the onions, garlic, pine and beet root extracts that were issued once a week since many prisoners were suffering from scurvy. After roll call I would put the women to bed, packing them together literally like sardines in a tin: I made them all turn on the same side and shift up as close to each other as possible. There was no room left for me, so at night I would go out with the workers to wash the floors of the prison corridors. After this work we were allowed to use the bathhouse and to wash our clothes there. Then I would sleep for two or three hours between breakfast and the midday meal.

For almost a year I did not see a newspaper and had no contact with the outside world. In the prison office where I washed the floors, I used to take old newspapers out of the wastebasket, but they were local papers with only a small circulation and did not tell you what was going on. Once, through the office window, I heard people shouting "Hurrah!" on the radio. Evidently it was a political meeting, but the loudspeaker was a long way off and the words were impossible to make out.

Our prison was the transit center for the Kursk Region. Each week, transports from the local prisons would be ferried in and ferried out, and our cell emptied and filled up all over again, but I stayed put. The prisoners had all spent a long time in jail or else were not greatly interested in outside events. One of the women criminals who had recently been free said that a war was going on somewhere in the Far East. That alarmed me.

I was sentenced without a trial to ten years' imprisonment, and no one even read the verdict to me. I thought I would be sent to a labor camp and was eager to get there as soon as possible. Then I could write a letter and get news of my relatives: in those years correspondence was forbidden to people in prisons, and not knowing what had happened to my daughter was torturing me.

After the departure of one of the large prison transports, sixteen of us were left. We were delighted. Now we could all have a place on the beds and, for a while, sleep stretched out and with room to move. Only Sigulda started a quarrel with her neighbor: "For the last six months I've been sleeping under the bed, so now I have the right to sleep on it the way I want to!" she shouted.

"Stop it," I said, trying to make her see reason. "When there were a hundred of us you had enough room, and now that there are sixteen, you don't."

At that moment the peephole in the door rustled, the locks slid back, and in walked the block officer. Everyone fell silent.

"What's all the noise?" he asked. "Cell leader, who was making that racket?"

He wanted the name of the troublemaker, I realized, so that he could make an example of her and insist on silence in the cell—something they had not worried about very much previously, because of the cramped conditions and the continual turnover. (Everyone was temporary, they thought, and would be gone the next day.) If Sigulda was put in the punishment cell,

I knew I would feel guilty and not be able to look her or the others in the eye. "Why does he ask?" I thought with irritation. "He was listening and heard every word."

"We weren't making a noise, we were chatting," I said, trying to be diplomatic.

"Who was chatting?"

"I was!" I said boldly.

"Three days in the punishment cell!" he shouted, incensed by an answer he had not expected from me.

"As you wish." I knew the layout of the prison and set off for the punishment cell without waiting for him.

The locks thundered shut, and I was left alone in a stone box with no windows. In the right-hand corner there was a bucket that had not been covered over or emptied by the previous occupants, and which was fouling the already stale air. I sat down on the stone floor. I began to feel so sorry for myself that I silently started to cry. I had not slept much for many months, and soon I dropped off, curled up on the floor because the cramped conditions made it impossible to stretch out full length.

The silence was quickly broken by the sound of a man being dragged along the corridor, growling and cursing as he tried to put up a fight. I heard sounds of a struggle—they must have been putting him into a straitjacket.

In the morning the prison director made the rounds of the punishment cells.

"And what are you in here for?" he asked me.

"Nothing," I replied.

"We don't put people in here for nothing."

"Well, you did in my case."

"Well, and here you'll stay."

"And here I'll stay," I answered doggedly.

The door slammed shut, but a short while later I was let out. Back in our cell, some were sympathetic and delighted to see me, but others were indifferent. Sigulda did not say a word, as though none of this concerned her. Fearing that I would succumb to misanthropy, I refused to carry on as cell leader. But the days dragged by unbearably, and I wrote two requests to the prison director, asking for a transfer to my labor camp.

People who knew their prison sentences and did not request a transfer used to spend the whole time in Kursk. Then, skipping the transit prisons at Kazan and Suzdal, they went straight to Vladimir, ready for convoy to the camps in Kolyma. This spared them much unpleasantness. Finally I was assigned to a convoy. To avoid sending me on my own under special escort, probably, as they were supposed to with such "deadly enemies," the documents that accompanied me did not indicate whether I had been convicted or was just awaiting trial. I was asked about this every time we were passed on to new convoy guards, but I did not know the answer.

We were taken up to Moscow, where we were unloaded and regrouped. I was led away on my own to a wagon on the sidings, where I was kept until evening, deeply troubled as I watched a gang of very young prostitutes. They were trying to climb up to the men whose wagon had been parked nearby, and were shrieking obscenities. One of them was so pretty that I could not tear my eyes from her face, and the more I looked at her, the more pained I felt inside.

Toward evening we were put on a train. The sleeping compartment was very crowded, and I had to clamber onto the top bunk. In the morning one of the elderly women sitting down below told us that she had been arrested because her neighbor, a Party member and state official, wanted to swap rooms with her. At first he promised money, then he arranged all sorts of difficulties for her, and finally he denounced her. She got eight years in a labor camp, but her room went to the security police, the NKVD. The neighbor came to visit her in prison and brought her a parcel of food, crying and begging her to forgive him.

Another old lady, now a pensioner, had been a textile worker in the Ivanovo Region and had worked all her life in a factory. She told us how she had become involved in the church in her later years and been a local church elder. Her investigator was a young boy who would thump his fist on the table and scream that he'd send her to a place where she could use her smart ass to pull out nails or melt the snow. "I couldn't resist asking—Why? Is my arse so much better than everyone else's?" We laughed at her story. The train came to a halt way east of Moscow, in Kazan.

Kazan

Why had they brought us to Kazan? I could not understand it. I and two others were called out of the wagon and taken through the streets on foot, of which I was very glad. The autumn morning was clear, sunny, and cool. For almost a year now I had not seen city streets, or people going off to work, or children on their way to school. I had never been in Kazan before and looked at all the streets and buildings with some pleasure. The two guards walking behind us were evidently decent young men. They did not pick at us and they took us along the sidewalk rather than the roadway, keeping to themselves and leaving us in peace.

At last we reached the prison, and the guard locked us, as new arrivals, in a box cell as usual. I was put on my own, in the middle of three, and my companions were locked up on my left. They did not interest me, as I knew that they were ordinary criminal offenders, but hearing someone else behind the thin partition on my right, I asked him who he was and where he came from. He was a worker from a collective farm, it turned out, and he told me all about his case. He had been accused under Article 58:8 (terrorism) of attempting to assassinate Stalin. "Oho," I thought to myself, "a big fish!"

"Where on earth did you see Stalin?" I asked.

"I've never seen Stalin in my life—I've never even been to Moscow."

A couple of young hooligans had climbed into this "terrorist's" loft and stolen his apples. He found out who they were (you can't hide that kind of thing in a village) and went to the village soviet to make a complaint. The hooligans then reported him to the district authorities for supposedly having threatened to kill Stalin. He was picked up and spent nine months in prison. Now he was being sent away, but where he did not know. I very much wanted to take a look at him. Suddenly we heard footsteps. The doors on either side of me opened, and a voice said, "Out!" Then they called me out, and I bumped into the neighbor I had found so intriguing.

He was a man of about forty to forty-five, of below average height, with a pale face sprouting sharp stubble. His unbelievably dirty, torn clothing was made of rough homespun linen and at one time had been padded with flax tow, which was now sticking out or trailing from innumerable holes. He exuded the sharp prison smell—rough tobacco, the stench of dirty clothing that has been heat-treated for lice again and again and slept in on the floor, and the sweat of a dirty body. Over the past year I had grown used to that smell, but it came off him in such a concentrated stream that it caught even my breath. On his head he wore a shapeless cap and on his feet, leggings and shoes of an unknown vintage, with curled-up toes. We nodded to each other and parted.

In the meantime the prison office had opened my envelope of documents. I was sent off to another place on my own with the same guards. I found all this rather entertaining, and never suspected that I was on my way to be buried alive for ten years. Finally we came to a different prison. It was in the middle of the town, and from the outside it perhaps did not resemble a prison. The gates swung open in front of us, and we walked in under an archway, turned to the right, and found ourselves in the duty office. A woman in uniform took my papers, read them, told me to hand over my things (I was carrying a small bundle of clean underwear in a kerchief), wrote everything down on a docket, and led me off.

For a long time we walked in silence down some corridors before we finally came to a bathroom. After only a hasty wash, because I was constantly being nagged, I came out of the bathroom and was given prison underwear, clothing, and a towel. Everything was stamped with three large numbers, signifying my block, my cell, and my personal number. This was something new. If my memory does not deceive me, my numbers were 365 —for block 3, cell 6, and my own number, 5. The underwear was new. The clothing consisted of a dark gray moleskin skirt with a brown stripe along the hem, and a blouse of the same gray with brown stripes on the collar, cuffs, yoke, and hips. The black stockings had no garters, or I guess I should say that they had tapes no longer than your finger sewn on to them which could not support the stockings. The boots were size 45 with no laces. I was also given an enormous padded jacket, made out of the same gray moleskin with a brown lining and brown stripes on the hem, collar, cuffs, and sides. The head scarf was dark gray calico, and for winter I was given an incredibly ugly padded hat with earflaps, also made out of brown moleskin.

The sleeves of the jacket hung to my knees, the boots clumped on the floor, parting company with my feet, and my stockings dangled around my ankles. The woman led me along the corridor looking like this, constantly telling me to hurry up or hissing: "Sssh . . . sssh . . . " We came out into a courtyard, then went into another building, entering a corridor with a narrow strip of carpet running down its center in the semi-darkness. Then, with the sharp snap of a lock, a door opened right in front of me into the gloom of a cell with a stone floor.

Opposite the door was a fairly large window with a grid of thick iron bars mounted between two frames. A wooden screen fixed to the outside blocked out all the light, and was covered with a fine mesh at the top. In the lower right-hand side of the window was a small ventilation pane. The window had no sill, and the wall sloped inward, almost as far as the iron table that was clamped to the adjoining wall by brackets. On either side of the table were two single iron seats, also bracketed to the wall. Opposite the table was an iron bench, which at a pinch could seat three people squeezed up tight. Along the right-hand side of the cell were four hinged metal bed frames, which were stowed up against the wall and locked shut during the day. Written beneath them in black paint on the wall were the numbers 2, 3, 4, and 5. Another bed frame was clamped lengthwise to the left wall.

In the right-hand corner nearest the door, a stove stuck out into the room; it was stoked from the corridor and heated two adjacent cells. In the corner next to it was a wooden bucket with a lid—the slop bucket. Down the middle of the cell there was a wide red strip that looked like linoleum, but in fact was made of stone. In the far right-hand corner lay a perpetual puddle. In the thick wall above the door, a listening vent, 40 centimeters by 40, had been cut and covered with a very fine black mesh. A 25-watt light bulb hung in this space, giving virtually no light in the evenings. The door had the inevitable peephole, and a "food hatch" underneath it. The sound of its flap falling open was like a gunshot, and it always woke us up in terror during the night.

To the right of the table a young woman of about thirty was sitting with a bandage around her cheek and wearing the same outfit as I was. We introduced ourselves. She was Zina and had come from Moscow by the same train, but under special escort, and so had arrived at the prison in a "Black Crow."

We began sharing our impressions, talking in low voices. Every minute the lid of the food hatch would open with a bang and someone would hiss, "Sssh!" An eye was constantly blinking at the peephole. We started to whisper. Again the food hatch was flung open and a voice said, "Sssh!" We purposely fell silent. In walked the guard, who ordered us to stand up and again said, "Sssh!" pointing to the regulations hanging on the wall to the right of the window, signed by the head of the NKVD, Yezhov. The rules said that we had to talk quietly and to stand up in the presence of the prison administration. Nevertheless, every fifteen minutes the guards would come in and order us to stand up and be quiet. Zina and I agreed that she would ask to see the head of the block. When he came in, we drew his attention to the fact that the guards were making us stand up every fifteen minutes, while according to the rules we had to stand up only for the administration. After that they gave us some peace.

Zina did not belong to the Party and, like me, was imprisoned on account of her husband. She had been tried by the Military Tribunal and knew what her sentence was: eight years' imprisonment. She came from Gorky (Nizhny Novgorod), and it was in prison there that she had come down with a toothache and become infected when the dentist extracted the tooth. She contracted periostitis and was transferred in serious condition to the Butyrki Prison in Moscow, where she was operated on: they had to remove all her lower teeth on the right side. Her jaw developed sepsis, and now she had a fistula near her ear, which was oozing pus and fragments of jawbone. Later on in Kazan she underwent another operation and the fistula closed over, but her face remained permanently twisted.

She had left two children behind at home, a girl of seven and a boy of four. They had been put in a children's home, and she missed them terribly. Zina was a slightly hysterical woman and not very well educated. She had been orphaned early on when her father and mother died of typhoid. Her uncle and aunt had raised her, and they turned her into the housemaid; thus she barely learned to read or write. She married young, but her marriage was also not happy. She had lived with her mother-in-law, who liked to drink, and her husband had drunk heavily too. He was a metallurgical engineer in a factory in Gorky.

In Butyrki Prison in Moscow, Zina had been kept for a long time in a hospital wing with some mentally disturbed women, and she spoke about them so often that her stories stayed with me. Two of the women there, according to her accounts, were young girls who had been arrested because of an erotic obsession. They had fallen in love with Stalin and thought they were going to marry him. They never stopped talking about him, and about how strong he was; and they kept going over his appearance and recounting dreams in which he had invariably taken part. Each was waiting for him to come and take her as his bride. Sometimes they would compete for him, and on those occasions they quarreled or even came to blows. Before prison they had not known each other, and they had seen Stalin only once, from a distance, when he was passing along the street in a car. In 1937 their strange outpourings obviously struck someone as counterrevolutionary, rather than the ravings of a deranged mind. They were denounced, and the machine went into action. Now they had been tried and put in prison, instead of receiving treatment in a psychiatric hospital.

Down to its finest detail, the entire regime in Kazan prison was calculated to suppress our individuality. For a corridor of ten cells there were five people employed just to look through the peepholes, and two corridor guards. We had to get out of bed at the seven o'clock bell, immediately dress, strip our beds, and stand next to them. The guard on duty would come in; we would raise our beds against the wall, and he would lock them. After that we would wait for our turn to slop out, then make our way to the latrines with our towels, walking in single file in dead silence, with our hands behind our backs. We also had to wait our turn to empty our toilet buckets. Toilet duty was supposed to take us all five minutes.

A guard would stand in front of the latrines and hand each of us a carefully cut square of paper, approximately 15 by 15 centimeters. This scrap of paper was always the cause of extraordinary scenes and must have been deliberately dreamed up by somebody in order to confound, intimidate, and humiliate. Perfectly civilized in itself, it had completely unforeseen ramifications. In the corner of the latrine there was a metal bin where we were supposed to throw our used papers, but as no one had told us, we naturally put them down the toilet. All the newly arrived prisoners did this, we later learned, and all of them went through what we did.

We returned to our cell, and a minute later the guard burst in: "Where's your paper?" We had already forgotten all about it. "What paper?" We asked.

"The paper we gave you."

"We threw it away."

"What do you mean, you threw it away?"

Women guards immediately appeared and began the most painstaking search—of our mouths, our hair, in between our fingers and toes, etc. Of course, we were dumbfounded. It would have been easier, naturally, for the prison staff to have warned us, but that was not in their interests. I should add that this totting up of our dirty pieces of toilet paper was carried out by full-grown adults, sound in limb and mind, both young and old, who all wore the military uniform of the NKVD. After each cell had slopped out, the guard would go into the latrines carrying a torch and shine it on the walls, to make sure nothing had been written there. While we were on toilet duty, our cell would be searched, and each time they went through our books and cigarettes. Inside the cell, we were not allowed to go up to the walls to keep us from tapping messages to each other; physical exercises were also forbidden. After slopping out, we would be brought 800 grams of bread and a pot of boiling water faintly flavored with carrot tea. Sugar was issued to us once a month, two cubes per day, and we used to keep it in special little bags with our numbers on them. Lunch was at two o'clock and varied little from one day to the next: it was either a watery pea soup, with pieces of beef lungs bobbing on it like corks, or a cabbage soup made of dried vegetables, followed by porridge or lentils. At six in the evening we had thin porridge and tea. I never had enough bread or sugar.

We were made to go to bed at ten o'clock, but before this happened there was a whole procedure to be gone through. At nine-thirty we would lower our beds, then stand next to them waiting for a signal with the light, which meant permission to make them up. At a second signal we had to remove our outer garments and sit on the bed, and only on the third did we have the right to lie down—but not to cover our heads. Toward ten o'clock the light bulb began to shine more brightly, and it would burn until morning. Several times a night we would be awakened by the crash of the flap to the food hatch, because someone at the peephole could not see our heads.

In the gray half-light and with nothing to do, the days dragged by painfully slowly. We grew tired of whispering. Winter evenings were yet worse: in the feeble glow of the light bulb, we were all but stumbling over each other. Even walking around the cell was impossible, because our huge laceless boots clumped on the stone floor. We were forbidden to open the ventilation pane ourselves and had to call the guard to open it for us. Noises flooded in from the street with the air: car horns, dogs barking, children's voices . . .

During the day we would be taken out for a half-hour walk in the exercise yard. It was covered in asphalt and walled off with a high plywood fence, and we were supposed to walk around in a circle with our heads bowed and our hands behind our backs. All it took was for one of us to raise her head, and everyone was taken back to the cell without finishing the walk. Our garter-less stockings were always falling down during exercise, but we did not have the right to stop and pull them up. Apart from the fact that it was already cold, it seemed humiliating to me to be walking around with a dangling stocking. I pulled mine up, and immediately everyone was led back to the cell. The deputy director of the prison appeared and asked each of us our names. When he heard mine, he flew into a rage: "Don't listen to her, she's a troublemaker. I'll break you! Five days in the punishment cell!"

The punishment cell was small and windowless. Like our cell, it had a little table screwed to the wall, a stool for one person, and a bare board fastened to the wall. The latrines were on the other side of the adjoining wall, and you could hear the constant sound of running water. Jackets and slopping out were forbidden in the punishment cell. The toilet bucket stood in the corner. I was given 400 grams of bread and some water, and just before it was time to sleep, they lowered the board. It was dripping wet from the dank wall, but I had to lie on it all night, since standing up or sitting down was forbidden. This made my dress damp, and the constant slight shivering of a fever shook my body. All my muscles grew tired, and I could not fall asleep. That was how I passed the five days, and toward the end my legs swelled up.

Prisoners with some money in their account had the right to subscribe to a newspaper, and once every ten days we were given books: a catalogue would be brought into the cell, along with a piece of paper on which we wrote out the numbers of the books we wanted. The library was extensive and consisted of requisitioned books—or so we inferred from the fact that the corners of the title pages of many of them, where book owners customarily write their names, had been cut off. If we had money in our account we had the right to buy things at the prison shop: soap, a toothbrush, an exercise book, a mechanical pencil (for some reason other types were not allowed), sugar and onions, or a textbook we had ordered. The soap was brought to the cell, cut up into tiny pieces. All this took endless requests and persistence. When we complained to the block officer that we had no newspapers, he would invariably reply, "There are none on sale. I don't have a newspaper myself."

Twice a month we were allowed to send letters, and twice a month we could receive them. Of course they were censored and often arrived with large cuts. The letters we looked forward to so avidly did not make us happy, because we had to give them back the following day. All five women in our cell devoured them with their eyes, each reacting in her own way.

Tanya would immediately burst into tears and say that of course everything was not as fine at home as they were making out; it was just that they did not want to upset her by telling her. Pelagea Yakovlevna would read through hers in silence, not sharing the contents with anyone, but now and again sighing and saying "Well, well" with a shake of her head, in answer to some thoughts of her own. Zina would ask me to read the letters she got from the woman at the home where her children were. She was not sure if she had read them correctly. Lena did not get any letters, and while the rest of us were reading ours, she would silently walk up and down the cell. I was never happy to get letters from home. My mother could not understand that I was in prison for nothing: she thought that if I had been given such a long sentence, I must have committed a crime, and she blamed me for it. At age sixty, it was hard for her to have to bring up my daughter, and on top of that she had to go out to work. My daughter, I knew, found it difficult to live with her grandmother, and this made me deeply unhappy. For me, the days we received letters were the most difficult, because my family rarely wrote, and I would be left with nothing to read while others were receiving theirs.

Eventually our life settled down, and we got into a routine. They began to let us read books. Pelagea Yakovlevna had some money in her account, and she used to subscribe to *Pravda*, the Party's daily newspaper. Then she succeeded in persuading the prison to buy Kiselyov's algebra reader, and managed to get permission to buy pencils and exercise books at the prison shop for Zina and me with her own money. She would also share the food she had bought with us. She was a remarkable person. Born into a family of proletarians, she was a textile worker from Ivanovo who had joined the Party in 1912 and was about ten years older than the rest of us. Her husband had been burned alive in a bonfire by the White Army during the Civil War. Pelagea Yakovlevna became an administrator in the textile industry and had received a decoration. She had two grown-up children, a son and a daughter, but of course, after her arrest, their apartment in Moscow was confiscated. Her son moved to Voronezh, got a job as an engineer, and did not write to her. Her daughter completed the tenth grade at school, then went to a village in the neighboring Ryazan region to work as a teacher. Pelagea Yakovlevna and her daughter kept up a correspondence. I always think of this courageous woman with respect: she taught us not to lose heart, not to fall to pieces, not to give in to despair, and, whatever the situation, to maintain our self-respect.

Of the women in our cell, only Zina and I had not been Party members. Tanya, a historian by training, had been in the Party since 1918, and Lena, who was the youngest, had been a Party member since 1928 or 1930. Both of them were from the Ukraine.

Pelagea Yakovlevna tried to get us organized. She suggested that she and I study algebra together, and since I had forgotten everything I knew, I agreed with pleasure. Zina did not even know the four rules of arithmetic and could not study with us, but I did mathematics with her in the evenings, when the semi-darkness made it impossible to read or write, and time dragged unbearably. We used to practice mental arithmetic, starting with our multiplication tables. This benefitted me, too: it was training for my mind, and I learned to add, subtract, and multiply three-digit figures in my head.

Before lunch I would be busy studying algebra with Pelagea Yakovlevna, and after lunch she, Zina, and I would work on Russian, doing dictations and memorizing rules. By half past three in winter, the cell would be dark, and the light didn't come on until six. In those days I still had good eyesight, and if I sat with my back to the weak light bulb, holding the book so the light fell on it, I could read to the others in a whisper. It was too dark for everyone else to read, and so they would all listen. Pelagea Yakovlevna wanted to stir some life into Tanya, as she never took part in any of our activities and was often in tears, and suggested that she give us a history lecture. But to my mind this historian, who claimed she had taught in a teacher-training institute, knew no more history than I did, and her lectures were of little interest. The fifth woman in our cell, Lena, was a great individualist. She did not want to join in anything; she said that our activities did not interest her, and that our whispering interrupted her reading. She often had stormy arguments with Pelagea Yakovlevna. They were of different generations, and each blamed the other's generation for what had happened to them.

That year saw the end of the Spanish Civil War, in which the best people of many countries had died fighting against fascism. At the 18th Party Congress in 1939, Stalin announced without a hint of embarrassment that he had personally ensured a 270,000-person reduction in the number of Party members. And the congress, in which my Party women had vested such hopes for redress and rehabilitation, gave a warm hand to Stalin. Judging from articles in *Pravda*, all the grassroots Party organizations had been hastily upgrading people to full membership and taking in new members before the congress opened in an effort to make up for the losses from their ranks. I was extremely surprised that my present comrades, former Party members, did not know what was going on in the country. When I used to tell them about the famine in Orenburg during my exile there in 1932–33, they would say that it was a lie, that I was exaggerating so that I could slander our Soviet way of life. When I talked about the "excesses" that had been allowed during the campaign to collectivize peasant farming, they used to say that I was a Trotskyite—although Stalin himself had already condemned these excesses in his article "Dizzy with Success." When I told them how I had been evicted from my home for no reason at all, and how much grief the introduction of the internal passport system had brought people in Leningrad in 1932, they used to say, "True, but that was the best way to deal with people like you."

I used to think, "Well, all right, Pelagea Yakovlevna lived in Moscow and might not know about the famine in Orenburg, or Uzbekistan, or the Ukraine." But how could Lena not know? She was a district Party activist employed in the political department. Weren't they the ones who were helping to sow hatred and distrust among people for the last ten years, or at least condoning it? Under the guise of increasing people's vigilance, they had been breeding suspicion and slander, and had whipped up the process to such a climax, it had eventually devoured them too. They thought I got what I deserved because I was critical of the excesses. Yet when the same happened to them, they thought it was a mistake that would be fixed— because they had never had any doubts whatsoever, and whatever instructions had come down from the top, they had always cheered and carried them out.

They used to tell me how in some Party branches as many as seven consecutive secretaries had been replaced in the space of one year, because they were expelled from the Party, or arrested, or labeled "enemies of the people." Their own hands would go up in favor of the expulsion of the first, the vacancy would be filled by a second, and in a couple of months the new secretary would also be expelled, not without a little help from them. A third secretary would come along and meet the same fate. And with them would go all the chairmen of the executive committees of the local soviets and their entourages: and again the hands of my Party women would go up.

Later the NKVD stopped asking their consent, as it knew they invariably agreed, and would simply arrest Party secretaries and their families at home or in the street, wherever was handy. But now my Party women thought this was a mistake which would be corrected. Some of them, like Tanya, would say, "It's what had to be done." They used to tell me how they would bump into each other on transports from district jails to regional or republican prisons, and joke that they were all off to the plenum of the Party's regional or central committee. Yes, for two decades these people had regularly traveled to attend such meetings, and they had known each other since the Civil War and the days when the Party was forced to operate underground. The older ones had gotten the young ones admitted to the Party, and the latter were often arrested because at some time in their life they had obtained references from old Party members who suddenly turned out to have been "enemies of the people." And when they were being expelled from the Party, none of them stood up for each other; they all kept quiet or raised their hands in support of the expulsion. It was some kind of universal psychosis. Many of them paid for it with their lives, and my cellmates were branded enemies of the people and did ten years just like me, a sinner.

Sometimes *Pravda* would publish a brief report about a trial. We used to entertain ourselves by reading out the background to a case and then guessing what the sentence would be. This was in the winter of 1938–39 and the sentences were, as they say, child's play compared to those we had been given in 1937. Then the psychosis began to abate. Each issue of the paper carried indignant reports from abroad that in this or that capitalist country, Communists were being sentenced to six months in prison or fines "just" for taking part in protests or putting up fliers or going on strike. My husband once warned me against drawing comparisons, and, truly, comparisons are terrible things. We had not taken part in any strikes and demonstrations, or put up any fliers . . .

Once a week we were taken to the bathhouse. Of course, even the bathhouse door had a peephole which was in constant use. There were three showers for five people, and we were given fifteen minutes to wash. I never was able to wash myself properly, and the bathhouse gave me no pleasure, but at least it meant variety. Once it was fairly muddy in the changing room, and we pulled our stockings on over dirty feet. Back in the cell, Tanya decided to rinse off her feet over the toilet bucket. She took off a stocking and asked Zina to pour water over her foot with a mug. Immediately the food hatch slammed open, and an enraged guard asked in a penetrating whisper, "What are you doing?"

"I'm washing my feet."

"Couldn't you do that in the bathhouse?" The food hatch banged shut, and we all got scared. In five minutes the block officer appeared: "What's happened here?" Tanya told him, and he left.

Two days later, Tanya was called out of the cell with her mug and towel, and till nightfall we waited, trying to guess what might have happened to her. Our Party women decided that a commission had come to sort out her case. When Tanya did not appear the following day, they decided that she had been called for a fresh investigation and transferred to Moscow, or to Vinnitsa in the Ukraine, where she had been tried. Zina and I, who were more skeptical, said that she was in the punishment cell. Our version was rejected with great indignation. As proof, we pointed out that the docket for her things was still in the cell. Toward lunchtime on the fourth day, the door opened, and in walked our Tanya. She was shivering slightly, with one eye bandaged, and burst into tears. She said that she had fainted and hit her eye on the corner of the board on which she was sleeping. Zina and I were proved right: the prison director had summoned her and read out a decree from Moscow—three days in the punishment cell. To all her pleas and excuses, he had said that he was powerless to alter a decree from Moscow.

I am writing only what I heard and saw, and am not adding a word. Apparently Moscow was taking a strong interest in our conduct, pondering crimes like foot washing over the toilet bucket, and deciding upon punishments, which even the prison director was powerless to revoke.

Once a month he would come around to the cells. He was already an elderly man, and had possibly been in the security service—the Cheka— soon after the Revolution. He spoke brusquely in a very coarse voice, and his answer to any question would be the Russian saying "When the head's gone, you don't waste tears on the hair." He was a martinet and a brute, and he was absolutely certain that we must be dangerous enemies if we had been put in prison like this for so many years. He hated us, because to him we were enemies of the Soviet regime.

One day Pelagea Yakovlevna, tired of struggling to get a reply to her latest request, said, "When the director comes around, let's not say anything." That same day he visited the cells, walked into ours, and barked, "Any questions?" We said nothing. His eyes moved over our glum faces one by one, then he abruptly turned on his heel and left the cell.

Our guards, in fact, might just as well have been prisoners like us. They also had to stay silent for days on end. They whispered to each other in the corridor, and sometimes we would hear the light tapping of a key on a belt buckle, which meant that the senior guard was calling over one of his staff to whisper an instruction.

Soon we were used to the daily routine, and Zina, who had been in prison longer than the rest of us and was more sensitive and high-strung, could always tell precisely what was going on out in the corridor. It was as though she were looking through the wall: she knew when it was almost lunchtime, if they were bringing the newspaper or books, or whether they were coming to hand out writing paper or letters from home. The guards called us by our numbers, not our names.

In the silence our hearing became extraordinarily acute. Sometimes we would hear a movement in the corridor and know that they were bringing in fresh prisoners, and how many. We could hear "the cells" going out to exercise or to slop out; our cell was in the middle. A couple of times we would hear a muffled scream and the noise of a struggle. They were dragging someone down the corridor. Someone else would be escorted by; we would hear sobbing, and evidently their mouth was then gagged.

At night when we went to bed, a scraping noise and cautious tapping would be audible in the silence—there must have been a bunk running along the wall of the next cell on the side where Zina slept. Zina would try to send an answer, but we would hiss at her to stop. What was the point? We were not trying to escape or set up an underground organization, and tapping for tapping's sake could result in punishments, including withdrawal of exercise, our books, or, worst of all, our correspondence.

My cell mates were astonished that I did not know my sentence. I had probably been sent to prison by mistake, they said, and they advised me to go to the director to find out what it was. I applied for an appointment, and the director received me in his office. It was worth seeing the gratification and feeling with which he read out, "Ten years' imprisonment for subversion, under Article 58:10." Strangely, I was left unmoved. His solemn enunciation simply amused me. Was this courage or emotional paralysis? I must say that I very rarely wept.

Our cell wrote appeals to have their cases reviewed and asked that their prison sentences be replaced with time in labor camps. They swore on their honor that they would justify their transfer with honest labor, etc. I did not particularly want to go to a camp by then. I did not know what I would have to do, or prove, to pay for the privilege, and even if letters from home came rarely in prison, it was books that helped me get through a lot. Before I was arrested, I had not been able to study; I used to read only at night, on the tram or when I was cooking at the primus. I was passionately seeking an explanation for everything that had happened to us. I used to think, Well, I am someone from a non-proletarian background, who has been unjustly wronged in my time, and at some stage I might be, or seem to be, a danger to society. But Pelagea Yakovlevna has dedicated her whole life to the revolution, without a moment's doubt or hesitation, and has always supported and carried out Party policy: How did she get here? What had happened in the country? In the twentieth year of the Soviet regime, why had its foundation—working people, and totally innocent ones at that—been plunged into this abyss? Even the arbitrariness only reflected the processes taking place in the country, because the people responsible could not carry on so long, scot-free, on such a scale, without some sort of force behind them. So what was this force? People were confused and had no information. Nor could books give me an answer to this question.

Soon I realized that it was impossible to study systematically here: books were allowed out only for ten days and the ones you ordered did not always appear when you needed them, because they had been given to someone else. Copying down excerpts also made no sense, because you got a new exercise book only in exchange for the old one. That left only one's memory.

But while it was possible to memorize a poem, prose was hopeless—any book that landed in the cell was in demand by everyone, and there was not enough time to commit the text to memory.

I applied to have five years taken off my sentence since I did not belong to the Party and could not have participated in a Trotskyite organization. I was merely the wife of Yevgeny Grankin, who had died nine months before my arrest. I referred to an article Stalin had written in the autumn of 1936, in which he said there were different sorts of Trotskyites, that those differences must be clearly understood, and that there were some people who had merely traveled the same road as a Trotskyite.

One day we came back from slopping out and noticed that Yezhov's signature on the prison rules had been pasted over. "Vainberg" was written on top. A month later the signature had changed to "Beria." My Party women whispered together, made wild surmises and suppositions, and awaited improvements. This time it turned out they were right.*

Suddenly our books were taken back before they were due. Half an hour later we were ordered to gather up our dockets, mugs, and towels, and go. Where? That was no business of ours, was the usual reply. We were half afraid, half elated. We were loaded into the "Black Crow" and driven off. At the rail station we were bundled into the "Stolypin" prison wagons, the inhabitants of all the cells mixed up together. We were deliriously happy. It was all so unexpected. Everything that had happened was like a hallucination. And although we were afraid of the unknown, we wanted to believe that things would be better. It was a complete mystery why they had taken such pains to hide us from each other and make us talk in whispers for years, if in the end we were all going to be thrown in together.

I was lucky. I had been living in those conditions since 25 October 1938, and when we left Kazan it must have been April 1939. That made a little more than five months, while many people were kept for three years in Yaroslavl prison. Kazan was a new prison, which had been specially built for people like us.

Our prison guards traveled with us. Of course it was a closely guarded secret where we were being taken. Eventually we reached some station and got off on a railway siding a long way from a town. Opposite the tracks there were huts, the town outskirts, and we saw women wiping away tears as they watched us through their windows. The guards were in a hurry. We were loaded into trucks, covered with tarpaulins like cattle, and driven off.

---

* In December 1938, Lavrenty Beria replaced Yezhov as head of the secret police.

Suzdal

The prison in Suzdal was an old security jail for political prisoners, northeast of Moscow, where, it was rumored, Fanny Kaplan, Lenin's would-be assassin of 1918, and Grigory Zinoviev,* among others, had been held at different times.

The gates swung open, then shut. We were off-loaded and led into an administrative building. There we got to know each other and shared impressions and conjectures. Some of us met people we had known on the outside, or in Butyrki Prison in Moscow. We tried to find out what had happened to our friends and loved ones. All of us were shocked by how much we had changed: many, at the age of thirty-five, were already gray-haired. The ritual of surrendering our belongings and getting prison issue began. Then they began to call us in alphabetical order into an empty cell.

In the middle, opposite the peephole, stood a table. Fifteen of us were called in. The duty officer came in and announced that anyone who attempted to resist would be severely punished, even shot. What might we want to resist? We could not understand. The guard left. In came two women in uniform, who began to search us. They looked in our hair, inside our mouths, and between our toes and fingers. Then they ordered us to get dressed again and left. Two other women guards came in. One was wearing a rubber sheath on one of her fingers, and the other was carrying a glass with liquid in it. "Take off your underpants and lie down," one of them said. Horrified, we huddled like sheep in a corner, not saying a word and trying to hide behind each other. Finally a young Austrian woman spoke up: "Oh, this is nothing to be afraid of!" she declared defiantly, and lay down on the table opposite the peephole. The cover on the peephole continually scraped open and shut. A vaginal search: we also had to endure that. All of us had been brought there from maximum security prisons, and none of us could possibly have had anything illegal to hide. This was a simple act of barbarism.

In all other respects, the routine in Suzdal and the conditions were much easier than in Kazan. We exercised, not in enclosed yards, but simply by strolling through the garden on paved paths. The walk to the bathhouse was long, past a glorious orchard of blooming cherry trees. The cells were light, with painted wooden floors. We slept on trestle beds with straw mattresses and were allowed to lie down even during the day. There were boards

---

* Bolshevik politician, close to Lenin, who was tried and shot in 1936 as leader of the "Trotskyite-Zinovievite bloc."

over the windows, but they were lower than in Kazan, with no wire mesh on top, so the tall trees in the orchard were visible. The ventilation pane, which had been the object of a continual unspoken battle in Kazan, was left open here, day and night. The food was better and more varied. True, the water was awful: cloudy, dark, and undrinkable.

We were issued pieces of toilet paper cut from the collected works of Lenin and all sorts of other literature. But here no one counted them. After our first slop out, we stood in bewilderment in the latrines with our dirty toilet paper in our hands, not knowing where to throw it, and debating what might happen if we asked the guard on duty. And to think that when I arrived in Kazan, I considered it humiliating to walk around with a droopy stocking. How are the mighty fallen!

Before we could summon her and ask, the guard opened the door, wondering what had happened to us. "What do you mean, where do you put it?" she replied with incomprehension. We sighed with relief. Later we heard whispering in the corridor and snorts of suppressed amusement. The guards were laughing at us because the same thing had happened with all the cells.

The composition of our cell changed. Tanya was gone, but where she went I don't know: she did not end up in Kolyma. She was replaced by Maria, who had been a Party member since 1920, and was a good, calm, and self-disciplined person. Maria had been arrested for her boundless faith in one man. He was an old Bolshevik and had recommended her for Party membership. She had known him for many years; he was the director of an institute, and she was the district Party secretary. When a campaign started against him, she continued to give him her support. He was expelled from the Party, and everyone turned their backs on him, but she insisted that he appeal his expulsion, that he fight it, and kept telling him, "It's a mistake, a misunderstanding." At one time, he admitted to her, he had been in an opposition group within the Party, and because of that he no longer wanted them to meet, for fear of compromising her. He foresaw that he would be arrested. "Nonsense," she said. "They can't arrest you. You haven't done anything." And he gave her his solemn word that he had indeed done nothing. He was arrested, and a month later, so was she. When they were brought together face to face in prison, she flung herself at him, crying, "Tell them it's not true!" "But you know that I recruited you into a Trotskyite organization," he replied.

In Suzdal the atmosphere in the cell was less tense because the conditions were better. Here we did not have to sit squashed round the table as in Kazan; and Lena could read lying down. Lena was not really a bad person so much as she was pathetic. But prison is like a ship, sailing for a long time without putting into port. The continual enforced proximity to the same people, all of different ages and cultural backgrounds, magnifies even minor human failings and weaknesses, so that they become unbearable for everyone else. On board ship, people have to work hard to stay afloat and stay on course to their destination. We were consigned to a pernicious idleness. In Kazan we had not even been able to read all day because it was dark by three o'clock; and we could not lie down in the daytime because the bunks were fastened to the wall.

Lena rarely spoke about herself or her family. Letters did not come for her, and in a cell where everyone else is receiving them, that is terrible. Once she told us how her daughter cried when she was leaving for work. Her daughter had died when she was about six or seven years old.

We had worked right through the algebra textbook with Pelagea Yakovlevna while we were still in Kazan, and we needed to set ourselves another goal. Maria suggested that we tell stories. She took on the tale of "The House of the Cat Who Played Ball," and I whiled away the time with "Faust."

Here we were not required to speak in whispers, but by now that had become second nature to us. I, unfortunately, began to feel unwell, because my correspondence had ceased with my transfer, and I started suffering from insomnia. Spring had come, there was almost no nighttime, and countless rooks flew into the orchard, squawking from sunrise to sunset. It must have been June when we were once again loaded into vehicles and, under cover of tarpaulins, transported to the nearby prison in Vladimir.

The next day we were given a physical. The doctor did not examine any of us, but asked, "Anything wrong with you?" and cleared us all. Then, under cover of tarpaulins once more, we were delivered to the railway line and loaded onto a freight train, seventy-five people to a wagon. We celebrated, laughing, singing songs, dancing, reciting poetry. We talked at the tops of our voices and asked each other, "Where do you think they are taking us?" Lena started reading palms. "What a fate line this woman has," she said when she looked at mine. "She's been to hell and back." I was amazed at her intuition.

The doors of the wagon were bolted shut, and looking out the window was forbidden. There were three-tier bed boards in the wagon, and it was fairly cramped. We did not know what was going to happen to us next, but we were happy.

The Transport

On the train, many women met people they had known at Butyrki Prison. They discussed acquaintances and found out what had happened to their families. I also met a friend from Leningrad, Polina, with whom I had shared a cell in the Shpalerka Prison there. Polina was three or four years younger than I. She was from a proletarian family; her father and mother had worked and lived all their lives in the Porokhovykh, a workers' district of the city. In 1918 Polina was left an orphan, along with her younger sister and brother, when her parents both died of typhoid. The girl went to school and brought up the little ones. Then she put them in a children's home, became a worker herself, and joined the Komsomol. In 1927 she used to go to open Party meetings, like everyone else, but she had no voting rights, as she was still not a member of the Party. By 1936 she was secretary of the Party cell in her factory workshop. She married a working man who had studied at the institute of aviation construction and become an engineer. Life was just beginning to go well when suddenly she was arrested.

Everyone knew Polina in the factory, just as she knew everyone else, and it was on this basis that they put together the investigation.

"Do you know so-and-so?"

"Yes."

"Did you know that he is an enemy of the people?"

"No, I didn't. I know he has been arrested."

"Who else do you know?" and so on and so forth. "Why do you know all the enemies of the people?"

"Because they worked at the factory . . ."

Polina signed all the records of interrogation, as many people did. They sentenced her to five years and dispatched her to the Solovetsky Islands in the White Sea. At first there was only a camp on Solovki, but then its inmates built a prison with their own hands and moved into it. Now all the political prisons were being disbanded and their inmates transferred to Kolyma. Polina's sentence ended in July 1941, but war had already broken out, and she remained a prisoner until 1946: a total of ten years instead of five. Her husband was exiled to the Krasnoyarsk Territory in central Siberia with his mother and their six-year-old son. There he lived in the woods, working as a lumberman, because he was not allowed to stay in a town or work at his own profession. His mother died in exile. That was how life treated Polina. And that was how life turned out for many people, because fifty percent of the women in our transport were former Party members, and many of them had been workers, promoted to administrative jobs . . .

In a short while we reached Yaroslavl, where four wagonloads of women from Yaroslavl Prison were coupled onto our train.

The journey across the country to Vladivostok is difficult even in normal conditions: you get tired in the course of ten days of constant travel. We were shunted around for a month, often without water in the July heat, with almost no hot food, in closed wagons. There was a diabetic in our wagon, who suffered from intolerable thirst. She died in Vladivostok. We had no bedding, and no personal belongings. We slept on the bare boards, spreading our jackets out beneath us and pulling them over us as covers. For days on end, if the train was moving, we would sit in just our underwear, suffocating with the heat. At night, if the train had stopped, we would be awakened by the sound of someone hammering the walls or running along the roof. The guards were checking that the wagons were secure.

We entertained ourselves as best we could. Natasha, our poet, composed an epic about our journey, with lines like "We contrived to clean clothes, hands and feet with a single cup of water." A singer, a mezzo soprano, sang romances and operatic arias for us; someone else told us stories. Yelena Tager endlessly recited poems, which so fatigued and irritated me. Now was not the time, it seemed to me, to convey someone else's thoughts and emotions, no matter how beautifully they were expressed. I was desperately seeking the answer to my own questions and an explanation for everything that had happened to us, but they were trying to run away from the questions and bury themselves in a mental haze, in the music of Blok, or in Akhmatova's or Gumilyov's poetry. Zhenya Ginzburg recited long poems from Pushkin by heart, and Nekrasov's "Russian Women."

Across the Ural mountains in Sverdlovsk, we were off-loaded and taken to a bathhouse, where, wearing only what we were born in, we were marched past two rows of young men—our transport guards. Some of us had sons their age. Farther east in Irkutsk there was another visit to a bathhouse. But either there had been a change of shift or the spectacle had proved uninteresting, because this time our guards stayed outside.

We traveled on and on. Woods and fields flickered past, and bridges and streams, tunnels and stations. We passed Lake Baikal at night. No one went to sleep in the wagon that night, because they all wanted to catch sight of the legendary inland sea. And there, through the bars on our tiny windows and the branches of trees, we glimpsed the paths the moonlight traced on the dark water.

We came to BAM, the Baikal-Amur railway that was being built by prisoners. We passed barracks surrounded by barbed wire. Watchtowers with searchlights and guards. All around was forest and grass, but in these areas everything had been trampled flat—there was not a blade of grass or a twig to be seen. Sometimes we saw people hard at work under armed guard, with mosquito nets covering their faces. We could not understand what this meant. The women who had come from Solovki said it was a camp. We peered through our barred windows and thought, Will we be abandoned in the same limbo for a whole ten years?

The farther we went, the more I was gripped by depression and hopelessness. I was unable to cry; I had forgotten how to, and that was what made the ache in my heart so unbearable. Once in the night, when my wagon mates were sleeping and I was tormented with insomnia, I sat up on the bed boards. As the wheels rattled, I buried my head in my knees and, trying not to waken anyone so that no one would see my weakness, I began to wail. I was sure I would not survive and that I was on my way to die.

We passed Nerchinsk, near the Chinese border. It was here, more than one hundred years ago, after the Decembrist revolt against the Tsar had failed, that the wives of the conspirators came to join their husbands, not as prisoners but as heroines, traveling over the winter roads in horse-drawn sledges. And to wish them godspeed, they had the enthusiastic approval of the best people of their day, and the fond remembrance of later generations. This trail had been blazed by the feet of thousands who had struggled for the nation's happiness. What a terrible fate it was to travel the same road as enemies of the people, yet knowing oneself to be innocent. Will future generations understand what torment we went through?

Then came Volochaevka, where the White Army was routed in 1922. We pressed to the windows, all of us wanting to glimpse a place commemorated in song. There was a woman in the wagon who had taken part in the battle, and she told us what had happened and even tried to show us the slopes where many heroes died in the February snows. But little was visible through our bars. We knew that some of the victorious survivors were now passing those slopes in the same sort of wagons as ours, or that they would do so in the future.

We passed Khabarovsk, and it became clear that we were being taken south, to the coast. We reached Vladivostok toward evening. The train stood for a long time in the station, then there was the handover to the transport guard, roll call, line formation, head count, and at last, in the darkness, late in the evening we moved off, surrounded by guards. We spent the night sitting in a building, then finally, when it was already afternoon, we reached the Vladivostok transit camp.

And at the Pacific Ocean
Their journey came to an end.*

In the camp there was a visit to the bathhouse and, of course, a medical examination. Prison trusties who had found themselves jobs with the hair-

---

* Lines from "Along the Valleys and Hillsides," a song honoring the soldiers who expelled the White Army from the Soviet Far East.

dresser there were delighted at the prospect of shaving off our pubic hair. But they were deprived of this entertainment. We produced our own hairdressers from among the women on the transport and got the administration's agreement to carry out this procedure ourselves. The medical commission assigned me to invalid work, as I was suffering from myocarditis. Now, I remember Vladivostok poorly. I was struck by the thousands of people passing through the place from all over the country, in a constant ebb and flow, like waves in the sea. Ours was the next to last large transport of women to arrive here before the war. We came together in one group, all of us with prison sentences, and left in three parties. The women who had contracted pellagra stayed behind, and a few chronic invalids remained there forever. The last large transport to arrive were "wives" (of enemies of the people), being transferred to Kolyma from the Mariinsk camps farther west, who were sent straight to the factories in Magadan. That was where they lived, and we hardly ever met them. After that, with the exception of odd prisoners who were being sent on to punitive camps, there were no more transports of women until 1944.

The camp made a gloomy impression on me. I kept thinking, surely this is not what our husbands and brothers fought for in the Civil War.

I remember intense heat during the daytime, vivid sunsets, and fairly cold nights. The barracks with their double- and triple-tier board beds were infested with countless bedbugs. There were so many of them that sleeping indoors was impossible, even during the day, and we would lie down outside, right on the ground, in pairs, so that we could spread one jacket beneath us and use the second one as a cover. But even outside it was difficult to get to sleep. You were continually being bitten by mosquitoes or rained on. Until nearly one o'clock in the morning, a patient in the hospital compound used to rant in a loud, impassioned voice. At first I thought it was the radio, but on closer listening I realized from the incoherence of his utterances, culled from phrases used in political meetings of the Civil War era, that he was crazy. However, soon afterward, we did not hear him anymore.

Half the transport had scurvy and could scarcely move on their bloated legs, glistening with dark blue blotches. The entire transport, except for two or three people, began to suffer from night blindness and so would try to prepare their bedding while it was still daylight. The approach of twilight struck unaccountable fear in one's soul. Two or three people who could see would be leading around whole processions of the blind as soon as dusk fell. Our doctors, of whom there were about ten, went to the camp administration and got a large bottle of cod-liver oil from the camp hospital. After a couple of spoonfuls, the blindness lifted.

Our food consisted of rye dumplings and herring. There were great quantities of sardines, which we fell on hungrily, as we had not seen them for three years. Shortly afterward, the symptoms of pellagra manifested themselves, and the serious cases were taken to the camp hospital. The others were allocated a barrack, where our own doctors and nurses looked after them. Our compound was surrounded by a fence. All around us were male prisoners, and among them many of the women found people they knew, or even their husbands. Our pale, starved appearance and the fact that we had no personal belongings with us amazed even the criminal offenders, and when we first appeared in the camp, many of them cried, and threw undershirts and shorts over the fence so that some of the women could change their clothing. This was the first time I heard the expression "Everyone for themselves." We all had arrived in identical prison clothing, with a mug and a towel in our hands, and with no personal belongings whatsoever. In a day or two, some women had changed their clothes and even begun to accumulate a small bundle of things. They later left the camp dragging suitcases full of possessions. But there were also women who served out their entire sentence, and emerged from the camp, wearing only prison clothing.

Incidentally, about personal belongings. Many people had arrived in prison with stuffed suitcases, because they were going away for ten years, and no one knew where they would end up. There were also some well-to-do people. The plundering of our possessions began while we were still in prison, and bit by bit they vanished, palmed off by one group of guards or the next. Some of us got our personal belongings back in Vladivostok; some had them handed over in Magadan. Then they lay in heaps under tarpaulins outside the barracks, with no one keeping an eye on them. Finally they were distributed any old way, and you would sometimes recognize your own things on someone else. Throughout the whole ten years, the question "Where are our things?" would ring out whenever a new person who we thought might be an administrator appeared in the barracks. At first we used to get the insolent answer: "What do you need your things for? You'll get them when you're released," meaning—first you have to survive the next ten years. After rehabilitation, a very few of the women who applied received compensation for their personal belongings.

Soon I was given a job at the clinic. The camp administrators were indignant that I came to work wearing prison clothes, and they drove me back, saying that I was just trying to make a point. I had no other clothes, I told them. They could not understand why not, when other people did. But a few days later, they sent me back to the clinic all the same . . .

There was a young Russian man working there as an orderly who had completely forgotten how to speak normal Russian. His whole conversation consisted of variations on the three nouns that people like him scrawl on walls and fences. I later would meet a lot of people like this, but at the time he was a novelty for me, and that is why I remember him. Also, it was while I was working as an orderly in the hospital that I saw my first dead body. The man was lying in the corridor on a stretcher, with a sheet covering his face. He was extremely tall, and his legs stuck out beyond the bottom of the sheet. I saw the wooden number tag on his ankle and thought, That is how my husband must have been buried, too. I worked there for about two weeks until I came down with dysentery.

When they finally reached Vladivostok, some people were called away for a reexamination of their case. And some people received rehabilitation there—for example, one of the women from our train who had been secretary of the Party cell at a collective farm in the Kalinin region. Once we were sent out to shift some logs. A few men who had come from Kolyma to have their cases reviewed were working alongside us. We questioned them eagerly about what it was like in Kolyma, but they were reluctant to tell us. I knew that we would have to work wherever we were, but I was interested to know if we would be given any bedding. I was tired of shivering under my jacket and sleeping fully dressed with no pillow, and the nights were getting colder. We would get bedding, they reassured me.

The first transport got ready to go, but I had a 40 degree temperature and do not remember it leaving. Seventy percent of our group left, leaving the doctors and sick prisoners. It became quiet and depressing. After about ten days another transport began to get ready, and I again had a fever. But this time I could not bear it and begged the doctor to include me on the list. Reluctantly the doctor put my name down, and after lunch on 25 August we set off.

There were about seventy of us political prisoners in all; the rest were criminals. Toward evening we boarded the steamship *Dzhurma*. The hold was packed with bed boards in three tiers. That night a woman went into labor, and we were awakened by her screams and moans. Yelena Kostyuk, our doctor, called for help, and she was taken off to the medical unit. The steamship was carrying a huge quantity of people and confectionery: candy, chocolate, and biscuits. Some criminal offenders who had been let out on deck to do maintenance work broke a lock and cleaned out one of the holds. Someone disturbed them, and to cover their traces, they set fire to the place. The painted wooden partitions began to burn. Nearby was a hold full of male prisoners. Choking from the smoke, they began crawling out, and the guards opened fire on them. Some simple ladders were crudely knocked together and lowered into the hold, but they could not take the men's body weight and broke. The ship's captain appeared, dismissed the guards, and gave orders to drag the men out with ropes. In the panic, many of them were trampled to death. People raced to put out the fire, dousing it with water from fire pumps, and finally releasing compressed steam into the hold, where many of the men were still trapped.

While all this was going on, two of the criminal offenders sneaked into our hold. There they found themselves some lady friends, treated them to chocolate, and got what they were after. One of them described what had happened to his new girlfriend. Our hold was under particularly close watch because it was above the fuel tanks, and we were taken out on deck. The girl dressed her pretty-boy in her clothes, and he left his jacket with her, but nevertheless the guards forced him out of our lines.

When we got back to our hold, she told her friend what he had said to her. A huge song and dance erupted. Everyone was screaming that she should be shot for going with an enemy of the people and selling us for a piece of chocolate—for wanting to get us all drowned, for being a "wrecker," and, of course, for being a Trotskyite. That last was the most convenient and familiar accusation of all. The same friends who an hour earlier had been covering up for her and eating the chocolate now flew at her and all but tore her limb from limb. A guard lowered his rifle muzzle into the hold and said that he would open fire. At that point one of the women ran out and shouted up to him, "Shoot the Trotskyites!" Eventually the guards came for the reckless romantic and took her away to the punishment cell. She stayed there until we arrived in Magadan, where she, the criminals, and the guards were put on trial—the guards for incompetence. She was given a second term—ten years—for complicity in a crime.

The ship was evidently in a perilous condition, because when the *Felix Dzerzhinsky* met us en route to Vladivostok, it turned back and escorted us. We were taken out on deck one more time and saw that all the non-prisoners were being issued life jackets. No plans were being made to save us. But fortunately the sea was calm, and on 30 August we put into shore at the Bay of Good Cheer near Magadan. Our escort was immediately withdrawn and arrested because the ship's captain refused to sign a statement saying that they had opened fire to prevent an escape. It was said that 120 men were trampled to death in the panic or boiled alive by the compressed steam. Our group of women was ordered to sew the bags in which they were dumped into the sea.

Translation by Marjorie Farquharson

VERONICA ZNAMENSKAYA

FIVE

Veronica Znamenskaya ————

To This Day

🌸 **About the Author**

A long, long time ago, in the early 1920s, Vera Znamenskaya and I were classmates. We went to school in an old town house on Znamenka Street across the way from the People's Commissariat of Military and Naval Affairs (the War Ministry). Sometimes we would see the Commissar, Leon Trotsky, arrive there by car. Once when the boys were playing in the schoolyard, the ball flew over the fence and landed right in the Commissar's open-topped vehicle. We were reprimanded and told to be more careful.

Vera was a girl of 13, a childhood friend and my first love. I used to walk her home, to the tall gray Art Nouveau apartment block where she lived. When I started visiting their large apartment, requisitioned from the previous wealthy inhabitants, I got to know the rest of the family.

Her parents struck me as unusual. Konstantin Znamensky wore his hair long, and in place of a tie he sported a handsomely knotted black bow. He looked like an artist. But in fact he was a quite ordinary office worker. Veronica's mother, Esther, was a woman of unusual beauty. Tall and stately, she always made me think of a queen. Her oval face was framed by black hair with two dangling locks, just like an illustration I remembered of Tatyana in Pushkin's Yevgeny Onegin. *Even more romantic seemed the slight, delicate figure of Vera's sister Dina (Christina).*

Today Veronica is a tall, handsome, and energetic woman. Life has been hard on both of us, in different ways; but there is one thing we share with many of our generation. My father was shot, my mother spent seven years in the camps, and for years I was branded the son of "Enemies of the People." It was chance that we both survived. We are elderly witnesses of a harsh and bloody epoch. But I want to recall others here.

It is the sacred duty of the living to honor the memory of those who died then. And not just the famous victims. We must remember all whose names are unknown but who, like us, could also feel, think, suffer, and sometimes rejoice—who, in a word, could have lived as ordinary human beings if they had not been prematurely deprived of life.

ALEXANDER ANIKST

My sister Christina was arrested in 1936. The warrant was signed by our Uncle Gena [Genrikh Yagoda, then head of the NKVD]. Dina (as we called her) was not arrested in Moscow but far away, in the south of Russia. She had only just gone there to join her husband, Volodya Golenko, a recent graduate from the Institute of Red Professors. As a biologist and geneticist, he had been sent to Salsk to do research on horse breeding.

Packing her small case before she left, Dina said to me, "I have the feeling I shall never come back."

On the railway platform she repeated, "Mama, something tells me we shall never meet again."

"Don't talk nonsense," Mother sharply replied.

But Dina was right. We never saw one another again.

Three days after she left, they came to our apartment with a warrant for her arrest. They stayed all night, until six in the morning, when news reached them from Salsk that Dina had been picked up there.

There were four of them, three men and a woman. All night they searched Dina's and Golenko's rooms, the room I shared with my husband, Vladimir Koritsky, and the dining room and sitting room that we all used. There was nothing to look for in the dining room. All it contained was a table, chairs, and an upright piano. They had so much time, and so little to search. Dina and Golenko possessed Lenin's collected works, specialist literature on genetics, old lecture notes, and the German-language textbooks that Dina was studying. Vladimir and I had physics and geology textbooks and summaries of lectures we'd attended. Dina and I owned so few clothes that a single glance in our modest wardrobes was sufficient: there was nothing to be found there, either.

They thumbed through the books, peeked into the bindings, and read our letters and the lecture notes.

Dina's husband Volodya returned from Salsk one week later. The week after, they came back to confiscate Dina's belongings.

This time there were three of them.

They stood in front of the opened wardrobe in bad-tempered perplexity. On the shelves to the left lay worn sheets and pillowcases, faded men's underwear, shirts with fraying collars, and a few feminine trifles: an opened bottle of perfume, a new powder box, several handkerchiefs, a new pair of stockings (a present from Mother), and several other pairs that were darned. To the right hung a brown wool suit, a dressing gown, a sleeveless "peasant" dress, and a jacket, now worn at the elbows and where it was creased, that was Dina's only winter coat. Below them stood patched shoes and felt overboots that had long gone out of fashion.

"They've managed to hide everything," one of them said at last.

"What did you say? Hide what?" demanded Dina's husband indignantly.

They did not even glance at him. One said something to another, who nodded, sat down at the table, and began to write out the record of confiscation, or whatever they call it.

"I shall complain about your behavior. You have no right to be offensive. I'm a Party member."

Golenko's lips were trembling, and he grew pale. This time all three turned threatening and hostile faces in his direction. Now there would be trouble and we might not be able to undo the damage. I grasped him by the elbow, but he shook free.

"This is all we have, everything. We only have our salaries. We've no way of getting rich, and anyway, we wouldn't try to . . . "

"Stop it, Volodya, don't say anything." I tried to draw him out of the room.

My husband stood in the doorway and called to him.

But Volodya went on: "We've hidden things? How dare you. We've never owned anything. And if we had, we would not have kept it for ourselves. You'll answer for this."

Poor, naive Volodya Golenko! He had an unquestioning faith in the law, in justice, and the printed word, especially if those words were published in a newspaper. Like all of them, he believed that Stalin was infallible. And in spite of his boundless love for Dina, he even believed that this was just retribution. They had arrested Dina, after all, because she had formerly been married to a Trotskyist. "What if it was ten years ago?" he argued. "We must still accept responsibility, however hard it may be! They had to do it. They consider it a necessary measure."

I managed to push him into the dining room and told my husband not to let him out.

Meanwhile, the NKVD men had spread out one of the neatly ironed sheets on the floor, exposing Dina's tidy patches, in all their touching helplessness. Into this sheet flew Dina's mended shoes, her calico dressing gown, and her darned stockings. Somehow I managed to grab a filmy kerchief with red spots from right under their noses and roll it into a ball. My whole body shaking, and gritting my teeth to prevent them chattering, I clasped it in my fist and kept my hand in my pocket, terrified of being discovered. I had to keep something to remember Dina by, no matter how small! They even tossed the opened bottle of perfume and the powder box onto this pile of pitiful objects. I concealed my "theft" from her husband. Knowing Volodya, I had every reason to think he would not only reprove me but force me to hand over the kerchief as well.

I have it to this day, Dina's red spotted kerchief.

"Tell Mama and Volodya that I can hold my head high," she wrote in one of the three letters I received from her, "and that I have no reason to ask forgiveness: I have nothing to repent and am completely innocent."

This letter reached us several months later: her husband was arrested only a few days after.

"If you see Dina," said Volodya as they led him away, "tell her that I am quite innocent."

It hardly needs saying that she never received his message and he never received hers.

Dina died in the camps. Her case was reexamined by the Military Tribunal of the USSR Supreme Court on 28 January 1958. The rehabilitation certificate states: "In the light of new circumstances, the sentence passed on Christina Znamenskaya by the Military Tribunal on 31 May 1937 has been annulled. The case against her has been closed for lack of any evidence of criminal activity. Znamenskaya is posthumously rehabilitated."

Volodya Golenko's son by his first marriage received a similar certificate. His parents, who had been Party members since before the Revolution, did not live to see him rehabilitated.

My grandfather Grigory Yagoda was a watchmaker in Nizhny Novgorod. He had three sons and five daughters, of whom my mother was the eldest. It was difficult looking after such a large family, so some of the children were sent to their mother's relatives in Rybinsk, a small town on the Volga north of Moscow.

There was an illegal press in Grandfather's apartment, and my father would print political leaflets there. Mother helped him, and that was how they got to know each other.

In 1902 Misha, the eldest brother, was sabred to death by the Cossacks during the "Sormovo disturbances," a protest by shipyard workers. The second son, Lyova, died in 1917. He was shot at the front for Bolshevik agitation among the soldiers of Kornilov's army. The youngest, Genrikh

Yagoda (or Gena, for short), survived. From the early 1920s onward, he worked in the Cheka and its successor, the OGPU. In 1934 he became head of the People's Commissariat of Internal Affairs, the NKVD.

In the mid-1930s I was a student and could not imagine the evil role being played by Stalin and his accomplices—his "comrades in arms" as they were then called. My uncle was one of that company, and the first of the unholy trinity to turn the bloody wheel of repression (being succeeded by Yezhov, and then by Beria).

When Yagoda was himself arrested in 1937, his parents and all his sisters were exiled to Astrakhan.

We were standing in the hall of Grandmother's apartment. The door was already open; only one more step, and no one would ever return there.

"If only Gena could see what they're doing to us," someone quietly said.

Suddenly Grandmother, who never raised her voice, turned toward the empty apartment, and cried loudly, "May he be damned!" She crossed the threshold and the door slammed shut. The sound reverberated in the stairwell like the echo of this maternal curse.

To this day that curse sounds again and again in my memory: "May he be damned!"

A year later they were arrested in their Astrakhan exile, and all trace of them disappeared. The same whirlwind swept away Grandmother's relatives in Rybinsk.

For some unknown reason, and to everyone's astonishment, I was left untouched. I was also fortunate in another respect: I managed to complete my studies and gain my diploma as a geologist. That was as far as my luck went, however. No one would give me a job, not even to go on a geological expedition to Yakutia in northeastern Siberia! This was because I always replied honestly on every application form, when asked whether any of my relatives had been arrested. Then I came across the Moscow Youth Theater. Their form did not contain this question, and they took me on.

My transformation from a geologist into an actress took place when my mother was still living in Astrakhan. In May 1938 I stopped getting any more letters from her, and she did not come to take calls at the telephone exchange. So I went to see her myself.

The room she had been renting was empty. Neither Mama nor any of her belongings were there. In the room next-door the owners of the house were drinking tea. With an air of indifference, the woman, a fat creature in a dirty woolen jacket, told me that when Mother came back from making a telephone call to Moscow at the post office on 6 May, they were already waiting for her. She struggled with all her might, and shouted and wept at the top of her voice. They had to use force to remove her. I had no intention of asking about her belongings—their fate was already quite obvious. But with striking haste the woman began to explain, looking me insolently in the eye, how "Esther Grigorievna took everything with her: all she left was that basin."

I stood for a little while longer in the bare room, trying to imagine my mother here, within these four walls, and said farewell to her once more. Then I left without another word. The man remained sitting at the table, slurping his tea from a saucer and crunching a lump of sugar.

I went to another address where the rest of the family were living.

It took a long time, wandering about the dusty outskirts of Astrakhan, along boarded sidewalks, peering through the gaps in solid high fences, before I found the house. It looked no different from its neighbors: not very large, solidly built and with a sturdy metal roof. I opened the gate and found myself in a small yard overgrown with tender new grass. It was very quiet. Immediately I sensed that the house had been abandoned. The door was ajar. I was about to enter, but then I halted and knocked.

"Who's there?" a man called.

I recognized the voice of Vladimir Mordvinkin, my Aunt Tasya's husband. The other sisters' husbands had all been arrested and shot, except for one who managed to shoot himself first. Only now did I remember Mother telling me in a letter that Mordvinkin had recently come to live with Auntie Tasya since they had dismissed him from the Main Repertory Committee, the theater censors' body, and evicted him from the apartment.

"Good afternoon," I said as I entered the room.

"Hello," he answered indifferently, as if we saw each other ten times a day and he could no longer be bothered to greet me.

He was the same as always. The indispensable pince-nez, the little pointed beard, and hair brushed back from his forehead. When I entered, he was reading something. Little Viola, their three-year-old daughter, was playing next to him: at the time it simply did not enter my head that this was my cousin. On the table were a blackened kettle, dirty plates and cups, and a saucepan of dried-up porridge. Two or three chairs stood at angles to the table. The floor was littered with rubbish and had not been washed for a long time. It was the room of a man who was not used to household chores and who could not give a damn.

Dina and I hardly knew him. We saw him only at family gatherings, around the dining table in Grandmother's apartment. Our relations extended no further than an indifferent "Good evening" on our part and a negligent nod from him. We disliked him intensely because it was he who had banned Bulgakov's *Days of the Turbins* from the Moscow Art Theater.

Perhaps he was not personally to blame. But at the time we thought he was. Dina and I had managed to see the play before it was taken off in 1929; I think we caught the last performance. Since then a vision of Mordvinkin rose before my eyes whenever Bulgakov's play was mentioned. Yet our past life and all its concerns now seemed as petty and distant as something seen through the wrong end of a telescope.

I took the tea towel off one of the chairs and, sitting down, realized how tired I was. The room was in semi-darkness and pleasantly cool.

"Want some tea?" asked Mordvinkin. "I think it's still hot."

I drank a cup of tepid watery tea and ate a piece of bread. My eyelids were drooping, and I wanted to sleep. We knew we had nothing to say to each other and kept silent. I sat, my head propped on my hand, staring mindlessly at the table. Mordvinkin looked at his book. The child turned and babbled something to her father. "My God!" I thought as I gazed at Viola, "Whatever did Tasya feel about leaving this little mite? She so wanted a child, and kept her immaculately clean, washing her only in boiled water!"

"When did they take them away?" I asked at last.

"On the sixth."

The same day as Mother, in other words.

"May I look at . . . " I did not finish the sentence, not knowing whether to say the house, the rooms, or whatever was left.

But Mordvinkin understood: "Go ahead."

He looked at his book again. But I don't think he was reading it, because he did not turn a single page all the time I was there.

The rest of the house was in chaos. Stockings, dresses, and newspapers were strewn everywhere, and in the largest room, which, I supposed, had been occupied by my grandparents, the entire floor was covered with letters and photographs. It was the lightest room in the house, and the bright sunlight made the chaos seem particularly awful. I could just imagine the boots stamping back and forth over the white pages and yellowing photographs that my grandparents had preserved as their dearest possessions. For many years, elderly hands had lovingly stored these letters and photographs in a wooden box and then brought them here: now someone had tossed them about like so much useless rubbish and trampled them underfoot. I picked up one of the photographs. Grandmother's sisters. On the back, an inscription in an old-fashioned, curling hand read: "To our dear Maria from her loving sisters." There was a date and a year (1909 or 1912?) Now "dear Maria" was 65 years old and in prison.

Mordvinkin told me where the prison was. We were allowed to hand over 50 rubles, he added.

I went right away. But Mama was not there. All the others were—but not she! They called this the Inner Prison. There was another one in the city, and people explained how to find it. Mama was probably there. Where else could she be? There was no third prison in Astrakhan.

As it was growing light the next morning, I approached an enormous open space crammed with people. Some were sitting, either alone or in groups. The earth had been stamped to dust, and only a few people were standing: probably they could not bring themselves to sit in the dirt, and hoped to stay on their feet for several hours. Somewhere in the distance, on the far edge of this field, a building could be seen. This was the prison, they told me. All these people were in line, and I should find out who was last.

For six hours, under the blazing sun, I moved toward the tiny hatch. For six hours I hoped to hand over 50 rubles: then mother would understand that I was here, and she would rejoice because I was still free, at least for the time being. Six hours later, I gave them mother's name and pushed 50 rubles beneath the barely raised glass of the hatch. But they would not take the money, and instead began checking their lists. I could hear the rustle of pages being turned. Then they said, "Not listed here. She's left. Next."

"What do you mean, she's left? Where's she gone? Check again!"

But they repeated, "She's left. Next."

The line surged forward, and I was pushed aside. Once more I was standing on that trampled field. Again the blinding light and intolerable heat beat down on me. Yet for some reason I saw everything in shades of black and felt a pounding at my temples. I took the tram, struggled back to the house, and the last thing I remember is the bed onto which, losing consciousness, I collapsed.

I came to when it was quite dark. Mordvinkin was asleep. My head was splitting. Feeling my way to the kitchen, I rattled the buckets in search of water, drank some, soaked a rag and pressed it to my head.

When I came back to Moscow and went to our theater, the first person I saw was Natasha. It was she who had brought me there, to begin with. We were friends and took turns playing Beatrice in A Servant of Two Masters. Natasha seized me by the hand and dragged me into a corner.

"Listen," she whispered, "They've arrested Inka!"

Inka was not only a mutual friend, she was also a relative of mine. She had married Dodik, one of Mother's clan, and since they lived nearby I knew them better than any of my other distant Rybinsk relatives. We often visited one another. He was a very good photographer, and I had many copies of his work. And now they had arrested Inka! I almost cried out but Natasha hissed, "Quiet!"

We stood among boxes, old set decorations, tattered "trees," and broken benches in a corner of the bare stage. The theater was empty, the curtain raised, and the auditorium yawned before us with its echoing emptiness. We were quite alone but kept whispering to one another.

"And how's Dodik?" I asked in a barely audible voice.

"Who?" Natasha did not understand.

"Dodik, her husband."

"Oh, her husband. But he was arrested before they took her away."

"And the child? They had a little girl. She was probably not even a year old yet."

We heard steps. Someone was coming down the stairs. We flew apart.

"Don't say a word!" Natasha managed to warn me.

> Certificate
> Military Tribunal of USSR Supreme Court
> 21 June 1957
> The case against Esther Grigorievna Znamenskaya, arrested on 6 May 1938, has been reexamined by the Military Tribunal of the USSR Supreme Court on 8 June 1957.
> The decree issued by the USSR NKVD on 16 June 1938 with respect to Esther Znamenskaya has been annulled, and the case against her has been closed for lack of any evidence of criminal activity. Esther Znamenskaya is posthumously rehabilitated.
> Colonel P. Likhachev

Fifty years later I learned from people with access to the KGB archives that when I was searching for my mother that summer in the prisons of Astrakhan, she had already been shot, on 16 June 1938.

Translation by John Crowfoot

VERA SHULZ

SIX

Vera Shulz ─────────────────

Taganka

🌺 About the Author

Vera Alexandrovna Shulz was born in Moscow in 1905. From her child-
hood she was fluent in several languages, and in 1926 she graduated from
Moscow University with a degree in language and literature.

During the 1920s, the stormy cultural life of the capital gave birth to
a new Soviet dramatic art. Bulgakov's Days of the Turbins *played at the*
Moscow Art Theater. The theaters of Vakhtangov, Chekhov, Meyerhold,
Tairov, and Mikhoels flourished, and scores of new theaters appeared. One
was the Ruben Simonov studio-theater, where Vera Alexandrovna started
her career as an actress. All ended with her arrest in 1938.

I first met "Auntie Vera" in 1953, when she returned to Moscow from
exile. My father, the USSR's first ambassador to Belgium, also returned from
the camps that year, and one day he said to me, "Auntie Vera wants to take
you to the theater to see The Bluebird.*"*

I was eleven years old at the time. As I settled into my seat in the stalls,
the back of which bore a metal plate with the words "K. S. Stanislavsky," I
was so captivated by the action on the stage that I almost forgot the old
woman sitting beside me and peering intently at me. After the play was
over, she walked me back to the metro station, handed me a piece of paper
with her telephone number, gave me a hug, and asked me to visit her. Her
image soon faded from my eyes, and I would never have guessed that she
had waited more than ten years for us to meet.

I was born in the spring of 1942 in a remote part of the Volga region,
where we had been evacuated. At the end of that year, my mother was killed
in a fire. Vera Alexandrovna heard of this while in exile in the arid wastes of
the Aral Desert in Central Asia, but she was powerless to help. Although

she had never met me, she felt an almost morbid love for me and thought of me constantly. As a helpless semi-starving exile, a mere number on the NKVD's books, there was nothing she could do, but she vowed that if she ever returned to Moscow, she would take me to see Maeterlinck's Bluebird, which she had loved so much as a child. The play had been a major event in the life of the Moscow intelligentsia in those years, and its benevolent humanism could not but inspire a young child with good feelings for her parents, for animals, plants, water, fire, and all of nature's gifts.

In the thirty years after our meeting, Vera Alexandrovna led a hard life. She lived in a small room with her son and her mother and taught foreign languages in a school, but she had huge problems in organizing her everyday existence in Moscow, which after sixteen years' absence had ceased to be her home.

She wrote these memoirs in the early 1960s. Neither of us could have imagined then that they would ever be published in our country. Closing the door carefully behind her and swearing us all to silence, she would read in a quiet, even voice these bitter lines.

ALEXANDER RUBININ
VERA SHULZ DIED IN 1989. —SV

I should like to call you all by name,
But they have lost the lists . . .

I have woven for them a great shroud
Out of the poor words I overheard them speak.

—Anna Akhmatova, "Requiem"

Taganka

The circle of light on the table is the first thing I recall about that terrible time in March 1938. That night will always be my personal Ides of March, filling me each spring with a dull sense of dread. It is impossible ever to forget this kind of cruel and senseless blow which affects the whole of one's life. Impossible to forget that one might at any moment become a powerless, humiliated pawn. Such psychic wounds never heal.

The time by the clock under the table lamp said 4:20 A.M. as the doorbell rang for a second time. My husband was away in Minsk for a few days giving some lectures. Throwing on my dressing gown, I went to the door. I was quite calm. Then I heard the janitor's voice asking me to open up. I did so. Standing out there with him were three soldiers, who showed me their search warrants. Since we had nothing criminal or forbidden in the apartment, I was still naive enough to assume that it must be all a mistake. I only later remembered my copy of Trotsky's *The Year 1905* on the bookshelf, which had been one of our university textbooks. I have no idea what would have happened to me if they had found it, but they carried out only the most perfunctory search, pulling out a few books, leafing through them, then putting them back and going into the other room, where they ripped open my mattress with a bayonet in search of hidden weapons. In hindsight, of course, I realize that they must have known quite well what kind of "criminal" I was; they did not even go into the room where our old nurse was sleeping with our six-year-old son.

When all the "formalities" had been completed, the soldiers handed me a warrant for my arrest, on which I was amazed to see the signature of Andrei Vyshinsky, the man who had been rector of Moscow University when I was there [but who was now Stalin's chief prosecutor]. Since it was several years since I had left the university, I found this most odd.

I set off on my sixteen-year road to Calvary—*sancta simplicitas*—with a suitcase containing a nightgown, a change of underwear, and a one-volume edition of Pushkin and Galsworthy's *Forsyte Saga*. Although the courteous agents of state terror knew full well that I would be living with seventeen others in a cell intended for three, where nightclothes were pointless and books forbidden, they did not forewarn me. I said goodbye to my son, warm and sleepy in his bed—he did not stir when I kissed him—wondering when I would see him next. It never occurred to me that I might never see him again.

Outside the gates of the building stood a car. We got in. Moscow lay in the grip of a winter frost, still sleeping in the violet hues of early dawn. We passed through deserted Okhotny Row, with just a few lights on here and there. I said I wanted a cigarette, and the car stopped and a Red Army man was sent off for some. I was surprised by their consideration. He soon returned and we drove off again.

We arrived at the Lubyanka. I was led down some high-walled corridors, up a staircase and down another corridor, where a tall door was thrown open and a man was led out toward me. It was my brother! Of course, this was a blunder on their part. He had also been taken in that night. He was amazed to see me, but he tried to joke about it, saying, "Well, fancy seeing you here!"

We were then marched off in opposite directions, and I never saw my brother again.

After this I was made to sit down behind a table in a room with cold high walls painted with green glossy paint. There I was left on my own with a piece of paper to give an account of my life and fill out innumerable forms. The fiction of legality was still being maintained, and everyone was very polite to me and treated me like a human being. But as the components of this hypocrisy were gradually discarded, one descended ever lower into a hell where one was stripped of all human dignity and turned into a speechless, powerless pawn.

More corridors, passages, and a staircase leading down to a room without windows, rather like a basement cloakroom. There I was searched. They confiscated my Pushkin and the Forsytes, and a young soldier tried to pull the gold and diamond ring—a present from my late father—off my finger, but it was so firmly stuck there that he finally gave up and left it. After this a woman guard came to search me more intimately; then I was handed back my suitcase and taken out.

We stopped at a door which was thrown open, and I was told to go in. Then the door slammed shut, and the key turned in the lock—the first turn of the prison key. I was all alone in a vertical pink stone box, with nothing to sit or lie on, so that I had to remain standing. Far above me glimmered a ceiling light behind a grill.

As my watch had been confiscated, I had no idea how long I was there, and remember only the frantic jumble of thoughts in my head. The time dragged intolerably, my legs became swollen from standing, and I felt painfully aware of my utter helplessness and isolation from my loved ones.

I was finally led out into the murky prison yard, where a Black Maria swallowed up a huddle of pale, unrecognizably altered people shivering with nervousness.

The legendary Butyrki, where we were taken, proved to be full, so the Black Maria drove on to the Taganka. For centuries this had been a criminal jail of the roughest kind, renowned for the primitiveness of both its living conditions and its staff.

At the Taganka I was searched yet again, then taken off to a room rather like a laboratory, where our fingers were smeared with black printing ink and pressed onto white squared paper for prints. It was an extraordinarily humiliating procedure, and although superficially calm, I was burning inside with rage and disgust. How dare they treat me like a bandit or a murderer! I felt as though they had trampled me into the mud. There are some occasions when humor comes to the rescue. But the heavy hand of tragedy seemed to allow no place for it. That first day of incarceration inflicted wounds which would never heal.

A woman guard marched us off to the prison building. The heavy iron-clad doors closed behind us, and the medieval bolts clanged. The inside of the prison was like a gray oval with tiered balconies running along it, several stories high, all enclosed in wire netting in case someone decided to spill their brains on the stone floor. Overlooking the balconies were the doors of the cells, each with its peephole, through which the male and female guards would occasionally peer as they silently patrolled the corridor.

Outside one of the cells on the ground floor, the woman guard stopped, opened the door, and pushed me inside. The door slammed shut, the bolt clanged, the key turned. It was all over. I stood like a poor relative in the space between the door and the slop bucket. It was impossible to take a single step forward, as the entire floor was covered by reclining bodies. In the dim light of the bulb constantly burning on the ceiling, I could also see three iron cots, each with three bodies on it.

It was late, and the whole cell had long been asleep, but now they were awakened by the scrape of the lock, and I saw what looked like the dark rippling surface of water, as matted heads and pale sleepy faces rose up from the beds and the floor. Rags rustled, and the cell stirred like a dark beast aroused in the night.

The arrival of a new prisoner is always an event, and in the grim darkness of the small cell, everyone was soon sitting up and showering me with questions:

"What Article are you?"

"Are you here as a wife or on your own account?"

"What's happening out there?"

"Are the mass arrests still going on?"

"Did they leave your family?"

"Have you met so-and-so?"

"What's your name?"

"What's your job?"

I was so upset that first night that I did not ask any questions.

Nine people were lying on the three cots. The rest lay on the floor, beneath and between the beds. Places were allocated according to a strict hierarchy, so that I spent my first night in the worst place, between the door and the slop bucket, moving gradually over the next few days, and finally some two weeks later finding myself in a bed.

Like all prisons in those years, the cell in which I began my "university studies" was like a bazaar from Babylon, with Russians, Ukrainians, Byelorussians, Jews, Germans, Hungarians, French, and English, and women from the Chinese Eastern Railroad, young and old, all mingling and jostling together in an endless stream of humanity.

On one of my first nights there, I lay on the floor wrapped in my light overcoat, my head teeming with an anguishing chaos of thoughts about my son and his father. I gritted my teeth, unable to sleep for the lump in my throat, and forcing myself not to betray what I was suffering. It was then that I heard a man shrieking in mortal agony, like an animal being slaughtered. The screams came from the basement directly under the floor, close to my ear. I struggled up and leaned on my elbow. The other women were all asleep. "They've stopped noticing!" I thought in horror. The cries went on, long and piercing. My heart pounded. Then suddenly I felt someone touching my back, and turning around, I saw an old peasant woman looking at me with sad, hollow eyes.

"Don't listen, darling—it'll break your heart! They scream every night, poor things. What can you do! That's the basement, where they do the interrogations. When people won't sign, the interrogators beat them even worse."

"But what if there's nothing to sign?"

"Makes no difference. Folks want to live and see their families again— they'll sign anything. It's still better to be in the camps than here."

I confess, to my shame, that I had only the haziest notion at the time of what Stalin's camps were like. That night was my baptism of fire, as the nation's tragedy began slowly to unfold before my eyes.

I later learned that the basement was quiet only on Saturdays and Sundays, when the torturers rested from their labors.

Every ten days we were taken to the bathhouse. This might have offered us a little pleasure, but instead it was turned into an extra torture, for we would be taken there at three in the morning.

They woke us roughly as we slept, warmed by the dreams that gave us some brief respite from our grief, and herded us outside into the cold and dark. The bathhouse was like a dark inferno. Its high black walls loomed up out of the darkness streaming with dampness, and naked bodies flitted through the steam like the souls of the damned. Troubled by an old heart ailment, I started to choke in the heat. The instinct of preservation made me rush to the locked door, put my lips to the keyhole, and gulp greedily for air. Then the guard pushed me away. One's life sometimes is in the hands of such people.

I remember another night. One particular guard at the Taganka was renowned for her cruelty to the inmates, and would punish weak, humiliated victims with a vicious, mindless violence. She had an inexhaustible hatred for the prisoners, whom she regarded as loathsome and dangerous enemies, and she would happily have killed each one of us with her bare hands. Why should she care for us? She saw us as her personal enemies. What a brainless, well-trained animal she was.

It was this guardian of the law who took us to the bathhouse that night. I staggered off half-asleep to find myself a bowl, and was starting to soap myself when the ring I was wearing flashed in the darkness. Suddenly the guard wafted before me out of the steam like an impure spirit and grabbed my hand, screaming, "What's this ring? Bringing gold into the prison? You'll pay for this!"

I explained that I had been given the ring many years ago when my fingers were thinner, and that the soldier at the Lubyanka had been unable to remove it and had left it on.

"Liar! We'll see about that! I'm not stupid. . . ! I'll show you," she yelled, and panting and swearing with exertion, she seized my hand, soaped my finger, and finally managed to screw the ring off.

I felt completely detached from her as she was doing this. I no longer cared about anything, even the fact that the ring had been a present from my beloved now-dead father. My present losses were nothing compared to everything that had already happened to me. I stood there like stone while my memory did its work, fixing certain moments forever in my mind.

After we had washed, this same guard handed me a piece of paper stating in an illiterate scrawl that she had confiscated a small brass ring. About two months later, I heard that she was now herself a prisoner for some offense. I confess that I believe in the idea of retribution, providing as it does some sort of balance between good and evil in this world.

The cell was like a Noah's Ark, crammed with women of different ages, nationalities, levels of education, interests, and personalities. Since we were forbidden to lie down during the day, we all had to sit squashed together on the floor. The days dragged horribly, and the monotony was broken only by being called out for interrogation, or to be transferred. There was a desperate need to escape from painful thoughts, especially at night, when the sleeping cell was filled with sobs and snuffles.

Our bread rations were generally a green half-baked glue, and we would sit one in front of the other, shaping this inedible clay into rough ashtrays, soap dishes, vases, little animals, and cockerels. It was strictly forbidden, of course, and the models would stay in the cell only until they were confiscated in the next search, so the next day we would have to start all over again.

Another forbidden activity was sewing. Needles were naturally banned, but we managed to make them by breaking the teeth from combs. The hole for the eye would be burned with a match by a woman who had smuggled in a safety pin (we were allowed to smoke, so we had matches), and we got thread by unraveling old stockings and underwear. I still have one of these pieces of embroidery to this day, as a memento mori of my life in prison.

But our favorite pastime was storytelling. We would listen with bated breath, transported into another reality, and the storytellers enjoyed the special indulgence of the cell. While I was there I heard stories by Chekhov,

Gorky, Turgenev, Maupassant, and others. *Jane Eyre* and Voynich's *Gadfly* were especially popular, as were the poems of Pushkin, Lermontov, Mayakovsky, Blok, Nekrasov, and Yesenin.

Even as a girl I had worshipped Anna Akhmatova, and I knew many of her poems by heart. I also loved the poems of Gumilyov. But despite these poets' remarkable qualities, they were not popular during those years. Akhmatova was then composing her masterpiece, the divine "Requiem," and I discovered it only in the 1960s, when it was being passed from hand to hand in *samizdat*. I knew almost nothing written by Pasternak, Tsvetaeva, or Mandelstam.

Four of us were especially in demand as storytellers. One was an elderly educated Russian woman named Fage, who had married a French writer living in the Soviet Union. Then there was a sharp, clever young Jewish girl called Lenochka. There was the Hungarian Iolan Yaroi-Groob, well past her youth but full of fire. And I before my arrest had been an actress at the Moscow studio theater of Ruben Simonov (formerly literary manager of the Vakhtangov Theater).

In our youth we lived without looking back. Borne along in the frantic rhythms of Moscow life and the delights of art, books, music, galleries, and theaters, we needed constant excitement to jolt us out of our usual routine. Then came the inevitable reassessment. It was only in prison that I discovered the true significance of human memory. Before that I had taken it for granted, like the air we breathe. I needed memory professionally, to pass exams and remember lines, but so far it had played only a small part in my life.

In the isolation of prison, memory was a blessing which I could share with other equally unfortunate people. Memory enabled me to populate the desert island of our prison cell with people and images from the great world of literature. It helped me to forget myself and immerse myself in another life. Some of my cellmates had had almost no contact with art and culture, yet I shall never forget the moments I spent with them as they listened with tears in their eyes, whispering, "That's good—it makes your flesh creep . . . "

Before I was arrested, I had been learning an excerpt from Mayakovsky's poem "Vladimir Ilich Lenin" for a concert performance. When I recited the poem here, I saw the tears in the women's eyes as they sat like dark angular birds on the bare floor. They listened with the same fascination to the part from Leskov's *Lady Macbeth from Mtsensk* where Katerina Izmailova, Sergei, and Sonetka set out on their last journey to Siberia—a passage with a special resonance for all of us in those terrible days.

But I was a listener, too. I remember how the usually reserved Fage would open up when recounting Chekhov's story "The Literature Teacher."

A different life would enter our dark stuffy cell, and instead of the tiny strip of blue sky visible through the metal plate over the window, we would hear the rustling lime trees in the old park around the estate, and see the enchanting young Maria Godfroi and her elderly landowner father. Lenochka would recite with blazing eyes from the immortal "Gadfly," and Iolan would describe in lively but halting Russian the interminable novels of the classic Hungarian writer Moor Iokai, with his haunted castles and romantic dramas.

Iolan was one of the most interesting of my cellmates at the Taganka. She belonged to the category of "wives," a tall, slim, youthfully elegant woman, with dark, graying hair, eyes that shone like moist cherries—like those of Yekaterina Maslova in Tolstoy's *Resurrection*—and an enchanting sense of humor. Her husband was a Hungarian Communist, a political émigré who had been living in Moscow and working for the Comintern. Iolan came from a proletarian family, and before emigrating with her husband to the Soviet Union, she had worked as a dresser at a Budapest theater. The Hungary of the Hapsburgs had made it hard for her to get an education—her parents had died when she was a child, and some distant relatives had packed her off to a convent. She soon realized that she was innately unsuited to convent life, but since she had nowhere else to go, she stayed on there until they kicked her out. After that, someone helped her to find work as a dresser, and she began to read voraciously. Then she met her husband, and before long they left for Moscow together.

In 1937 they were both arrested. Her husband was in poor health and much older than she was, and she wept constantly for him, convinced that she would never see him again. "He's so sick, so sick . . . He'll die in prison!" she used to say, rubbing her eyes with her fists.

I wonder what became of Iolan. Did she lay down her head in the Far North, or Siberia? I suppose she must be dead by now.

It was one day some two weeks after my arrest that I was led downstairs for my first interrogation. During the day, the basement did not seem so terrible. Daylight flooded in through the windows that lined one side of the long, wide red-carpeted corridor. On the other side were the doors to the interrogators' offices. The soldier led me into one of these.

A young man in a military uniform sat on a chair in the middle of the room, his legs planted wide apart in a pair of gleaming polished boots, and his gray eyes glaring menacingly at me.

"When did you arrive in the USSR?" he demanded.

His question showed that the guardians of the law had not bothered to establish the most elementary facts about me, since I was born in Moscow and had spent over thirty years of my life there.

"Never!" I said ironically.

"How is that?" the interrogator shifted on his chair.

"Quite simply because I was born here in Moscow, and have lived here all my life. In three buildings: one is now the Commissariat of Foreign Affairs, on the corner of Kuznetsky Most and the Lubyanka; another is the Stroganov College, on Myasnitsky Street; and the third is on Levshinsky Lane, between Kropotkin Street and the Arbat, where I was arrested for some reason I still do not understand."

I was absolutely calm as I spoke, and I looked him straight in the eye. He had clearly not expected this, and was very put out. He asked me several more ridiculous questions, which I have now forgotten, then summoned the soldier from outside the door.

My first interrogation had obviously ended badly for him, since he had failed to make a foreign agent out of me and would now have to think of something else. I was led out of the room.

After this the days dragged by unbearably slowly, and I sometimes felt as if they had forgotten about me. I was obsessed with thoughts of my son. It was terrible not to know if he was on his own, and if his father had been arrested on his return from Minsk.

Then one morning I was handed a greasy slip of green paper, and a soldier in white overalls told me that this was a voucher for the prison shop, and that I had been sent some money, which I could spend on bread, herring, cigarettes, and rusks. I ordered a few things, but all I could think of was how to get my hands on the piece of paper so that I could read the signature. It was as if my life depended on it. My hands trembled, my eyes blurred; then at last I saw at the bottom of the paper the familiar elegant signature of my husband. So he must be free, and my little boy with him! I collapsed against the metal rail of my cot and wept for joy.

Strangely enough, I blessed fate at such moments that it was I who was following this path of suffering into an unknown future fraught with peril. I had been used to life's hardships since childhood, when I had endured the chaos and hunger of the 1914 war and the Civil War. My husband, who was older and accustomed to a more comfortable life, suffered occasionally from neurasthenia. Prison would have killed him. Hard-working and highly qualified, he would be able to make a good life for our son. A boy needs a father's hand.

I was overjoyed that he had drawn the winning ticket in this bloody lottery, and that he had not renounced me, as so many people did then. Instead he had set out on his own road to Calvary, and this showed a considerable degree of heroism in those years. I later learned that he had visited all the prisons in search of me, as well as the Commissariat of Internal Affairs, the procurator's office, and numerous tribunals, pointing out that they had made a mistake and that I was innocent.

Our only link over the months that followed was the regular arrival of the green slips of paper bearing his signature. I sobbed over them at night and treasured them for the rest of my life.

One day humor entered our cell. The bolt clanged, and there in the doorway stood a little old woman. We clustered around and offered her a seat, while she peered warily at the gang of women surrounding her. She was one of those illiterate village women, destined by poverty to a life of hard physical labor and endless anxieties about the harvest, her family, and her home. She was an embodiment of *sancta simplicitas,* like the old woman who brought a bundle of firewood to the pyre where Jan Hus was to be burned.

When one of us asked her why she was in prison, she replied eagerly, and it was clear that she had been forced to be silent for a long time.

"It's all because of my boy, my darling son. Why it happened, I still don't know. Maybe you can help a simple old woman to understand why they take me hundreds of miles from home. A soldier drives us here in a lorry. 'Why are you dragging me to these distant parts, my dear?' I ask him. 'And Lord help us, what do you need that gun for?'

'Hold your tongue, gran,' he says, 'We're not allowed to talk to you! You're an enemy of the people!'

"So we don't say anything for the rest of the journey.

"As soon as we stop, they lock me up in a little cage. There's one bed in there, and two women sitting on it—they're not from our parts, and they're chattering away like rifle fire; you can't make out a word of it. So I said nothing.

"Next morning they take me off to be questioned. I'm in a right state— I cross myself, wrap my shawl around my head, and off I go. The soldier orders me to put my hands behind my back, then we go into this room. There's a soldier sitting at a desk.

"'Name?' he says.

"'You can call me Matryona,' says I.

"'Sit down old woman,' he says. 'I'm the interrogator.'

"I look at him, sitting there in silence sorting through his papers. Then suddenly he looks up all angry and says, 'Tell me when you joined, old woman!'

"'What?' I say.

"'When did you join? Answer me!' he shouts. I have no idea what he's going on about.

"'Forgive me, dear sir, for the love of Christ! I don't follow you, I'm just an ignorant old woman . . . '

"'Did your son make you join?'

"By now he's completely crazy. He's staring like a madman, and I'm trembling all over. "I'd better do as he wants," I think.

"'I did join, sir, that I did!' I say.

"'There, see, you can't fool me! So you did join!' And he grinds his teeth like he's got the plague.

"'Yes, sir, I did!' God knows what I'm getting myself into.

"Then I put my mark on the paper, and he calms down right away and lets me go. I'm that happy—maybe the Lord will take mercy on an old woman . . . '

She was over seventy at the time. Before long she was taken off, given her sentence, and driven out to alien lands to await death.

O Russia, here is your meekness, your timorous non-resistance, your gentleness, and your faith in God. Yet how much more precious is the image of that simple, illiterate old woman than of that other Russia which besieged me in my cell.

There were also two German women there. They were typically Germanic, with blond hair and blue eyes, and despite prison life they kept their rosy complexions, their plump dimpled cheeks, and their twittering speech. They knew just a little conversational Russian, and could say only a few things in our language. They were both married to German Communists who had emigrated to Soviet Russia after Hitler came to power, and had been arrested in 1937. They were in a strange land, with strange people and a strange tongue, yet they never lost heart. One of the women was called Marie. Even in the cell, where our lives were ravaged by fate and our hearts broken by despair, she would sing popular German songs in syncopated operetta style, stamping her feet and waving her arms about. At such moments the shadow of a smile might cross people's faces. But only a shadow. Soon there would be a rap at the door, and the guard would order her to stop. Singing was strictly forbidden in the prison, and anyone doing so risked the punishment cell.

Not once did I see those two women despair. Did they really have such a powerful faith in the logic of events? Did they really believe they would be acquitted of their nonexistent crimes? Had they not heard the march of history? Did they regard the whole thing as some ghastly burlesque? I think not. I think for them it was a matter of character.

I turn the kaleidoscope again and see Agafya Petrovna, the wife of a railworker on the Chinese Eastern Railroad. She and her husband had both been arrested. In the mornings Agafya's eyes would be red, for she did all her crying at night, and she did her utmost to be cheerful during the day. She was from a worker's family and had left school at an early age to look after another family's children. An ordinary simple Russian woman, she had enormous inner strength, energy, and willpower, and always tried to cheer up those who were not so strong. She firmly believed that everything was merely a temporary aberration, and she tried to convince others of this, too. She never mentioned the name of Stalin, refusing to console herself or others with the myth that he knew nothing. There were a few who were taken in by this myth, but their protestations would meet with a cold response, and they would lapse into silence. I still remember that woman's kind, broad face, her auburn hair, her invariable maroon flannel dress, and her felt slippers. "The truth will win!" she used to say.

There was another railworker's wife in the cell, a young Byelorussian named Lyubinskaya, who had only recently left her village for the town. Pale and transparently thin, she seemed physically detached from us in a state of numbed silence. A few months before her arrest, she had given birth to a baby boy. Now, separated from the infant, she was on the verge of madness. Unable to comprehend what had happened to her, she ate, drank, slept, and got up in the morning like a sleepwalker. Agafya Petrovna took the woman under her wing, comforting her and talking to her with the utmost sensitivity.

In this hothouse of human energy, I recall the frail, girlish figure of Jewish Lenochka. Black-eyed and clever, she would occasionally collapse into paroxysms of despair at the way her young life, her intelligence, and her hunger for knowledge were being drowned in the mindless absurdity of prison. Although the youngest among us, she had already been in prison for six months and had come in contact with the common criminals, from whom she had picked up a few things. In those days of whispering and fear, we were astonished by the carefree pleasure with which she told us how they interpreted the initials of the USSR as "Kill Stalin, Swine of the Revolution." Fortunately there were no informers among us, but her story made me realize how well ordinary people already understood the Stalinist terror. Whether Lenochka survived or was buried in a common grave, I do not know.

Though I am now in my fifties, and carry my past on my back like an old tortoise carries her shell, the memory of old Akutina still fills my heart with grief. Maybe it is is a higher form of "universal conscience," the instinct of responsibility, indeed guilt, which an educated person must bear for the evil done to others. Moreover, fate brought me and Akutina together on three occasions, each of which threw a fierce light on fragments of this old Russian woman's life and the shameful things going on all around.

One day a little gray-haired old woman with a round face and button nose was led into our cell. She stood at the door by the slop bucket, as I too had once done. Her pale, nearsighted eyes were kind, her smile was shy and beseeching, and she radiated a calm, inexhaustible goodness. Her name was Tatyana Pavlovna Akutina.

All alone in the world, with no home of her own, she had gone to live in a village near Moscow as housekeeper for a well-off elderly woman, for whom she performed various simple household tasks such as lighting the stove, drawing water from the well, feeding the cow and chickens, and preparing the meals. Both the women were Baptists, and they used to go off to pray together. They lived a quiet life, keeping to themselves and not causing any harm to anyone. Then in 1938 they were arrested.

The old woman accepted her fate with uncomplaining gentleness. Having being educated by the Soviet state as an atheist, I knew almost nothing about religion or the role that religious faith might play in someone's life, but I realized what a consolation it was to Tatyana Pavlovna.

Small and homely, with often watering, blinking eyes, she once came up to me and shyly asked, "Look in my hair, will you, Vera darling? I can't stand it; I keep scratching. It's the lice, accursed that I am. With your young eyes . . . "

I lifted a knot of thin hair, and went through her graying yellow locks, crushing the lice. I did not find it disgusting, for she was so gentle and I was eager to help her. She had been happy to answer all our questions when she appeared in the cell, but then spent most of her time sitting in silence with her head bowed.

I was ordered to "get my things" before she was, and after saying my final farewells to all my friends, I left them and the cell forever.

More than a year passed, and I was living in exile in Kazakhstan on the shores of the Aral Sea, working in a local school teaching Russian to little Kazakhs. The town of Aralsk, if this collection of straw and clay huts spread out under the blazing sun could be called a town, drowned in the arid sandy wastelands around the Aral, and I felt constantly homesick for the green of central Russia, blinking back the tears whenever goods trucks passed by loaded with Russian birch logs.

One day as I struggled across the sand in the sweltering heat, I saw an old woman hobbling toward me in the distance. She walked with a stick, and when I got closer to her, I saw that it was old Akutina. I flung my arms around her as though she were a relative, crying, "Tatyana Pavlovna, my dear friend, so we meet again. . . !"

She blinked up at me. "Is that Vera, my little daughter? What a joy! I never expected to see you . . . !"

She told me that her group of prisoners had arrived just a few days earlier. "They let us off the train—most of us old women—and handed us over. When we saw there were no trees or grass, we fell to their feet, saying, 'Where have you brought us? There's nothing but sand and wind. How will we live? You've brought us here to die! Why don't you shoot us here and now!'" But the soldiers just handed the old women over to the local NKVD, who found them somewhere to live.

My third meeting with old Akutina was more bitter. I was lying ill with tropical dysentery in the epidemic ward of the Aralsk hospital. There were no drugs for the illness, and I did not expect to live. Yet I was saved in the most improbable way, as though some higher power did not wish me to die. One of the exiles, a former nurse, had just been sent the right drugs from Moscow in case she fell ill, and since she was desperately short of money, she sold me the precious vials that saved my life.

The hospital barracks stood on the edge of the town, right by the sea. A white clay hut stood a little farther off, and beyond it stretched an endless sea of sand. When I felt a little stronger I started to sit outside the barracks in the mornings, sheltered from the tropical heat in the shade they cast. It was here that one of the patients told me that an old woman exile, a Baptist apparently, had recently died. Before her death she had given instructions that she was to be buried in a simple white shift, which she had laid out in her room for the purpose. She was now lying in the morgue, and I was directed across the sea of sand to the white clay hut.

I pushed open the unlocked door and stood at the threshold. On the floor in the middle of the room lay a small body shrouded in white, frozen into the stern immobility of death. It was old Akutina.

I stood for a long time in the doorway looking at her. At such moments one sees things with special clarity. This should never be forgotten or forgiven. Would the cup of evil ever be full? When would retribution come? Why had this simple peasant soul been torn from her native land? Why had she been condemned to die, knowing that her body would not rest in the long grass of her village plot, topped by a gray rain-washed wooden cross, knowing that she would never see the weeping birch or the rowan tree before finally closing her eyes—knowing that she would lie not amid tilting crosses, twittering birds, wandering horses with burrs in their tails, chattering Easter sparrows, and brightly painted eggs, but in alien salty sands where weeds and thistles flourished, where the water was sour and brackish as urine, and wise-eyed camels, exotic and incomprehending, stalked past on tall gouty legs. Why? What for? Had not the idea of the "guilty without blame" achieved here its most tragic and universal resonance?

My second interrogation was about two months later, in the morning—

the nights apparently being reserved for the more dangerous "criminals." This time I had a different interrogator, an extremely affable young fair-haired man who took a completely different tack from the first one and asked me all about my work in the theater.

The charge against me now was that I had been employed as an agent of German counterintelligence, which had also supposedly recruited a distant relative of mine named Boris B. (the son of my grandmother's niece or one of her friends), who had been a teacher in the town of Engels. He had hardly ever been to Moscow, and his last visit there had been five years earlier, in 1933.

According to this fantastic scenario, I had given the Germans information about when members of the government would be at the theater. I protested to my youthful interrogator that since it was a small, young theater that had only just come into existence, not one member of the government had ever been there.

"That's beside the point!" he replied.

All through the interrogation he was constantly scribbling away, and finally he asked me to read what he had written and sign it as a record of the cross-examination.

"No, I can't sign; there's not a word of truth in it."

"Sooner or later you will," he said with a grin. "All right, I'll give you another chance. But the sooner you sign, the better it will be for you."

On my way back to my cell, a strange thing happened. The soldier suddenly ordered me to face the wall, and as I did so a key grated in the lock, a door opened, and I was pushed into a small windowless room with the usual light behind a grill on the ceiling. Then the door closed behind me. The cell was empty except for a stool against the wall, and I sat on this stool for what seemed like an eternity. Had they forgotten about me, or was the interrogator merely giving me "one more chance?" When I was eventually taken back to my cell, everyone was lying down for the night. Of course they all woke up and started asking questions, and it was a long time before I finally managed to get some sleep, having eaten nothing all day.

During my third interrogation, when I again refused to sign the nonsense put before me, the man suddenly assumed a quite different tone, a tone of friendly persuasion, which as a good Soviet citizen I was supposed to understand.

"Look, we all know none of this is true," he said. "But our government desperately needs you to sign! As a Soviet citizen, you can't refuse to do this for your country!"

The full cynicism of his words struck me only later. At the time my only thought was that a mere stroke of the pen could load this guilt onto me, and turn an honest person into a dishonest one. My honor was at stake. I refused to sign.

At this point the pleasant fair-haired man changed completely. His face contorted with rage, he jumped from his chair, unbuckled the belt from his tunic, and started waving it around, thrusting out his lower jaw, and screaming with bared teeth and blazing eyes, "For the last time, sign—or else. . . !"

"Wait!" I shouted. "Wait!"

My mind raced. If he struck me, I knew that I would never forgive or forget it. It wasn't him—he was just a pawn. Or my country—my country was sick and suffering. People signed because there was no other way for them to live. Then suddenly I saw a little ray of hope, and knew what I must do.

"Give me some paper," I cried, "and promise not to change what I write! Promise me that, and I'll sign!"

He gave me a sheet of paper, and I wrote that everything I had signed was a lie, that there was not a word of truth in it, that the interrogator had forced me to sign by threatening to beat me, and that I lived in hope that my case would someday be reexamined and my name cleared.

I could hope till the Second Coming, although at the time I had no doubt of my powerlessness in this struggle with Leviathan. Yet time proved me right in submitting to the historical course of events. There was nothing else I could have done. Beatings and needles under the fingernails would change nothing.

Shortly after my third interrogation, I was ordered to "get my things," and I packed and said my farewells, knowing that I would never return to this cell again.

After receiving my sentence—five years exile in Kazakhstan as a "socially dangerous element"—I was moved to a new cell with new people. The short time I spent there has dissolved in the mists of time. But my "universities" continued.

My paternal grandmother was an Englishwoman whose mother had died when she was six years old and whose father had moved with his children to Russia. This meant that she spent virtually the whole of her life in Moscow, Russian became her mother tongue, and she spoke with a perfect Moscow accent. Since my own parents separated when I was eighteen months old, it was she who brought me up. She loved me dearly, and was like a real mother to me.

Grandmother's father—a real Dickensian type, to judge from the photographs—died when she was just eight, and the little orphan was sent to

Vera Gasparovna Brok's educational establishment on Ostozhenka Street in Moscow. Since there were no specialist foreign-language establishments in Russia at the time, girls were trained as governesses to teach languages to the children of rich merchants and landowners. Grandmother taught me everything she had learned, and after 1938, it was this that saved my life. Despite my university degree, I could not get a job because of a secret government circular that banned exiles from teaching Russian literature. There was no such ban on the teaching of foreign languages, however, and so life gave me a new profession, and I learned from bitter experience the wisdom of Marx's words that knowing a foreign language is a weapon in the struggle for existence.

After being sentenced, I was moved to a new cell, and it was here that I had the most profound encounter of my entire prison life. My eye was drawn to the boyish figure of a fair-haired, highly intelligent-looking young woman with a cunning glint in her bright green eyes. In this cage of suffering she had managed to retain her bright eyes and her inner calm, and I felt instinctively drawn to her. In the evening we would lie side by side on the floor, whispering so as not to disturb the others, who were getting ready to sleep, two sad souls talking long and passionately and discovering each other in the emptiness.

Her name was Carol Mityanina, and she was Australian. She came from a humble family of white-collar workers and had spent her childhood near Sydney, on the shores of the Pacific Ocean. In the early 1930s she married an official at the Soviet Embassy named Mityanin, and when he was recalled to Moscow, she followed him there. By 1937 they had two children, and lived just off Kropotkin Street, a few yards from where I myself had lived, although we had never met. When she and her husband were arrested, her two sons went to stay with their grandmother, but she had had no news of them. What faith she had in the infallibility of our great country! She believed passionately in people's honesty, and was convinced that there was some sort of logic to world events. Her husband had done nothing wrong, she said, everything would eventually be sorted out, and if in the meantime they both died, the state would take care of her sons and make men of them. I never for a moment doubted her sincerity, and told myself that her incomprehension of so much evil was the result of living in a foreign country, with a strange language and very few friends. Besides, if as a wife and mother her faith in justice was some sort of consolation to her in these terrible circumstances, who was I to destroy it? Such things could not assuage our grief, but we found comfort in our passionate discussions together.

I told Carol about my English background and my grandmother. My English was poor, as was her Russian, so we communicated in a strange and passionate mixture of the two, and we began to sense a growing kinship, as though we had known each other for years. I do not know if our talks were anything more than exalted ravings, but they enriched us immeasurably in those terrible times of loneliness and despair, and as we fell asleep in each other's arms on the dirty stone floor of the cell at the Taganka, we would no longer feel alone.

Carol already knew her sentence, ten years in the camps. She had heard nothing of her husband. It was only the beginning. Ahead lay the common-place cruelty of cold, hunger, and back-breaking labor. But we knew nothing of all this yet.

All things must come to an end, and one day Carol was ordered to "get her things." We embraced and said farewell, and through eyes misted with tears I gazed at her dear face, which I had grown to love so much. The cunning gray-green eyes smiled at me for the last time, and that was the end. I still do not know if her bones have been swallowed up in the permafrost at Magadan or Kolyma, but to my dying day I shall recall with a fierce and unforgiving anger my prison friend who was so unjustly punished.

Soon I too was ordered to "get my things," and my road to Calvary continued.

Translation by Cathy Porter

GALINA ZATMILOVA

SEVEN

Galina Zatmilova ──────

A Part of History

🌸 About the Author

I first got to know Galina Zatmilova in Chukotka. As a young geologist, I had been sent from Leningrad to work at the far northeastern tip of the Soviet Union. The hotel room was crowded, I was sleepy, and my head ached. But through the noise I heard someone discussing the Italian cinema. In the mid-1950s, Italian neo-realism was a breath of fresh air for us, and I could not resist joining in. The speaker, it turned out, was Galina Zatmilova. We became friends, there and then, and remained friends until her death in 1982.

Since she preferred to talk about public events, I can only offer the following incomplete biography. Galina Ivanovna Zatmilova was born in 1906 in Saratov, into the family of a minor government official. She studied at the Urals Polytechnic Institute in Sverdlovsk and until the late 1920s was an active member of the Komsomol. Then she got to know exiled socialist opponents of the Bolsheviks. She married one of them, and they moved to Ufa, where she became especially close to the Left SR leader Irina Kakhovskaya. The former Socialist Revolutionaries were no longer active as public or political figures; many of them were now working for a variety of Soviet institutions. In February 1937, they were all arrested. That was the last time Galina saw her husband, but she shared a cell with Kakhovskaya for four months, and 19 years later they would find each other again.

After ten years in the camps, Galina was "fortunate" not to be given a second sentence, like so many others. However, she had no wish to leave Kolyma: there was no one waiting for her in Russia. She remarried, this time choosing a "dekulakized" peasant who had also served his sentence in Kolyma. In 1957 they returned to his home area of Rubtsovsk in southern Siberia, where she helped him bring up his orphaned nephews and nieces.

After his death, and that of Kakhovskaya in 1960, Galina began to spend the summers in Moscow and Leningrad, sometimes accompanying me on geological expeditions and cooking for us.

NATALYA GROMOVA

It is difficult to begin these memoirs. I know quite well that I have little ability to depict people who played an important part in the history of the Revolution, let alone produce a literary memoir. I am almost the last person alive who knew them, however (apart from Bertha Babina). That, and my own love and respect for them, forces me to begin this record.

Until July 1930 I lived in Sverdlovsk. I had a husband, I belonged to the Komsomol, and I took both marriage and my Komsomol membership seriously. Indeed, for me, the Komsomol was probably even the more important. I was happy, I thought.

Then, in autumn 1929, I was put in charge of literacy classes at the Aromil cloth mill. The collectivization of agriculture was already under way, and, consequently, so was the expropriation and exiling of the "kulaks." The rural soviet and the factory, though side by side, were controlled by different authorities, so I was not directly involved. But I saw for myself what collectivization and "dekulakization" actually meant. Until then I had no serious disagreements with the policies of our government. Cracks had already begun to appear, though.

The debates within the Party in 1927 did not really affect me. I didn't know enough to get involved, and, besides, not many fundamental issues were raised in the Komsomol. Discussion was restricted to the membership groups for each year or department, and I don't remember any meeting of all the students. The resolution we adopted, of course, was always in support of the "general line." After the month of discussion had ended, the groups expelled all the oppositionists from the Party and the Komsomol. At the time this struck me as just. I thought it was impossible to belong to an organization if you did not share its program. Next the oppositionists were expelled from the institute. That I could not possibly accept. The first cracks thus appeared in my Komsomol "view of the world." I was still very far, however, from a sober understanding of what was going on. So far, in fact, that when a fellow student whom I greatly respected said, "Do you know where they went, our mates whom they expelled from the institute? They're all in Verkhneuralsk, in the political detention center." I angrily replied, "Don't you ever say things like that to me—I refuse to believe them!"

Then I saw dekulakization and collectivization with my own eyes. It left a terrible impression, although I later learned that the Aromil rural soviet was much less brutal in its actions than was the case elsewhere. Those crowds of people driven out of their homes, the wild howling of the women, and the wailing of the children, were so awful that I did not recover for long after. I applied to leave the Komsomol. Neither the reproaches of my comrades nor the knowledge that I was condemning myself to oblivion could alter my decision. They expelled me. I had loved belonging to that large organization; now I was on my own. Next came my divorce, which had been brewing up for some time. I could not stay in Sverdlovsk anymore. In July 1930 I left for Shadrinsk, a town some three hundred kilometers away.

It had been a noisy existence in the Komsomol, with constant arguments and debates about what socialism would be like—our lives then would be fine, we had no doubt, and, most important of all, fair and just. Now, especially after divorcing my husband, I felt very lonely. One day a young man came up to me and we got into conversation. "Are you in the Party?" I inquired.

He looked at me intently. "Not the party of the Communists," he replied.

It was like a bolt out of the blue. I didn't know what to say: "How do you mean?"

He did not conceal his amusement: "Did you really think that all the other parties just vanished into some hole in the ground?"

I was not offended. All my time in the Komsomol, I never once had wondered, "Where had they gone, the political parties that existed before the 1917 October Revolution?" Now curiosity overwhelmed me. Who was he? What party had he belonged to? How had he ended up in Shadrinsk? I found out that he was an SR, a member of the Socialist Revolutionary Party. He had been exiled for organizing a student group, and his name was Arkady Stepanovich Petrov.

Later, when visiting him once, I found two other people there. One introduced himself as "Yegorov, Pavel Alexandrovich," to which Arkady added, "Left SR."

I sank into a chair: "Now I'm totally confused. SRs, Left SRs, Anarchists, Maximalists—it makes my head spin!"

"Don't worry," said Arkady, "Pavel Alexandrovich will tell you all about himself."

Later Pavel Yegorov would indeed tell me of his life in Kazan. He had attended the seminary there but left, without completing the last two qualifying years of study, and enrolled instead at Kazan University. In late 1917, when he was seventeen years old, he joined the Left SRs, and he remained loyal to that party until his death. His declaration of love came as a great surprise.

"I love you very much, Galina, and will do anything for you. But I have no intention of altering my status as an exile. I shall remain in prison and in exile until the authorities have ceased persecuting dissenters." After a pause he added, "Wives are not sent to prison in our country, but they have to deliver parcels there for their husbands." We married on 11 January 1931, and three days later Pavel was forbidden to live in a large number of towns.

Both of us thought it inconceivable to go somewhere else if none of our comrades were living there. Yet they were scattered, for the most part, in distant northern areas—to which, of course, we had little desire to go. We wrote to Nikolai Zheleznov, another SR, for advice. Although he could not be sure, he replied, the party "elders" had apparently been moved from Tashkent to Ufa. He recommended that we join them. By "elders" he meant the four Left SR leaders whom the GPU had not separated since the mid-1920s, when they were exiled together to Samarkand: Maria Spiridonova, Irina Kakhovskaya, Alexandra Izmailovich, and Ilya Mayorov. We were not at all confident of finding any comrades in Ufa. But we had little choice, so off we went.

On arrival, we applied to the city information bureau, and they gave us the addresses of Kakhovskaya and Spiridonova. It was close to 4 P.M. Since offices then closed at 3 or 3:30, we set out immediately to find Maria Spiridonova.

She and Ilya Mayorov lived in a large communal apartment. After the bright sunshine, we almost had to feel our way down the long corridor. One of the doors opened, and a small delicate woman came out. After a quick glance, Pavel said, "Good afternoon, Alexandra Adolfovna."

Alexandra Izmailovich looked at him hard: "Is that you, Pavel Yegorov? I recognize you from the photograph you sent us."

Still talking, we entered the room. Mayorov and Spiridonova were there; soon Irina Kakhovskaya appeared.*

By the autumn of 1933, Irina Kakhovskaya managed to rent quite a large apartment in a very old and decrepit little house standing above the Belaya River. We found a place to live nearby, on the very banks of the river

---

* Irina Kakhovskaya (1888–1960) was a member of the SR's Fighting Detachment and was sentenced in 1907 to 15 years' imprisonment. Released after the 1917 February Revolution, she organized assassination attempts on Eichhorn, the Kaiser's viceroy in occupied Ukraine, and against the White generals Denikin and Kolchak.

itself. Often, on our way back from work, we could not resist dropping in for at least half an hour.

An entire commune set up house in Kakhovskaya's apartment. In addition to the Novikov family, Alexandra Izmailovich, Nikolai Podgorsky, and Mayorov's son Lyova also lived with her. Spiridonova and Mayorov remained in their old apartment but would come, each day, right after work and share the evening meal. On weekends, others such as Boris Belostotsky dropped by, and mealtimes were noisy and cheerful occasions.

Kakhovskaya gave Lyova Mayorov all his lessons. He was an educated boy, advanced for his age, and no one doubted that he would pass the entrance exam for any institute. However, he was to face a quite different test. Arrested soon after the rest of us, he was broken, either under interrogation or in the camps. When Irina Kakhovskaya managed to trace him much later and send him a letter in 1957, he wanted nothing more to do with her.

Often we went on walks together, and each year Kakhovskaya led a large group of us, always accompanied by two or three GPU men, out into the forest to celebrate May Day. Once all of us went to the cinema and saw *The Captive Earth*. Afterward, we sat in the unheated summer room of Irina Kakhovskaya's apartment. "It's unbearable," commented Nikolai Podgorsky sadly, gazing into the distance. "Our country is no freer than it was before the Revolution, probably less so." The silence that followed was so tense that no one could help but feel it. Then Pavel and Boris Belostotsky started talking about the Kuban. Entire villages were full of boarded-up houses: most of the inhabitants had been deported to Siberia, to Narym or Igarka; some had died of hunger, and a few managed to escape to the towns. The terror had reached a catastrophic level. "I don't know how we can stand it," said Boris Belostotsky. But after a moment's silence he added, "Still, we're really very lucky! There aren't many people in the USSR who can get together and say all they think, without fear of being denounced to the GPU!" This was the everyday mood of the exiles. They did not expect that they would be allowed to say or do anything much in the near future, but they did not abandon hope altogether.

In the summer of 1936, I went away for a holiday. On my return I found a great many friends in our apartment. "Why are you all looking so upset?" I asked, sensing that something was wrong. "Haven't you heard? There's a trial going on." Grigory Zinoviev and a number of leading Bolsheviks were accused of planning to assassinate Stalin and several other Soviet leaders. Our friends were dumbfounded by this travesty of justice. How could the accused have publicly confessed to such crimes? Ilya Mayorov immediately said that Grisha Zinoviev had never been a decent person, and so there was no reason to expect him to behave properly now.

"Well, that's Zinoviev. But what about the others?" objected Kakhov-skaya.

The NKVD came to our apartment on the night of 7 February 1937. They arrested Pavel and conducted a thorough search, which ended at ten in the morning. It was our practice, once they were gone, to visit someone else and find out if other comrades had been searched, or only us. As soon as I was alone, I went to the Novikovs, who lived a few houses away. There I fell into a trap: they had eight "guests," and this time no one let me go. Someone drove off to the procurator and came back with a warrant for my arrest. Before I went to prison, I told them, I had to pack some clothing for Pavel and myself. They drove me home. There I washed, changed my clothes, packed for the two of us, and told them I was ready.

The interrogations began on 11 February. At seven or eight in the morning I was called out. But by nine A.M., when it was light, I was already back in the cell. The first cross-examination was only to acquaint me with the charges, and the next day was the interrogators' day off. On 13 February they began in earnest. The interrogations might go on for five days at a time, and I would return to my cell only on the morning of the sixth. The day off, I should add, was far more torment than the interrogation: "Don't sleep, don't sleep!" repeated the jailers (there were four of them for eighteen cells), as they peered through the peephole. Yet it was then that I wanted to sleep more than ever. During interrogation, a certain nervous tension was maintained either by the questioning itself or by the savage bellowing and obscenities that the interrogators used to wind themselves up and to stay awake.

An interrogator would cross-examine me until one or two o'clock in the morning. Then he went either to the buffet, to drink tea with brandy, or else home to sleep. His place was taken by a sergeant who only ever said one thing: "Don't sleep!" I do not remember the surnames of my interrogators. There were five of them during the whole period; one, it seems to me, was called Yapatov. They kept me on the "conveyer," under continuous interrogation, for a month.

What did they ask, you wonder? There were, in fact, few questions. More often they yelled at me, demanding that I "surrender," admit everything, and be truly penitent. One of the intelligible questions was about the political conversations we had. To begin with, I replied that they themselves knew better than I, since their agents had listened under our windows and handed in regular reports. My interrogators denied this. Later, however, they convincingly explained that they could use such information only for their own purposes. For the court, the participants themselves had to provide testimony.

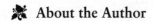

HAVA VOLOVICH

came my cellmate. As yet she knew little of prison, and compassion for another's suffering saved me from myself. Then I was taken to the transit block. On the way there we called in at the office, and I was informed that I had been sentenced to an unlimited period of exile in the Krasnoyarsk Territory. For me the news was like being born again.

In the transit block we were allowed to play checkers, but I could not join in. The almost daily interrogations had left their mark. Even the level of confrontation (no matter how innocent!) in a game of checkers reminded me of my interrogator's questioning.

Everyone must accept and obey the system unquestioningly, thought the country's rulers, and each Soviet prison was packed with those who obstructed this goal. Layer by layer, this "human material" was accumulated there and removed. During my three periods of imprisonment, I gained a thorough acquaintance with these "negative" layers.

In spring 1949 I was in the transit block of Kharkov Prison, which was yet again filled to overflowing. There I encountered what was for me a new category of prisoner—the followers of Stepan Bandera, the Ukrainian nationalist leader, or, to be more precise, the families of his former supporters. There were also, of course, the "second-timers," who by then formed entire groups in the transit cells, and the criminals. However, I most remember the strong, silent, dignified young women from the Western Ukraine, who viewed their surroundings with contempt. Among themselves, they maintained a friendly solidarity. Some wore blouses of rough homespun linen, and their hair was plaited and concealed by kerchiefs. They were handsome and strong, as though they had grown straight out of the land and the forests. They never squabbled over their food ration, accepting what they were given. At the same time, they stood their ground, and the criminal inmates kept well out of their way.

They did not mix with us, the "intelligentsia." Crossing themselves, they would whisper prayers, and sometimes they gathered together and sang. I can remember to this day the words of one of their songs:

Siberia, Siberia, so far away!
We shall go there on foot, and come home again,
And see our friends once more!

Of course, their songs also talked of prison, parcels from home, their mothers, and their far-off homeland; they sang of hope, memories, and love. These young women radiated a great inner strength and unbending determination.

The transit cell of Kharkov Prison was on the top floor, and was known among the prisoners as "heaven." It was narrow and long, with the toilet bucket by the door and open windows on the opposite wall. Fresh air rarely reached the other side of the cell, however, where, in accordance with prison tradition, the newest arrivals had to live. We lay squashed together. Someone was taken for transfer, and I moved nearer the window.

But I did not get my share of fresh air before my own journey into semi-freedom began, first to Kuibyshev and then on to Krasnoyarsk, Igarka, and Yermakovo, where I began my life as an exile.

Translation by John Crowfoot

ANNA BARKOVA

ELEVEN

Anna Barkova ——————
Selected Poems

❊ About the Author

*Anna Alexandrovna Barkova (16 July 1901–29 April 1976) was born in
Ivanovo-Voznesensk, where her father worked as a watchman at the gymnasium. Barkova was later to attend the same school herself.*

*She began publishing in local papers in 1918, and soon was able to
place her work with major literary journals. In 1922 the first and, as it
turned out, only collection of her poetry was published. Its title was* Woman, *and it had a preface by Anatoly Lunacharsky, People's Commissar of
Enlightenment.*

After moving to Moscow, Barkova went on to publish work in Krasnaya
nov, Novy mir, *and many other major literary journals; from 1924 to 1929
she worked for the Communist Party daily* Pravda.

*But then came difficult times. Barkova had a rebellious character, and
she was unable to keep silent or to say "yes" when her heart cried "no." In
December 1934 she was sentenced to five years in the camps. In 1939 she
was freed, but sent into exile; then in 1947 she was again arrested, and
given a further sentence, this time of ten years. She was sent to the Far
North, and it was there, in one of the camps, that we met.*

*There were many remarkable people in the camp where we were serving
our sentences, but even here Anna Alexandrovna's original mind and scathing tongue made her stand out.*

*She was a small, ugly woman, with a cunning look in her narrowed eyes;
she wore an oversized prison jacket and padded knee socks, and always had
a hand-rolled cigarette hanging out of her mouth. She didn't have any relatives "outside," so she had no one to send her parcels or money. But she
never complained; she was unfailingly courageous, and never lost her sense
of humor.*

Barkova was released in 1956, and went back to Moscow, but there was no welcome for her in the capital. All her efforts to get a residence permit or somewhere to live were in vain. Finally she agreed to go off with a friend of hers from the camps and find somewhere to live in the provinces. By this time Barkova was officially rehabilitated.

The friend was a dressmaker who worked from home. One of her clients decided to get out of paying a bill by denouncing this woman and Barkova to the authorities. Other "witnesses" also came forward to testify that the two had "disseminated slander about the Soviet press and radio." So in 1957 Barkova and her friend got yet another ten-year sentence—and all because of a bill for 120 rubles.

In 1965 Anna Alexandrovna was rehabilitated for this "crime." As someone in poor health without relatives to care for her, she was placed in a home for the disabled in Mordovia. However, after the intervention of two well-placed writers, Konstantin Fedin and Alexander Tvardovsky, she was able to return to Moscow. She was allocated a room in a communal apartment in the center of the city and a small pension.

Every morning ("It's like going to work," she would say) she went to the Dom Knigi bookshop on Kalinin Prospect; she spent her entire pension on books. Books filled her whole room. Someone had given her an old refrigerator, but she never turned it on; even that had been pressed into service as a bookcase . . .

Anna Alexandrovna offered her poems to several Moscow literary magazines, but no one would take them: they were "not life-affirming and lacked optimism."

Although she was a difficult and prickly person, Barkova was never lonely: her company was always in demand, and she was popular with young people too.

It is very difficult to track down Barkova's poems: many are probably lost for good. How many scraps of paper covered in her decisive, angular hand must have been swept up, scattered, and carried off by the "winds of Russia"!

IRINA UGRIMOVA
NADEZHDA ZVEZDOCHOTOVA

1.

Scarlet blood and yellow bile
Feed our life, and all we do;
Malignant fate has given us
Hearts insatiable as wolves,
Teeth and claws we use to maul
And tear our mothers and our fathers;
No, we do not stone our neighbors,
Our bullets rip their hearts in two.
Oh! Better not to think like this?
Very well, then—as you wish.
Then hand me universal joy,
Like bread and salt, upon a dish.

1925

2.

What's the point of faith to some fatherland,
Why pretend that we've one settled home?
Now, facing life's judgment, each one of us
Is merciless, indigent, strong.

With a sneer of disapprobation
We'll remember our fathers' mistakes;
We know now that our sainted relations
Were gambling for worthless stakes.

And with a slave's quiescence
We shall pay our blood-stained toll,
In order to build a useless
Heaven of concrete and steel.

Behind a door hooped with iron
In the dark of our tortuous hearts
A priest conducts godless rituals,
A suffering saint, and a liar.

1932

3.

In the Prison-Camp Barracks

I can't sleep, and blizzards are howling
In a time that has left no trace,

And Tamburlaine's gaudy pavilions
Strew the steppes . . . Bonfires blaze, bonfires blaze.

Let me go, like a Mongol tsaritsa,
To the depths of the years that have fled;
I'd lash to the tail of my steppe mare
My enemies, lovers, and friends.

And you, the world that I'd conquered,
My savage revenge would lay waste;
While in my pavilion the fallen
Ate the barbarous meats of my feast.

And then, at one of the battles—
Unimaginable orgy of blood—
At defeat's ineluctable moment
I'd throw myself on my own sword.

So I am a woman, a poet:
Now, tell me: what purpose has that?
Angry and sad as a she-wolf
I gaze at the years that are past.

And burn with a strange savage hunger,
And burn with a strange savage rage.
I am far from Tamburlaine's bonfires,
His tents are far away, far away.

>   Karaganda 1935

4.

The Heroes of Our Time

Our time has its own heroes,
Not twenty, not thirty years old.
Such could not bear this burden,
No!
We're the heroes, born with the century,
Walking in step with the years;
We are victims, we're prophets and heralds,
Allies and enemies.

We cast spells with Blok the magician,
We fought the noble fight,

We treasured one blond curl as keepsake,
And slunk to brothels at night.

We struck off our chains with "the people,"
And proclaimed ourselves in their debt:
Like Gorky, we wandered with beggars;
Like Tolstoy, we wore peasant shirts.

The troops of Old Belief Cossacks
Bruised our backs with their flails,
And we gnawed at the meager portions
Served to us in Bolshevik jails.

We shook when we saw diamond emblems
or collars of raspberry hue:
We sheltered from German bombardment
And answered our inquisitors, "No!"

We've seen everything, and survived it,
We were shot, beaten, tempered like steel;
The embittered sons, angry daughters,
Of a country embittered, brought low.

      (no date)

    5.

He lived in a cold back garret
In Judea, in ancient Greece.
"I shall borrow the warmth of a lamb's breath,
Warm my blood with a match's heat."

He gazed at the constellations,
Was a beggar, sang hymns to life;
Who murdered Osip,* life's lover,
Yet chose to leave me alive?

With all my heart I curse life,
But just as intently hate death.
Who knows for what I am searching,
Who knows for what reason I battle on?

---

* The poet Osip Mandelstam, who died in the Vladivostok transit camp in 1938.

No doubt on the Day of Judgment
I shall laugh to myself in contempt
When I hear the seraphs talk nonsense,
And see that their harpstrings are frayed.

The refuse of denunciations
Has been sifted by God himself,
And the acting Procurator
Is the Master and Chief of the Devils.

    1976

    6.

Forgive, O Lord, nocturnal spirits
(I don't remember who wrote this)

Forgive me, my nocturnal spirit,
Take pity now,
All around it's quieter, thicker,
The darkness grows.

I'm traveling to asphyxiation
To November fogs.
Forgive me my nocturnal spirit,
My only love.

Sleep. I'll eavesdrop on your reveries,
Full of disquiet.
Forgive me my nocturnal spirit
Wherever you are.

    21 January 1976

Translation by Catriona Kelly

TAMARA PETKEVICH

Tamara Petkevich ────────

Just One Fate

❧ About the Author

Tamara Vladimirovna Petkevich was born in Petrograd in 1920. During the Civil War, her parents fought in the same Red division: they were captured by White forces loyal to General Kolchak, but managed to escape.

In the 1930s Tamara's father was director of a peat works near Leningrad. In 1937 he was arrested. As the daughter of an "enemy of the people," Tamara was driven out of the Komsomol; only one school friend, Ilya Granovsky (later an eminent art historian), did not meekly raise his hand in favor of her expulsion. Tamara's life became intolerable. NKVD agents pursued her, urging her to become an informer. Finally, on her mother's advice, she left secretly for the Central Asian town of Frunze. There she married and enrolled as a student at the Medical Institute. Eighteen months later, during a lecture, the NKVD came for her. She was thrown into prison and, after lengthy interrogation, sentenced to ten years in a strict-regime labor camp.

Tamara's gifts as an actress would help her to survive later in the camps of the Far North, and the theater director Alexander Gavronsky, who was also a prisoner there, took her on as a member of his troupe. After her release, Tamara worked in the theater for several years. She now lives and works in Leningrad.

VLADIMIR GALITSKY

The night before our transfer from Frunze, none of us slept. They spent the time checking our documents, shaving our heads, and handing out our ration: 500 grams of bread and two stale, discolored herrings. The sun was already shining in the prison yard, and still we had not been lined up to leave. One of the women, determined (for some reason) to find out our destination, overheard that they were taking us to the Djangi-Djir women's camp.

"Any idea how far it is from Frunze?"

"Oh, about a hundred kilometers."

"What will we ride in?"

"Ride? You don't feel like walking, then?"

The reason for the delay soon became clear. A woman was brought out of the punishment block, her swollen face blue and yellow from a recent beating. She staggered and closed her eyes against the light; it was obvious that she had been given a very thorough going-over.

The young baby-faced commander of the transport shouted out in a piercing voice, "Everyone, look over here! Everyone! This freak tried to run! She'll get what's coming to her later. Now she's going to lead the lot of you, and if we make you walk an extra 70 versts, you've only got her to thank. Is that clear? I said, is that clear?!"

The woman, who took no notice of her surroundings, was placed at the head of the transport.

They counted us again. The square column, ten rows by four, surrounded by armed guards and dogs, was ready to leave. As we set off, the young commander yelled, "Try to run and we shoot! One step to right or left is an attempt to escape! Got it? I repeat: One step to the right or left, and you're dead."

The prison gates opened, and we marched out through the town. As the landmarks of Frunze disappeared behind us, it felt as though my emotions, everything that still made up my old life, were being physically and violently wrenched apart. What ungodly alien force was leading me off in this column, where and what for? Why must we submit to its demands?

On and on we walked. No one spoke to anyone else. Only the youthful commander continued to shout at the poor stumbling woman who was dragging herself along, in front of the column and ahead of the guards themselves.

Until about ten o'clock, the going was fairly easy. But gradually everything we had found so pleasant after four months inside—the air, wind, and sun—became a punishment. The light blue sky turned heavy and dark, and pitilessly poured its molten lava on our heads. Each step forward, and the constant wind, kicked up sand, which got in our mouths, eyes, and hair. Sun, sand; sand, sun. There was nowhere to hide.

We had already passed the limits of our strength and endurance, but we were not allowed to stop. One woman fell, then another. The guards shouted, "Stand up, or we shoot!" Those still unable to get up were heaved onto the two carts bringing up the rear. It was then we realized why they had been added to our transport.

I don't know how many kilometers we walked before we were allowed our first break and crawled under the carts, where the sunstroke victims lay covered in sacking. We dug into our bread and stale herrings, and since we were not permitted to drink, we turned away when the guards unscrewed their flasks and poured water down their throats.

My face was already burned by the sun; my skin throbbed as if covered with one large boil; and my swollen eyelids reduced my eyes to slits. "I brought out a Pole," laughed the commander, "and she'll be a Mongol when we get there!" Then we set off again, the sun dissolving everything in its path.

Exhaustion. An effort beyond endurance. The nightmare of that waterless frenzy!

I had no idea how much I could stand, and what would prove beyond me. I felt like some strange figment of the absurd. "Forget you're a woman!" the "lady in the caracul overcoat" had advised when she arrested me. Now I had an opportunity, it seemed, to forget that I was human, too. It was to keep this knowledge alive that I dragged myself on and on, driven by a crazed inhuman stubbornness that amazed me.

I was the youngest prisoner in the transport. Beside me walked old women. Each of us forced herself to the limit. If someone fell, she made no sound or complaint. Here you immediately realized that you were all alone. When night came we lay down on the earth and snatched a few hours' rest. "We can sleep when we get there," we all consoled ourselves.

The next morning we arrived at Djangi-Djir. The village stood to the left. Ahead of us loomed two large barracks and some outbuildings enclosed in rows of barbed wire. The four watch towers were manned by guards with machine guns. But it was not this which made the blood freeze in my veins and sent a chill creeping through me. There behind the barbed wire was a row of creatures, distantly reminiscent of human beings. They stood motionless in the blazing heat of the day.

Who or *what* were they?

Exhaustion, pain, and all other sensations receded and evaporated before this. We drew closer, and now we could make out more clearly: yes, not *what* but *who*; these were indeed human beings. There were ten of them, skeletons of various sizes covered with brown parchment-like skin, all stripped to the waist, with shaved heads and pendulous withered breasts. Their only clothing was some pathetic dirty underpants, and their shinbones projected from concave circles of emptiness. Women! Hunger, heat, and hard toil had transformed them into dried specimens that still, unaccountably, clung to the last vestiges of life. Is this what they brought us here for as well?

After we were let through the gates, it was impossible to avoid these parchment people. Walking past, we were amazed to hear intelligible human speech: "Are you from the outside? What is it like out there?"

"We don't know; we've been in prison for six months."

Then we were allocated our barracks. I was sent to the workers' barracks, where the walls were lined with two tiers of plank beds. There was no one in there but the barracks orderly. The others were still out in the fields.

The "shadows" followed me in. Three came up and touched me with their bony fingers.

"I've got a daughter like you out there," said one.

Others I reminded of a granddaughter or a sister. Some stood at a distance, gazing at the newcomers with numb detachment and a frightening gleam in their eyes.

How many limits, how many boundaries, had they already transgressed?

These women were classified as invalids. Many were deemed unfit for work and were due for release. Yet they remained in the camp and were still working, sitting on the plank beds in the invalid barracks spinning yarn.

I knew then that every sorrow I had experienced up to that moment was child's play, a lie, and a sham. This was the real thing, the truth, the first letter in the alphabet of human suffering and grief. I was shaking all over, whether out of compassion for these human relics or from horror, I do not know.

The prisoners at the Djangi-Djir camp did not work only in the fields. There was also a factory, housed in a large closed barn, with three looms for processing hemp. Another, similar machine stood in the middle of a field, operated by a separate work brigade.

The preparation of the cruder Deccan hemp was a more complicated business. A huge quantity was first stored in artificial reservoirs, where it would lie soaking for two or three months. During that time a thick white layer of seething worms appeared on the surface of the water. A wooden jetty was then built across the reservoir, and the hemp was laid on this and beaten with a wooden bat. The result was a dazzling silky white fiber.

Prisoners on this job became covered in cuts and wounds. The worms and the stinking water not only had an appalling effect on their hands and feet, but also left sores all over their wasted, skeletal bodies. We would implore the foreman and even go to the work distributor, begging them to let us off.

Both had recently been appointed. Our new work distributor was a beautiful Polish woman, Marina Ventslavskaya, who still bore all the traces of her former prosperity. The foreman, Mikhailovsky, was also Polish, and the only man in this all-woman camp. Both of them were prisoners, but they lived in their own quarters, not in the barracks. They were both fairly benevolent, and to all appearances were having a serious love affair.

Soon I was moved from the field brigade to the factory. It operated around the clock, and we all dreamed of the night shift, which brought some respite from the stifling heat. The drawback of this work was the innumerable needle-like fibers that worked their way into every pore of the body and stung unmercifully. It was impossible to shake them out of your clothes; you simply learned to put up with them, sleeping and waking, night and day.

The most difficult task in the factory was distributing the hemp stems over the shafts of the loom and feeding them in. That was now my job. The machines would roar and clatter, filling the building with a haze of dust and needles, and making it virtually impossible to see the woman who collected the fiber from the other side.

Through the roar, an unearthly, animal-like shriek would sometimes suddenly be heard. Exhausted by her twelve-hour shift, one of those feeding the machine had failed to extricate her hand (or both hands) from a noose of tangled hemp. The whole arm was pulled into the whirling steel shafts, and there was no time to stop the machine—or to help, either. The woman lost her arm, the blood gushed, and most often she died not long after.

Every once in a while they were late bringing the hemp. Then for some minutes work would halt. The machines stopped, one after another, and a sudden hush fell. We were allowed to leave the factory and lie on the compressed bales of fiber, which were ready to be taken away.

I shall never forget those moments. We lay surrounded by the fantastic moonlit night of Central Asia. It was as if we were floating in the clamorous sea of the steppe, which hummed with the rustling of sand and grass and the chirping of the cicadas. No one spoke. We were lulled by the warmth. Our half-starved condition prompted neither forgetfulness nor exaltation, but a feeling that you had disappeared and existed only in the sights and sounds of that vast universe.

At that time I was constantly haunted by several inexplicable associations. The roar of the looms conjured up the rumble of trains at the station in Leningrad when we set off for our summer holidays at the dacha. Each day when I reached the factory, I relived the same emotions I used to feel then.

I would give into the moment, pretending I was transported to the Rostov house in Tolstoy's *War and Peace*. I was Natasha hiding behind the flower pot before her meeting with Boris, and I dreamily immersed myself in her joyful mood of anticipation. The incomprehensible radiance of that scene descended on me, and it became my secret refuge from our everyday existence. It was as if I did not hear or see the reality of camp life.

But it did not let one out of its grasp for long.

The guards who took us out to work were all different. Some were good, but most of them were not. One was especially terrifying—young, cold, and sharp as a knife. People called him the Beast. It was said that he had recently killed a prisoner, after raping her, and that she was neither the first nor the last.

One night, he was sitting above us on some bales of fiber, with the moon shining into his face and his machine gun at the ready. I gazed up at him, without a thought in my mind. Suddenly I heard myself ask, "How many people have you killed?"

What made me say that? I have no idea. Everyone turned to look and held their breath. I sensed immediately how stupid I had been. The Beast did not lose his temper: "If I shoot you, that'll make five," he coldly replied.

The hemp soon arrived, and we had to get back to work. The women headed off to the toilet, which stood about thirty meters away. I was about to follow them when another prisoner touched my elbow: "Don't go! He'll say you were trying to escape; he couldn't give a damn."

I took her advice. And I was grateful, for not many prisoners had the energy for compassion then.

Soon our daily bread rations were reduced. The maximum was now 600 grams. Our clothing was scorched by the sun and tattered, and we were not issued any uniforms. The war went on, but we had no idea what was happening at the front.

Once I saw my reflection in a glass door at the medical unit. I did not immediately realize who it was. But there was nobody else around. I simply had not noticed myself turning into a skeleton. It was almost impossible to recognize anything familiar in that reflection.

The prisoners made different use of their daily bread ration. Some, like me, ate it all in the morning. The others divided it into three or more pieces, and made it last the whole day. They were probably the more sensible, for it meant that they had something to eat after work. When I came back from the factory, I would lie down immediately, to stave off the pangs of hunger with sleep.

Only once was I ever let off work, because of a high temperature. Apart from the barrack orderly, I was alone and lay on the top tier of the plank beds. Opposite me, next to the folded bedding of another woman, lay a 200-gram hunk of bread. No matter which way I turned, I could not get it out of my mind. The desire to eat was unbearable. Then, making myself stare straight at the bread, I forced myself to say, "That's someone else's bread! If I lay hands on it, I'm a thief! Never! Do without! Be patient. . . !"

The bread loomed insistently and mockingly before my eyes . . . Then I floated away from the suffocating pangs of hunger: I knew that I had escaped disgrace.

The food situation deteriorated still further. Bread supplies were erratic, the work was becoming unbearable, and we grew even more skeletal.

One evening after work, the foreman came into the barrack. We were all lying motionless on the planks, trying to conserve our energy. "Who wants to do some work at the collective farm? They need a new vegetable store built. They'll feed you for it."

After a pause, six women agreed to go.

"What about you?" He turned to me.

I knew this meant a chance of surviving, but it was so hard to get up. Overcoming my desire to stay put, I crawled down off the boards. It was seven in the evening, and the heat was abating as we walked the two kilometers to the farm.

There they explained that we had to make bricks first. We dug a trench, and mixed clay and straw. Some brought water, others dug out the foundation. We did things at our own pace. We had no norms to fulfill, no soldiers watching over us, and the work was not arduous.

They were pleased with what we'd done, and it was dark by the time they sat us down at a table under a canopy in the yard. Each of us received 200 grams of bread, and they brought out some salt, watermelons, and cucumbers. We had long since forgotten such things!

We heard children's voices, and the rattle of buckets and milk churns. A woman came home from milking the cow. A baby started crying. The lights went out in one of the houses.

Ordinary human life! How far we had come from anything of the kind . . .

Translation by Cathy Porter

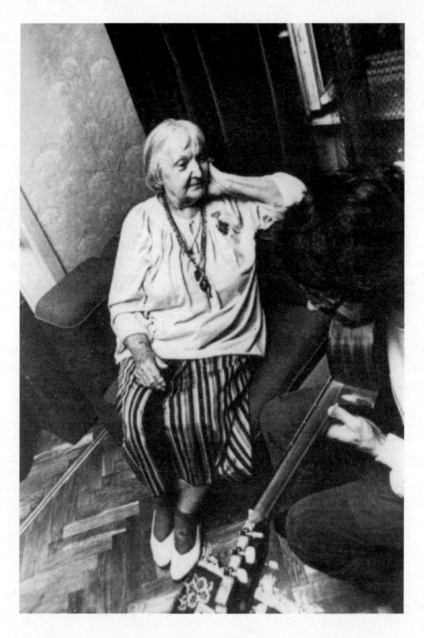

TATYANA LESHCHENKO-SUKHOMLINA

Tatyana Leshchenko-Sukhomlina—

Selections from "My Guitar"

🐾 About the Author

"How your words delighted me . . ." goes the old song. One can say this of few people, but Tatyana Ivanovna's words constantly delight with all the warmth, clarity, and sincerity of Russian speech.

Her family lived in Moscow and Pyatigorsk. Her mother, Yelizaveta Nikolaevna, a member of the Kostroma nobility, was a concert pianist and teacher. Her Cossack-born father, Ivan Vasilevich, a graduate of the Petrovsk Agricultural Academy and a pupil of Timiryazev, played the violin and guitar. And her uncle Vladimir Steklov, a mathematician and physicist, had a fine singing voice.

Between 1924 and 1935, Tatyana Ivanovna lived abroad. She graduated from the Columbia School of Journalism, joined the American actors' union in 1929, and appeared on the stage of New York's Theater of New Playwrights. Thereafter she moved first to Paris, then to Majorca and London, and in 1935 she returned to Moscow with her young daughter and her husband, the sculptor Dmitry Tsaplin.

During the war, Tatyana Ivanovna traveled around Siberia, singing and playing her guitar in the hospitals of Novosibirsk and Barnaul, and in 1943 she gave her first solo performances in Moscow. Then in 1947 came arrest, prison, and the camps at Vorkuta.

After her rehabilitation in 1956, she returned to Moscow, where she lives to this day. She translates from French and English. Her version of Wilkie Collins's Woman in White *has gone through many editions, and her translation of Georges Simenon's* The President *marked the beginning of her friendship with the author.*

Tatyana Ivanovna gives public concerts and has a large repertoire of ballads and old songs and songs she has composed herself. I help her with the accompaniments on my guitar. Recently, when I arrived at her apartment for our regular rehearsal, she greeted me: "I've got to leave, Seryozha. I'm acting in a film—they've offered me the part of the Queen of France!"

SERGEI CHESNOKOV
TATYANA LESHCHENKO-SUKHOMLINA DIED IN 1998. —SV

On the evening of 30 September 1947, I had returned home late from seeing Yelizaveta Khenkina. It was drizzling but warm, and the street lights were swaying in a haze of rain. I went in. My daughter Alyonka was already asleep, and I sat down in the kitchen to drink some coffee and play a game of solitaire.

It was after midnight when I heard the knock at the door. I went over and threw it open, assuming it would be my neighbor Zhenya wanting to make a telephone call. Instead I saw five people, including three men in military uniform, and a young woman (it turned out to be our janitor, who was evidently there as a witness). I silently stepped back, my first thought being that they were robbers. They followed me into the room, and one said, "Your passport!" Smiling, I said, "Thank heavens, I thought you wanted to rob me. You're checking passports? Here you are!" I passed it to them and they examined it. Then the soldier in charge produced a sealed document from his pocket and handed it to me. It was an arrest warrant. Suddenly everything went very quiet and empty, and the light seemed to shine more brightly. I slumped silently into a chair. There was a deep silence as I stared blankly at Granny's lace lampshade.

"What's the matter with you? Get packed!" they said.

"For how long?" I asked.

"I don't know. A week or two, maybe."

I packed a soft towel, a toothbrush, some soap, a change of underwear, and a pair of silk stockings. Then I changed into my best black dress and put my coat on.

"Let's go!" said the soldier.

"May I kiss my daughter?" I asked.

"Okay, but be quick!"

He followed me into Alyonka's room. She was asleep, and when I kissed her she moaned and stirred, and said, "Mama, where are you going?"

"I have to go out for a while. I expect I'll be back soon. Take care of your brother!" Then I left.

Outside the building a car was waiting. The streets were silent and empty as we drove to the terrible Lubyanka building, which I had always passed so blithely before. The soldier rang the bell, the door slammed behind us, and I was led into a tiny room with no windows, a naked electric light glaring on the ceiling, and one chair. The key grated in the lock, and that was the start of a long and senseless nightmare.

I have no words to describe that night. The worst thing was the noises that rang out into the sepulchral silence of the prison. The soldiers were not allowed to speak, and I could hear them signaling to each other by clicking their tongues. Then there was a sudden wailing, shrieking sound, which quickly died down. Apparently people shriek like that when they are suddenly taken off drugs.

All the lights were on, and the "box" in which I was sitting had no windows, so I lost track of the time and have no idea how long afterward it was that I was taken upstairs in the elevator. The sinister empty corridors and staircases were enclosed in wire netting to stop people throwing themselves down, as the authorities did not want us to kill ourselves.

I spent a month in the Ministry of State Security's prison at the Lubyanka, and was interrogated there by a young man named Captain Panteleyev, about whom I have no particular complaints. From the Lubyanka I was taken to the Lefortovo jail, where I spent another three months in solitary confinement. My cell on the third floor was roughly twelve foot by six, and from the little barred window I could see a small patch of sky and birds. After Lefortovo I was taken back to the Lubyanka, this time to a shared cell, but Panteleyev had now been replaced by a crazy, vicious, red-haired little rat named Lieutenant Colonel Polyansky. He was a sadist and a sex fiend, and his language was far fouler than that of any of the robbers I met later in the camps. One night toward dawn, after several nights without sleep, I said to him, "Now I know what you remind me of—a lynx! Even your color!" To be honest, I was merely exhausted and had not intended to offend him, but he was beside himself with rage, lunging at me, kicking my leg, and howling, "Now I know you're a spy!"

Two months later (Panteleyev was back again), I was led out to be cross-examined by the procurator, which must have meant that the investigation of my "case" was nearing its conclusion. The cross-examination was very mild, and I was amazed to discover that, in contrast to my previous interrogations, they had recorded my replies accurately. I thought I would probably get a maximum of five years, for I was still naive enough then to believe in justice. I said that I had been coerced into signing a confession based on Nadezhda Volynskaya's evidence against me, and I now demanded a meeting with her. I also lodged a complaint against Colonel Polyansky for striking me during the interrogation.

I saw Panteleyev pale, and when I was led out, he appeared beside me murmuring, "If only you knew what you've done!" In fact I had always sensed that despite his cruel questions, young Panteleyev felt sorry for me and even wanted to help me. Polyansky, on the other hand, was nothing but a cynic and a scoundrel.

One night a week later, I was taken out of my cell for yet another interrogation. As I entered a large dark office, Polyansky rose from behind his desk and came up to me, rubbing his hands and smirking, "At last I've got you to myself! The lynx will really go to work on you now! Complained about me to the Procurator, did you? I'll show you what happens when you tell tales about your interrogator!"

Later that night I was taken back to Lefortovo and thrown into a terrible solitary cell in the basement. Months of cruelty and delirium followed. Polyansky insulted me to his heart's content, punching me in the face, tearing my blouse to shreds, screaming at me, and threatening to shoot me.

For days on end I saw nobody but him, the guards, and soldiers. Once, in the middle of the night, he stared at me in silence for a long time, then said in a muffled voice, "You know what I'd like to do? I'd like to f**k you, then trample you into the ground!" I've remembered his words all my life. In fact he never touched me in that way, but I realized that I was in a madhouse and he was a maniac. I often heard the shrieks and groans and prayers of people being beaten and tortured beneath me in the basement.

On 11 September 1948, after a year in prison, with two three-month periods of solitary confinement, I was taken from Lefortovo to some mysterious destination.

On a heart-rendingly beautiful glowing autumn day, twenty male prisoners and I were driven in a Black Maria to what turned out to be the Northern Station. I had to sit separately from the others in the cramped pitch-dark cabin at the back of the van, but as we were driving along, a soldier opened the back door a crack, and through it I could see the lively streets of Moscow bathed in sunlight. Something like joy stirred within me. Anywhere would be better than prison!

Compared with Lefortovo, the jail at the Lubyanka had been a haven of peace, with proper beds rather than plank boards, and a parquet floor, not stone, as in my second period of solitary confinement at Lefortovo. Life was hard at the Lefortovo—gloomy, dark, and lonely, with nothing to do, all the books read and reread and learned by heart, and time weighing on my shoulders like a suffocating physical presence. Lord, if only I could do something! I used to think. Moving boulders would be better than this! To vary the monotony, I would pick fishbones out of my soup, tear off a strip of sheet, pull some blue threads from the edge of my towel, and do some sewing. I made six handkerchiefs there, some of which I gave away at the Kirov transit prison, but one of which I still have somewhere.

The soldiers, or rather guards, did not torment me, apart from one, a youngish man with the face of a deranged monster, who would peer at me for hours through the peephole in my door, occasionally opening it and coming in, or cursing me vilely from the corridor outside. One young soldier, a kind soul, used to find excuses to give me scissors and a needle and thread, for sewing was a good diversion. Once I asked to see the doctor and the dentist, and I was taken there and given some medicine. Receiving books and food parcels was an immense joy, of course, but this did not happen for a long time, and I discovered later that I had been forbidden for several months to receive parcels. I was desperately hungry, especially for sugar, and I could not help gobbling up my daily two lumps first thing in the morning with my tea. My bread ration I would cut into pieces with a piece of thread and eat throughout the day, to the last crumb. Every day the food was the same: soup, tea, and a little gruel with vegetable oil. Sometimes, especially after an interrogation, I would miss dinner, and the guards would bring me an extra-large helping or pour more oil into my soup. I was grateful to them, and knew they felt sorry for me. Prisoners were taken out for twenty minutes' exercise, and I never missed it once. It was terrible living in the basement, exposed to the shouts and screams of the interrogation rooms.

There was another cell behind mine, and when I was taken to the washhouse I would pass three other cells around a bend in the corridor. In one of these I once heard a man screaming to be let out. During the day I could hear a crazy German shouting wildly in German. The interrogators' offices were just across the corridor, and at night they could be heard cursing and yelling. The guards evidently put on phonograph records to drown the shrieks, for muffled groans and sobs would occasionally be mingled with the strains of music.

One day I was moved to a cell on the first floor, which was already occupied by an old woman and a young girl. The old woman had absolutely no idea why she was there, and talked incessantly of her daughter Frieda. The girl told me that an Abyssinian prince had fallen in love with her and asked her to marry him, but she had turned him down. Her parents had ordered her to stop seeing him, but she loved dancing and going to the theater with him, for even though he was black, he was exceptionally handsome. She had not liked the idea of living in Abyssinia, though, and had decided to marry a Russian instead. She had been studying English at the Institute of Foreign Languages, and it was there that she was arrested and taken to the Lubyanka, where she had spent five months.

That day all three of us were led out of our cell, taken downstairs to a "box," and called one by one into the office next door. The first to return was the old woman, half-dead with shock. "Ten years!" she said, wringing her hands. I was next. A stiff young man in civilian clothes with a totally expressionless face read out something from a piece of paper.

"Sorry, would you read it again? I didn't understand," I said, for I had grasped nothing of the strange words written there. He repeated, "Eight years in a corrective labor camp for anti-Soviet agitation. By verdict of the Special Board."

"Agitation?" I demanded. He nodded.

"What a sad job you have," I said thoughtfully.

He looked at me in silence, his face grim and motionless as before. "You understand what I have read out to you?" he asked after a pause.

I replied: "Eight years—I get eight years in . . . what do you call it?"

"A corrective labor camp," he replied.

I said nothing. He looked at me again as though he were a million miles away; then the soldier led me back to the "box." I felt nothing. The other day I had told my cellmates of a dream I had had in which some people were seated around a table arguing about whether to give me eight years or five, and I thought it would be five. The young girl came in last, sobbing with rage, and said, "Two years' exile in Kolyma! I'm ill—I have TB! It's monstrous! What for?" At this I burst into tears. But I felt sorrier for the poor old woman. At that moment I wished that I were the only one to be suffering, and in years to come I often recalled the sadness I felt at being surrounded by such unbearable quantities of human grief. I felt this especially keenly some five years later, when they started handing out sentences of twenty years' hard labor merely for trying to escape from exile. I was at a transit prison at the time, and they started bringing in women and girls devastated by grief, facing the prospect of twenty years away from their children, their husbands, their families . . .

Things became a little easier after we returned to our cell, where we wept and comforted one another that things were bound to change, that they were sure to reduce our sentences and let us go home.

A few days later, we were again called out one by one and sent off. I hugged the sobbing old woman. I never met her again, and will never know if she ever saw her Frieda again. I kissed the girl, saying, "Don't you dare be sad—you've got exile, and for only two years! Make the best of it!" I never met her again, either. I was the last to be called. I wrapped my tiny bundle of things in my towel. The black high-heeled shoes. The black dress. Nothing for my head.

"All the best!" said the prison governor, who was supervising our departure.

"Thanks!" I responded.

The dazzling brightness of the street embraced me in its warm September arms. The prison was finally in the past.

We were taken out of the Black Maria at some railway lines behind the Northern Station, where a prison car was standing on a line parallel to a pale blue express train. The guards clapped a pair of handcuffs onto one of the prisoners, a squat, stocky man with dark hair, a rough beard, and narrow eyes blazing like coals, and he laughed, radiating strength and toughness. Later, at the Kirov transit prison, our surnames were called out, and he turned out to have several. "Aka or Also Known As Potyomkin," they called him. "Aka Potyomkin" then strutted like a lord around the large waiting room where the newly arrived prisoners had to spend the next two or three hours together. Someone whispered to me that he was an "Article 59-er." I had no idea then what that meant, but later, when I learned what the most important articles stood for, I discovered that Article 59 was for "armed robbery with murder," and that the man had innumerable previous convictions on his record.

We were loaded onto the prison truck, and I found myself in a car with barred windows looking out onto the corridor, whose windows were also barred. It was occupied by a young woman and about seven young girls. At the sight of these girls, I threw my arms around them, sobbing, for they reminded me of my Alyonka, and I finally realized that I was being taken away from her, from my home, and from Vanya, possibly forever. I must not die there, I told myself; I must see them again, I must survive!

The most terrible part was over, prison and interrogation were behind me, and now I was gripped with a fascination for everything about the new life unfolding before me, and for the land and people where I would be living. Yet my heart was seized with anguish at the thought of losing my children, my parents, my sister, and my friends. My children, my children! My past had sunk without a trace.

At the Kirov transit prison, I remember making friends with a young Moscow woman named Yevgeniya Schmidt, who wanted to hang herself. I said to her, "A million rubles wouldn't buy you a ticket for this. It's fascinating! And they feed you for free. . . !" She didn't hang herself. A former Moscow dancer, she worked at the "Gornyak" camp as a loader, swineherd, and stoker at the bathhouse and the bakery. She used to smuggle out potatoes in her coat for Lena Ilsen and me, and we would boil them and eat them with our bread-in-water. It must be said that although she had previously been a rather spoiled and capricious young woman, she proved herself in the camp to be a loyal, hard-working person and a good comrade.

On my first or second night at the barracks at Vorkuta, they asked me to sing, and it was a joy to do so again, and to see the women criminals weeping with happiness. But by then I was so weak that I had to be packed off to the sickbay, where I slept continuously for two months.

Afterward, they arranged for me to do an audition at the Vorkuta theater, and as a result I was taken into the cast. This was a great stroke of luck, for it meant working in a warm building and countless other benefits, and we staged shows that earned praise even from jaded theatergoers used to the best Moscow theaters. We had some extraordinarily talented people working with us, and we not only loved our theater but were terribly grateful to it, for it was our refuge and afforded us some contact with art. Not by bread alone . . .

Before me I see a long line of actors, singers, musicians, and scene-shifters. My closest friend there was Yevgeniya Dobromyslova, an elderly intellectual who had been arrested in Leningrad merely on the basis of her "origins." She was a marvelous pianist, and like me she had a touching faith in rumors of our imminent release. She soon died of food poisoning.

The star of the cast was an enchanting, slightly crosseyed Moscow ballerina by the name of Lola Dobrzhanskaya, whose husband, an actor called Martinson, still prospered in Moscow. Brilliant and sharp-tongued, Lola had lived purely for her own pleasure, but had had the misfortune to fall in love with a handsome foreigner. As she lay dying of polar jaundice, she asked me to contact her son Sasha in Moscow if I survived, and to give him greetings from his mother. When I was released, I did so.

After Yevgeniya Dobromyslova's death, Lola became my best friend. The criminals worshipped her, as did everyone in the theater. She was a dashing hussar, fearlessly leaping onto the stage from great heights, to be caught in midair by the Moscow dancer Vanechka Bogdanov, another prisoner. She was buried, yellow as saffron, in a coffin that her theater friends had lined with silver paper, and following prison rules, she was accompanied to her grave by just one soldier.

Georgy Zhiltsov, a teacher from the Chita region of Siberia, had been arrested as a Trotskyist in 1937 and sentenced to ten years in Vorkuta. After his sentence was completed, he was permanently exiled to the region and stayed to work in the theater as chorus master. Needless to say, he was never a Trotskyist. A gruff, severe old man, he was demanding and meticulous in his work, but in his time off he was a clown and a joker who drank to excess. In 1950 he finally drank himself to death—may he rest in Heaven, if it exists, for his life here on earth was hard indeed.

Kolya Soroka had escaped from a German prisoner-of-war camp and gone to Italy, where he joined the partisans. After the war he returned home, where he was immediately packed off to "voluntary exile" in Vorkuta. He played the violin, and after Zhiltsov's death he became our chorus master. Kolya was always very good to me, and once when I had the scurvy, he brought me a little bag of potatoes. He was in love with a beautiful Baku dancer named Almaza Balta. He hanged himself one day in January 1951. May he also rest in peace.

Kostya Ivanov, a Leningrader, had also escaped from a German POW camp and ended up at Vorkuta, but in the camp. A handsome, talented actor, an intellectual and a good person, he hanged himself in despair in 1950 in the attic of the theater. How sad it all was. I can see him so clearly now, walking past me that day in the corridor with a face like a thunder-cloud, and I longed to run up to him and say a kind word to him, but did not dare. When my fellow prisoners were being taken back to the camp, they couldn't find him at first, and were about to announce an attempt to escape . . .

I have warm memories of so many good, intelligent people and talented actors—Valentina Tokarskaya, Rafail Kholodov, and many more—but the most talented of them all was undoubtedly Izrail Vershkov, or Izya.

When Izya was arrested, he was just 23, a "Stalin scholarship-boy" and a third-year student at Moscow's State Theater Institute. Clever, good-looking, and innocent of any crime, he was charged under Article 58:10 (anti-Soviet agitation), given eight years in a camp, and sent off to Vorkuta. "You must play Romeo," his teacher Zavadsky had said to him at the institute before he left.

He came from a poor Jewish family in Kiev, where his father was a tailor. When he arrived at Vorkuta, a fellow prisoner named Doctor Nimburg, from the camp hospital, called me in to introduce me to Izya and begged me to persuade Marmontov, the theater's manager, to take him on. I agreed at once, for I confess that I have an infallible eye for talent. Marmontov immediately started giving Izya the leading roles, and people in the theater and the town loved him. His mother, a young Ukrainian beauty, once came to Vorkuta and managed to have a secret meeting with him. One evening after the show—he was playing the lead in the operetta *Akulina*—I saw him standing in the wings looking very sad, and he said, "I so much want to talk to you, Tatyana Ivanovna. Can I meet you in the library tomorrow?" That morning, as the prisoners were being taken to the theater, he ran out to help push a truck out of a snowdrift, and it crushed him to death.

Prisoners and non-prisoners alike wept for this poor boy, barely twenty-five years old, crushed, like millions of the best people in Russia, by the evil epoch of Stalin. In June, when the snows had melted, his mother came, no longer young and beautiful now but an old woman. She collapsed by the staircase in the theater and crawled up the steps, sobbing, "This is where his feet once trod. . . !"

What oceans of human tears!

During our midday break at the theater when we were taken back to the prison, I would sometimes plead that I had to practice an accompaniment or transcribe some notes, and would give vent to my grief on the piano. Music could not heal the suffering, but it had a wonderfully soothing effect. I also wrote poems—or rather, they sang inside me and wrote themselves.

I was well treated at the theater, even by strict old Marmontov. He had a sense of justice, as we had several occasions to observe, and although he was curt with us, he was unfailingly correct. There was no place for intrigues or boorishness at the theater, and since informers did not flourish, the management must have actively discouraged it.

The sets were all painted and constructed by an exceptional Moscow theater designer named Bendel, who was assisted by several scene-shifters, all of them prisoners.

We had two conductors, Vielgorsky from Kiev and Mikosha from Moscow, both of them prisoners, professional musicians, and good people. Our chief director was a non-prisoner by the name of Nikolai Bykov, an actor from Moscow's Kamerny Theater, a highly educated man and an excellent director. He had kind, intelligent eyes, but naturally we never had a close relationship with him. We used to rehearse in the morning and perform almost every evening, and we had a huge repertoire, which included the operas *Yevgeny Onegin, Rigoletto* and scenes from *Prince Igor,* as well as a number of operettas such as *The Merry Widow,* and a list of Soviet and classical songs too long to mention.

Vorkuta was a grim town. Blizzards would rage as though the earth were howling in mortal agony, and the wind would roar and lash as one stumbled along, thrusting one's chest into the maelstrom, gasping, falling, getting up again, blindly feeling the way, grasping on to life with all the fibers of one's being, and knowing that to stop meant death.

I would have to return from the theater to the camp in the middle of the night. I had a long way to go, across the river and over several hills, and all in the pitch dark, with not a soul in sight, and with only the shafts of light from the electricity station lighting the darkness as it loomed above the town and the river like a ship sailing into Eternity.

At that time the dressmaker and I were the only two women prisoners in the theater, and I had just been allowed to go on my own from the camp to the theater with no guard, following a prescribed route and returning late at night. I was terrified. It was seven kilometers in savage frosts and storms.

Sometimes the green northern lights flickered and dissolved in the night sky above my head.

I remember once in a blizzard collapsing on the road from cold and exhaustion, and howling into the wind at the fear that I would lack the strength to get up and would freeze to death under a snowdrift. The thought of my children forced me to get up and continue on my way, and when I finally arrived back at the camp, the guard at the gate said, "We thought you didn't make it . . . "

On Christmas Eve 1950, a party was organized for the non-prisoners at the theater, and I took a fir branch back to the camp to cheer up the primeval chaos of our huge women's barracks beside the Vorkuta River. That night the building had been broken into by a gang of murderers and thieves, who had raped the women, then fought among themselves.

(I saw many murderers, men and women, and I think I can spot them by their faces, a certain deadness in the eyes).

There were not many of us politicals in the barracks. I and the dressmaker Yelizaveta Mikhailovna lived there permanently and had passes to work at the theater, but since this was a transit camp, most of the others kept coming and going.

The moment I went in that night, I was struck by how quiet and clean it was. All the women were kneeling on the floor. A group of politicals from the Western Ukraine had been brought in two days before, and now everyone was kneeling and the Ukrainians were singing hymns. I shall never forget the beauty of their singing, in four-part harmony, without music. As we listened to them, even the most terrible "lifers" fell silent and became human for a while. Then we moved the tables together and spread them with white sheets, and each of us contributed some little treat. We put my fir branch in a bottle, hung it with sweets and even a tangerine, and put the end of a candle on top and lit it. Then we sat down at the table, and everyone was quiet and at peace as food and mugs of tea were passed around . . .

Translation by Cathy Porter

HAVA VOLOVICH

FOURTEEN

Hava Volovich —————————————

My Past

🔥 About the Author

*Hava Vladimirovna Volovich was born in 1916 in the small town of Mena,
in the Ukraine. After leaving school, she worked for a while as a typesetter,
then as a sub-editor with a local newspaper. She was arrested in 1937.*

*After her release from the camps in 1953, she spent three years in exile
before being allowed to return home. Here she had various jobs, looking
after pigs, and working as a night watchman and a stoker at a factory; she
also ran an amateur puppet theater at the local Palace of Culture. Today she
still lives in Mena.*

Simeon Vilensky

When I was young, I dreamt, like nearly all the young people of my
generation, that when I grew up I would get a job working a lathe in a big
factory somewhere. When I was twelve, I actually tried to join a factory
"college"—a misleading term, because all they taught was how to make
stools—but they wouldn't take me on. This didn't bother me for long: making stools was far too prosaic; it smacked of a cottage industry. What I
needed was a big factory, with smoke pouring from the chimneys—that, or
somewhere where I could fell trees in the snowy taiga (I'd seen something
like this once in a movie). Or—and this was the height of my fantasies—
I wanted to go on an expedition somewhere, anywhere—to Africa or to
the Arctic.

Later I was to have a basinful of it. Woodcutting in the taiga, Arctic cold
(it was just as well for me that there's nothing comparable to Africa in the
Soviet Union). "Go to it!" they used to urge us in the 1930s: dig mines and

build factories and towns in Siberia and the frozen North. Well, I went to it, but it turned out to be as inspiring as a punch in the face.

In 1931 I passed the graduation exams for the seven-year school. That same year, they opened a printing press in the nearby town, and my father fixed me up a job there as a trainee typesetter. God, when I think how pleased I was with that job at first! I used to walk home with my red scarf and my inky nose, all puffed up with pride and self-importance. I wanted everyone to see that I was a worker, one tiny cog in the great machine of proletarian dictatorship.

In those years a hail of directives, decrees, statutes, and regulations was raining down from the Kremlin. I spent days at a time setting the texts; these were my first lessons in political literacy. And that's not all. I learned where babies came from that way too. Seriously. While I was setting a directive on putting mares to the stallion.

In 1932 and 1933, life became increasingly difficult. Horses wandered the streets looking like skeletons, their skins a mass of scabs. The peasants had nothing to feed their horses, so they would take them to other villages or into town and abandon them like so many unwanted kittens or puppies. Peasants who wouldn't join the collective farms had every last kernel of grain taken away; all their potatoes, and even their dried beans, were seized. In the hunt for concealed grain, the authorities would pull apart stoves and sometimes demolish entire houses.

By 1933 there were no private peasant farms left, let alone any kulaks. So then they started to "dekulakize" the collective farmers themselves. Every individual collective farm member now had his own grain production norm, not just the collective farm as a whole. Never mind the fact that individuals had no land beyond a tiny allotment for vegetables. There weren't fixed overall norms; so as soon as the basic norm was completed, they slapped a "voluntary" one on top of it.

These "voluntary" norms were a typical example of the criminal lies that lay like a black cloud over those dreadful years. The idea was that the collective farms—that is, the peasants themselves—were dissatisfied with the "insultingly small" norms they had been asked to fulfill, so they volunteered to hand over every last kernel of grain. As though we were talking not about "our daily bread" but about chocolates, something you could perfectly well live without. And those responsible for perpetrating this lie strode around the villages confiscating everything they saw. They even took the very last loaf, which was made half from flour and half from goosefoot and bark. They shoveled up the seed corn from the collective farms' grain bins. If people said, "We haven't any," they would answer, "There's no such word as 'haven't'! You're stuffing your own faces and don't want to give the state a share."

It was like a cholera epidemic—people dropped like flies. But it was hunger, not cholera, that was killing them. Do people still remember this? I don't know. They don't talk to me about it.

The sister of a friend of mine, a girl of fifteen, "fell in love with" a policeman. "Love" isn't the right word, of course: Dunya was trying to find a way to keep from starving. At sixteen she gave birth to a baby daughter, and her husband sent them home to his father, who was a parish priest in some distant village.

A year later, back Dunya came to her mother. Her husband's parents had been sent into exile, but since her marriage hadn't been officially registered (she was then underage), she was left behind. Dunya had been cast to the four winds. The village authorities wouldn't let her leave with one crumb of bread or a single stitch of clothing. One of the activists grabbed the blanket the baby was wrapped in, tipped the child out on the bare bedstead and flung the blanket on to the pile of confiscated goods.

You can get used to your own troubles, as you can to a chronic illness. It's other people's misfortunes that sometimes make you cry. No, it wasn't Dunya's troubles that got to me. She left her baby with her mother and went off to find something better. Her father died, and the whole family was starving to death. If the mother got hold of any food, she gave it to her own children. She gave Vera, her granddaughter, nothing: that way she'd die quicker.

Verochka turned into a living skeleton, with a coat of whitish fluff covering her yellow shrunken skin. Day after day she lay in her cot, eyes wide open like shining glass buttons on her corpse's face. But still she would not die. Her mouth, which hadn't yet learned to form the word "mama," whispered "issi"—she wanted something to eat.

I was the only person in my family who was getting a ration—thirty pounds of flour a month. It was a reasonable amount for one, but far too little for a family of seven. The only way we could make it last two weeks was by preparing a thin gruel with it, flavored with goosefoot and sorrel. But often even this miserable meal stuck in our throats. Crowds of starving people from villages farther south would gather around the window, rending our hearts with their long-drawn-out piteous wails of "Give us, give us, hungry!"

I saved Verochka a small share of my food if we had anything to eat at home. She would fasten her skinny hands (they were like chicken feet) on the bowl and swallow the contents in seconds. Then she would point at the window. My friend would carry her out and put her down on the grass in the sun. Verochka would roll over on her belly in an instant. With her yellow old woman's hands, she'd start snatching at the grass and stuffing it in her mouth.

That child was made of iron!

A grass diet finished off many, many other children and adults. But Verochka survived; she lived on into better times and turned into the most gorgeous little girl. (Later on, when I saw people in the camps with pellagra, I remembered Verochka lying on the grass, and marveled at how her infant brain had hit on this way of staving off malnutrition.)

As I set the texts letter by letter, I would think about what they said, and try to grasp what it all meant. "Grain levy." "Voluntary norm." The phrases were commonplaces of the time. But what terrible things they concealed.

"Voluntary norm" meant collective farms ruined before they'd had a chance to get started. "Grain levy" meant crowds of starving people wandering from place to place in search of food. It meant hundreds of deserted villages. It meant corpses on the streets, abandoned children, heaps of naked skeletons on hospital wagons (no one even bothered to cover them with a sheet) that were carted straight to the graveyard, then tipped like rubbish into the same pit.

I always tried to use the long way back from work, round by the vegetable gardens and the cemetery, rather than going the more direct way down the main street. I couldn't bear having to avoid the eyes of starving people all the time. But once I saw a little boy about six years old by the cemetery fence. His greenish puffy face was covered in cracks, out of which some kind of liquid was oozing; his bloated, cracked legs were running in it too. Something green and wet was trickling out from under his homespun trousers. It must have been the grass he'd just eaten. His stomach had atrophied, and he could no longer digest anything at all.

The boy stood immobile. From his half-open mouth came a thin cry: "ee-ee-ee!" It wasn't a call for help; he didn't expect that from anyone. He'd seen adults—who were supposed to take care of children, not exterminate them—come and snatch his family's last crust of bread, condemning them to death by starvation. People were enemies; he was afraid of them. And so he'd come away from the busy streets, where there was nothing for him, to the cemetery fence, perhaps hoping to find something to eat. But it was death that had found him.

Did the bread they snatched from such children's mouths help Soviet industrialization in those years of world economic crisis, when even in rich countries grain couldn't find a buyer and so was dumped in the sea? I don't know. But I doubt it. The grain lay rotting in the elevators. But instead of returning at least some of it to the people, they opened a gigantic distillery and began pouring vodka down the throats of those still capable of drinking and still able to afford it.

The Great Wise Chief didn't want the people to think he was the Big Bad Wolf. He understood that he had laid it on too thick. That was the reason behind his famous article "Dizzy with Success" [written by Stalin and published in *Pravda* 2 March 1930]. This shifted all the blame from the wise leader to "those who couldn't think straight," that is, the local authorities. Yet these authorities didn't even dare breathe without orders from above, and they would bust their guts as soon as a directive arrived! Correction: it wasn't their own guts they'd bust; it was other people's.

No one in authority, from the village right up to the leaders of the Soviet republic, dared to lift a finger without a command from the Chief. But as the commands rolled down, they ran smack into whole dung heaps of servility and careerism, becoming encrusted with "voluntary" this and "additional" that; these, in turn, brought agriculture to rack and ruin, and caused hundreds of thousands of deaths by starvation.

Of course, it was hardly my miserable business to pass judgment on leaders and geniuses. Nor did I. But my naive belief in the inviolability of the truth was such that I spoke quite openly and frankly about what I saw with my own eyes.

By now I had been transferred to editorial work. The reason was that the copy and sub-editing were done by unqualified people, who often weren't too strong on grammar and spelling (the colleges taught such things in slipshod fashion in those days). The translations from Russian into Ukrainian were done roughly. I would stand in front of my typesetter's frame, alter the punctuation marks, get rid of the grammatical howlers and the worst stylistic errors (though that wasn't my job at all), and correct the translations. I even wrote a couple of columns myself. They really weren't too bad; they certainly were up to the standards of our local rag.

And when yet another copyeditor, this time a mathematician by profession, left his job to go and work in a school, the chief editor promoted me. That was how I set off, in all innocence, to meet catastrophe. I don't want to say anything, good or bad, about my former colleagues. I hope that they're enjoying a peaceful old age, if they've survived to see it; if they haven't, may they rest in peace. But I'd have been better off spending my whole life humping type than to experience what petty envy people feel at someone else's success.

The editor praised the copy I wrote, and had it sent straight into print without any corrections. Then he slammed the literary efforts of two of his own colleagues, young men with whom I'd enthusiastically read Ostrovsky's *How the Steel Was Tempered* and sung "The Cool Morning Greets Us" ("The Factory Siren calls us to work . . ."). Now they were my enemies.

"I've worked here for twenty-five years," said the head of the print shop, "and no one's ever said I'm good enough to be given a 'clean' job. But this little girl don't even have to work two years before they stick her with the intellectuals!" I often caught the machinist at that old printer's trick, switching the type around so that the words become a dangerous political joke. I once had a real row with him about it.

But my worst enemy was my own tongue.

The year 1935 was one of relative calm and prosperity, a year of triumphalist hymns. But everyone had been shocked by Kirov's murder in December 1934. Then there was the first wave of the Great Terror; day by day came more and more outbursts of slavish reverence and love for the Leader. Finally, they started executing the heroes of the Civil War, the Revolution, and the first years of the Soviet state.

There was reason to be shocked; and there was reason to be thoughtful. These were the heroes of our childhood. They hadn't feared for their own lives; they'd spilled their blood for the Soviet state. Now, suddenly, on the threshold of its final triumph, they had become enemies.

I had not entirely stopped using my head, so doubts stirred. I consulted my elders and the chief editor about them. No one could tell me anything; they just advised me to keep quiet. "They don't condemn people for nothing in this country!" others were saying.

The atmosphere in the office become unpleasant, oppressive. The lies weighed me down. There were lies at every step. I'd be sent to interview some old partisan or model worker on a collective farm. He would have his say, then I would have to write something different altogether.

In the summer of 1937, dreadful events began happening in our district. All the district chiefs bit the dust, including my chief editor, a man for whom I had the greatest respect. I couldn't stand living there anymore. Just then, Valentina Khetagurova's article calling girls to go and work in the Soviet Far East appeared in the newspapers. I decided I would go. I was tired of merely reading about great construction projects: I wanted to go along and build something myself.

My family's protests, my mother's tears, were all in vain. I began visiting the local NKVD to arrange a permit to travel to the Far East. I knew everyone in our small town, but one day I saw two unfamiliar NKVD men in the commandant's office.

I never went back home.

Well, there you have it. They had to take some people all warm and sleepy from their beds at night. I went along myself, and spared them the bother.

Everything that happened to me after that fateful day, 14 August 1937, was like a dream. And just as in a dream, I didn't so much directly experience what was going on as observe it from a distance.

Like many other people who went through the same experience, I didn't think that they would keep me long. Yet at the same time I understood that my life was ruined for good. I held the commonly held belief that even the shortest stay in prison brands a person forever. I was still curious to learn what was going to happen to me. But when I got to know the interrogator and realized what they wanted from me, this childish curiosity was replaced by a quite adult feeling of doom and despair.

To my astonishment, the cell where they put me was light and clean. There were six beds, each covered with an old flannelette quilt. Six women's faces turned toward me, six pairs of eyes.

Behind me, the guards were bringing in another bed and more bed-clothes. The door slammed shut, and I stood where I was on the threshold, not knowing what to do next. The women welcomed me delightedly; they made my bed, let me wash up, and offered me something to eat. I refused the food. I hadn't had a bite for two days, and the very thought of eating made me feel sick.

Who were they? What were they here for? I looked to be the baby among them. What could that statuesque woman with the gray streak in her brown hair have done? She was lying on her bed smoking a home-rolled cigarette and gazing at me calmly from under her puffy Chinese-looking eyelids. No doubt she was a fervent Trotskyist. Or maybe that other woman was, that one with the long plaits. She had a glint of gray in her hair, too, though her face still looked very young.

No doubt they all had something on their conscience; they must have, for they'd obviously been here for ages, their faces were so pale and drawn. I was a shorn lamb among these women! I hadn't done anything wrong, and I would soon be out of here.

"What are you here for?"

What should I reply? If I said I didn't know, they would never believe me. The warmth, friendliness, and support with which they'd greeted me would all evaporate. And I needed all that so badly. They would say, "They don't put people in here for no good reason!" and start shunning me as a liar. If these kindly criminals were to accept me as one of them, I had better think of something quickly.

"Sabotage," I said modestly.

"What kind of sabotage?"

"Arson!"

But oddly enough, instead of flinging themselves at me with open arms, the women drew back and went on with their own private affairs and con-versations. No one paid the slightest attention to me after that. I was crest-fallen.

I felt very tired after the two days I'd just been through, and when the signal to sleep sounded and the women started getting into bed, I lay down too. But scarcely five minutes later, the guards came for me. I was loaded into a prison van and taken off to the interrogator. It was the same man who had arrested me. He was obviously responsible for gutting his own fish.

I had a vague idea of what they wanted by now. Back in the district office, he'd asked me about my relationship with the editor—or, as he put it, "your criminal links with this Ukrainian nationalist and chauvinist." I was flabbergasted: what, our editor a nationalist and chauvinist?

If that was so, then why on earth had he defended me from the loutish junior Party officials, from that pig of a machinist, and from the manager's filthy abuse? Why had he given my father coupons to buy shoes and trousers in the special Party shop, when he had no decent shoes himself during the summer? Because he was a kind man, and kind people couldn't possibly be criminals. He was the most honest, the most honorable man I knew. What kind of fool could slander him as a nationalist and a chauvinist?

"Tell me about the organization you and the editor belonged to. I need the names of the other members of this organization."

What an idiot this interrogator was! I would explain to him that there couldn't be any "organization" in our small town. Things were simply too ordinary for that. The people were too busy trying to earn a living; the authorities had plans to think about. Everyone adored Stalin and condemned the enemies of the people. Where on earth would a subversive organization get its members from? But he just wouldn't believe me; over and over again he asked the same questions, stopping only when he got sick of the whole thing himself and started wanting his dinner.

But today's interrogation brought a new question: "Did you not say that voluntary norms were ruining the collective farms?"

"Yes, I did. But it's the honest truth!"

"You had the nerve to criticize the Party?"

"But it wasn't the Party that thought up the norms, individual members did."

"You're too young to reach conclusions like that by yourself. Who gave you such ideas?"

"No one. I made up my own mind."

"Against whom was your terrorist campaign to be directed?"

"If I had joined some organization, I certainly would never have picked a terrorist group. I can't even bear to squash a beetle."

"One of your girlfriends has testified: 'In 1935 Volovich decided to steal a revolver from the editor in order to engage in terrorism . . .'"

"How interesting! I belong to the same organization as the editor, but I decide to steal his revolver? He could have simply given it to me! And if she's such a patriot, then why didn't she report that right away, in 1935?"

"We have already taken steps. She has been arrested for withholding information."

"Can I see her?"

"We will allow you a meeting at the appropriate time. Now I want you to tell me . . ."

And it would begin all over again.

I was desperately tired, but he wouldn't let me go and sleep. Only when it was growing light and the sounds of morning traffic could be heard did he call in the guards and have me sent back to the prison.

I had barely entered the cell when the bugle sounded: it was reveille. The women leapt up from their beds, straightened their bedclothes, and sat down in readiness, holding their washing things and toothbrushes. I lay down intending to get some sleep, but right away someone nudged me in the ribs:

"Toilet duty!"

"I don't want to go."

"Later they won't let you."

Unwillingly I got to my feet and stumbled after the others to the lavatories.

I didn't touch breakfast. Why should I bother to eat in prison? Better to starve myself and die as quickly as possible.

I tried to lie down again, but they made me get up for inspection. The senior guard told me that it was against the rules to sleep in the daytime. Even leaning against the wall and closing your eyes was forbidden.

"But they kept me up all night at the interrogation!"

"That's not our problem."

Ignoring the rules, I lay down again, and paid no attention to the guard's knocking at the peephole. I refused to take any soup at lunch, but he left me alone, and I did manage to snatch a little sleep.

After supper I was sent for interrogation again. And so it went for a whole week. My head was buzzing, and all I wanted was to lie down anywhere—the wooden floor would have done—and sleep, sleep, sleep. Chekhov's story "Sleepy," about the young nanny who smothered the baby who wouldn't let her sleep, kept running through my brain. Perhaps I should try smothering the interrogator? I had to bite my tongue to keep myself from laughing. What an idiot to think of something so insane . . .

"How did you get yourself in such a mess?" The interrogator asked his formulaic secret policeman's question, yawning widely.

"You helped," I answered, also yawning.

When I finally grasped that they just didn't want to believe me, I stopped trying to convince them. I either said nothing, or gave some obviously facetious answer, or looked away and yawned.

"What's your interrogator's name?" one of the women in my cell asked me one day.

"Rzhavsky."

"What's he like? Does he shout at you a lot?"

"No, not at all. He just keeps asking me stupid questions. He seems civilized enough himself; he just has a dirty job to do."

"Civilized, my foot!" the woman answered bitterly. "You should have heard him swear at me—I've never heard language like that in my whole life."

She walked away, muttering, "It's all right for those who really do have something to answer for."

I blushed.

"Look," I said to the interrogator one day—by now my eyelids were so swollen from lack of sleep that I could hardly keep them open—"I've had enough of this. Write down whatever you want. Just keep everyone else out of it, all right? If even one other person is mentioned, you'll be wasting your time . . ."

"What's the hurry? We've got plenty of time."

They weren't much interested in me as a person. I wasn't someone who was going to bring them honor and glory by myself. Their orders were to slap together a local "show trial," and the "masterminds" had to be tracked down.

I survived the sleepless nights of interrogation and the days of enforced idleness in the cell on sheer nervous tension. If I let go for one moment, I knew that I would be plunged into a shameful fit of hysterics.

I misbehaved in the cell: I would sit down on my bed and doze, or even lay my head on the pillow. But every time the guard banged at the peephole, I leapt to my feet. In the end, though, I lost patience. One day, when they brought me in at reveille as usual, I flung myself down on my bed, and wouldn't stir for toilet duty, breakfast, or inspection. I slept like the dead till midday. Some big wigs were paying a visit to the prison. My cellmates shook me awake with difficulty; when I found out what was going on, I lay down again. When the big wigs came into our cell, there I still was, lying face to the wall.

There was the usual round of questions. "Have you any complaints?" Having been assured that there were none, the big wigs turned their attention to me.

"Why won't that woman get up?"

"She's ill," someone said, trying timidly to stave off trouble.

"If she's ill, she should be in the hospital."

I'm not ill," I said, propping myself up on my elbows. "They haven't let me sleep all week, that's all."

An hour later, they came and took me to the punishment cell.

The punishment cell looked much more like I'd imagined a prison than the big light cell I'd been in at first. A small basement room with a low sloping ceiling, it had a barred window without any glass in it; the rudimentary bed was bolted to the concrete floor.

I stretched out on the bed and fell asleep at once.

During the night I woke up feeling terribly cold. The only clothes I had were those I'd been wearing when I was arrested: a print blouse, a cotton sateen skirt, and shoes worn without stockings. I will never forget that first experience of prison cold. I can't describe it; I'm not capable of it. I was pulled one way by sleep, the other by cold. I would jump up and run around the cell, falling asleep on my feet, then collapse on the bed again, where the cold would soon force me up.

In the morning they brought me bread and water. I refused to take it. The guard ignored my protests and put the mug and slice of bread down on my bed, but I threw the bread out the window and used the water to splash my face and hands.

The next day, and the next, I did likewise. On the third day they brought me a bowl of thick rich soup and a hunk of white bread. I still wouldn't take anything.

"Tssk, you silly girl!" the guard grumbled.

The head guard on the block came in with the prison doctor, and they asked me what I thought I was doing.

I said that I was going to keep refusing food until they let me read books, or at the very least do some sewing or embroidery to pass the time. They exchanged glances and walked out.

A moment later, an elderly guard who had also been present during this exchange came back into the cell and put a roll-up down on my bed.

"Here, smoke this! It'll make you feel better."

I'd never tried smoking before and had absolutely no idea why anyone would have wanted to. I thought that you swallowed the smoke like food, and I found the whole idea disgusting. But I didn't want to rebuff a kindness; I would have swallowed a rag if he'd asked me. So I started to swallow the smoke. It sank in waves into my stomach, making my head spin and arousing feelings of nausea, but at the same time making me feel blissfully drowsy and relaxed.

I was still refusing to eat, but when the same guard was on duty, I asked him to give me some more tobacco. He probably thought that I was a hardened criminal who had smoked since I could walk; at any rate, he never turned me down.

I took no food for ten whole days, only water. I was not hungry at all. I felt ready to fly away at any moment, I was so light. I became as frail as a twig; I have absolutely no idea where on earth I found the strength to keep moving.

The head guard and the doctor came in regularly. I would meet them with my head held high, though my hair was as tangled as a haystack (they had taken my comb away). The cold in the cell was just as bad as before.

Then one day I told the head guard that I had decided to make a full confession; I said that I would need a pencil and a lot of paper.

Instantly they brought what I'd asked for. I wrote down that, yes, I had been in the organization all along; in fact, I wrote, I'd been the organization's secretary and its treasurer. We had a secret printing press, concealed (along with a large supply of funds in hard currency, sent to us from abroad) in the pit of a recently demolished public latrine next to the old synagogue. They would find a full list of the organization's members hidden there, too.

I had this effort sent on to my interrogator.

Late that night I was taken off to see him. He was alone in the office. I stared at him impudently.

"Why did you lie to us?" he asked.

"Well, the truth doesn't seem to suit you."

I wasn't called for interrogation again after that.

On the morning of the eleventh day, they let me out of the punishment cell and took me back to the cell, though by rights I should have had another four days in it. The women (some more had now arrived) greeted me warmly, teased the tangles out of my hair, and made me eat a little food.

A day or so later, the whole investigation block was rocked by some astonishing news. One of the cells was occupied by a group of "Shostkenites," factory workers from the town of Shostka who had been accused of industrial sabotage. They had all declared a hunger strike in protest against the beatings and torture they had suffered during interrogation. The night before the strike began, someone threw a note through our window during exercise. It invited us to join the strike. The next morning, we too began refusing food.

Appeals were scratched on the lavatory walls: "Wives and sisters, join our protest!" "We're being tortured!"

Hardly pausing for thought, I stuck my oar in, too, scratching in large letters "Protest against the beatings in the NKVD!" and "Ivan the Terrible had his hirelings; the NKVD do Stalin's dirty work!" And I signed my name, very clearly. Then I added, "Our entire country is turning into one vast Fooltown, headed by Gloom-Grumpy, its mayor."* Naturally all these compositions were carefully copied down and passed on to my interrogator. But they didn't put me back in the punishment cell.

The tensions of the day, compounded by the women's fears for their husbands, defiance of the authorities, and the hunger strike itself, culminated that evening in a general outburst of hysteria. And there our hunger strike ended. The following morning, we women shamefacedly accepted our breakfast.

On the whole, the atmosphere in our cell was very friendly; as a matter of fact, I don't remember any quarrels or fights in any of the various cells for political prisoners that I was in during my two years in jail. It wasn't all tears and sorrow. We kept ourselves amused, too: we told stories from books we had read and passed messages between cells by knocking on the walls.

I developed an enormous appetite. My emaciated body was desperate for food, but the prison diet grew worse and worse. Sometimes all we got for dinner was a mess of hot grits. Fortunately every two weeks we were able to buy pork fat, sugar, rusks, and cheap tobacco in the prison shop.

In the autumn of 1937, the prison began to fill up quickly. They put wooden shutters up outside the windows, and the cell became dark and gloomy. At night we would hear terrible screaming. Several people from our corridor had already been taken out and shot. One of them was Reva, the former chairman of the local Soviet committee.

In November I was formally charged: bad behavior while in custody. I began awaiting the trial.

Shortly afterward, the wives of NKVD men began to arrive in the cell next door. Almost the entire local section, including Teitel, the director, had been arrested. My interrogator and the public procurator who had signed the charge sheet were among those arrested.

In January 1938, a new charge sheet arrived, signed by another public procurator. Now I was being charged under Article 58:9 and 10 (Part II) of the Criminal Code [Sabotage and Anti-Soviet propaganda].

There was no one in the room when I was brought into court. At one end was a long table with a green baize cloth; close to the chair where they had me sit was a small table. On it was a sort of rubber bag with an opening

---

* A reference to the 19th-century Russian satirist Saltykov-Shchedrin's "The History of a Town."

at one end like a collar. I'd heard rumors in my cell that when they took you out to shoot you, they put a rubber bag over your head.

I began trembling all over. My ears seemed to have stopped up. When the judges came in (there were three of them: the fourth man was the clerk of the court), I was told to stand, but at first I couldn't understand what I was supposed to do. All this lasted no more than a few seconds. As soon as I heard the first question, "Give an account of your counterrevolutionary activities," I was able to pull myself together.

A charge of deceiving the investigating authorities was read (my story about the underground press next to the synagogue), and I was asked, "What was your purpose in doing this?"

"I wanted to get up the nose of idiots like you!" I snapped.

No sooner were the words out of my mouth than I understood that I really had done it now. I could have bitten my tongue off.

Their faces were purple with rage, their eyes narrowed . . . I took one look and sat down, though this was a breach of protocol: I should have remained standing.

The member of the tribunal who read the sentence—fifteen years' imprisonment in corrective labor camps—stopped at frequent intervals to see how I was reacting.

I listened with indifference; this didn't seem to have the slightest relevance to me. But when I heard the phrase "confiscation of personal property," I smiled: I hadn't managed to get hold of much of that during my short life!

When I got back to the cell and told my cellmates what they'd given me, there were cries and wails all around, but I said, "You can expect to live seventy-five years on average. Fifteen years out of seventy-five isn't all that much when you think about it."

After that I was shunted from prison to prison—eleven in all—before being sent off to Kotlas.

As I climbed down from the railway car there, I sniffed the air; it was cleaner than anything I'd ever smelled at home. It was so sweet and transparent that you wanted to drink it like water. (They say that these days Kotlas is one of the smokiest and dirtiest cities in all of northern Russia.)

So now I was in the huge Kotlas transit camp. Winter was almost over; there was still a hard frost outside, but the prison barracks, made of boards and tarpaulin, was warm. A bright fire burned in the iron stove.

I spent six weeks in the transit camp. In mid-May I was sent with a group of ten elderly intellectuals to the nearby Koryazhma camp. They barely made it from the camp to the truck that we were to be loaded in. One in particular kept getting behind. Bent double and clasping his little bundle of possessions to his chest, he lagged a few steps behind no matter how hard he struggled. Then something happened which to this day means I can't call some scoundrel a "dog," because that would be an insult to animals.

The transport guard, a young boy hardly old enough to wipe his own nose, rushed up to the old man and hit him on the back with his rifle butt. The old man swayed on his feet, but managed to remain standing. Staring straight ahead, and keeping the same distant expression on his face, he walked on unsteadily to the truck; the rest of us helped him up. He died three days later. I heard that he was a famous law professor, but I can't remember his name.

I didn't stay long in Koryazhma. Two weeks later I was sent farther north, this time in a mixed transport of politicals and ordinary criminals. We went through the forest on foot. We were greeted by a collection of drafty barracks with bed boards crudely made of wooden poles. The floors were of poles also, with a coating of mud to make them level. We were served a foul swill made from grits dressed with vegetable oil.

It was evening when we got there. Officially we were supposed to get a day's rest after the journey, but the next day we were divided up into brigades and sent to clear branches and debris off the forest road. I rather liked the work at first. There didn't seem much to it: you grabbed hold of a log or branch that you could manage and dragged it away, piling it on a heap with the others. There were pines and firs all around, sunshine and grass, birds and butterflies. The only problem was that you needed heavy trousers and boots for work like that, and I hadn't been given any. I was still wearing canvas house shoes, with no stockings, and a light dress. By evening my arms and legs were covered with deep bloody scratches.

The next day we were given "real" work to do. We were sent off into the bog to take off the top layer of vegetation. This layer was about eighteen inches thick and soggy with stagnant water. We had to slice it into pieces with our spades, then load it onto stretchers and, up to our ankles or knees in water, carry it forty or fifty yards off to the side.

I was paired with an exceedingly thin gray-haired woman. Panting, she would hurriedly load the stretcher with a drenched mass of peat; she took the front end of the stretcher and stumbled as she went, making me stumble as I followed her. My arms felt as if they were being dragged out of their sockets by the dreadful weight, and yesterday's scratches stung like mad. They hadn't healed overnight; in fact, they had gotten puffy and infected.

"Why are you making such an effort?" I asked my partner. "We'll never last the whole day like this."

"Not long ago they told us at roll call that record-breaking workers would be freed early. I'm a Communist, you know. Mind you, I don't think they'll keep me here so long anyway. It's all a mistake; the Party will soon sort it out . . ." She paused, then added, "Why couldn't they have asked me to volunteer to work out here; do they really think I would have refused? All I would have asked was to bring my son along."

That very day Malakhov, the camp director, paid a visit to the track. He had the reputation of a hard, brutal man. The common criminals especially hated him; they called him the Bloodsucker.

Shyly, the prisoners made their requests: could we have boots, trousers, mittens. He said nothing, then he narrowed one eye, making his face look deformed, and swept his gaze over the prisoners' heads, checking up on the work that we'd done. Finally he hissed, "We don't have any trousers and boots. Or mittens. This section must be clear in three days. In twelve days' time the embankment must be ready." Then he turned on his heel and went to inspect another brigade.

By evening my partner's zeal had abated. She put smaller and smaller pieces of peat on the stretcher, and her panting grew louder and louder. I felt no better myself. My shoes were sopping wet, and I had had to tie them with string to keep them on my feet. My palms were covered in oozing blisters.

Next day I didn't go out to roll call. Half an hour later, the work distributor took me to the office. When I was asked why I hadn't gone to work, I said, "Because no one told me to bring boots with me from home. And on top of that, I can't cope with your norms."

"We put malingerers in the punishment cell here. It's a pit full of water. Three days in there and you rot."

"If I've got to die, then it might as well be quickly."

To my intense surprise, the work distributor didn't take me to the punishment cells. Instead he took me into the sewing workshop. A few old men and women were sitting among heaps of remnants, making patches for shirts, underpants, trousers, and mittens from rags.

I'd been working there for a couple of days when I heard some news. Malakhov had been transferred to a new section of the track, and was taking a team of workers with him. He would be choosing them himself. The elderly, the goners and anyone else who didn't suit him, would be left behind; this camp would be turned into a medical block. Prisoners who were no longer able to work would be sent here.

Every prisoner prayed to God that Malakhov would reject him and that he wouldn't have to go on to the new labor camp. After supper all the prisoners were lined up in front of their barracks. Malakhov and the work distributor went around carrying each prisoner's sentence and began to make their selections.

Malakhov waved people to one side or the other: "his" prisoners were sent to the right, the others to the left. Having picked out about two hundred men, he came over to the women's line. About forty of us were waiting to learn the worst. Again a wave of the hand sent people to the right or the left. He came up to me and waved his hand without a second glance. I had ended up on the right.

The new camp was different from the old in the sense that it really was new: spanking new. The hastily constructed drafty barracks were still running with resin. On all sides tree stumps had not yet been dug up. Wood chippings and litter were scattered everywhere.

We weren't given a chance to rest. Hardly had we swilled down our carelessly cooked slops than we were rounded up to clear the camp area. That evening the work distributor read out the lists of who was working in what brigades or had what job in the camp. I didn't think I had anything to look forward to, but I was dumbfounded to hear that I had been selected to work as the camp switchboard operator. The easiest, the cleanest, the "softest" job in the camp! The switchboard was in the guardroom. As I took my place there in the mornings, I would watch roll call and the march out to work in progress.

Though it was now the height of summer, most of the prisoners had scurvy. The food got worse by the day. Often there would be no bread for three days in a row. We were fed twice a day—they served us what was supposed to be "soup" followed by "stew": a liter of watery stewed grits, followed by a half-liter of thick grits. People's legs became covered with hard raised purple areas which quickly turned into pustulant sores. Many of the prisoners couldn't get up off the bed boards in the mornings; they would be dragged up to the gates like sacks of potatoes, with plenty of kicks as encouragement. Once past the gate, some would struggle to their feet and go to stand in line with the other prisoners, but others would just lie there. Then a horse with a drag behind it would be brought up; the sick person would be tied to the drag and hauled over the stumps and bumpy ground until he had either given up the ghost or gotten to his feet. Most people did get up.

The sight of it filled me with dread, but also with shame. I was ashamed to be sitting in the guardroom wearing my earphones while other people were smashed to bits on the bumpy ground, slaving away felling trees, and giving their all to clear the road, before dying of exhaustion, heat stroke, or hunger. I knew that I was going to have to go there myself, to join them. But I kept putting it off, as a bather puts off the moment when he must jump into cold water.

After the prisoners had gone out to work, Malakhov sometimes came into the guardroom. I used to sit watching him with my headphones on. At last I plucked up courage to say, "How can you treat people like that? They're sick."

"We've got sixty percent sick just now," he replied, "and soon we'll have ninety percent. Do you think I should close the road for that? You don't cure scurvy with bed rest. Scurvy cases need as much movement as they can get."

One day a telephone call came in from the dock: a load of flour had come in for the camp, along with a load of wheels for the wheelbarrows. Which load should they send first? "The wheels!" Malakhov ordered, although the bread had been used up the previous day, and the prisoners had had nothing but gruel for twenty-four hours.

That did it.

"Citizen director," I said, "I'm quite fit enough to go work on the road now."

"Right," he rapped out, and left the guardroom.

There were not many women in the camp—only enough for one brigade. The rest were working as camp personnel. So I said nothing to the work distributor; I simply turned up the next morning at the gates and stood with the other women. The work distributor looked at me, said nothing, and added my name to the list. I went out to the line with the others.

Out I went to the quarry, the wheelbarrows, the spades. The emaciated prisoners, covered in the ulcers of scurvy, didn't have the strength to complete even half of their work norms.

The administration tried another way of pushing those who didn't fulfill their norms. Prisoners who lagged behind especially badly were put right into special brigades. They were left to work all night on the road, with no sleep or rest. Only the guards changed shifts. It was about as much use as putting a poultice on a leg with gangrene. The miracle didn't happen: those on their last legs didn't find an ounce of extra strength or work any harder. They simply started bringing loads of corpses into the camp in the mornings.

A medical commission arrived to inspect the camp. They weeded out a whole transport of invalids and had them transferred to the medical block. They found that I had symptoms of scurvy, too, and recommended that I be added to the group. Malakhov refused to agree, but he did have me transferred to work as an accountant for the tractor brigade.

On the track itself, things continued as before. In rain or blazing heat, in fierce frosts or snowstorms, the work went on. The shouts of "Get to it," the nasty slops for food, the torn rags and the green faces of the prisoners were all just as before. And all in aid of the record-breaking construction of a railway line linking the oil and coal of Ukhta and Vorkuta with the heart of Russia.

Time passed. Places which till then had been covered by impenetrable forest and bog were now crossed by a railway that had cost thousands of lives. (A corpse under every railroad tie is what former prisoners figure.) Whole new settlements grew up along it. If everything had been done properly, it might have been possible to take pride in our work. But no one who spent time in the camps feels any sense of pride; we don't much like remembering the past at all. Judging by my own feelings, I would say that this reluctance to remember isn't simply caused by the desire to shut out years of torment and deprivation; it's also prompted by a sense of shame. Our emotions are those of a girl dishonored by the man she loves.

I have no intention of idealizing the prisoners en masse. There were all kinds of people in the camps, especially after the war. But we were all tortured just the same: the good, the bad, the guilty, and the innocent. I'm not denying that people who were responsible for bloody atrocities during the war deserved to be punished severely. But, as Ukrainians say, "You worry only about your own misdeeds." The terror that Yezhov and Beria organized was every bit as bloody and vicious as the deeds of those punished after the war at the Nuremberg trials for crimes against humanity.

To give an example of what I mean, I must skip a few years, to the time when I was working in the theater company in Knyazh-Pogost. We were on a tour of the camps when we happened to see the following incident in Ukhta.

We were making our way to the club at an oil refinery. From far away you could see a slogan painted on the walls in huge letters—it was a quotation from the Soviet Constitution: "In the USSR, work is a matter of honor, a matter of glory, a matter of achievement and heroism!"

Strange noises floated over to us from somewhere. They sounded like the moans of a sick giant. When we got closer, we realized that these were no moans: they were the sounds of people chanting, "Heave, heave." A crowd of ragged prisoners burst out from behind the club. They were harnessed between the shafts of a huge sledge built for hitching to a tractor. It was piled high with peat. All of them were wearing chains on their arms and legs: they were from a labor camp.

Whenever anyone talks about the speed with which socialism was built in Russia, I see before me the extraordinary crowds, the herds of ragged, yellow, puffy creatures belonging to that unique breed known as zeks. (A plague on those who selected and bred this species!)

I see a former member of the Academy of Sciences, with lowered eyes, walking slowly in a column of other living corpses to his place of work.

I see a famous lawyer, whose articles are still cited by specialists, drinking thin gruel from a rusty tin.

I see a jowly camp guard hit a skeletal prisoner in the face because the man had put a potato in its furrow the wrong way, "ass end down."

I see the women from the collective farms crying over letters from their children, the very children for whom they had gleaned a handful of corn during the famine, receiving eight or ten years in prison for their pains.

I see the truck that spent the entire day going between the medical block and the cemetery. There are twelve coffins in the truck. At the cemetery the corpses are tipped out of their "boxes" into a common pit, and the truck goes back for more.

Human rights, dignity, pride were all reduced to nothing.

There was only one thing that these stock-breeders from hell could not exterminate: the sex drive. Indifferent to regulations, to the threat of the punishment cells, to hunger and humiliation alike, it lived and flourished far more openly and directly than it does in freedom.

Things that a free person might have thought about a hundred times before doing happened here as simply as they would between stray cats. No, this wasn't depravity of the kind you might expect in a brothel. This was real, "legitimate" love, with fidelity, jealousy, suffering, with the pain of parting, and with the terrible "crowning joy" of love—the birth of children.

The childbearing instinct is both beautiful and terrible. Beautiful if everything has been done to greet the arrival in the world of this new human being; terrible if this child is condemned, even before birth, to torment and suffering. But our reason was by then too blunted for us to think very carefully about the fate of our offspring.

Our need for love, tenderness, caresses was so desperate that it reached the point of insanity, of beating one's head against a wall, of suicide. And we wanted a child—the dearest and closest of all people, someone for whom we could give up our own life. I held out for a relatively long time. But I did so need and long for a hand of my own to hold, something I could lean on in those long years of solitude, oppression, and humiliation to which we were all condemned.

A number of such hands were offered, and I did not choose the best of them, by any means. But the result of my choice was an angelic little girl with golden curls. I called her Eleonora.

She was born in a remote camp barracks, not in the medical block. There were three mothers there, and we were given a tiny room to ourselves in the barracks. Bedbugs poured down like sand from the ceiling and walls; we spent the whole night brushing them off the children. During the daytime we had to go out to work and leave the infants with any old woman whom we could find who had been excused from work; these women would calmly help themselves to the food we left for the children.

I believed neither in God nor in the devil. But while I had my child, I most passionately, most violently wanted there to be a God. I wanted there to be someone who might hear my fervent prayer, born of slavery and degradation, and grant me salvation and happiness for my child, at the cost of all possible punishment and torment for myself, if need be.

Every night for a whole year, I stood at my child's cot, picking off the bedbugs and praying. I prayed that God would prolong my torment for a hundred years if it meant that I wouldn't be parted from my daughter. I prayed that I might be released with her, even if only as a beggar or a cripple. I prayed that I might be able to raise her to adulthood, even if I had to grovel at people's feet and beg for alms to do it.

But God did not answer my prayer. My baby had barely started walking, I had hardly heard her first words, the wonderful heartwarming word "Mama," when we were dressed in rags despite the winter chill, bundled into a freight car, and transferred to the "mothers'" camp. And here my pudgy little angel with the golden curls soon turned into a pale ghost with blue shadows under her eyes and sores all over her lips.

I was put to work felling trees. On the very first day, a huge dead pine fell toward me. I saw it begin to fall, but my legs turned to water and I couldn't move. Next to me was a huge tree that had blown down in a snowstorm and I instinctively squatted down behind its upturned roots. The pine crashed down right by me, but not even a twig touched me. I had hardly scrambled from my shelter when the brigade leader rushed up and started yelling that he didn't need sloppy workers in his brigade, and that he certainly wasn't going to answer for cretins. I let his abuse wash over me; my thoughts were far away from the pine that had so nearly killed me, and the tree-felling, and the brigade leader's bad language. I could think only of my sick daughter in her cot. The next day I was transferred to the sawmill right next to the camp itself.

All that winter I sat on a frozen block of wood clutching the handle of a saw. I got a chill on the bladder and terrible lumbago, but I thanked my lucky stars for the job. I was able to take home a little bundle of firewood every day, and in return I was allowed to see my daughter outside normal visiting hours. But sometimes the guards at the gates took my firewood for themselves, causing me intense anguish.

My appearance at the time could hardly have been more miserable and wretched. To avoid getting lice (a ubiquitous delight in the camps at the time), I had shaved off my hair. Few women would have done that without being forced to. The only time I took off my padded trousers was when I was going to see my daughter.

In return for my bribes of firewood, the children's nurses, whose own children were also there in the group, would let me see my child first thing in the morning before roll call, and occasionally during the lunch break— besides, of course, at night when I brought back the firewood.

And the things I saw there!

I saw the nurses getting the children up in the mornings. They would force them out of their cold beds with shoves and kicks. (For the sake of "cleanliness," blankets weren't tucked in around the children but were sim- ply thrown on top of their cots.) Pushing the children with their fists and swearing at them roughly, they took off their night clothes and washed them in ice-cold water. The babies didn't even dare cry. They made little sniffing noises like old men and let out low hoots.

This awful hooting noise would come from the cots for days at a time. Children already old enough to be sitting up or crawling would lie on their backs, their knees pressed to their stomachs, making these strange noises, like the muffled cooing of pigeons.

One nurse was responsible for each group of seventeen children. She had to sweep the ward, wash and dress the children, feed them, keep the stove going, and do all sorts of special "voluntary" shifts in the camp; but her main responsibility was keeping the ward clean. In order to cut down on her workload and allow herself a bit of free time, she would "rational- ize" her jobs: that is, she would try to come up with ways in which she could reduce the amount of time she had to spend on the children. Take feeding, for instance, which I saw once.

The nurse brought a steaming bowl of porridge from the kitchen, and portioned it out into separate dishes. She grabbed the nearest baby, forced its arms back, tied them in place with a towel, and began cramming spoon- ful after spoonful of hot porridge down its throat, not leaving it enough time to swallow, exactly as if she were feeding a turkey chick. The fact that there was a stranger present didn't bother her: this "rationalization" had evidently been approved by someone higher up the line. No wonder there were plenty of empty beds in the infants shelter even though the birth rate in the camps was relatively high. Three hundred babies died there every year even before the war started. And how many were there during the war!

It was only their own babies whom these nurses carried around in their arms all the time, whom they fed properly, patting their bottoms tenderly; these were the only babies who lived to see freedom.

There was a doctor working in this House of Dead Babies too. Her name was Mitrikova. There was something odd and unpleasant about this woman: her movements were hasty, her speech was jerky, her eyes were always darting around. She did nothing to reduce the death rate among the infants; she cared only about the ones in the isolation ward, and even that was only for form's sake. I don't suppose the "rationalization" with the hot porridge and the loose blankets, when the temperature in the ward was only eleven or twelve degrees above freezing, was done without her knowledge either.

The few minutes that the doctor did spend in the infants' house were allocated to the groups of older children. These feeble-minded six- and seven-year-olds had somehow conformed to Darwin's law of the survival of the fittest, and they lived on despite the hot porridge, the kicks, the shoves, the washing in icy water, and the long sessions when they were left sitting on their potties tied to their chairs, a practice which meant that many children began suffering from prolapses of the large intestine.

Mitrikova did spend some time with the older children. She didn't give them any medical treatment—she had neither the wherewithal nor the skill for that—but she got them to do dances and taught them little poems and songs. Well, it was meant to look good when the time came to pack them off to an orphanage. All the children really learned in that house was the cunning and craftiness of old camp lags. They learned how to cheat and to steal, and how not to be caught doing it.

Before I had figured out what sort of person Mitrikova was, I told her how badly some of the nurses treated the children, and begged her to do something about it. She looked thunderous and promised that the guilty parties would be punished, but things remained exactly as they had been, and my little Eleonora began to fade even faster.

On some of my visits I found bruises on her little body. I shall never forget how she grabbed my neck with her tiny skinny hands and moaned, "Mama, want home!" She hadn't forgotten the bug-ridden slum where she first saw the light of day, and where she'd been with her mother all the time.

The anguish of small children is more powerful and more tragic than the anguish of adults. Knowledge comes to a child before he can fend for himself. For as long as his needs and wishes are anticipated by loving eyes and hands, he doesn't realize his own helplessness. But if those hands betray him, surrendering him to callous and cruel strangers, his horror has no limits. A child cannot grow used to things or forget them; he can only put up with them, and when that happens, anguish settles in his heart and condemns him to sickness and death.

People who find nature tidy and readily understandable may well be shocked by my view that animals are like small children, and vice versa

—that is, small children are like animals. Both of them understand many things and suffer much, but since they cannot speak, they cannot beg for mercy and charity.

Little Eleonora, who was now fifteen months old, soon realized that her pleas for "home" were in vain. She stopped reaching out for me when I visited her; she would turn away in silence. On the last day of her life, when I picked her up (they allowed me to breastfeed her), she stared wide-eye somewhere off into the distance, then started to beat her weak little fists on my face, clawing at my breast, and biting it. Then she pointed down at her bed.

In the evening, when I came back with my bundle of firewood, her cot was empty. I found her lying naked in the morgue among the corpses of the adult prisoners. She had spent one year and four months in this world, and died on 3 March 1944.

I don't know where her tiny grave is. They wouldn't let me leave the camp compound to bury her myself. By clearing the snow off the roofs of two wings of the infants' house, I earned three extra bread rations. I swapped them and my own two rations for a coffin and a small individual grave. Our brigade leader, who was allowed out without a guard, took the coffin to the cemetery and brought me back a fir twig in the shape of a cross, to stand in for a crucifix.

That is the whole story of how, in giving birth to my only child, I committed the worst crime there is.

I kept on working, not sensing now whether I found it easy or hard. I did various jobs, feeling neither hunger nor the need for company.

At one of the regular medical checks, they diagnosed dystrophy and gave me two weeks' leave, but I was beyond understanding, and kept turning up to work even though I could hardly stand; eventually a doctor turned me back at roll call. Just then a transfer warrant turned up for me from the main camp at Knyazh-Pogost.

When the baby and I were still at the camp with the bedbugs, I'd gotten involved in amateur theatricals and had made friends with their organizer, a delightful elderly professor named Alexander Gavronsky. When he was rehearsing with me, we would spend hours talking about everything under the sun, while little Eleonora crawled around his boots, trying to undo the laces.

He had been transferred from the "bughouse" to Knyazh-Pogost, and they had given him another ten years in the camps before promoting him to director of the newly formed variety theater troupe. When he got there, he thought of me, found out where I was, and arranged a transfer warrant for me to Knyazh-Pogost. How could he have known how completely I had changed? How could he have known that my desire to act, and my talent for acting, had both died with my daughter's death?

You don't get a choice in the camps anyway. If a transfer warrant comes, you go where they send you. Carrying an empty wooden suitcase, and wearing sturdy canvas boots over my bare feet and an old pea jacket, I walked to the station in August 1944 with no more feeling than if I had been walking to the fields or to cut wood.

Neither my love for the stage nor my ability as an actress returned to me in Gavronsky's theater. The kind old man often called me in to see him. Partly he wanted to cheer me up, but what interested him most was having an audience so that he could think aloud (he was writing some sort of academic treatise). He would launch into long monologues, read me lectures for half an hour at a time; it all went in one ear and out the other. What use was all the philosophy in the world now that little Eleonora was gone?

And he would sit smoking his home-rolled cigarettes and talking and talking, till at last I felt as though I were hanging upside down from the ceiling, with the floor spinning far below me.

I was cast in roles that were totally unsuitable for the way I felt then: I had to play "positive heroines," ladies who were vivacious and dewy-eyed, the prosperous permed wives of army officers. Where had the pre-war heroines, in their shifts and their short hair, gone to?

Now if I'd been cast as a peasant woman pulling the plow in place of a horse. . . ! But there were no parts like that. Nor were we given plays like that to perform. The truth was being varnished, even in 1944, when the towns lay in ruins, people lived in earth dugouts, and women on the collective farms were pulling the plows themselves.

We "serf actors" lived quite differently from the other prisoners. Our food was far better. And when we were on tour, for up to ten months at a time, conditions were good in every way. We were given our rations "dry." This meant that we actually ate almost all the food we were supposed to get. While we were on tour in some places, we were treated to our meals; in others they made arrangements for us to eat at their canteen.

It was terrifying to think of going back to the dirt and the lice in the ordinary barracks, to soup made from nettle and willowherb, to the slave labor and the continual degradation. But I knew what was going to happen. I couldn't get into my parts, and I acted like a trained parrot. I knew perfectly well that the troupe didn't need me; I didn't even need myself. I knew that I would be dismissed as soon as the tour finished, and that I was no longer in condition to last out the rest of my fifteen years. When we got back from the tour, I tried to kill myself. The memory still makes me blush with shame.

I stole a heap of sleeping pills from the theater manager, and when everyone else had left the hostel to go to a concert, I swallowed them all. But it's hard to kill yourself if you don't have your own bedroom. An old friend of mine had lost a book, and he decided that he must have lent it to me. He and his wife came over to the hostel and started trying to wake me up. My unusually heavy sleep aroused their suspicions; they raised the alarm.

I'm going to digress a little and tell you a bit about this friend. A few years before I arrived at Knyazh-Pogost, I'd had a job in the kitchens at another camp. One day a transport of new prisoners arrived. There was not a worker among them: all were scholars, academics, publishers' editors, and the like.

The prisoners' elder was a small, thin man with a remarkably clear, charming, and friendly smile. When he arrived in the kitchen with his bucket to collect dinner for the group, this smile would always make me want to do something nice for him, and I would try to pour an especially large and thick portion into his dish. He organized an amateur theatrical group right away, and I found myself involved as well. Later, working on the track, we were put in the same brigade. He was the only man in the whole camp whose company made me believe that it was possible for men and women to be real friends. Afterward we got split up, but we found ourselves together again in the theater troupe. He and his camp wife (they stayed together after being released as well) saved me from death by suicide that time; later they remained my guardian angels, supporting me against the various blows delivered by ill fortune.

We were in different theater groups. They worked in the puppet theater, which was more or less separately organized (and later was to become separate even in an official sense). While I was recovering in the hospital, they and Gavronsky persuaded the director of the puppet theater to take me on.

She was an interesting woman. The former wife of the famous Georgian theater director Akhmeteli and at one time a well-known actress herself, she was a kind and sensitive woman. She used to smile so broadly and sincerely when she was in a good mood that it was infectious. It was Tamara Georgievna Tsulukidze who made me want to start living again.

Her theater used to put on one-act comedies using live actors as well as puppet dramas, and she gave me a part in one of these short plays. It was entirely thanks to her that later on, in another camp in Siberia, I was able to run a culture brigade myself, and that I made quite a successful career in the theater after being released. The most important thing, though, was that I fell in love with the puppets.

But this spell in puppet paradise didn't last long. The end of the war brought changes in politics and ideology, and these began affecting absolutely everything. I'm not entirely sure why they closed our theater. I think that the Minister of Culture in the Komi Republic decided that he wanted to take over the theater—but without its prison workers, thank you very much. The puppets that we had made with our own hands were taken from us and sent off to the Komi capital, Syktyvkar, and there they soon found their eternal rest in the stomachs of rats.

Tamara Tsukulidze and Alexei and Mira Linkevich (the friends I had made in the puppet theater) were all due to be released shortly; they stayed on at Knyazh-Pogost. I was sent off to an agricultural camp at Kyltovo, hundreds of miles away; then, not long afterward, I was picked to go on a transport to Siberia.

Getting there took nearly a month. Everything went according to tradition: they gave us salt fish to eat, but hardly any water. Not that there was much of the fish, either. The women criminals and the guards swapped our food supply for vodka and white bread; then they would drink and eat together, and have a good laugh over how green we all were.

These women criminals were allocated in lots of eight or ten ("lots" is the right word: they were barely human) to thirty or forty politicals; they terrorized the politicals however they could, stealing whatever they wanted. No one dared utter a word: they all had knives. Most of the prisoners in my railway car were "Westerners," that is, Poles, Lithuanians, Estonians, and Latvians. There were eight of us "Soviets", and ten criminals. We "Soviets" decided not to let the criminals give us a hard time.

The criminals started with the Westerners. There were a lot of the latter, and most of them were fit-looking young women. They could easily have crushed the criminals. But no! When the criminals were working one of them over, her neighbors would move out of the way to make it easier for the bandits. All right, the criminals did have knives, as I said, but would they ever really have used them?

It was Easter Saturday. The bandit girls had just stolen a pregnant Polish woman's "mommy rations," which they were devouring in their lair on an upper berth. One of them, who was the spitting image of a witch just back from her coven, but who had a crucifix hanging around her neck, stopped chewing her cud for a moment and said, "Eh, girls, what we done! We just robbed a pregnant woman on Easter Saturday!"

But after another moment's thought she added, "Never mind. God won't hold it against us!"

We eight politicals decided that we had to get rid of them. We knew that it was useless to appeal to the guards or expect them to do anything; they were all in cahoots anyway. So we came up with a rather mean trick (but I don't suppose God will hold that against us either!). At one of the stops we threw a letter out of the car saying that we had reason to believe that the criminals in our wagon were planning an escape; they were going to pry up the floor of the carriage with their knives and jump out while the train was moving.

Half an hour later, the guards rushed into the car, body-searched the criminals, found the knives, and put the women in the punishment van. We had peace and quiet for the rest of the journey.

After our month's journey, we reached the Suslovo agricultural camp, where we were immediately put into quarantine. If you weren't infected before you got there, you were likely to be afterward: the quarantine hut was stuffy, thick with black mud, and swarming with fleas and bedbugs. There weren't enough plank beds to go round, so people had to sleep on the floor underneath them.

One day, the head of the culture and education section of the camp administration came into the hut to round up people to work in his culture brigade. One of my traveling companions "betrayed" me, and when we got out of quarantine, I was assigned to make puppets in the tiny studio attached to the club for the administration personnel. (The Suslovo camp was officially registered as a state farm, and the camp administration was treated as the state farm office, so to speak.)

The only difference between this camp and the others I had been in was that it had a large medical section and a big club. The barracks were just the same as everywhere: full of bugs and fleas, with straw-stuffed mattresses, no sheets, and torn blankets. In contrast to the northern Russian camps, these were hardly heated in winter, so people slept on their plank beds fully clothed, in their quilted work jackets, padded trousers, and felt boots.

I did relatively well: I lived in the club. It was a big tumbledown rat-infested building that was impossible to heat. We burned what we could to keep warm: old scenery, newspapers, furniture. Once during a play reading, one of the boys stepped out for a moment; when he got back, his chair had vanished into the stove. No matter what we burned, though, if you spilled water or a bowl of soup on the table, it would freeze immediately.

In 1949 this became the first ordinary rather than punitive camp to be divided into compounds by sex. The boys now needed a special pass to come to rehearsals (the club was in the women's section). The power of forbidden love became particularly evident at that time. Men and women would crawl through the barbed wire to reach their lovers; often people were hit by bullets and crippled, but that didn't stop anyone. Later still, the women were all moved out of this camp, and it became single-sex. The culture brigade was closed down.

This was a major blow for me, because I had been very happy in this group. It was very different from the theater brigade: the difficulties here had united us into one big family, where jokes and laughter reigned and where we played silly tricks and looked out for each other.

I probably owe it more to this group than to anything else that I'm still alive today. I came down with acute pneumonia; the doctors had nothing to treat me with, so they were going to leave me to die. But the people in the culture brigade who were allowed out of the camp went out and scoured two villages for sulfa tablets; then they took turns sitting by my bed and giving me the medicine on time. I owe my life to them.

I wasn't forced out into the fields even after that. After the culture brigade was closed, a transfer warrant came for me, and I was moved into the administration's "serf theater."

So how did they find out about me?

I had gone with the puppet theater to Mariinsk during one of the annual arts competitions held there. We presented a play with live actors as well, in which I acted the part of a dreadful empty-headed little woman, the wife of an important official. Before, when I'd acted this part in our own camp or on tour in other camps, I had had only moderate success with it. But here, on the big stage, all my inhibitions seemed to melt away. I gave such a lively, convincing, and relaxed performance, and managed to be so funny at the same time, that I was cheered off the stage. That was when I was offered a transfer to the administration theater. But I wouldn't have swapped the Suslovo group for anything. However, when the Mariinsk theater learned that the Suslovo brigade had been disbanded, they sent a transfer warrant for me.

The Mariinsk theater had three sections: drama, singing, and choreography. I had always been pretty indifferent to dance. But in Mariinsk I fell in love with it. The ballet master was every bit as much of an artist as Moiseev. But the real star of the group was a dancer whose studies had been interrupted by the war. She was a Hungarian, and her father was a Jew; when the Nazis invaded, she and her family had had to flee in different directions.

She began working as a cabaret dancer in some small provincial town. As the Soviet Army approached the Hungarian border, she decided to escape across the front to the Soviet Union. She managed to get herself right to the Soviet trenches, where she ended up falling into the arms of some soldiers. These men first raped her, infecting her with a venereal disease as an additional little bonus; then they handed her over to the authorities. She was tried for spying and sent to a prison camp.

When they unloaded her from the transport train at Mariinsk, she was seriously ill. She was transferred directly to the sanitary quarters; when she recovered, the theater people fished her out.

What a dancer she was! She performed folk and character dances as well as ballet. It is hard for me to describe the technical perfection and beauty of her dancing. I don't have the vocabulary, and anyway I don't know much about choreography, but I've never seen anything like Dolly Takvaryan either before or since. The gulag chiefs themselves used to fly down from Moscow just to see her perform.

While working for the Mariinsk theater, I got to play parts that were much more in my line: Manefa and Galchikha in plays by Ostrovsky,* Dunyasha in Gogol's *The Wedding*, Lukerya in *The Dowry*. But before we went off on tour, I was made to take part in choral and dance numbers at the big variety shows that they put on for public holidays. I liked that about as much as a dog likes being whipped.

But I did play my parts with enthusiasm. You can't really tell how well you're acting yourself. But I would often hear the musicians or dancers talking about some play that had been in the repertoire for ages and saying, "Let's go watch Galchikha (or Dunyasha) before we go to bed."

Things were really not half bad at the theater. The hostel was clean, and we were paid a direct salary (once our living expenses had been deducted). There were some old pros there, such as the actresses Morskaya and Malinovskaya, who said they would rather stay at this theater till they died; they didn't much like the idea of the so-called freedom they would get outside the camps.

But then there was some more alarming news. Hundreds of prisoners who were on their second or third stretches had been rounded up and packed off to the Mariinsk transit camp. Here they immediately got involved in an all-out war against the Vlasovites.** They fought one another to the death with axes.

The head of the transit camp gave the order that the "war" must be stopped, whatever it took: he issued machine guns to the camp guards in the watchtowers which they used to mow down people at random. Quite a few innocent bystanders were slaughtered, too. About three hundred prisoners were butchered, some killed by machine-gun fire, others by the axes and knives of their fellow prisoners.

It all created such a big scandal that the order came down from above to find a scapegoat—the usual practice in such instances. The person selected was the head of the transit camp, who, it was rumored, got twenty-five years—after being dismissed from his post.

---

* Character roles in comedies by Alexander Ostrovsky, the most famous and prolific 19th-century Russian playwright.
** Soviet prisoners of war recruited by the Nazis to fight against the Red Army.

Not long afterward, they began rounding up the politicals. The station was full of prison trains, all of them packed to the roofs. No attention was paid to whether people were in shape to travel, to the gravity of the offense that they had committed, or to the length of sentence that they had been given.

They took decrepit, half-dead old men and post-operative patients from the hospitals, dragging them to the station on stretchers, or forcing them to hobble there on crutches or on foot, and they crammed them, in their indescribable rags, into the icy railway cars until they could fit no more in.

This lasted through January, February, and March of 1951. The whole camp was in high tension. Rumors flew that all the politicals were to be exterminated, or at the very least transferred to somewhere unheard of, to the wildest, most desolate, and waterless corners of the country; there the fierce regulations and the indescribably difficult conditions would lead to mass exterminations without the need to resort to gas chambers and rifles.

No skills or services to society saved politicals from being sent on these appalling journeys. There was a young surgeon named Grinko (imprisoned for his contacts with Bandera's followers) who worked in the medical unit. He was famous throughout the Mariinsk region: his scalpel had saved hundreds from certain death. Most of those on whom he'd operated were not prisoners, and his patients had included many officials and their families. But despite the protests of the head surgeon, Startsev, a Communist from pre-Revolutionary days, and the petitions of his own former patients, Grinko too was rounded up and packed off to the station.

They soon started on the theater. It became clear when they read the lists in the club that this amounted to a complete purge. They took everyone except the technical staff, those on short sentences, and those who were in the last year or two of their sentences. But for the moment Dolly Takvaryan and I were not on either of the lists.

We already knew the worst at the theater: some of the free employees were friends of ours, and some of them had been assigned to the transports as escorts. They told us where the transports were going: to Djezkazgan, in Kazakhstan. There were copper mines there, on the waterless Solonchak steppe.

There was a prisoner in our camp who until recently had worked as a gulag official himself. He came to the women's hostel where we lived. Most of the people from the theater had gathered in the little building for a tearful farewell party. This man told us what was behind these round-ups. This is what he said: Eleanor Roosevelt, who knew about the huge numbers of political prisoners in the Soviet Union, had come to the country and asked to visit the camps and see for herself. This request had been categorically refused.

In the UN, questions had been raised about Soviet violations of human rights, and there had been talk of sending a special commission to investigate. Our representatives at the UN had stalled for all they were worth, but the home authorities had become alarmed and begun to collect the "rubbish" and dump it as far away as they could—in places like Djezkazgan.

There had been mines there for a long time, but the exceptionally harsh living conditions (especially the lack of water) had meant that it was next to impossible to find workers, and the mines were limping along feebly. But now there was a supply of prisoners, to whom ordinary human rights did not apply. All you needed was rolls and rolls of barbed wire, handcuffs, machine guns for the guards, Alsatians . . .

The groups went off. The transport guards came back and brought us a note from our friends that told us what had happened to them. They were living in hard labor camp conditions. They all had to wear numbers, just like in the German concentration camps. They were working in the mines. They were allowed two meals a day, and a liter of water for drinking and washing every twenty-four hours. A healthy person might stand it for a month, but anyone not in perfect health would be finished in two weeks. Grinko was ruining his surgeon's hands doing rough work with a pick and spade. One of the ballet dancers from our theater had gone mad.

The news was shattering. The rehearsals were going badly. If we were going to put anything on at all, we all had to double or triple up the parts, but all of the actors were too depressed to feel like working. Many had loved what they did all their lives, but now it seemed pointless and distasteful.

Not long before all this, I had had to go into the hospital for a serious operation. While I was still there, the whole wretched business with the transfers started. Anyone who could still walk at all was kicked out of the hospital. I was kicked out too, although I was still learning how to walk again after the operation. But I gritted my teeth and decided to show everyone (including myself!) that I could do it.

It turned out that I could, too. With the exception of Galchikha, all my parts required me to move around a lot. No one who saw me at the rehearsals would have believed that only a few days ago I'd had difficulty walking the few feet between two hospital beds, with my breath coming in gasps and my heart racing. But I paid for it after the rehearsals: I collapsed on my bed and lay like a wet rag.

When trouble hit the theater, I was overcome by feelings of hopelessness, terror, and depression. I was afraid on account of my own physical weakness; I was terrified at the thought of the guards driving me on with their bayonets, and I loathed my damn heart because it wouldn't just burst and let me die. It was the sort of fear felt by a stray dog threatened with a stick, by a wounded hare screaming like a baby in the hunter's hands out of pain and the fear of still worse pain to come. May those who can cause such fear be eternally damned—no matter whether they cause it for a hare, a dog, or another human being.

Of course, outwardly I didn't give my feelings away; we were all long hardened into not showing what we felt. But when you find your hair gone gray one morning after a sleepless night, lines on your face that weren't there before, and your mouth wrinkled up like an old woman's—those are things you can't hide.

To cut a long story short, my forebodings turned out to be justified. The core teams had already gone off, and things seemed to have settled down, but the administration was busy tying up the loose ends.

We had somehow managed to put together a program that we could take on tour, but then we received an unexpected and uniquely painful blow: Dolly Takvaryan, the star of the theater, its mainstay, was to be sent away. A few days later it was my turn, though I had only just over a year left on my sentence.

It was late spring by the time I left Mariinsk for the transit camp. There were a few other women with me, all strangers. It was a warm, sunny day. Our luggage had been loaded on a cart; the guards made no attempt to hurry or push us. We had only a couple of miles to walk to the transit camp in any case. Fear and anxiety had vanished: all that was left was an odd sense of detachment and an indifference to everything in life.

Dolly had already left the transit camp by the time I got there. Yet another disappointment. I suddenly felt terribly sleepy. I threw my things down on a bunk and slumped on top of them; I slept nearly the entire two weeks in the transit camp before we were sent off. I had to sit down or lie down for only a moment and I was out. Luckily they didn't make me go to work.

I woke up properly only when we reached Taishet. Here I learned that Dolly had been sent off to work on the track only a few days before. It wasn't clear which camp she was in. Not long after that, I was sent off to Bratsk with a big party of other women.

From about the mid-1930s, the official name for the Soviet prison camps —"corrective labor camps"—had lost its original meaning. To be sure, even in the early days they had been more like camps for extermination by labor than camps for corrective labor, but a measure of humaneness—even in the limited sense in which one could use such a word in the case, say, of Malakhov—had softened the officials' "educational" aims.

The camps were not separated by sex, and people who weren't too exhausted and beaten down by work had the chance to forget themselves for a while in love's embrace; the authorities often turned a blind eye to this as long as the prisoners continued to fulfill and surpass their work norms.

Then there were the amateur theatricals, in which the camp administrators took particular pride; these were the professional companies that they themselves had founded, and they loved to show them off to their colleagues. The lucky actors in these companies might feel that they were second-class human beings, but at least that meant that they were some sort of human beings. They used to show films as well. Inside the camp the windows weren't barred (except for those on the solitary cells and in the morgue); the doors weren't locked, and you could walk freely throughout the camp.

The new system organized by the Beria-Abakumov gang was not a shining example of originality: they had copied everything from Hitler, except for the gas chambers.

As soon as we got to the camp, we saw the bars on the windows and the locks on the doors. Next to the lavatory, which is where we all rushed off to as was usual with new arrivals, big buckets were lined up. We didn't have to think hard about what those were. They were the slop buckets: the arrangements here were the same as in prison.

There was hardly anyone in the camp. After the camp commandant had given us a sermon on the rules and regulations, in which the two most common words were "forbidden" and "punishable," we were told to sit down in the baking heat right in the middle of the camp and wait there. No one was to wander off.

Immediately a huge swarm of midges flew down on us. They were monstrous, fearless creatures whose bites tore out chunks of flesh. But it wasn't the clouds of insects that dimmed my eyes. It was the sight of the women coming toward us with lists in their hands: a doctor and two supervisors. The doctor's white coat had a rag with a number on it sewn on the back, and another on the front, on the seam by her knee. The supervisors had numbers on their dresses, too, and so did the few women we could see run past.

Why should a bit of cloth with a number on it, sewn to your clothes, make such a difference? Well, those bits of cloth took away your name, your surname, your age; they turned you into a branded beast, an inventory number—or maybe something worse than that: a table with a number on it is still a table, a branded cow has its own nickname, but from then on we were allowed to respond only to our numbers. You were severely punished for not wearing your number in the proper place.

By that evening we had been divided up among the barracks. There was no washdown for us, there being no water. It had been crowded enough in the barracks as it was, especially since the plank beds were continuous shelves without any divisions. Now that we new arrivals had come in, there was hardly room to breathe. No medical inspection had been performed, and some of the women had already served sentences; some of them were sick with syphilis or TB. The barracks were locked at night, and they put the slop buckets in. The close, stifling atmosphere was made still worse by their frightful stench.

In these new camps, amateur theatricals and films were forbidden; the prisoners were also not allowed newspapers, books, cards, or games. After supper we were all sent off to roll call and were kept there in formation until the order came to sleep. Reveille was at half-past five, and on days when the duty guard was bored with picking his nose, and felt he might start dozing off on duty, he would move reveille forward an hour.

There was another scourge here, too: the lack of water. Water was brought in tanks from a river five miles away. Two tankers were not nearly enough to fill the needs of two big camps and the villages as well. The free employees and the guard barracks had first call, then the camp kitchens. They would bring a small barrel of water into each barrack first thing in the morning; the strongest women then fought over it. In the evening the same barrel would come in again, this time full of boiling water colored faintly with ersatz barley coffee. You were allowed into the bathhouse once a month and given half a bowl of water; as for a laundry—forget it. Every puddle of rainwater was precious, and when they wanted to wash their clothes, women would carry their bowls around the camp and get their friends to piss in them, then use the urine to wash a sweater or a skirt.

Everyone without exception was made to do hard labor: old and young alike. What was interesting was that there wasn't any fuss over plans and norms here. They didn't punish you for not doing enough, or reward you for doing more than your share. They just made you work ten hours straight, till you collapsed. There were so many prisoners that there often was not enough work to go around. When this was the case, they thought up Sisyphean tasks for us to do; never mind that the work didn't need doing, it "kept you out of trouble." The most trifling offense, such as not having your number sewn on, got you sent to the "special regime" cell.

Of the three men who ran the camp, the political organizer was the most humane. He used to threaten us too, but his threats were more in the way of a warning than anything else, and he could calm and encourage desperate people with a single word. He somehow managed to keep the drunken regime supervisor and the clinically insane camp commandant on the straight and narrow, or nearly so.

There was an epidemic of suicides among the camp inmates. For the most part these were young Westerners; they poisoned themselves with bleach or hanged themselves in some out-of-the-way corner.

One more winter had passed; now it was summer again. August 1952, the date when my sentence was officially supposed to end, had come and gone. I had lived through the anniversary without feeling any joy or sadness. I had long since gotten used to the idea that there was no way out of this. They were no longer bothering to go through the mockery of imposing new sentences, as they had before. (They used to call a prisoner in, congratulate him on finishing his old sentence, and ask him to sign on the dotted line for a new one.) Now they just didn't release anyone: it was as simple as that.

But one day the head of the special department called me in. With a pained smile, he told me that I had been summoned so that "my contract might be terminated." I ought to say that at that time the simple word "freedom" had been replaced by the words "termination of contract."

So there I was, freed, with my own name turned by a clerk's slip of the pen into one that one might give a dog. Now I was "Alma!"

That was on April 19, 1953.

Translation by Catriona Kelly

NADEZHDA KANEL

FIFTEEN

Nadezhda Kanel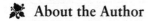
A Meeting at the Lubyanka

🏵 **About the Author**

Nadezhda Kanel's father, Venyamin (1873–1918), a Bolshevik from 1903 on, was a doctor in local government service before being appointed surgeon at the Yekaterininskaya Hospital in Moscow. After the October Revolution, Nadezhda's mother, Alexandra Kanel (1878–1936), also a doctor, became chief consultant at the hospital for the new Kremlin elite.

In 1939 both Nadezhda and her sister Yulia were arrested. Yulia died in prison in 1941. Nadezhda was released in 1953, and the following year she appeared as a prosecution witness at the trial of Beria's closest secret police associates, Abakumov and Komarov.

At the time of this writing, Nadezhda Veniaminovna lives in Moscow, where she is a doctor.

SIMEON VILENSKY

To begin with, I should explain how I found myself at the Lubyanka.

I suppose it was preordained as far back as 1932. In that year my mother, as chief consultant at the Kremlin hospital, together with Doctor Levin and Professor Pletnyov, refused to sign the falsified death certificate of Stalin's wife: it stated that Nadezhda Alliluyeva had died of acute appendicitis.* Stalin never forgave any of them for this. The fate of Levin and Plet-

---

* Nadezhda Alliluyeva shot herself on 9 November 1932.

nyov is well known: they were later accused of having murdered Maxim Gorky.* My mother was dismissed from her post in 1935, and she died the next year.

Three years later they arrested my sister Yulia, her husband, and me.

As part of her job, mother had taken Polina Zhemchuzhina, Molotov's wife, abroad to see some renowned foreign specialists, and had also accompanied the wives of Kamenev and Kalinin when they went to Berlin and Paris, respectively. The interrogator now claimed that she had been working for three European intelligence agencies, and had also recruited her daughters.

Naturally, I denied it all—and they beat me.

During one interrogation, I was shown the "confession" Yulia had made: I realized how they must have been torturing my Lyala!**

I was also shown a statement by Yulia's husband, Doctor Weinberg. He "confessed" to having been recruited by my mother, Alexandra Kanel, and to having divulged the secret of how malaria was spread in the USSR (in fact, his article on the subject had recently been published in a widely available medical textbook).

For a long time I had no idea what had happened to my own husband, Adolf Slomyansky. Was he free or had he also been arrested? We had no children: I was pregnant when I entered prison, and they forced me to have an abortion. Fortunately they didn't touch Adolf. He took in Yulia's two children and began to care for our elderly aunt. Meanwhile he completed both his master's thesis and his doctorate. Fifteen years he waited for me, and finally I came back.

My first three months at the Lubyanka were spent in endless interrogations. Then, suddenly, some light entered my prison existence: I met Alya— Ariadne Efron, the daughter of the poet Marina Tsvetaeva. This happened on 2 September 1939 when they moved me to a different cell.

Sitting on the floor in front of the door was a girl who looked to be about eighteen years old, with long blonde plaits and huge blue eyes. It was a very Russian face, but somehow she struck me as a foreigner—she was dressed simply, but her black skirt, white blouse, and red sleeveless sweater were obviously of foreign make.

"Ever since she was arrested a few days ago, she's been sitting by that door, waiting to be let out," one of the women said to me.

I asked the girl where she worked.

---

* At the 1938 show trial of the "Right-Trotskyist bloc," the doctors were found guilty of murdering Gorky. Levin was shot immediately, Pletnyov in September 1941.
** Affectionate diminutive used in the family for Yulia; Nadezhda was known as Dina.

Ariadne Efron

"On Strastnoi Boulevard, at the Magazine and Newspaper Combine."
"I know quite a few people there," I said.
"Oh. Who?"
"Mulya Gurevich, for instance."
"He's my husband!"
"He can't be—Mulya's married to one of my closest friends!"
"He and I have been together now for a year . . ."

I can remember her saying, "I was such a good girl—everyone was so fond of me, and then, suddenly, they arrested me . . ." At the time I thought, "All of us are good girls, and we are all being arrested." I soon realized, however, that there really was no one quite as good as Alya.

We were together for six months, until February 1940. Alya had been accused of spying. She realized that her father had also been arrested, and feared that they would imprison her mother as well. Yet the constant nervous tension evidently heightened Alya's powers of observation, and her inexhaustible humor served as a sort of defense. In any case, I can't remember ever laughing so much in my life. Alya made me laugh from morning to night. She parodied every visit the guard made to our cell, and when she demanded: "Name! Initials in full!" we could not help laughing out loud.

Despite the frequent interrogations and the sheer tedium of our life in prison, Alya and I didn't take things seriously at all. Knowing that we were completely innocent, we were sure that the most they could give us was three years' exile. We agreed to meet up after our release and even decided where—in the town of Voronezh, for some reason.

Alya was still thoroughly immersed in the life from which she had been abruptly torn; she thought constantly about Mulya, her first great love. "Even though I'm in prison," she used to say, "I'm glad I came back to Russia and that I have my Mulya. The last two years of my life have been so happy!"

Later she wrote to me, "Remember when you and I read together and talked endlessly, about everything and anything, as if we were trying to store up our friendship for all the years we would be apart? Little did I know then that a time would come when I would be all on my own. Despite the frightful circumstances, I was still very happy as long as we were together."

Alya and I saw in the New Year of 1940 together. She even managed to make a cake using some biscuits that she bought at the prison shop, with a mixture of butter and sugar for the filling. We listened to the Kremlin clock on Red Square strike midnight.

In 1974, the year before her death, Alya sent me a letter: "It's almost the New Year again. At this time I always think back to the extraordinary New Year's Eve that we celebrated together: the remarkable circumstances (even I find them hard to credit now) and the remarkable closeness we felt for one another; the Kremlin chimes (I can hear them still), and hearts filled, in spite of everything, above all else, with faith, hope, and love . . ."

Starting in August 1940, Alya spent three months with only a young Latvian woman, Valya Freiberg, for company. Then the two of them were moved to another cell. "I can still vividly recall the scene," Alya later wrote:

> Valya and I entered a small cell, which for some reason had its own wash basin. One of the women stood there washing. As soon as the door closed behind us, I asked, "Have any of you met someone named Kanel?"
>
> The woman at the basin turned around, her face pale, and said, "My name's Kanel!"
>
> "Lyalya?"

"Lyalya."

"Dina sends her greetings."

We were not together long, only a few days—but long enough for me to capture a living image, and bring it back to you. She was sure I would do that and, Dinochka, that made her last moments easier to bear . . .

At the end of 1947, when Alya was living in Ryazan, she once came to see me in Moscow and gave me the details of her meeting with Yulia. She told me all that Yulia had gone through during her terrible interrogation, and how she was forced to sign awful false confessions. Alya spoke of her own losses, too—the deaths of her mother, her brother Georgy (or Moor, as they called him), and her father. "I've no more tears to shed," she told me.

We never met again. At the beginning of 1948 I was exiled from Moscow, and, in July 1949 I was arrested for the second time.

In 1953 I was being held in Vladimir prison, and although the newspapers we were given were many weeks out of date, we knew that Stalin had died, and that Beria was now in control. The prisoners all wrote petitions asking him to review their cases, but since I knew that Beria had been behind my arrest, I naturally did not do so.

On 16 August I was suddenly summoned for interrogation. We had to walk to a different block: as I crossed the yard in the drizzling rain, I had a terrible premonition of fresh misfortune.

Inside I was greeted by a man of about fifty, who introduced himself as Procurator Volodin. "Have you ever discussed your case with anyone else?" he immediately asked. I assured him that I had not.

"What about Ariadne Efron?"

I went cold. Surely Alya had not betrayed me?!

"Tell me how you and your sister were arrested in 1939, and how the investigation was conducted."

"I've forgotten all about that . . ."

"You have nothing to be afraid of. You can tell me everything. We know that you and your sister weren't guilty of anything. Beria has been unmasked. Write down everything that happened to you. Ariadne Efron wrote to the USSR Procurator General's Office from Turukhansk, and this has speeded up the review of your case."

The next day I left prison and took a taxi all the way to Moscow.

Soon I began receiving letters from Alya, who had been exiled to Turukhansk, in the Far North:

Over the years, my mind has learned to understand it all, but my heart refuses to understand a thing. In short, every noble act seems natural to me, while all that is now accepted as normal strikes me as unbelievably base. I consider our friendship, your relationship with Adolf, and Adolf's treatment of Lyalya's children and Aunt Zhenya, entirely natural. It seems entirely natural to me that every time the ships can come here,* poor, old, chronically sick Aunt Lilya scrapes together a parcel for me—although it is now fifteen years since she started helping first Mama, and my brother Moor, and now me! Yet, by the standards of recent times, it would have been entirely normal for Adolf to remarry in 1940, for the children to be put in a home, and for Aunt Lilya to have disowned me fifteen years ago . . .

I'm afraid that I once broke the promise I made to you and Lyalya. On the day after Beria was unmasked, I sent a registered letter to the USSR Procurator-General's Office, briefly telling them everything I knew about you both. I so wanted for you to return home as quickly as possible, my darling . . .

Translation by Cathy Porter and John Crowfoot

---

* Turukhansk was accessible by sea and river only during the summer months from June to September.

ZAYARA VESYOLAYA

SIXTEEN

Zayara Vesyolaya ━━━━━━━━━━

7:35

🌸 About the Author

We became friends in 1947, when we studied together at the Potyomkin Teacher Training Institute in Moscow. At the end of our second year, Zayara suddenly stopped coming to class. We soon discovered that she had been arrested. I remember my horror at the thought that each one of us could just as suddenly end up behind bars.

Zayara was not sent to a camp, but she endured the Butyrki and Lubyanka prisons in Moscow, transit prisons elsewhere, and exile. There is nothing gloomy about her memoirs, though; the tone throughout is one of innate optimism and an ability to laugh at herself—a well-known means of defense.

This is especially true of the ending, which has not been included in this excerpt. Zayara had been allowed to change her place of exile from Siberia to Kazakhstan. Failure to report to the commandant's office by the date given in the document she carried with her would be considered an attempt to escape, and punished by twenty years' hard labor.

"I had to walk the sixty kilometers to the station," she writes. "As I set off, escorted by a document that took up half a notebook page, those ten days of freedom made me feel like that poor dog in the Chekhov story: I've swallowed a piece of meat with a string attached, and it can be pulled back out of my throat at any time. Still, I was looking forward to every moment."

There were several delays along the way, and her allotted time was already running out, but finally she managed to buy a train ticket to her destination. "The conductor of the soft-seated carriage, looking askance at my rough laborer's boots and quilted jacket, and my canvas bag with its string straps, examined my ticket very thoroughly, all but testing it with his teeth. When the train moved off, I thought that fate must be on my side, for now I would definitely make it in time. Unless, of course, the train derailed . . ."

Zayara Vesyolaya's memoirs read as vividly as pages from a diary, recreating the past as though she were writing them the day after.

NONNA DRUYAN

My Arrest

In 1949 I was in my second year at the Moscow City Teacher-Training Institute, and my elder sister Gaira was in her final year at university. That April she successfully defended her graduation diploma, so we invited some friends to come over the following Saturday to celebrate.

I don't know why—perhaps the heart really is a prophet—I began to persuade her to hold the party on Friday instead. Gaira objected, saying it was easier to have people come over on a Saturday, before our day off, and, more important, I had to keep Friday free to study for my Latin test the next day. But I was so stubbornly insistent that in the end we invited our friends for Friday, 22 April.

Since our mother's arrest, my sister and I had been sharing a room in a communal apartment on busy Arbat Street in the very center of the city, where all roads then met. There were few evenings when someone did not come by, and it was not unusual to get a friend to ring from a pay phone after ten in the evening, saying "We're here with Valya and Mila—you don't know them—and we missed the last film-show. Can we come over?" "Of course!" we would tell them.

Our friends and our friends' friends, who were mainly students, would come to visit us. We would take turns reading poems aloud, swap books, and wind up the gramophone (our favorite records then were "Solveig's Song" and Oginsky's polonaise "Farewell my Country," which we played over and over again).

In Moscow tradition, our guests were always served tea, but unless Minka, my best friend and classmate, brought something tasty, we rarely had anything to go with it except bread. Minka's parents gave her extra money, so that she could spend her stipend however she liked, whereas my sister and I had nothing else to live on, and we were always hungry.

That Friday, however, to mark this special occasion, we had bought plenty of sausage, cheese, cookies, and sweets, and put two bottles of wine on the table. (We could afford all this because not long before, we had taken our sewing machine to a second-hand shop.)

The party was a great success, and our guests were reluctant to leave. But since the metro closed at midnight, most of them eventually started making their farewells. Only those who lived nearby remained: Minka, an old schoolfriend of ours named Oleg, and Dima, a student from the Institute of Foreign Relations whom we had never met before, who had come with one of my girlfriends and had the misfortune to stay late.

The table had been extended to seat all our guests, and the five of us sat together along one side drinking our now cold tea; deep in conversation, we quite forgot the time.

Suddenly there was a knock at the front door. The clock read a quarter past two.

Gaira and I exchanged glances, and I went out into the hallway to open the door. When I came back, I was accompanied by an officer and several lads in Ministry of State Security uniforms. They were followed by the janitor and his wife—witnesses.

There was a brief mute scene, as our guests stared in bewilderment at the new arrivals. The good-looking officer, who resembled the hero Kadochnikov in the popular film *Exploits of a Secret Service Agent*, glanced quickly around the room, then introduced himself: "Major Potapov." Nodding toward the messy table, he asked jokingly, "Celebrating Easter?"

"Not likely!" I retorted, stung by the suggestion. We weren't old ladies—and besides, Easter wasn't until Sunday! What was the matter with him?

"I've just defended my graduation diploma, so we're celebrating," explained Gaira.

"Well, that's a good cause, isn't it. Which one of you would be Zayara Artyomovna Vesyolaya?" The major handed me a search and arrest warrant.

For some reason I wasn't alarmed, merely surprised. But Gaira was terrified. "Wait, what does Zayara have to do with it? It's me they should be arresting, not Zayara!"

To Major Potapov, and indeed all the others, her outburst probably seemed rather strange, to say the least.

While she was student teaching at a secondary school, Gaira had said in a history class that during the 1905 Revolution the more backward segments of the population had taken part in pogroms against the Jews. One of her fellow students considered this to be slander against the Russian people and reported it, appropriately embellished, to the student Party organization. The matter was taken up, and after being publicly criticized several times by various authorities, Gaira was expelled from the Komsomol.

For the past few weeks, therefore, my sister and I had been living as if on the edge of a volcano. True, we never thought that she might be arrested; we merely feared that she would not be allowed to graduate. Since she had been granted her diploma, after a brilliant defense, we assumed that the worst was over.

"You must have gotten the names mixed up," Gaira firmly told the major. "It's a mistake!"

The major assured her that there was no mistake, and ordered me to pack my things.

"Don't take much—just a change of underwear and . . . well, just the bare essentials. Don't forget a warm cardigan," he added solicitously. "And bring some money if you have any."

His lips gone pale, Dima started mumbling that he had never met us before, that it was the first time he had ever been in our apartment. Gaira and I swore that he was telling the truth. We felt desperately sorry for him for having gotten caught up in this mess.

Oleg stood loyally by us, observing everything that was happening with silent interest. Minka immediately shook out all the money in her purse and gave it to me. Seeing me rummage in the dresser in a futile search for some spare underwear, she went into a corner, casually called out "Don't look!" and slipped off her dress and her silk petticoat. She pulled the dress back on over her bare body and stuffed the petticoat into the pillowcase that, for want of a traveling bag, I was putting my things in. She then removed her nylon stockings. These were the very height of fashion, and hardly anyone had them yet. I was about to protest that she couldn't possibly go home dressed like that (it was a cold April, and the nights were sometimes frosty), but she waved aside my objection.

"Ready?" said the major. "Then say your goodbyes!"

At that moment I remembered next morning's Latin test, and was overjoyed to be getting out of it.

Number 12 Krivoarbatsky Street was a typical apartment building of the beginning of the century; it was six stories high, with a gray granite facade. I loved our house. The only thing it lacked was an elevator. It probably had been built not long before the First World War, and there had not been time to install one in the space created for it, so the staircase wound around an empty shaft.

I was led out by two of the young MGB men, while the major and the others for some reason stayed behind in our room. As we walked down from the fourth floor, I was about to put my hand as usual on the bannister, but one of the MGB men silently steered me toward the wall, so that he was nearest to the stairwell. "Are they really afraid that I'll jump?" I thought in amazement. "You would think they'd caught a spy! V-e-e-ry interesting!"

As I descended the dimly lit staircase between the two guards, I could not help noticing the theatricality of the whole event. The scene would have been far more striking if I had been dressed more elegantly. My light overcoat with its sagging pockets, which I had been issued during the war, and my refugee's bundle totally ruined my image.

As we emerged from the entrance I surveyed the street. I had never seen it at such a late hour before.

No, that was not quite true. Once, during an air-raid alert in July 1941, Gaira and I had dashed along a similarly deserted road in the middle of the night, to the bomb shelter on the corner of Krivoarbatsky and Plotnikov streets. Mother was on night duty at the maternity hospital where she worked at the time, and my sister and I were sleeping so soundly that we did not hear the sirens: the neighbors had to wake us as they left for the shelter. In my sleepy state, it took me a long time to get dressed. Gaira tried to hurry me, but I insisted on standing in front of the mirror to put on my red Pioneer scarf. "Why are you doing that?" demanded Gaira. "To spite Hitler!" I replied. When we eventually dashed out of the house there was not a soul around. Holding hands, we ran toward Plotnikov Street, pursued by the wail of the sirens.

It was also in the dead of night that Mama had been taken away the previous year, and that my father had been arrested eleven years before.

My parents met in Moscow and married in 1922.

Mama left school in her home town of Kriukov, in the Poltava province of southern Russia, after the fourth grade. She worked for several years in a children's home, and then was sent to Moscow to train as a teacher. But she failed her exams, and went to work at a stocking factory instead.

At that time Father—the writer Artyom Vesyoly—had just been demobilized from the navy. He had brought the manuscript of his first novel, *Rivers of Fire*, to Moscow. It was published in 1923 in a magazine, and the next year it came out as a book.

My parents separated after only a few years, but they remained friends. I often saw my father and remember him well.

We celebrated the New Year of 1937 at his dacha in Peredelkino, the new writers' village outside Moscow.

The dinner table had been opened out ready for the traditional New Year meal. For the moment it was covered up with piles of colored paper and bright scraps of material. Gaira, our stepsister Fanta, and I made toys to decorate the tree. Father and his younger brother Vasily had chopped down a fir tree right there on the still wild grounds of the dacha, and now it

Zayara Vesyolaya

stood in the diningroom, its tip brushing against the ceiling. Its resiny fragrance drowned out all the other New Year smells: paint, glue, tangerines, and Granny's hot pies.

To keep us going we ate a simple evening meal in the kitchen, where Granny had kept the stove going. Then, Father went upstairs to his study, returning with several boxes of expensive Kazbek cigarettes.

"That's it! I'm giving up smoking!" he said. Opening the door of the stove, he flung the cigarettes into the flames.

"How can you? They're Kazbeks!" Uncle Vasya cried out in dismay, and we gasped in horror as he snatched the boxes out of the fire with his bare hands.

After the meal Father lay down on the gray soldier's blanket in his study. My sisters and I snuggled up to him and began vying with each other to tell him what we were doing at school (I was in the first grade then, and it all seemed extremely important to me).

After a while he said, "Now just imagine the following scene." It is all engraved in my memory. Speaking steadily as if he were reading from a printed page, he stared intently out the window as though he could see something in the darkness.

"In a tent on the steppe sat a Tatar Khan and a young Russian slave girl. The Khan plied the girl with food and wine, but she refused everything. Then suddenly she said, 'Give me bread.' He gave her bread. 'Give me meat.' He gave her meat. 'Give me a knife!' He gave her a knife. She cut the bread and meat on a board, and said to the Khan, 'Take it!' The Khan stretched out his hand"—at this point Father stretched a hand out toward the dark window—"when suddenly the girl swung down the knife and impaled the Khan's hand on the board. The Khan howled, and his bodyguards rushed in. They would have seized the girl, but she slithered out of the tent, as lithe as a snake, leaving them clutching her clothes. Around the Khan's tent were camped the countless warriors of his army, and a thousand fires blazed into the night. They gave chase, but the girl—naked, her hair flowing down her back—jumped over one fire after another, running until the night steppe swallowed her up . . ."

When I later recalled this story, I thought it was an episode that had not appeared in *Flow, Swift Volga!*, his novel about how Yermak and his Cossacks conquered Siberia for the Tsar. It was only recently, when I explored what was left of Father's archive, that I realized it was an excerpt from an entirely different novel, the manuscript of which had been confiscated when he was arrested.

I don't remember actually seeing in the New Year. I may simply have slept through it. Nor can I guess what Father was thinking about when he walked around Peredelkino with us on the first day of 1937. But there can be no doubt that he foresaw his tragic end, for people were being arrested all around him.

That summer, when he and my sisters returned from their usual trip down the Volga in a small fishing boat, they said that, unlike previous trips, Father had avoided visiting any of the big towns, and he had stayed close to the great floating rafts of timber when he sailed under the sentry-guarded bridges. He was afraid that if he were arrested, his daughters would be left alone and far from home.

Father spent the rest of that August in Peredelkino, where his second wife, Lyudmila Yosifovna, and two of their children, Lyova and Volga, were spending the summer. I was staying there, too, with my grandparents.

Komsomolskaya Pravda had just published a review of father's greatest novel, under the headline "A Slanderous Work: Artyom Vesyoly's *Russia Bathed in Blood*." Realizing that his arrest was now imminent, he began to prepare. Some of his papers he took to his elderly parents and steve-dore brother Vasya on Pokrovka Street, assuming that they would not be touched. In this, thankfully, he was proved correct.

Grandfather died during the war, Grandmother in 1948. Father's young-er brother, our Uncle Vasily, stayed on Pokrovka Street with his wife, Klav-dia. They were the only ones who knew of the existence of this archive: it was considered an act of sedition to harbor papers belonging to a convicted "enemy of the people." They kept them hidden under the bed in a wicker clothes basket. Vasily and Klavdia were far from literary people. Yet this stevedore and his canteen worker wife not only loved Artyom as family, but had boundless respect for his work, believing that these papers would be valued and needed when he was released from prison. The materials they saved were invaluable: manuscripts, documents, letters, photographs, and the various editions of his works that were published during his lifetime.

The last time I saw my father was in September or October of 1937. He came by right after I returned from school. He was silent and focused. He slowly took off his coat, paced around the room a few times, then sat down, took a little paperback book from his pocket, and laid it before him on the table. Seeing that it was one of the "Book by Book" series that I was collect-ing, I happily reached across the table for it. But Father put his hand over the book: "Sit down and listen. Yanko the Musician," he announced in a tone of mournful solemnity.

Father read aloud to me, something he had never done. I had learned to read on my own at the age of four. I listened, blinking back the tears, and when he came to the last line, "The birch trees rustled over Yanko's grave," I burst into sobs.

He soon left, and I was not sorry at the time—I could not wait to read the story of Yanko again.

Father was arrested at the end of October. Soon afterward, Lyudmila Yosifovna was sentenced to eight years in the camps, and their children were placed in a home.

For many years we knew nothing about Father's fate. Our regular visits to the NKVD Inquiries Office at 24 Kuznetsky Street invariably met with the same standard reply: "Alive and working; sentenced to ten years with-out rights of correspondence." This was repeated without explanation even when his sentence had expired. After he was posthumously rehabilitated in 1956, the date of his death was given as 2 December 1939. According to information we received from the Military Collegium of the USSR Supreme Court only in 1988, however, he was shot on 8 April 1938.

Mother was arrested at the beginning of 1948. She was not jailed in 1937, although she had been expecting it because of offenses committed much earlier. While working at the Moscow Electric Lightbulb Factory in the 1920s, she had once spoken out in support of the opposition at a meeting there. For this past misdeed, she was expelled from the Party in the mid-1930s, and lost her job. Unable to find any other work in Moscow, she was forced to sign up for a year in Karakalpakia in Central Asia. She left me in the care of a friend from her days at the stocking factory, and Gaira she left with her parents. Mother returned to Moscow at the very height of the mass arrests. Every evening she warned us not to worry if they came for her during the night, and she would put money under Gaira's pillow "just in case, to keep you going." But they left her alone at that time.

After the war, Mother worked as a nurse at a polyclinic, where she earned extra money by giving injections. One day she was talking to a patient over the telephone in the hallway of our communal apartment, telling him that he should try to get some American penicillin, because it was much better than ours. A neighbor overheard and reported her.

Mother was accused of anti-Soviet agitation. Because of her previous misdemeanors, she was sentenced to the maximum of eight years in the camps. She ended up in Mordovia, in the Potma women's camp. She was not deprived of the right to correspond, but she was limited to sending only two letters a year. They also allowed her to acknowledge our food parcels with a single line on a postcard: "Received your parcel, Mother." One very brief letter (it had clearly been censored) had already reached us. She told us that she was alive and well, doing gang labor, and she thanked us for the parcels. She was worried about us, she added, and begged us to write more often.

My sister and I used to send her parcels every month. We were given the money for them by a close friend of hers, but were sworn to the strictest secrecy: he was an Old Bolshevik, a factory director, and he ran a huge risk by helping a prisoner. We had hoped that once Gaira finished the university and got a job, we would be able to take on full responsibility for helping Mother ourselves.

Outside the entrance to our building stood a black sedan. The door was thrown open in front of me, and I found myself in the back seat between the two soldiers. The car sped off down the Arbat, along Vozdvizhenka Street, across Manege Square past the Kremlin, and drew up outside the large building on Dzerzhinsky Square. We had stopped outside entrance number 3.

The Lubyanka

It was only after I became familiar with prison and its terminology that I realized I had spent the night in a "box." At the time I thought this windowless little cubbyhole was the standard cell for one. There was a stool and something like a bedside table. But no bed. "I expect they'll throw me a straw mattress," I said to myself. "Just think, I'm in prison!"

I was in a state of nervous excitement, expecting something dramatic to happen that would explain my mysterious arrest.

It amused me to think that we would never have had our party if we had not changed it to Friday. I was glad that the knock in the night did not come when my sister and I were fast asleep, as had been the case for Mother. In hindsight, I was surprised that they had not searched the apartment.

Time passed, and nothing happened. My excitement gradually began to give way to anxiety. I tried to think of reasons why I might have been arrested. During the visit we had been allowed to make to Mother in prison before she was sent off to the camps, she had managed to hint which of our neighbors in the apartment was the informer. Maybe I had blabbed something over the telephone and he had heard and reported me also? Or perhaps he had simply invented some accusation against me? How would I get the chance to clear my name? Either my arrest was a mistake, and they would sort things out and let me go, or . . .

I sat staring at the wall, beginning to feel the oppressive effects of the glaring electric light overhead and the total silence—it made my ears ring.

Over the last year, while standing in lines for hours at various prison inquiry windows, I had overheard snatches of conversation from which I learned that political prisoners did not face a trial in the normal sense. Their sentences were handed down by the "Special Board."

Why was I sitting here for so long without being called? Had they forgotten about me, or what? What if the Special Board had already sentenced me to solitary confinement? In that case I would stay where I was. I began to feel afraid.

There was no window in the cell, and soon I lost all track of time. Suddenly I felt myself in the grip of some sort of psychosis: the most important thing was to find out right away whether it was night or day outside.

I went up to the door and knocked. The lock or bolt clanged open and a guard peered in. "What's your problem?" he said.

"What time is it?"

He looked at me dumbfounded and slammed the door. The bolt clanged to.

I felt a lump in my throat, and it was all I could do not to burst into tears.

But soon the lump disappeared. Things were starting to happen.

First I was taken to the shower. This was evidently merely for appearance's sake, since the water was barely warm, and when I complained about it to the guard, he merely shouted from outside the door, "You don't have to wash if you don't want to—just make sure to wet your hair!"

Next I was searched. A sullen woman in a military uniform and a beret shook the things from my pillowcase onto a large table. The nylon stockings immediately caught her attention.

"Been running around with an American, have you?"

I swore that there had never been a single American in my life, but she clearly did not believe me. I bit my tongue and regretted that I had not maintained a haughty silence.

Under the left cuff of her tunic I glimpsed a watch.

"Please, could you tell me the time?" I asked her. It was as if she had not heard. She looked through the stockings at the light with feminine interest, then stuffed them back in my pillowcase and said grumpily, "My daughter doesn't have anything like that . . . Get undressed."

"What?" I gasped.

"You heard me—everything off." With deft, practiced fingers she felt the seams, collar, and cuffs of my dress, and cut off the buttons. Then she ripped the elastic out of my knickers and set it to one side, along with the belt from my dress, my scarf, and my garter belt.

The whole time I stood in the classic pose of the modest bather.

"Get dressed!"

I hurriedly pulled on my dress and plain cotton stockings and was reaching out for my garter belt, when she silently scooped up the things she had set aside and tied them up in a bundle.

I knew that belts and straps were confiscated from prisoners to keep them from hanging themselves, so the removal of my scarf and belt seemed appropriate. But pieces of elastic? I realized then that these were taken away not to prevent suicides but purely in order to humiliate and demoralize us. My knickers were somehow kept up by my tight dress, but as soon as the guard led me with my bundle back down the corridor, my stockings started to slip to the floor, and I stumbled along, bending over every minute to pull them up with my free hand.

I was taken back to my box. Soon, however, I was called out ("Leave your things!") to have my photograph and finger prints taken. I continued to ask what time it was.

"I don't know," the soldier taking the finger prints growled sullenly.

"At least tell me if it's night or day."

"I don't know."

The photographer also said that he did not know, but he gave me a guilty glance as he did so.

"Please tell me!" I implored him. "You're wearing a watch!"

He said nothing, and looked away. To this day I cannot understand why it was such a secret.

I had been sitting in my box for what seemed like an interminably long time. I realized now that this was a temporary accommodation, for I had heard that a cell must contain a slop bucket. It appeared that they would be moving me. I hoped it would be soon. I was already fed up with this cubbyhole.

Suddenly the order came: "Collect your things!"

I happily jumped up from the stool, grabbed my bundle, and emerged with a beating heart. Where were they taking me now?

The guard led me down the corridor. We went up some stairs, down another corridor, then down some more stairs and along yet another corridor, where we stopped in front of a door with a peephole. The guard flung it open, and I anxiously stepped in—it was the same box!

Someone once observed that when it came to matters of hygiene in prisons and camps, priority was always given to clean floors. Among the prisoners, this tireless obsession of the administration became the butt of many a joke. Later, I realized that I had been taken out of my box for a few minutes so that it could be cleaned—the floor was gleaming wet. At the time, I interpreted the fact that I had been made to walk up and down stairs with that ridiculous bundle and my falling stockings—only to be brought right back to where I had started from—as a deliberate attempt to humiliate me.

The door slammed behind me, and I burst into tears. Hurling my bundle down on the table, I buried my face in it . . .

Having cried my eyes out, I sat staring vacantly at the wall. I did not want to sleep, but my head was ringing from being awake so long.

Suddenly, so suddenly that I did not believe my ears, I heard the voice of my sister Gaira. It was followed immediately by a hissing voice, "Sh-sh!"

I jumped up and threw myself at the door.

"You have my sister here; they took her away last night." Gaira spoke in a very loud voice, evidently hoping that I would hear and would at least know that she had also been arrested.

"Sh-sh!"

"She forgot to bring soap. Can I give her some?"

"Sh-sh!"

I banged on the door with my fists: "I'm here, Gaira, I'm here!"

"Zaika! Zaika!"

A door banged, and all was quiet again.

A minute later—I was still clinging to the door—a furious fat sergeant burst into the cell. Pushing me away from the door and closing it firmly behind him, even then he muffled his voice: "What were you yelling about?"

"My sister's there!"

"Sh-sh! There's nobody there."

"But I heard her voice!"

"Sh-sh! If you can't keep quiet, I will put you someplace where you'll roast alive!" (Or perhaps he said "freeze to death"; I don't exactly remember now, but the threat was definitely connected to the temperature of this "other place.") I am not the bravest of souls, and I was a little bit scared, but to keep him from guessing this, I dug in my heels, gritted my teeth, and stared him right in the eye. Casting one more threatening glance at me, the fat man left.

It was all over! Now that Gaira had also been arrested, it was foolish to hope that they would sort things out and release us. Did this mean that they had a reason? How treacherous the handsome major had been! Obviously he had come to our apartment with two search and arrest warrants, so why had he not said so right away, instead of putting on a performance? He must have stayed on after I was taken away. There had been a search after all.

But what luck that Gaira and I had heard each other! They had wanted to fool us (or rather me, by making me sit there thinking that Gaira was still free), but their plan didn't work! It's no wonder the fat man was angry; we had probably gotten him in trouble.

I even cheered up a bit for a while, but then I thought of Mother, who was doomed without our support—it was said to be impossible to survive the camps without food parcels.

Soon the guard brought me some food—the day's allowance of black bread, two lumps of sugar, and a mug of something hot. I had no desire to eat or drink, and just gnawed on the sugar.

I remembered Gaira saying that they had come for me at night. It was probably now morning, and this was breakfast. So the daily prison routine had begun. How long would it last? Eight years? Ten?

I must have been exhausted after the night's adventures. A strange feeling of indifference came over me, a mixture of anger and elation: *So be it!*

The door opened. "Get your things!"

I dragged my bundle off the table and stumbled to the door, without my previous sense of anticipation.

"Take your bread," the guard reminded me.

I went back, stuffed the bread into my pillowcase, and went out into the corridor. I again was led through a series of corridors and down some stairs;

then we crossed a yard (it was broad daylight, and I immediately felt better breathing in the fresh air) and went up to the second floor, where we came to a grille that partitioned off a rather wide corridor.

A sharp smell of disinfectant (the same kind that railway sleeper cars are sometimes washed down with) assailed my nose, mingled with the stench of urine, and I realized that behind the doors beyond the grille on both sides of the corridor were cells.

At the grille I was handed over to the guard in charge of this corridor, and he led me to cell number 10.

"Face to the wall!" he ordered. As he fiddled with his key ring, I tried to imagine what it would be like behind the door. I pictured a huge room with a stone floor and a dark vaulted ceiling, with prisoners—their heads shaved, and wearing striped vests and trousers—lying on board beds. (For some reason it never crossed my mind that the men might be kept separate from the women in prison.)

I entered the cell shrinking inside with fear, but managing somehow to keep my chin up.

It was a fairly small room, of some twenty square meters, with a waxed parquet floor. (I learned later that the building had once contained furnished apartments.) Instead of board beds there were iron cots, similar to hospital beds, and by the wall was a large table covered in oilcloth. In the corner by the door was the slop bucket, a lidded zinc tank like the kind you boil underwear in. On the outside wall was a window covered with a metal panel (known in prison slang as a "muzzle") which was mounted at a slight angle: it fit close to the windowsill, but leaned out slightly at the top. Thus a little bit of fresh air came through the open ventilation pane, and even a tiny amount of daylight which, after the "box," I found especially comforting. The radiator recessed in the wall was covered by fine wire netting.

I took in all these details only later. At the time I felt mainly a huge sense of relief at seeing, not a crowd of men in prison stripes but five educated-looking women. When the guard had locked the door behind him, the youngest woman came up to me and said, "Aren't you from the university?"

"No, I'm from the teacher-training institute," I replied. Thinking that she herself might be a university student, I added, "But my sister's at Moscow University."

"What's her surname?"

"Vesyolaya."

"Gaira?"

"Yes!" I nearly threw my arms around her.

"I was studying history too. She's in her last year, isn't she?"

"She was. She's in prison now . . . "

"Oh Lord. . . ! What's your name? I'm Natasha Zaporozhets."

My sister had never mentioned Natasha. But Natasha knew Gaira, and that was enough to fill me with quiet confidence: I was no longer all alone in prison. They had taken me under their wing.

The blinding ceiling light stayed on all night (the other women tied bandages over their eyes before going to sleep) but the glare did not bother me that first evening. I fell asleep the moment my head touched the pillow. I did not hear the door open (which it always did with a particularly malevolent clang), and woke only when someone began shaking my bed.

A woman guard was standing next to me.

"Surname?" she demanded.

I told her.

"Initials in full!"

"Wha-at?"

"Initials in full!" she repeated impatiently. I could not understand what she meant.

"First name and patronymic!" Natasha whispered from the next bed.

"Zayara Artyomovna," I said.

"Interrogation."

There was a set routine: The guards never addressed prisoners by their surnames; the prisoners had to identify themselves. This, I was told, was because if a guard opened the wrong door by mistake and called Ivanov "Petrov," Ivanov would know that there was a Petrov in the next cell, and they might be friends or even "accomplices." At night, when everyone was asleep, only the prisoner they needed would be awakened and asked his name. During the day the ritual was even more complicated. Addressing no one in particular, the guard would ask, "Surnames beginning with K?"

"Me," someone would reply.

"Name?"

"Kuznetsova."

"Initials in full!"

If there were several surnames beginning with K, the guard would point at each person in turn until he got the right name.

There might also, of course, be people with the same surname, and even the same initials; hence initials "in full" would be meaningless.

At the grille the woman guard handed me over to a soldier, who led me through some endlessly long corridors. Whenever we approached a turn in a corridor or a flight of stairs, he would loudly click his tongue: I felt as if nails were being driven into the back of my head. The purpose of this clicking was to signal that a prisoner was approaching; they wanted to ensure that two prisoners did not meet.

"So, Zayara, you've been breaking our prison rules, have you?" the interrogator said to me affably as I entered his office. We looked at each other. He wore civilian clothes, and could have passed for an ordinary official doing some ordinary job. "Banging on the door, shouting—we don't allow that kind of thing in here. You have no soap; is that the problem? We have a prison shop—you can buy some there. Sit down." He pointed to a chair by the wall facing his table.

Having introduced himself as Melnikov (I don't remember his rank— lieutenant, I think), he warned me that I should address him as "citizen" rather than "comrade" investigator. Then, getting right to the point, he said, "Well, now . . . confess your crimes."

It was not the words themselves that surprised me—I had expected something of the kind (it would be strange not to ask about crimes at an interrogation)—it was the calm, expressionless, matter-of-fact tone in which they were pronounced. As I would later learn from my prison friends, this was not the only time Melnikov had used those words that night.

Shrugging my shoulders and unwittingly lapsing into the same languid tone, I replied, "I have nothing to confess."

"Think about it," Melnikov said. Ignoring me, he began to rummage through some papers.

There was a long pause.

Finally he got up from his desk and handed me a slip of paper. "Here are the charges against you."

As the daughter of enemy of the people Nikolai Ivanovich Kochkurov (alias Artyom Vesyoly) and the criminal Gita Grigorievna Lukatskaya (convicted under Article 58:10), the paper said, I had been charged under Article 7:35 ("SDE").

Were it not for the words "enemy of the people" and "criminal," the document in my hands might have been a copy of my birth certificate. And this was the accusation?!

I asked what Article 7:35 covered and what the initials SDE stood for. Those charged under Article 7:35 were "Socially Dangerous Elements," Melnikov replied. (Since Articles 7 and 35 were always spoken of together and were similarly abbreviated even in official documents, I had always assumed that it must mean Article 7, clause 35. They were in fact two separate articles of the Criminal Code. Article 7 referred to people against whom "measures had to be taken in the public interest," and 35 specified what those measures should be.)

I handed the document back to Melnikov with a grin, saying I could hardly deny that I was my parents' daughter.

He did not pursue this subject. He ordered me to sign in acknowledg-
ment that I had familiarized myself with the charges, then he summoned the
guard and ordered that I be taken back.

As we strode down the long corridors ("Hands behind your back!"), I
realized that the charges were not as ridiculous as they had first appeared.
In 1937 they had jailed the wives of enemies of the people, so now it must
be the children's turn. At the time I did not know that they had jailed adult
children in 1937.

But Stalin had clearly said that a son cannot answer for his father. Why
had I not recalled those memorable words before? The interrogator did not
have a leg to stand on!

When I was taken back to his office a day or two later, I immediately
asked him about this.

Making it clear that I was not supposed to ask questions ("I ask the
questions here!"), Melnikov nonetheless gave me a very detailed reply. Although a son of course could not answer for his father, he explained, it had
been necessary in this case to temporarily isolate my sister and me from
society. It was something that "had to be done."

I cannot recall his exact words, but the gist was that since I probably felt
sorry for my imprisoned parents, I might easily nurture a sense of grievance
or anger ("One never knows!")—in other words, I might have developed
"anti-Soviet attitudes."

"It may be that you are free of such attitudes," Melnikov continued.
"But you might have them. It's possible, isn't it? In principle?"

I said, "In principle, yes."

"There, you see! Think what would happen if such attitudes were ex-
ploited by agents of a hostile power. You must understand how complicated
the present international situation is!"

I did understand. What I did not see was what possible use I might be to
"agents of a hostile power." I could hardly contradict a man like Melnikov,
however. He worked for the Ministry of State Security and naturally had a
far better grasp than I of the problems of hostile powers and socially dangerous elements. And as he said, one never knew.

When I returned to my cell, I went over Melnikov's arguments again and
again in my head.

"I suppose he's right," I thought. "One can't dispute the obvious: The
interests of society must always outweigh those of the individual."

I was kept at the Lubyanka for a whole month, until 23 May. During
this time I was taken out for interrogation two or three more times, for
some reason always in the middle of the night.

My interrogator behaved impeccably. I was grateful to him for this; I
was also pleased that it was he, and not someone else, who was in charge of

Gaira's case. The women in my cell said that some interrogators shouted and cursed, but in 1949 I did not hear of anyone being beaten or tortured.

Melnikov conducted each interrogation in a slow, unhurried manner, recording his questions and my answers in his neat handwriting. His questions were monotonously repetitive. About almost everyoné who had ever visited our apartment he would ask whether or not they had "anti-Soviet attitudes" or had raised seditious topics in conversation.

He paid special attention to those whose parents had been arrested: "Really? But her father is in prison," he would say. "Surely you must remember something. No? All right. Read this and sign."

One of his questions made me wonder if there had been an informer among our student friends. In hindsight I began to have my suspicions about one of the boys.

He had a habit of asking endless questions: where I was yesterday and with whom, who else was there, what their names were, where they studied, and what we had talked about. I assumed it was me he was interested in, and since I liked him, I was happy to answer. At times, however, I exclaimed, "How curious you are!" to which he would reply, "I have an inquisitive nature!"

One evening Gaira and I decided to clean out the drawers in our writing desk. We collected a pile of papers to be thrown away, including several letters. I said that letters should not be thrown in the trash; they should be burned in a fireplace. We didn't have a fireplace, so instead we put a bowl in the middle of the floor, threw the letters in it, and lit them. At that moment the "inquisitive" student dropped by. He began jumping around the bowl, trying to save at least one sheet of paper from the flames. He wanted to see what secrets we were hiding, he said. We laughed and pushed him away.

If he really was an informer, he could easily have used his imagination to make things difficult for us; since Mother's recent arrest and Gaira's expulsion from the Komsomol, surely we had been under surveillance. (The neighbor who informed on Mother about the "American penicillin" had added some accusations of his own invention.) But in all fairness to him, he evidently did not make anything up. Neither my sister nor I had ever harbored so much as a seditious thought; we had both willingly accepted and believed all we were taught by the Soviet educational system and, more important, by Soviet literature.

I was sure that Father was not an "enemy of the people." I had read his books and loved them, but despite what the interrogator said, I had never felt the slightest hostility toward the Soviet authorities or even the NKVD, either right after Father's arrest or later. Since childhood I had accepted the then-universal aphorism "You have to break eggs to make an omelette."

Ever since I became a Young Octobrist (at the age of seven) I had known about the capitalist encirclement of my country and the sharpening of the class struggle within it; at school assemblies I would read with genuine emotion Sergei Mikhalkov's poems about Young Pioneers who caught spies and saboteurs. Spies and saboteurs had to be caught and imprisoned. Of course the arrest of my father had been a mistake—and that of Ira's father, and Marina's grandfather. But you had to break eggs . . .

Since I was convinced of my father's innocence, I never hid the fact that he had been arrested. On the contrary, I didn't mind who I told. Only on one occasion did I keep it quiet.

During the war, Mother and I were evacuated from Moscow to a small village in the Urals. Mother worked on her own, without a doctor, at a health-care office in the area, and because of her medical skills she enjoyed enormous authority among the local collective-farm peasants. Whenever she was asked about her husband, she would avoid false rumors by saying nothing about the divorce or his arrest, merely telling people that there was no news of him. Strictly speaking, that was quite true, but since the phrase was used only of soldiers at the front then, it made it seem as though Father were away fighting in the war. Mother also asked me not to say anything, convinced that if people in the village found out that he was in prison, they would become suspicious, and she might lose her job. I promised to hold my tongue.

It was there that I finished primary school. That spring the day came that I had long dreamed about: having turned fourteen, I could join the Komsomol. I would have considered it an unthinkable sacrilege to conceal anything from my Komsomol organization. But I could not break my promise to my mother. I announced that I would not be joining the Komsomol. At first I responded with dispirited silence to people's attempts to change my mind. Then suddenly I thought up an excuse: I told them that I wanted to join at home in Moscow, not here while in evacuation.

I never did join the Komsomol. I was too mediocre a pupil in the top classes of my Moscow school, and when my Komsomol membership was being considered during my first year at the institute, my mother was arrested. I told them about it when my application was discussed, and that was the end of that.

Melnikov was naturally interested to know why I had not joined the Komsomol, but when I told him, he let the matter drop.

I was the only "7:35er" in our cell.

My cellmates assured me that it was a "light offense," and that in all probability my sister and I would simply be exiled from Moscow.

Secretly I was delighted that unlike the others, who were all "58ers," I would not have to face the camps. But I could not help feeling a sense of guilt, like a healthy person in the presence of someone who is terminally ill.

It was impossible to imagine that any of the women in cell number 10 was a spy or a saboteur.

Maria Alexandrovna, a college teacher, was in despair at being separated from her schoolboy son. Her husband, a professor, was also in prison.

When Tonya and her husband were both arrested, their three-year-old Genka was left behind. There were relatives, but would they take the boy in? Or was he already in a children's home? His father had told a joke to a group of people, Tonya said, and someone had denounced him. Now he was in prison for "anti-Soviet agitation," and Tonya for "failure to report" him herself.

But the most tragic case was that of a woman whose name I no longer remember. After her arrest, her twelve-year-old daughter was left totally on her own in Rostov-on-Don; during questioning, the interrogator told her that the child was now a prostitute. We all tried to comfort the unfortunate woman, saying that this was inconceivable, impossible; the girl was most likely in a children's home. She would stare vacantly into space and reply barely audibly, "I think so, too. He's lying."

Natasha had no children, but she was pregnant. When she was fourteen, her parents had been arrested, leaving Natasha and her younger brother in the care of their elderly grandfather. Essentially they had had to fend for themselves, and they lived in desperate poverty. When war broke out, Natasha volunteered for the army and fought in the Battle of Moscow. Then she enrolled at Moscow University, studied history, and completed her master's thesis. She had just gotten married—and now here she was at the Lubyanka.

Natasha and I spent a month together in cell number 10, and we are friends to this day. What happened to her after we parted she told me when we met again several years later.

She had refused to sign the records of her cross-examination fabricated by the interrogator, Makarenko. He would force her—and she was heavily pregnant!—to remain standing for hours on end. She would lose consciousness and fall, and they would bring her to with a whiff of ammonia, then prop her back against the wall again. But she never did sign. She was sentenced to five years' exile in the Kokchetavsk Region of Kazakhstan. The prison doctor said that her pregnancy was by then in jeopardy, but instead of keeping her in the hospital until she gave birth, they forced her to leave at once. After a month of unbelievably hard traveling, she finally arrived, and gave birth that same day to a stillborn baby.

Even today one still hears it occasionally said that under Stalin there was more law and order, or there was better food in the shops, or the vodka was cheaper . . .

One day the six of us returned from our walk around the prison yard to find a middle-aged woman sitting in the cell weeping. She had just been arrested, as it turned out. Raising her head as we came in, she pointed at me and exclaimed, "God, now they're even taking schoolgirls!"

I leapt to the defense of the Soviet state: "Nonsense, I'm not a schoolgirl—I'm a student!"

May arrived. It became unbearably stuffy in the cell, and the stench from the slop bucket grew intolerable. The empty days dragged on, and we became accustomed to our prison routine, which only made the monotony more oppressive.

We didn't have a single peaceful night. Sometimes one of us would be taken off to be interrogated (the clank of the lock would jolt us all awake). Sometimes it was my fault that we were all awakened.

According to the rules, prisoners had to sleep with their hands on top of the blanket. I once asked my cellmates why this was, and they replied with a grin, "So you won't slash your veins under the covers."

Every evening I would conscientiously lie down with my hands outside the blanket. It was awkward and uncomfortable, and made it hard for me to fall asleep (moreover, we were ordered to bed at a much earlier hour than I was used to). As soon as I dozed off, however, I would instinctively pull the blanket up to my chin. The key would grate in the lock, and the guard would shake my bed: "Hands!"

The sleep of youth is deep, and though I was sorry that everyone else had been awakened because of me, I would quickly go back to sleep. The others, as Natasha would tell me in a whisper the next morning, tossed and sighed irritably for a long time before finally dropping off—only to be awakened once more: "Hands!"

We had to get up the minute it grew light, at six o'clock we were told, although none of us had a watch to check by. Waking at such an early hour was a torment for me, and I would yearn to sleep for the rest of the day. But sleeping, or even lying down, was strictly forbidden; we were permitted only to sit on the cot. Sitting all day was especially hard after a night of interrogation. Then we would long to lie down. The old hands, though, knew when it was possible to snatch a ten-minute nap.

We were familiar with the individual personalities of all the guards, and we had a nickname for each of them. "Hurrah!" somebody would say: "Amalia's on duty today!" This meant we could catch up on our sleep or even read on the bed, for Amalia, if she even looked through the peephole, would take no notice and move on.

The most vicious of the guards was a ruddy-cheeked girl with a severe six-month perm; although she was only of medium height we knew her, for some reason, as "Silly-Shura-Taller-than-All." On one occasion we had a good laugh at her expense. Tonya wasn't feeling well and she lay down. Silly Shura burst noisily into the cell. "Get up! Lying is not allowed on the bed!" Tonya obediently sat up. But the moment the door closed behind Shura, she lay down again. The door opened with an even louder crash, and Shura bawled, "Get up! Don't you know the rules? Is this your first time in prison?!" Obviously she had meant to say "first day." Tonya, pretending not to notice this slip of the tongue, replied with exaggerated meekness: "Yes, it's my first time." We all burst out laughing, and Silly Shura shot out the door.

"Better not lie down again, Tonya dear," Maria Alexandrovna advised. "She'll only complain to the superintendent—and he'll close the ventilation pane." Closing the ventilation pane was their way of punishing the whole cell for one person's misdemeanor.

Our day started with "lavatory drill"—a group visit to the lavatory. This event, which was repeated in the evening, proceeded according to a definite ritual. The guard would look in: "Get ready for lavatory drill!" This meant that those from the neighboring cell were in the lavatory, and we were next in line. We would line up in pairs behind the door. The door opened a second time, and we were allowed out.

The first pair—those on duty—would pick up the full slop bucket, and the entire procession would make its way slowly (so as not to spill any of the contents) and almost solemnly down the long corridor. I would look at the doors of the cells, from which not the slightest sound escaped, and try to guess which of them contained Gaira. (We were told that our floor consisted entirely of women, and was the only one of its kind at the Lubyanka.) At the lavatory door, the guard would hand each of us a tiny scrap of paper and lock us in.

Those were the best moments of the day—unsupervised, with no peephole in the door. My acquaintances who were also in the Lubyanka at that time told me later that there were indeed peepholes in the lavatory doors, and women described the humiliation of having the guards stare in at them. But I could not conceive of anyone using the peephole in that situation, so I have no memory of it.

Lavatory drill lasted about ten minutes, in which time we had to do the essential, wash as much of ourselves in the basins as possible—using only cold water, of course—and (though it was strictly forbidden) rinse out some of our underwear. (The bigger things we would wash when we were taken to the bathhouse every ten days, though that was also forbidden.)

After lavatory drill came breakfast. A mug of hot brown water—tea? coffee?—our daily ration of black bread, and two or three lumps of sugar. Since these lumps were all of different sizes, the guard would carefully line them up in seven piles, attempting to make sure that they were as equal as possible. To guarantee complete fairness, a second guard would turn his back to the table, and the first would point to a pile and ask, "Whose is this?"

"Tonya's."

"And whose is this?"

"Zaika's."

And so on.

Then each took her ration. You could gobble it all up at once, or make it last till evening.

Another morning event was the visit of the senior guard. At this time one could ask to see a doctor, or to use a needle. (I will return to the needle in a moment.)

Once I asked to see the dentist. I was taken there by a very young guard, who looked like a peasant boy. From the clumsy, earnest way he clicked his tongue, and his air of self-importance, I realized that he must be a new recruit; he was obviously enjoying his new role. He took me into the medical unit, but instead of waiting outside the door, he evidently had instructions to accompany me into the treatment room itself. There he stood by the chair and—from simple-minded curiosity, I assume, rather than by order— literally peered into my mouth. I found this unpleasant, and I hoped that the dentist, a sullen middle-aged woman, would tell him off. But she said nothing. (She said not a word to me, either, and I imagined that she probably wore an MGB uniform under her white coat. I might add that when this doctor—or was she just a nurse?—made her occasional visits to our cell accompanied by the guard, she also eyed us with a certain hostility.) When the dentist started drilling my teeth and I howled with pain, the soldier mimicked me and burst out laughing.

"It's all right for you!" I said a moment later, but he went on enjoying himself at my expense until the end of the visit. When he began to lead me back "home" down the corridor, however, he puffed up importantly again, shouting loudly, "Hands behind your back!" and once more earnestly clicking his tongue.

Around a corner in the corridor ahead of us came the sound of more tongue-clicking. My guard whipped open a little door in the wall and shoved me inside a tall narrow box—like a vertical coffin. I could hear two people walking past, one striding forcefully in boots, the other dragging himself along with a heavy shuffling gait. I assumed that the soldier must be leading

an elderly man. To the doctor? To be interrogated? Who was that old man?
. . . For some reason I often wondered thereafter about him, and felt sorry
for him.

The high point of the day, not counting mealtime, was exercise period.
There was no set time for it, but it was treated as a sacred right: whatever
the weather, those who wanted it were allowed their twenty minutes outside. We exercised in a small enclosed yard, walking single file in circles
next to the wall. There were often ashes floating in the air; papers were
being burned somewhere nearby.

Once the whole day passed without our being called out to exercise.
After the order to sleep, perplexed and indignant, we had just lain down
when a guard suddenly appeared and asked encouragingly, "You don't want
your walk now, do you?"

Five of the women refused, but Natasha and I maliciously responded,
"We want to go!" We were taken not to the yard but—for the first time—up
to the flat roof. It was surrounded by a continuous parapet, so we could not
see what was going on below, but the sky was glowing with the lights of the
city, in the distance—on the higher outskirts of Moscow—we could see
lighted windows, and from below we heard the sound of car horns. We felt
as if we had stumbled onto a celebration of some kind. Unfortunately, it
lasted only twenty minutes.

Once every week or ten days we had a visit from the librarian, a silent
old hunchback who would let us each have one book. He would sometimes
bring a particular title, having somehow managed to remember a request,
but usually he just handed out whatever he had, and we would then swap
the books among ourselves. The prison library was actually very good; it
was said to consist mainly of books confiscated from those arrested in the
1930s. It was curious that authors who were forbidden outside could be
freely read by those in prison. They might bring works by Zamyatin, Mer-
ezhkovsky, Bruno Jasienski, or Pilnyak. Even the longest books would be
finished instantly, and there were never enough to last us until the next
library day.

We talked endlessly, of course, but even talk eventually palled, especially
since some things tended to be said over and over again. So we would think
up ways to vary the monotony.

One of us, for example, might ask the superintendent on his morning
rounds for a needle. The following day a guard would take the woman into
a "box," where she would be given a needle and two pieces of thread, black
and white, with which to mend a hem, patch a hole, or sew on a button
made from bread. The remaining scrap of thread was smuggled back to the
cell, where we frequently sewed and mended things in secret. We made our

illicit needles from fish bones. (We were served "fishy soup" for supper every day). The technology was simple: we would dig a staple out of the spine of a library book with our nails, then use it to make a hole in the bone. These homemade needles did not last long, so the staple would be carefully hidden away in case we were searched. (We would remove staples only from the most dog-eared books, of course.) Liza, the only one in our cell who smoked, even managed to knit some mittens using matches and thread spun from the cotton wool that we received by special dispensation from the doctor.

Natasha and I found our pleasure in poetry. She would read me verses she had written; I had never written any myself, to my eternal regret, but I knew a great many poems by heart. Since I was a schoolgirl, my favorite poet had been Mayakovsky; I used to read him each day, and had memorized every line of his "Good!" and "Vladimir Ilich Lenin." But although I uncritically accepted this kind of sloganizing art, emotionally I was always more attuned to the older, humanistic culture.

In the first years after the war, some of my classmates and I went through a period of "great revelations," as we discovered the symphonies of Tchaikovsky, Beethoven, and Grieg, the paintings of Levitan, Nesterov, Vrubel, and Renoir, and the sculptures of Paolo Trubetskoi and Rodin. We passed around books by Hemingway, Aldington, Rolland, Bunin, and Kuprin, and we were familiar with Blok, Esenin, the early Mayakovsky, Akhmatova, and Gumilyov. Akhmatova and Gumilyov were not being published by then, but one could still get hold of prerevolutionary anthologies of their works, and we used to copy them down and learn the verses we particularly liked by heart. Recitals by young soldier-poets were the latest novelty then, and we tried not to miss a single one.

I used to recite to Natasha some poems by young poets, and during my first days in prison I would repeat to myself Evgeny Eliseev's "No Way Back":

Amid the precarious joys
What now seems suddenly a mistake
Has saddened my lips with
The trace of an unhappy smile. . . .

It was about something else, of course, but it very much matched my mood at the time.

Once when the women were feeling rather gloomy, I offered to do an Oriental dance for them. They agreed. Throwing someone's shawl over my shoulders, I wrapped a towel around my head like a turban, went over to the slop bucket, where there was more room, and started to dance. I accompanied myself by drumming my knuckles against the bottom of a green enamel mug in place of a tambourine.

Suddenly the lock clanged, and the superintendent entered the cell along with Silly Shura (she had probably summoned him).

"Who was knocking?!"

We all froze.

Later I learned the reason for the superintendent's fury. The authorities were concerned that inmates awaiting trial might follow prison tradition and tap out messages to each other through the walls. Yet no matter how many people I asked, I could find no one who knew the "prison alphabet," and I finally decided that the tradition must have died out. It seemed perfectly understandable—there was no longer any need for it. Under tsarism, real opponents of the regime were held in prison, and they had something to communicate to their comrades in other cells. But what would a person imprisoned merely for telling a joke have to pass on to the person in the next cell?

Or so I thought at the time—and as it turns out, I was wrong. Several people assured me later that they had communicated in this way with their neighbors, and it must have been true; otherwise the guard would not have burst in on us with his eyes popping.

"Who was knocking, I said?!"

"I was," I replied.

"Who to?"

"No one . . . "

"What do you mean, no one? Which wall were you knocking on?"

I grew frightened. Did they really think I had an accomplice to the right or the left of me? Damn it, there might be a real spy in the next cell!

This was the beginning of my new life, and I was still convinced that although some prisoners—everyone in my cell, for example!—were arrested by accident (the famous omelette theory), the vast majority were there for a good reason.

"Well?"

He was waiting. I had to say something.

"I was tapping the cup, not the wall."

"Why?" He seemed slightly taken aback.

"Just because," Natasha chimed in, trying to be helpful.

Ignoring her, he glared at me. If I told him the truth, he would never believe me. What kind of normal person would dance in a remand prison!

I stood with head bowed, like a bad schoolgirl at the blackboard, twisting the unlucky mug in my hands. Then suddenly I noticed some spots of rust at the bottom where the enamel had worn away. "I was chipping away the enamel!" I said.

"What for?"

"To clean off the rust. See, the whole bottom of the cup is covered in it." He did not interrupt, and I went on the offensive: "If that's not allowed, you must give me another mug: someone could get poisoned in here!"

He took the mug, peered into it, and handed it to Shura: "Give her another one. And so that they don't knock again, close the ventilation pane!"

Shura rushed to the window to carry out her orders. The pane closed with an unpleasant scraping sound, and the two of them left.

What a mess! Several long minutes passed. No one uttered a word, and no one but Natasha even looked in my direction. The air seemed to become tangibly more and more oppressive.

I took the other women's silence as condemnation: Why did I have to play the fool? Now they would have to spend the whole day without fresh air because of me, and life was hard enough as it was.

Cursing myself for my frivolity, I sat with my face propped on my fists, wondering how to make things better. Then I had an inspiration.

I waited for the peephole cover to flutter open, then I stood up and said in a loud voice, "In that case, I'm going on a hunger strike!"

"So am I!" joined in Natasha.

Abandoning their stunned silence, our cellmates started to persuade us in a friendly way not to bring more problems down upon ourselves. But nothing could stop us now, and we proudly rejected all appeals to common sense.

It was just before lunchtime, and we were very hungry. I sat down on Natasha's bed, and whispered so that the guard outside the door would not hear, "Let's have a proper meal first, then start."

Natasha agreed. Two days before this, we had bought food from the prison store. Anyone who had money saved up in the prison office (I do not remember if we were allowed to receive any money from outside, but I still had some of Minka's left) could spend it three times a month on food, which was delivered to our cells. The selection and quantity of this food was strictly limited: sugar, cheese, smoked sausage (all available, as far as I recall, in 300- or 400-gram portions), white bread, onions, soap, and cigarettes.

Constantly hungry, Natasha and I would eat up almost everything we bought in the first two days, but that morning we had a loaf of bread left and, luxury of luxuries, half a sausage, which we had intended to make last the whole week.

Sitting shoulder to shoulder on the bed with our backs to the door, we divided the bread and sausage between us and gobbled it up. Then we looked into each other's eyes, and silently vowed to stand together in whatever trials might lie ahead.

Literally a minute later, the senior guard appeared again with Shura. Shura set a new mug on the table. The guard turned to me and said severely, "Don't let this happen again." Then to Shura he said, "Open the ventilation pane!"

For many days afterward, Natasha and I teased each other about these events, and the others had a good laugh at us at well.

In the middle of May, Melnikov told me that the investigation of my case was concluded. He sat me down at a small table and set a folder in front of me containing the records of all my interrogations. He asked me to read through them again and sign that I had done so.

The folder itself amazed me. It was an ordinary cardboard office file with the word "Dossier" printed on it, but stamped above this were the words "To be kept forever."

"Have you read it and signed it? Then that's it for now. Next the procurator will cross-examine you, and then there'll be a verdict."

I think that I must have looked scared, because Melnikov said reassuringly that although he could not vouch for the outcome, he did not think that it would be too bad. "7:35ers" were generally only exiled, he said, so I could probably continue my teacher training in another town somewhere.

"We can't all live in Moscow, can we?" he said.

I responded with utter sincerity, "No, of course not."

The first thing that caught my eye in the procurator's office was the unusually informal photograph over his desk of a pipe-smoking Stalin. Behind the desk sat the procurator, Daron, and next to him, bending over respectfully, stood Melnikov, murmuring in his ear and leafing through a file which evidently contained my case.

The procurator asked me if I had any complaints about the investigation, and I said that I had none. There was no cross-examination as such, and the whole procedure lasted no more than two or three minutes.

All that remained now was the verdict. According to my cellmates, my sister and I would then be "allowed out" and given a couple of days to get ready and choose between a number of Siberian towns (that, they remembered, was how it used to happen in the 1920s).

Every day I waited for the prison gates to be flung open (for some reason it was always these mysterious gates that I imagined opening, rather than the door of our cell), and for someone solemnly to announce, "You may leave now—you are free!"

Instead a guard came into our cell one day and demanded: "Whose names begin with 'V'?"

"Mine."

"Name?"

"Vesyolaya."

"Initials in full!"

"Zayara Artyomovna."

"Collect your things!"

"So this is it!" I thought exultantly. "Not as solemn an occasion as I imagined, but never mind. The main thing is to get out of here. I'm going to see Gaira!"

I said goodbye to everyone, kissed Natasha, and almost ran to the door.

The guard led me to a "box" on the same floor, and before long a pale skinny girl came in, also with her belongings in her hand. Deciding that we must have been put together by mistake, I quickly and quietly asked her, "Which cell are you from?"

"Number 20," she said.

"Was a Gaira Vesyolaya in there with you?"

"Are you Zayara? She kept worrying about you . . . "

"So she's in number 20?"

"She was. She left a week ago."

"Left? Where to?"

The girl shrugged. "How should I know? To a camp, I suppose. Where else?"

"A camp!?"

"What did you expect?" she demanded with a hint of gloating malice in her voice.

Soon the guard came for us, and we were taken down to the yard, where we were bundled into a gray van with bars over the back window.

Butyrki

The prison van deposited us in the courtyard of Butyrki Prison.

Inside we found ourselves in a large lobby with a tiled floor and rows of doors on either side. The doors were arranged close to each other, and my prisoner's instinct told me that these must be "boxes." I was put inside one of the "boxes" along the left wall.

I cannot say how I spent the rest of that day and part of the night, for I suffered a complete memory lapse and was evidently in a state of shock. I had indeed found myself outside the gates of the Lubyanka—but in another prison, and with the prospect of the camps ahead!

Eventually the door opened, and a middle-aged woman guard said soft-
ly, as though she were a nurse addressing an invalid, "Come on, I'll take
you to your cell."

"What time is it?" I asked her.

"Just after four."

We went out of the lobby into a small inner courtyard. Dawn was breaking, the morning was cool, and there was a fresh smell of vegetation in the
air. In the middle of the yard there was either a flower bed or a ring of trees,
and as we walked past them, from one door to the other, I managed to gulp
down some lungfuls of fresh air. How large the leaves were! The last time I
had seen trees, they were only just coming into bud. On the branches sat
swarms of little birds, making a deafening row with their singing, chirping,
and twittering.

We went up to the second floor. I could not help comparing this prison
with the Lubyanka. Unlike the Lubyanka's windowless corridors, this one
reminded me rather of a school hallway. On the left was a row of doors, and
on the right a row of wide windows. And instead of clicking her tongue, the
guard rapped her keys on the buckle of her belt. She led me down the corridor and let me into cell number 93.

In the dawn light peeping through the two "muzzled" windows, I saw a
large cell with a tiled floor and a high ceiling. I don't know how many
prisoners the architect had intended to occupy the space, but on that morning there must have been at least fifty women there. They were all sleeping
side by side on mattress-covered boards laid out from window to door, on
both sides of a wide passage, in which stood a table. The women all faced
the window, lying so close together that if one turned, they would all have
had to turn together.

When I went in, some of the women propped themselves up on their
elbows and looked toward the door. I stood there confused, my bundle in
my arms. There was no room there even to sit down. Then suddenly I heard
a voice: "Zaika!"

"Gaira!"

Our meeting defies description. Words fail me, as they say in books.

As a newcomer to the cell, I would normally have been given a place by
the slop bucket. But this was a special occasion; our meeting so touched
everyone that they made an exception to the rules, and I squeezed in between Gaira and her friend Maya Peterson. During the week they had been
there, they had already moved from the slop bucket almost all the way to
the window.

Maya had been in her third year at Moscow University, studying ancient
Greek. She was arrested because of her father, R. A. Peterson, who was in

charge of security at the Kremlin for a number of years after the October Revolution.

Nina Zlatkina was in prison through no conceivable fault of her own. She had been convicted under Article 7:35 because of her aunt's husband—none other than the Old Bolshevik Alexei Rykov.

Both Maya and Nina were arrested on the same night as Gaira and I. At first this seemed a mere coincidence, but we soon met other arrested "children," and none of them had been picked up before 23 April. That, evidently, was when the campaign had started.

At the Lubyanka we had not been permitted to make the slightest sound. Here at Butyrki, our cell was unimaginably noisy from morning to night. In one corner, people sat chatting; in another, someone told the tale of her unhappy life; and in another, women laughed over jokes. In the remand prison, everyone had been too terrified of stool pigeons to make a sound; here they could let their hair down.

There was a girl there with a lovely voice who had studied at the Moscow Conservatory, and we used to ask her to sing for us. All talk stopped at those times, and our hearts missed a beat at Martha's prophetic words: "You will endure punishment and prison in a distant land . . . "

At Butyrki I was overwhelmed by an avalanche of new impressions. At first I enjoyed the crowded cell, but I soon began to find it oppressive. Everyone, understandably, was in a state of extreme nervous tension, and from time to time petty squabbles broke out. Yet whether out of solidarity (we understood each other's grief) or out of an instinct for self-preservation, we never let quarrels get out of hand. The last thing we needed was to fight among ourselves!

Also, strangely enough, I cannot recall anyone in our cell ever crying. The predominant mood—superficially, at least—was one of excitement rather than depression: there were times when everyone would be overcome by hysterical mirth, as we played tricks on each other or laughed at ourselves or at the most elementary joke.

In our little group, Maya Peterson's account of her arrest provoked loud laughter. She had recently married a fellow student; after she was taken away, he renounced her. There was nothing funny in that, of course, but when they were leading Maya out of the apartment, she told us, she had cried, "What for?!"

To those of us, including Maya herself, who had learned the hard way, this question now seemed the height of naiveté and irrelevance, and so we found it funny. From then on we used to cry "What for?" on any pretext

—when a stocking ran, or when it poured down rain during our exercise period.

There were a number of pretty girls in the cell who had been arrested under the same article as us students. They were considered "socially dangerous" because they had had intimate liaisons with foreign men. When the woman at the Lubyanka had suspected me of "running around with an American" because of my nylon stockings, she obviously had not been making it up.

A few years later, a former camp inmate noticed a scar left on my neck by an outbreak of boils (from which I used to suffer terribly in prison). Knowing under what article I had been convicted, he made a slicing movement across his throat and asked sympathetically, "Knife?"

The girls hotly denied that they were prostitutes; they each had a story to tell of a touching love affair with some Fred or Otto. I did not doubt their words for a moment and was outraged by this slur on their characters. One of them seemed to be an educated girl, but the others were very primitive creatures with a fairly rough past, and I soon lost interest in them. They tended to keep to themselves, sharing their own private jokes and conversations.

Our exercise periods were also freer at Butyrki than at the Lubyanka. Here we did not follow each other in circles, but just wandered around in the yard, warming ourselves in the June sun. We were given books, although the noise and commotion in the cell made it almost impossible to read. We were also allowed to receive parcels, and Minka used to bring us both food and money.

Gaira and I had different ideas about our future. We still hoped to escape the camps, but we no longer dreamed of being "allowed out," because if this were going to happen, we obviously would not have been moved to Butyrki. We were inclined to think that after choosing our place of exile (we both fancied Irkutsk, for some reason), they would send us off there for a fixed period straight from prison, at government expense, so to speak. I had somehow convinced myself that our sentence would be three years, possibly because young specialists were sent on to their first job for three years after graduating, and this is what we, too, had been preparing to do in our former life.

One day ten of us, including Gaira, Maya, Nina and me, were called out "with our things." At last!

"You'll get your sentence now," said the others.

"Chin up!"

"Here goes!"

We were taken downstairs to the lobby, where we were all locked up in the same "box" and then led out, one by one, to hear our sentences. I did not expect to see a judge in a robe and white wig, of course, but I did imagine that there would be a certain solemnity to the occasion.

There was nothing of the kind. In a small room little bigger than a "box," an officer from the Ministry of State Security read from a piece of paper: by decree of the Special Board, Zayara Vesyolaya has been found guilty under Article 7:35 and sentenced to five years' exile in Novosibirsk.

I felt as though someone had clubbed me over the head. Novosibirk was fine. It made little difference in the end whether it was Novosibirk or Irkutsk (although I was disappointed not to be given a choice). But five years! Not three, but five whole years!

At that moment I forgot about my mother, who was serving eight years (and not in exile but in a camp!). My five years seemed to me beyond the limits of the imaginable.

Later, when I had more time to think, I tried to understand why the verdict had seemed such a catastrophe to me. I realized that I had lived the whole of my conscious life, not counting childhood, in the 1940s—the war, the upper classes at school, the institute—with only the last digit of the year changing. But at the time 1954 seemed like a totally different era to me.

After the sentence I was led to another "box" next door to the first one. Soon Maya joined me: "Five years in Novosibirsk!" Then Nina: "Five years in Novosibirsk! What about you?"

"The same. At least we'll all be together."

Gaira was the last to come in.

"Five years in Karaganda!" she said.

"Karaganda? I'm going to Novosibirsk."

We were stunned. Could it have been an accident? Could the officer handing out the sentences not have known we were sisters? Or was it a deliberate act of cruelty toward us?

We were taken to another building, where five of us were locked into a cell so small it was possibly intended for solitary confinement; when it was time to sleep, an ordinary folding cot was set up between the beds.

Gaira and I immediately wrote letters to the Minister of State Security, Abakumov, requesting that she be sent to Novosibirsk, not Karaganda. But three days later, we were all sent off to our different places of exile.

The First Stage of the Journey

In prison terminology, convicts being moved under armed guard from one place to another are described as "in transit."

We were first taken from Butyrki to the Kuibyshev transit prison. Gaira and I traveled this far together.

The Black Crow in which we were driven to the Kazan station in Moscow was so packed with prisoners, sitting in the individual cubicles and standing in the aisle, that there was no room for Maya and me. The two soldiers who were meant to sit by the barred door at the back had to squeeze together on one seat and give the other to us. This allowed us the unexpected pleasure of enjoying a final farewell look at the streets of Moscow.

As the van stopped at a traffic light at the approach to Komsomol Square, I looked out and saw Volodya Kotov, a final-year student at our institute, which was just around the corner on Gavrikov Street. He was strolling along the pavement eating a pretzel. Although we barely knew each other, I was as happy to see him as if he were a relative. My first impulse was to call out (because of the hot weather, there was no glass in the barred windows), but common sense quickly prevailed. No one in his right mind would want to be hailed by someone in a Black Crow . . . !

Up till then I had always assumed that the cars with barred windows at the head of every passenger train were the mail cars. I now discovered that they were used not for letters but for prisoners, and were still sometimes called "Stolypin" wagons (after the tsarist minister in charge of putting down the 1905 Revolution).

These were basic sleeping cars, but re-equipped with special features. Instead of the usual windows, there were small openings level with the top berths, and iron bars separated the compartments from the corridor. A single soldier patrolling the corridor could see everyone at a glance. I don't know how many prisoners altogether were crammed into our car—the other compartments were for men—but our compartment contained twenty women.

When the train moved off, I tried to compose myself in an appropriately somber mood. Leaving Moscow was an important moment, after all! But I couldn't manage it. It was hot and stuffy, Nina had developed an acute kidney infection and was writhing and groaning from the pain, some women on the top berth were shouting obscenities, and men's voices could be heard demanding to be allowed to use the lavatory. (When our turn came, we discovered that the lavatory door had to be kept wide open, with a soldier standing outside by the window.)

It seemed to me that we were traveling very slowly, and for a long while (although, since this was an ordinary passenger train, we were actually moving at the right speed). Finally we stopped at a large station, and someone managed to make out the name: "It's Kuibyshev!"

"You mean Samara," said Gaira, who, as a true Volga native, preferred the town's old pre-revolutionary name. Father had grown up here, and as a child she had visited it several times with him.

Kuibyshev

The Kuibyshev transit prison consisted of a few long wooden barracks filled with two tiers of bare bed boards. We were given places on the bottom tier. Above our heads, bedbugs scurried across the boards day and night, but the floor was immaculately clean. It was unpainted, and it was scrubbed down every day with a besom and sand till it gleamed a dull yellow, like the table of a good village housewife. When I looked at this floor, I realized to my horror that one day it would be my turn to wash it.

In the barracks we joined some women from Moscow whom Gaira and Maya had gotten to know at Butyrki. I remember two of them, Inna and Sofia Sergeevna.

Inna, a final-year physics student at Moscow University, was in exactly the same position as we were. Her father, A. I. Gaister, a vice-president of the Academy of Agricultural Sciences, had been shot in 1937. They also came for her on the night of 23 April, but she was sleeping over at a friend's apartment because the next day she had to defend her graduation diploma. She duly did so, and afterward she was summoned to the personnel department, where a young man in civilian clothes who had been present at the ceremony congratulated her and asked her to accompany him outside. Excited by her success, and assuming that he wanted to discuss her future job assignment, she followed him into the street. As they strolled chatting up Manege Square toward the House of Unions, the man recalled the professors' flattering assessment of her work. They parted in the inquiries office of the Ministry of State Security on Kuznetsky Street. There another young man handed her a warrant for her arrest.

At the Lubyanka, both Inna and my friend Natasha Zaporozhets shared the same interrogator, Makarenko. With Inna he was extremely affable, since he was not trying to extract information about others from her, and she obviously did not deny that she was her parents' daughter. She told us that during the interrogation he suddenly started to consult her on Stalin's "Marxism and the National Question;" he was obviously preparing for some political exam. After only ten days at the Lubyanka and Butyrki, she was sentenced to five years' exile in the Kokchetavsk Region of Kazakhstan.

Since her documents had been mislaid, Inna spent a longer time than the rest of us in the Kuibyshev transit prison. There she had the misfortune to witness three women criminals taking their horrible revenge on a comrade whom they suspected of informing on them. They beat her to death with tin bowls before the eyes of everyone in the barracks.

Sofia Sergeevna caught my attention because she had known Mayakovsky in her youth. Occasionally we would recite his poems to each other. She was a so-called "repeater." I would meet a lot of them in years to come, but this was the first I had heard of such a category.

A prisoner sentenced in 1937 might serve his eight or ten years and be released, but with a "minus," which banned him from living in Moscow and various other cities and large towns (I cannot remember exactly which, but one can easily guess). Unable to return home to their families, most would settle as close to them as possible, but not too close: they had to remain beyond the 101-kilometer limit.

Here I must mention my Uncle Borya.

Boris Lvovich was the husband of my mother's sister Maria, or Aunt Manya as we called her. Arriving in Moscow in the early twenties, he went to a workers' school, then to college, and until 1937 he was employed as an electrical engineer. In that year he was denounced as a spy—either for Germany or Japan, I forget which. It must have been hard for them to make the charges stick, because he—a spy!—was given the same sentence they gave to "wives" (of enemies of the people): eight years. All the same, almost all of his teeth were knocked out during interrogation. In the camp he developed a stomach ulcer and lost the rest of his teeth.

When he was released, he settled in the town of Alexandrov. (They had left Aunt Manya, his wife, alone, and she continued to live in the Sokolniki district of Moscow, where she worked all her life at the local library.) Since employers were afraid that Uncle Boris might be a saboteur, he found it impossible to get work as an electrical engineer, or even as an ordinary electrician. For a long time both he and Manya had to live on her pitiful wages (their son Lyasya had been killed at the front during the first days of the war). Then finally Borya had a stroke of luck. He got a very modestly paid job as a stoker. To save money on housing, he moved into the boiler room itself, a dark and windowless basement. Once a month he would visit his wife. Gentle and timid by nature, he probably felt as though he were crossing some sort of state frontier when he came to Moscow, and he never dared to stay the night. Since Aunt Manya lived in a communal apartment, and they were both terrified of the neighbors, they tried not to spend too much time there, and after a quick bite to eat they would go out for long walks in Sokolniki park. I once saw them on one of these walks: Uncle Borya responding monosyllabically to his wife's questions, then falling silent, his faded blue eyes shining, a blissful toothless smile on his face. After spending a few hours in the capital (never forgetting for a moment that while he was enjoying life there, his absence might already have been noticed in Alexandrov), Uncle Borya would return home until his next Moscow escapade. They lived like that for years.

Uncle Borya died in Moscow, not long after he was rehabilitated. He had managed to live at home for a little while (in that same apartment with the spiteful neighbors). When he died, Mother had to telephone everyone she knew, because there was no one to carry his coffin.

In 1949 many former camp inmates were thrown back into prison (they may simply have forgotten about Uncle Borya in his basement) and—on the sole grounds that they had served time before—were again sentenced this time to exile, but with no fixed term: "until further notice." These exiles were known as "repeaters." Two years later, the vague formula "until further notice," which gave the "repeaters" some grounds for hope that their fortunes might eventually take a favorable turn, was officially replaced with the words "for life," which left no room for hope at all.

In Kuibyshev we found ourselves together with common criminals (those who had been convicted on social rather than political charges), and some of them were hardened criminals. We also met several "Ukazers" there. In 1947 a government "ukaz," or edict, was issued that made small thefts of government property a criminally punishable offense. One prisoner was said to have been imprisoned for stealing a spool of thread, another for taking a few handfuls of rye from a collective-farm field.

As soon as we had settled into our barracks, two young criminals sat down beside Gaira and me.

"Where are you from, girls?" they asked.

"Moscow."

"Which street did you live on?"

"The Arbat."

For some reason this sent them into ecstasies.

"Is that true? You aren't lying?"

"Why would we lie? We lived on Krivoarbatsky Street. What about it?"

It turned out that they used to frequent Moscow, and now they wanted to test us. We passed with flying colors—of course we knew the names of all the Arbat's cinemas! This test had an unexpected result: convinced that we really were from the Arbat (it was an obsession of theirs!), one of them said, "When it's your turn on duty, we'll wash the floors for you!"

"Well, thank you!" we said.

July came. It was a very hot summer. Fortunately there was a wide barred window directly opposite our bed boards without any glass or "muzzle" on it, and fresh air poured through, especially at night. We were delighted, most of all, that the window was "unmuzzled." During the day I could lie staring up at the drifting clouds, and in the evening I enjoyed looking at the lights in people's windows: a steep hill was visible beyond the prison fence, on which there were two apartment buildings painted a cheerful shade of bright yellow, one a couple of stories taller than the other. In the evenings, multicolored lights would appear in the windows (colored silk lampshades were all the rage then); the buildings themselves were invisible in the darkness, so the lights seemed suspended in mid-air above the hill.

Some twenty years later I visited the town again; this time, as the daughter of Artyom Vesyoly, I was an honored guest at the opening of the new Kuibyshev Museum of Literature. I met people who had known my father; I recorded their recollections; and I simply wandered about the unfamiliar city. I wanted to see what the transit prison looked like from the outside. I did not know the address or the general location, of course, and I would not have felt comfortable asking passers-by "How do I get to the prison?" So I set off on my own, looking for the tall hill with the two large buildings on top. And I found it! The two buildings were still there, but the prison, I was told, had long since been demolished, and in its place they had built the Volga Hotel, where I was now staying!

At the beginning of our stay in the transit prison, Nina Zlatkina had casually mentioned that she had some distant relatives in Kuibyshev, a married couple, both of them college instructors. Since the food we were given was terrible even by prison standards, Nina began to think about her relatives more and more often. I don't know how she managed it, but she finally got one of the civilian prison employees to smuggle out a note asking them to send her something to eat. We watched with interest as events unfolded (such contact with the outside world was, of course, illegal). Nina's relatives were clearly afraid to reveal their connection with the notorious Rykov family by delivering food to the prison in person. But they were too kindhearted to ignore her appeal, so they got someone else to take it instead. Nina ended up with a messily wrapped parcel and a "list of contents," a crumpled scrap of paper on which someone had scribbled in a barely literate hand, "Sadines—2, Sweats—200 grams."

Nina clutched her head. "Someone has obviously switched the parcels. Now they'll milk my poor relatives unmercifully, and all because of me. When will we get where we're going so that I can write and tell them! What have I done?"

We comforted her, saying that surely she soon would be able to write. We had already been in Kuibyshev for two weeks, and we were expecting to leave any day on the next stage of our journey.

I had mixed feelings about this. On one hand, I wanted to reach Novosibirk as soon as possible. I had a dilemma: whether to go right into the third year at the Novosibirsk Teacher-Training Institute, in which case I would have to take all the spring exams (which I frankly wasn't too keen on), or to resign myself to losing a year and starting the second year all over again. On the other hand, I was terrified about being separated from Gaira. We agreed to correspond through Aunt Anya, Mother's younger sister. (We did not want to write to Aunt Manya for fear of incriminating Uncle Borya, and I did not remember Minka's address.)

The day finally came for the two of us to say goodbye. The prisoners leaving for Novosibirsk were led out into the yard, while the rest were locked in their barracks.

"Move over! More! Make room!" shouted the soldiers, as they stood us elbow to elbow in tarpaulin-covered trucks and drove us to the station.

The Special Train

It was at a siding some way from the station that they loaded us onto the freight cars that made up our "special train." (The guards may have ridden in ordinary passenger cars. As our car was at the back and I could not see the whole train, I don't know.)

They put us on in alphabetical order. I was third. The two best places, by the windows on the upper bed boards, were already taken, of course. I use "upper" to refer to their location, for there were no actual lower bed boards; people whose surnames came farther down in the alphabet had to find a space on the floor. I took the third place from the window, reserving the second for Maya Peterson, and from then until the end of my Siberian exile, the two of us were inseparable.

Nina preferred to stay below, since her bad kidney made it hard for her to climb up and down.

We waited for hours in the suffocating heat with the door securely closed, and it was only late in the evening that we finally moved off. We soon made a very unpleasant discovery: there was no slop bucket in the car, only a narrow opening in the wall opposite the door, into which had been fitted a tilting wooden trough made of three rough planks. Since we were crazed with thirst and were given a mug of water only when there was a long halt, there was no way to flush it out. It was a real circus act to try to hit the trough while the train was bumping and swaying from side to side, and few managed it. One can well imagine what the floor around the trough was like within a couple of hours of setting off (there were forty of us in the car), and our trip lasted ten days. The stinking stain spread wider and wider, and for those who had to sleep on the floor, there was no getting away from it.

We on the upper boards were naturally in a far better position, although we too found the stench unbearable. Moreover, the roof, which one could touch with one's hand when lying down, became as hot as an oven during the day.

Maya "lived" to my right, and to my left were three nuns (or so we all assumed them to be)—two middle-aged, rather featureless women and a smiling, fussy old woman with a pleasant, kind face, named Baba Stepanida. I do not know if they really were nuns. They volunteered little about themselves, saying merely that they had been persecuted for their faith, but all three dressed entirely in black, and they would occasionally whisper intensely among themselves; presumably they were praying. I was feeling bored, so I asked Baba Stepanida to teach me a prayer. She eagerly agreed, and to her delight and amazement, I could soon recite the whole of the Lord's Prayer without a mistake.

Once I decided to "re-educate" the nuns, and boldly informed them that God did not exist. "What do you mean, He doesn't exist? Where do thunder and lightning come from then?" Baba Stepanida retorted, smiling craftily at this incontrovertible proof of God's existence.

Brought up short by such blissful ignorance, I tried to stammer out some explanation about natural phenomena and religion, but in the process I unexpectedly confronted the depths of my own ignorance. I discovered yet again the wisdom of the old proverb, "Look before you leap."

I learned another folk saying from Baba Stepanida that I have recalled on numerous occasions: "When the fox falls into the trap, it's time to look up at the sky"—trust in providence when all else fails.

I should have asked Baba Stepanida to tell me about her life, as a young woman and since the Revolution; but at that time the fate of some religious old woman was of little interest to me.

The train spent more time standing on sidings than on the move. Sometimes when the waiting became unbearable, I would ask the woman by the window if I could get a breath of air, and we would change places for a while.

This window, right under the roof, was a small rectangular opening the size of a ventilation pane, with no glass in it, and with two strips of metal hammered crossways from corner to corner instead of bars.

Once I was sitting by the window as we waited at a station, and a passenger train from the East moved past us on the next track, braking slowly to a halt. When it stopped, one of the passenger car windows was directly opposite me. The first thing I saw were packets of food and a bottle of fruit juice on the table. A woman's face appeared at the window. Seeing me, she said something to the others in her compartment, and two more women and a man peered out. They eyed my window with nervous curiosity, obviously realizing that this was a prison train. I started making faces, tragically knitting my brows, biting my lips, and grasping the metal strips with my fingers. The man said something to the women (the upper part of their window was open, but I could not make out what he said), and their expressions changed to unconcealed pity. One of them felt around on the table, possibly looking for a cake or an apple to give me. It is wrong to mock human compassion, but as our train moved off and the faces receded, I could not help feeling a vindictive pleasure at briefly disturbing the peace of those fortunate people who were traveling in the opposite direction, quite possibly to Moscow.

Even from my own place on the boards, I would look through the window from morning to night. Each view that unfolded was better than the last. After the blank walls of the cells and prison yards, the scenes of nature would have given me great pleasure, had it not been for the rusty metal strips, black against the light, which seemed to negate all that I saw outside the window.

It was on the train that I wrote my first poem:

I could gaze every minute through the window
Forgetting all hunger and pain
But all the things that I see there
Are twice scored by heavy black lines:
The trees and the sunset above them
The fields and paths cutting through . . .
Crossed out by rusting metal
My life scored by black iron bars.

Novosibirsk

We had wondered how our transition from prisoners into exiles would occur in Novosibirsk. Would they release us immediately, at the station? Or would they first take us to the local State Security branch and give us back the passports and student cards they had confiscated when we were arrested?

We were taken off the train just as we had been loaded: at a siding, and in alphabetical order. We were ordered to line up in rows of five. Since I was third on the list, I was in the first row; the men lined up behind those of us from the women's car.

Glancing back at Maya, I noticed some men in gray-green uniforms standing near one of the cars. Germans! Until then, except in movies, I had seen Germans only once, when the prisoners-of-war were paraded through the streets of Moscow.

The Germans briskly lined up in rows of five, and then were led past our column and put at the head of it. The middle German in the last row was directly in front of me, so close I could have reached out and touched his back.

A guard shouted, "One step to the right or the left will be considered an attempt to escape; the escort will shoot without warning!" Then off we marched along the tracks, past some warehouses, and finally through the streets of the town.

There have been two occasions in my life when I wished that the earth would literally swallow me up. The second was in June 1953, when I returned to Moscow after being amnestied. Following a short period of celebration, I started to pick up the pieces of my life again and looked for a job as a typist or an accountant. Day after day I went from one office to another, responding to "help wanted" notices. But no one took me on. As soon as people learned that I had been in exile—and I told them the moment I walked in—they would suddenly remember that they had hired someone else for the job, or simply turn me down flat, without any explanation.

One day, in response to yet another advertisement, I went to a small publishing house that handled technical literature. For some reason I spoke not to the personnel manager but to the editor-in-chief. I told him that I had just returned from exile and was looking for work. He seemed clearly embarassed, but being too polite to immediately show me the door, he opened my work record—then suddenly looked up at me: "You're Artyom Vesyoly's daughter?"

He sat me down in an armchair and we started talking. Though he had not known my father well, they had met in publishing circles, and over the years their paths had crossed many times. Recalling better days, he looked sad and said, "He was a true writer!"

In the end, he took me on as a clerk, at 450 rubles a month. My coworkers must not know that I had been in exile, he added ruefully, or he might get into trouble.

It was not hard to keep my secret. None of my co-workers showed any interest in my past (or my present, for that matter), apart from one woman who asked me on my first day whether I was married. I replied ingenuously, "For a long time, more than two weeks!" which made the women roar with laughter and earned me their approval.

The work was not difficult. I earned less than anyone else there, but I was happy to have the job. All went well until our trade-union meeting. The day before it, the chairman of our union branch told me I would have to join, and I gladly agreed. When the time came to discuss the new members, the chairman rapidly read out my application, then asked me to tell them about myself.

I had not expected this!

My benefactor, the elderly editor, sat hunched in his chair, staring at the floor. I fiddled with the buttons on my cardigan and said nothing.

"Speak up, we're all listening!" said the chairman with a yawn.

"No," I said.

"What do you mean, No?"

"I'm not telling you anything."

The meeting livened up; people stopped jabbering with their neighbors, dozing, and rustling their newspapers, and everyone looked at me with varying degrees of disapproval or amused bewilderment.

After a moment's confusion, the chairman spoke to me gently as though I were unwell: "Perhaps you didn't understand what I said, Zayara Artyomovna. It's nothing bad we're asking of you—just tell us about yourself."

"No."

He threw up his hands.

It was then that I wanted to sink through the parquet floor. After much whispering and shrugging of shoulders, they nevertheless accepted my application for membership in the trade union.

The first time I had wanted the earth—or rather the asphalt road— to swallow me up was in that June of 1949, when I was driven through Novosibirsk with the German prisoners-of-war.

We made our way slowly though the streets, automobiles passed us. The soldiers held their machine guns at the ready, and the column was escorted by several German sheep dogs. People stood along the sidewalks. I don't know what kind of expression was on their faces as they looked at us. I saw no one. Gritting my teeth, I kept my eyes fixed on the gray-green back in front of me.

We spent three or four dreary and uneventful days in Novosibirsk Prison. Maya and I got our hands on a volume of Pushkin's works, and were particularly drawn to a letter he had written to Vyazemsky from house arrest in Mikhailovskoe: "I need to learn English, but one of the disadvantages of my exile is that now that I have the time to study, I don't have the means. Shame on my persecutors! Like André Chenier, I can strike my forehead and cry, 'Il y avait quelque chose là . . . '"*

Afterwards we would often strike our heads and cry, "Il y avait quelque chose là . . . ," flattered to think that we had joined the ranks of history's persecuted!

The Final Stage of the Journey

One morning all the doors along the corridor were flung open, and the guards shouted, "Everyone out! On the double! With your things!" About a hundred of us, men and women, were led out into the yard and ordered to sit on the ground. Nobody knew what would happen next, but various suggestions were offered, with the word "transit" the most commonly heard.

I listened to these rumors without interest. Nothing more could possibly happen to Maya and me. We had arrived in our place of exile, Novosibirsk. Now we had only to collect our passports and walk out of the gates.

The gates opened, and some trucks drove into the yard.

We were all given a hunk of bread and a little packet of granulated sugar (I somehow managed to immediately spill mine on the ground), then we were put into the trucks and driven off.

We were let out on the bank of the river Ob, a short distance from the wharf. No more than five or six soldiers had come with us as an escort, and they kept to themselves more than usual, huddled together talking and paying little attention to us. The exiles acted like passengers waiting for a boat; huddling together in small groups, strolling along the shore, chatting and smoking. (We did not wander too far, though, as if restrained by some invisible barrier.)

Nina, Maya, and I stood a little apart from the rest.

I was furious with myself. God, what a fool I had been! I had really believed the interrogator when he said that this would be just a change of address. (I had actually nodded in agreement when he said that we couldn't all live in Moscow!) It certainly didn't look as though they intended to return our passports and student cards. No, the fox had certainly fallen into the trap this time!

---

* "There was something in here . . . " Tradition says these were Chenier's last words before he was guillotined in July 1794.

I won't say that I had a revelation on the banks of the Ob and could suddenly see everything clearly. That didn't happen. But I no longer found a satisfactory explanation for everything in the formula "That's the way it must be," which I had formerly taken on faith.

Did they really have to drag us through four prisons, and then drive us out of the town to which we had been exiled? What else was going to happen to us?

Suddenly a youth with his hands in his pockets stopped in front of me. For a while, we stared at each other in silence, he with an insolent smile, I in dazed incomprehension. He was short, dark, and muscular; his shirt was unbuttoned, and his cap sat at a rakish tilt. He had a scar across one cheek, a gold tooth, and tattoos across his arms and chest.

He spat a stream of saliva through his teeth, then began to speak: "So tell me, do you know the name of this river?"

"The Ob," I replied.

"Right. And you know which way it flows?"

"To the north."

"Right. It flows into the Arctic Ocean. It also passes through the vast expanses of the taiga. Do you know what they're going to do with us now?"

"No."

"I'll tell you. The same thing they did some time ago to the kulaks. Know what that was? We'll wait here until they load us onto a barge and float us down the river. Somewhere in the middle of the taiga, they'll dump us ashore, give us saws, axes, and spades, and say, 'Build yourselves a home, make a life for yourselves and be fruitful.' That's what. I'll mow the field, and you'll carry the whetstone. You know what a whetstone is?"

"No," I replied numbly.

"Don't know much, do you? It's what you use to sharpen the scythe. Never mind, you'll learn! Stick with me now."

I did not have time to become really frightened, because at that moment we were joined by a man in a black hat who was carrying a violin. He called the tattooed youth aside and said something to him. The youth vanished instantly.

The man with the violin came back.

"Nikolai Biletov's the name," he said. "You can call me Uncle Kolya."

"Are you a violinist?" I asked him.

"I am an artist," he said. "I just play the violin for pleasure. Before I was sent here, I asked my wife to send it to me. I'm a repeater;—they arrested me in Kalinin. Where are you girls from?"

Nikolai was thirty-seven years old and had been in and out of camps and prisons since he was a teenager. A jack-of-all-trades, vigorous and enterprising, he could instantly find his bearings in any situation and could stand up for himself and others. He was also a gentle and benevolent man who helped me greatly in my first year in exile.

I was naturally very grateful to Nikolai for extricating me from the prospect of having to carry the whetstone. I confessed with a bitter laugh that up to that moment my main concern had been which course to enroll in at the Novosibirsk Teacher-Training Institute.

"Will we really be dumped in the middle of the taiga, like that character said?" I asked him.

"We'll see," Nikolai replied vaguely. "The main thing is not to lose heart. Do you know what was inscribed on King Solomon's ring?" He answered himself, pronouncing the words clearly and solemnly (later he often repeated them when trying to cheer us in difficult moments): "'This too will pass . . .'"

Meanwhile the boat had moored at the wharf. The passengers embarked first, and then they put us on.

We sailed off down the river. As I stared at the billowing water beyond the stern, I remembered the net stretched across the stairwell in prison to prevent us from jumping, and I thought, "This is true freedom—being able to dive headfirst into the water!"

Nikolai went down to the buffet and got us a bag of sweets to console us. With him was a modest, quiet young man whose name was Pasha. Unlike everyone else, he was lightly clad in just a shirt and no jacket; perhaps his clothes had been stolen in prison.

For some reason I have absolutely no memory of the wharf where we disembarked, neither what it looked like nor what it was called; I remember only that it was on the left bank. (Checking the map now, I see that it must have been Kolyvan.) We walked the short distance to our first stopping place (they promised to send trucks for us in the morning) in a forest clearing, where we spent the night under the open sky, glad that it was not raining. Pasha, Nina, Maya, Nikolai, and I slept side by side on the grass, with two overcoats spread out beneath the five of us and two on top. Even so, the summer night proved teeth-chatteringly cold.

In the morning Baba Stepanida came up to Nikolai. (We had not talked to the nuns since our trip on the prison train; we had been in separate cells in Novosibirsk Prison, and had only nodded to each other from a distance at the wharf.) She held out to Nikolai a treat fit for a king—a large, hot potato baked in the coals of a bonfire that still glowed to one side—and said, "Now, you be nice to our Zaika, Nikolai Leonidovich."

I gratefully embraced the old woman, and Nikolai, who also seemed touched, swore that his intentions were entirely honorable.

Soon the trucks arrived. They loaded us on and we drove off.

The potholed road wound over the flat treeless plain. Only here and there could be seen isolated clumps of stunted birches, with marshy tussocks between their trunks. This was the beginning of the Vasyugan marshes, someone knowledgeable said.

"Exile, ha!" I picked up a conversation between two old men who looked like peasants. "Exile's nothing like the camps. Where did you do time?"

"North of Kotlas."

"I was in Kolyma." He sighed. "Exile, ha!"

"You just wait. They'll send you to some collective farm, make you work like a slave, and you'll starve to death. You got fed in the camps."

"No, I reckon there's nothing worse than the camps." He sighed. "We'll keep ourselves fed somehow."

Gradually, others were drawn into the conversation. All agreed that no matter how hard exile proved, it could not be worse than the camps. They began to recall various events from life in the camps. An old man who had served his sentence in the North told us how they sometimes dealt with prisoners there who "broke the rules": they were stripped naked, tied to a tree out in the taiga, and left overnight to be bitten and chewed to death by the midges and mosquitoes.

I could not believe it: "In our camps? That can't be true!"

The old man glanced my way, gave a wry grin, and did not answer.

I realized that he was telling the truth. It was incredible, but that was what happened.

Translation by Cathy Porter and John Crowfoot

AFTERWORD ━━━━━━━━━━

The women in this book were, in some sense, fortunate. Unlike several million others, they survived exile and the camps. And on their release in the mid-1950s, the Soviet authorities formally withdrew all charges against them (with the understandable exception of Bertha Babina). Many others would have to wait until Gorbachev's perestroika, if they lived that long, for such confirmation of their innocence.

Official certificates of rehabilitation did not entitle former prisoners to publicly discuss their experience, however, or to pursue justice and the punishment of their tormentors. After 1964 there was a perceptible drift backward, toward the rehabilitation of Stalin himself. For thirty years those who dared to write, distribute, or simply preserve writings on this forbidden subject risked prosecution under Article 70 of the Criminal Code. Repealed only in 1989, this article provided sentences of exile or up to seven years' imprisonment for the offense of "slandering the Soviet system."

For the epigraph to *The Drowned and the Saved* (1988), his last book, Primo Levi chose a passage from *The Ancient Mariner*:

> Since then, at an uncertain hour
> That agony returns,
> And till my ghastly tale is told
> This heart within me burns.

At the personal level, the compulsion to record a traumatic experience could not be more clearly expressed. Here, though, these words echo with a wider resonance. Stoicism and endurance are as evident as passionate determination in this volume; for these women the "uncertain hour" was immeasurably lengthened, and became something that, in the words of the book's epigraph, "to this day, continues to loom over our lives."

The authors offer various explanations for writing their memoirs. There is a strong sense of obligation to others. They must speak of, and for, the many that did not return. Often deprived of families themselves, they feel a compelling duty to pass on to others the unique and terrible knowledge that their generations possess: that "these things did happen"—and thus could happen again.

Yet in this case, the obstacles faced by those writing in the West about their experience of Nazi atrocities—a reluctance to speak out, personal reticence, public disbelief and indifference—were compounded by an officially enforced amnesia that for decades continued to deny and ignore the individual and collective trauma, suffered by millions. With little hope of ever living to see publication, it required stubborn persistence to record and preserve these testimonies.

The Nazi regime came to an abrupt and decisive end, when it was still at its most virulent. It was condemned as unequivocally evil and that judgment remains central to our view of the twentieth century. The older and longer-lived Soviet system seems relegated, once again, to the periphery of our concerns and perceptions. Perhaps, its influence is still too large to grasp: "The revolution of 1917 has defined the shape of the contemporary world, and we are only now emerging from its shadow" (Orlando Figes, *A People's Tragedy, Russia 1891–24*, 1997). The ideals proclaimed by the Soviet regime were shared not only by the women in this book. Their tale of disillusion and of trust betrayed is as good a place as any to start reconsidering the century's lessons.

It is not easy to read such testimonies, though. Surely, many will add, there is now little new that can be said on the subject. Yet this book is different.

Its strength lies partly in its cumulative effect. What is, in a sense, the same story, is told many times over, but by women of such different character and outlook that each time some new facet, dimension, or understanding is added. Moreover, the message is not one of despair. The first in an intended series, this volume was devoted to women's memoirs because they offered a humanly approachable introduction to a horrific and alien world. The authors recount how, after the initial shock of imprisonment, mistreatment, and loss, concern for the family and friends they had left behind was extended, in compassion, to those who now surrounded them—an assertion of human values in the face of an impersonal system of numbing scale and barely credible inhumanity.

Till My Tale Is Told also alters perceptions of two other established and classic texts about the Soviet era. The book is directly related to their history, and itself adds a further sixteen distinctive voices to two that are already well known to Western ears.

Yevgeniya Ginzburg's *Into the Whirlwind* appeared in the West long ago, but she was also among the Kolyma fellowship who gathered in Bertha

Babina's flat (and a chapter from her memoirs was included in the Russian edition of this volume). Her friend Olga Sliozberg began her own memoir as far back as the 1940s, and it is a rather different kind of work, which rivals that of Ginzburg in its conviction and power of expression. "When I began to write my book in 1958," commented a former prisoner of the postwar generation, "I knew of no memoirs or works of literature dealing with the camps." During the decade that followed, Alexander Solzhenitsyn "gradually got to know the *Kolyma Tales* of Varlam Shalamov and the memoirs of Dmitry Vitkovsky, Yevgeniya Ginzburg and Olga Adamova-Sliozberg." His other two hundred witnesses in *Gulag Archipelago* remain anonymous. Several were among the authors included here.

When they eventually became acquainted with Solzhenitsyn's interpretation, some of the women felt that their experience had been misrepresented. The response of the Soviet authorities left no opportunity for discussion. Yevgenia Ginzburg's *Into the Whirlwind* was published abroad in 1967, in Russian and in an English translation. After several of Shalamov's *Kolyma Tales* appeared in émigré periodicals, however, the author was forced to publicly renounce his work: as "an honest Soviet citizen who fully appreciated the significance of the 20th Party Congress," Shalamov declared in February 1972 that "the issues raised by *Kolyma Tales* have long lost their relevance." Two years later Solzhenitsyn was expelled from the Soviet Union. Today, Russian and Western audiences can read those testimonies for themselves, and draw their own conclusions.

Still, for a generation and more, these testimonies, the memoirs of Yevgenia Ginzburg, Shalamov's *Tales*, and almost all of Solzhenitsyn's writings could not reach the most important audience: their contemporaries and fellow citizens in the Soviet Union. When, in 1989, the Russian edition of *Till My Tale Is Told* was finally published, it would sell one hundred thousand copies, but half of the authors were no longer alive.

In the intervening years the tragic events of the Soviet war against Nazi Germany were increasingly invoked, by society and the regime, as a unifying and healing source of common pride and memory. This was something all could agree on, it seemed, and which legitimated the Soviet system at home and abroad. The wartime heroism of men and women, united against a common enemy, and armed by their government, bears little immediate comparison to what is described here—an unrelenting and protracted campaign waged against unarmed, divided, and often demoralized individuals by a merciless and seemingly omnipotent regime. Nevertheless, an event in June 1996 made a moving link between the two experiences.

In that month, Ernst Neizvestny's monumental sculpture, *The Mask of Sorrow*, commemorating the dead of Kolyma, was unveiled in Magadan.

Among the few surviving former prisoners who traveled thousands of miles across Russia and Siberia to attend the opening were Simeon Vilensky and Paulina Myasnikova, one of Babina's Kolyma fellowship. At the ceremony the local authorities, slightly nonplussed as to how best to mark the occasion, solemnly presented Simeon and Paulina with commemorative medals: these had been minted in the United States from Kolyma silver, and issued a year earlier to all surviving veterans of the Great Patriotic War.

Note on the Text

This volume was abridged by Simeon Vilensky, with the help of Zayara Vesyolaya, from the 600-page Russian edition, *Dodnes' tyagoteyet*, volume 1: *Zapiski vashei sovremennitsy* [A Burden Borne to This Day, volume 1: Notes of Your Woman Contemporary] published in Moscow in 1989. While the overall structure and sequence of materials have been carefully maintained in the English edition, for reasons of space seven authors were not included: Yulia Sokolova, Mira Linkevich, Yevgeniya Ginzburg, Hella Frischer, Ada Federolf-Shkodina, Ariadne Efron, and Natalya Zaporozhets. English translations of several of these memoirs can be found in other publications. The memoirs by Linkevich, Frischer, and Efron appear in a French selection from *Dodnes' tyagoteyet* published as *L'aujourd'hui blessé* (Lagrasse: Verdier, 1997).

The texts included in the Russian edition were selected and edited by Simeon Vilensky, and the authors or their heirs gave him full authority to choose and prepare their words for publication. When compiling the book, he recalls, the contributors displayed an exemplary readiness to surrender parts of their texts so that more authors could be represented. The original manuscript and typescript memoirs from which Simeon Vilensky chose the present extracts can be found in the archive of the *Vozvrashchenie* organization in Moscow and in the International Institute for Social History in Amsterdam. The annotations, glossary, and list of important dates included here were prepared by John Crowfoot.

Much credit for the present edition is also due to Janet Rabinowitch at Indiana University Press, who, with great tact and patience, nursed this complex and demanding project from beginning to end.

JC

IMPORTANT DATES ━━━

1904–1905 The Russo-Japanese war, ending in defeat for Imperial Russia.

1905   The first Russian Revolution. Tsar Nicholas II agrees to a written constitution and a legislative assembly with limited powers.

1914   August. The First World War begins. Russia, in alliance with France and Britain, goes to war against Germany, Austria-Hungary, and Turkey. St. Petersburg is renamed Petrograd.

1917   The February Revolution. Abdication and arrest of the tsar. A "provisional government" is formed until a new democratically elected legislature can be established. Bolsheviks and other revolutionaries return from internal exile or from abroad, and support the rival power of the Petrograd Soviet.

The October Revolution. The Bolsheviks and their allies seize power and establish the Soviet regime.

In November, elections are held to the Constituent Assembly; Bolsheviks win a quarter of the votes.

1918   In January, the Constituent Assembly meets for the first and last time; it is dispersed by Bolshevik troops.

In March, the Bolsheviks sign a separate peace treaty with the Germans at Brest-Litovsk, giving them most of Ukraine.

In November, Germany agrees to an armistice; the First World War ends.

1918–1920 The Civil War (July 1918–November 1920), pitting the Bolsheviks and their allies against the White Armies, which receive some support from intervening American, British, French, and Japanese troops.

The Bolsheviks win the war, at a cost of seven million lives.

1921–22   The Bolsheviks ban all other political parties.

The first permanent Soviet concentration camp is established, on the Solovetsky archipelago in the White Sea; famine in the Volga region.

1922   The first Soviet show trial of Right Socialist Revolutionaries.

1924   Lenin, having been ill for several years, dies. Petrograd (St. Petersburg) is renamed Leningrad.

1929   Stalin defeats his rivals within the Communist Party; forced industrialization of the first Five-Year Plan (1928–32); the remaining private enterprises are nationalized.

In autumn, collectivization of agriculture begins.

1932–33   Widespread famine and hunger, as a result of collectivization; it is particularly severe in Ukraine and the Kuban, where several million die.

1933   In March, the Nazis win 44 percent in the German elections; Hitler comes to power, and begins to set up his own concentration camps.

In May, the White Sea Canal is completed; writers, led by Gorky, praise this use of the forced labor of 100,000 political and criminal prisoners.

1934   In December, the Party boss in Leningrad, Sergei Kirov, is shot.

1936–39   The new Soviet elite itself becomes the victim of arbitrary arrests, trials, and execution, and major figures in the Party leadership and Red Army command are tried and shot.

By 1939, the prison and camp population numbers at least 2 million; there is high mortality, and wave after wave of arrests supply new labor to the lumber industry, mines, and construction projects.

The first major Nazi atrocity: 70,000 mentally handicapped Germans are killed in a euthanasia program.

1939   In August, Nazi Germany and the Soviet Union sign a non-aggression pact. Under its terms, Soviet troops occupy half of Poland (western Ukraine and Belorussia) and part of Rumania (1939), and Latvia, Lithuania, and Estonia (1940).

On 1 September, the German invasion of Poland marks the beginning of the Second World War.

1941   On 22 June, Hitler attacks the Soviet Union; the beginning of the Great Patriotic War.

First on Soviet territory, then in special extermination camps, chiefly in Poland, Nazis begin the systematic mass murder of all Jewish inhabitants of occupied Europe.

1945   The Soviet Union, in alliance with Britain and the United States, defeats Nazi Germany. Many surviving Soviet prisoners of war in Germany are sent to labor camps.

1946   The Nuremberg Trial of the Nazi leadership.

1947   The beginning of the Cold War.

1949   China becomes Communist.

1952   The Doctors' Plot: As part of a new cycle of repression, plans (announced publicly in January 1953) are made to bring a group of largely Jewish doctors to trial.

1953   In March, Stalin dies.

In May–August, prisoners in the Norilsk special camp refuse to obey the camp administration.

In July, there is mass disobedience in the Vorkuta camps.

1954   Mass acts of disobedience by prisoners in Kengir (Central Asia), where tanks are used to suppress their protests.

1956   In February, speaking before the 20th Party Congress, Nikita Khrushchev denounces Stalin's crimes (but the text of his speech is not published in Russia until 1988).

In October–November, the Hungarian uprising is crushed by Soviet troops.

1964   Khrushchev's brief and ambivalent "Thaw" ends; rehabilitations cease.

1986   Communist authorities led by Mikhail Gorbachev introduce *glasnost*, a novel but still limited freedom of expression.

1990   Other political parties are permitted to exist; censorship is formally abolished.

1991   In August, there is a coup attempt by diehards; a temporary ban is imposed on the Communist Party.

        In December, the USSR is replaced by the Commonwealth of Independent States.

GLOSSARY ━━━━━━━━━━━━━━━━━━

Article 58. The section of the 1926 Soviet Criminal Code that dealt with "counterrevolutionary" crimes, conferring political status on a prisoner.

Bolshevik. Before the October Revolution, the faction in the Russian Social Democratic (Marxist) Party led by Lenin; after October 1917, the ruling Communist party of the Soviet Union. *See* Party.

Butyrki. Largest prison in Moscow.

Cheka. The Soviet secret police or security service (an acronym for Extraordinary Commission). From its creation in December 1917, it grew steadily in size and influence, taking over the functions of the courts, prisons, and regular police, and building a vast empire of forced-labor industries. It underwent six changes of name:

> Cheka, 1918–22
> GPU, 1923–24
> OGPU, 1924–34
> NKVD, 1934–45
> MGB, 1945–54
> KGB, 1954–91

Except for the first three years of its existence, its headquarters were located at Lubyanka Square in central Moscow.

collectivization. The violent campaign that forced millions of individual peasant farmers to join the collective farms or kolkhozy in 1929–33.

Commissar. Title given to officials under the Bolshevik regime, including (until 1945) government ministers who headed People's Commissariats.

Decembrists. A conspiratorial group of Guards officers and their sympathizers who attempted a coup in December 1825, following the death of Alexander I, to force reforms.

dekulakization. *See* kulak.

GPU. State Political Administration, the title of the security service in 1923–24. *See* Cheka.

Gulag. Main Administration for Corrective-Labor Camps.

gymnasium. A pre-revolutionary classical secondary school, on the German model, providing excellent education.

Komsomol. The All-Union Leninist League of Young Communists. An organization for those in the 14–28 age group, primarily students. Younger schoolchildren belonged to scout-like organizations such as the Octobrists and Young Pioneers.

kulak. "Rich" peasants who were "dekulakized" during collectivization, i.e., dispossessed and sent, with their families or without, to camps or into exile. In practice, the term was vague, and those so punished were usually the most efficient and energetic agricultural producers.

Lefortovo. A prison in Moscow.

Left SR. *See* Socialist Revolutionaries.

Lubyanka. Headquarters of the Soviet secret police (and today's Russian security service) in central Moscow. In tsarist times the building housed an insurance company. It was taken over by the Cheka in December 1920.

May Day. International Labor Day, 1 May. A major Soviet holiday, together with October Revolution Day (7 November), International Women's Day (8 March), Lenin's Birthday (22 April), and others.

Menshevik. Before the October Revolution, the more moderate faction of the Russian Social Democratic (Marxist) Party; banned in 1921 by the Bolsheviks.

MGB. Ministry of State Security, post-war title of the security service, 1945–54. *See* Cheka.

NKVD. People's Commissariat of Internal Affairs, title of the secret police, 1934–45. *See* Cheka.

OGPU. United Main Political Administration, title of the secret police, 1924–34. *See* Cheka.

Party. The Communist Party; from 1921 to 1990 it was the only permitted political party in the Soviet Union.

passport. Internal identity document, restored in December 1932, without which an individual could not legally settle in a new area or travel freely.

People's Commissar. *See* Commissar.

Pravda. The daily paper of the Soviet Communist Party.

procurator. Official who combined the functions of a public prosecutor with legal supervision of all other bodies.

Red Army. Established in January 1918, led by Trotsky, and transformed with the help of former tsarist military officers into an effective fighting force.

rehabilitation. A process of largely administrative importance, given the weakness of the legal system, that enabled released prisoners to resume their former work and place of residence.

Socialist Revolutionaries. A non-Marxist socialist party, founded in 1902, that continued the tradition of the 19th-century Russian populists (or Narodniks). The party won the largest number of seats in the 1918 Constituent Assembly but was divided between Right and Left factions.

soviet. Literally "council." The term denoted the new revolutionary form of elective political organization that was to become the institution of state power and local government in the Soviet Union. In 1917 and following the Bolshevik Revolution, other left-wing parties protested Bolshevik manipulation of the Soviets. The Supreme Soviet, formally the highest authority in the land, was in practice little more than a rubber-stamp assembly.

Special Board. Extra-judicial body that passed sentence in the majority of political cases. *See* troika.

SR. *See* Socialist Revolutionaries.

Stakhanovites. "Shock-workers" who exceeded their plan targets in output; named after a miner, Alexei Stakhanov.

Supreme Soviet. *See* soviet.

Taganka. A prison in Moscow.

troika. Extra-judicial body, Cf. Special Board, that passed sentence in the majority of political cases until 1934.

Trotskyist, or Trotskyite. Literally, a follower or supporter of Lev Trotsky, Civil War leader of the Red Army and, in the 1920s, Stalin's first major opponent within the Bolshevik Party. In practice, "Trotskyist" became a severe term of abuse; often, those so named and condemned had no connection with Trotsky, his supporters, or his views.

White Army. Armed forces, led mainly by former tsarist generals, that fought against the Red Army of the Bolsheviks and their sympathizers in the Civil War. In political terms, the White Army represented all shades, from nationalists and monarchists to democrats.

Young Pioneer. *See* Komsomol.

USSR (1945 Boundaries)

INDEX

Adamov, Nikolai Vasilievich, 65–66, 78–79, 83–84

Adamova-Sliozberg, Olga: on Altunin, 60–61; arrested, 4–7; arrested as second-timer, 70–74; at Butyrki Prison, 16–25; at Galya Prison, 51–65; at Kazan Prison, 34–38; at Kolyma Prison, 48–51; at Lubyanka Prison, 7–15; at Suzdal Prison, 42–44; on Basya, 54–55; decision to survive by, 38; exile in Kazakhstan, 78–79; goes home to family, 67–71; influence of memoirs by, 337; journey to Karaganda, 74–78; on Lena Vladimirova, 90–92; life reflections by, 1–2; marries Nikolai Adamov, 65–66; rehabilitated by Decree/then denied, 56–57; rehabilitation and release of, 83–86; released from prison, 64–65; sent to Solovki Prison, 28–34; on tragedy suffered by nanny, 2–4; travels from Suzdal to Kolyma, 44–48; trial and sentencing of, 25–28. *See also* prisoner memoirs

Akhmatova, Anna, 158

Akulina (operetta), 237

Akutina, Tatyana Pavlovna, 164–65

Alexandrovna, Maria, 306, 308

Alexeeva, Shura, 34

Alliluyeva, Nadezhda, 13–14, 279

"Along the Valleys and Hillsides" (song), 135

Altovsky, Arkady, 107–108

Altunin (Olga Adamova-Sliozberg memoir), 60–61

The Ancient Mariner, 335

Andreev, Pyotr, 194

Anikst, Alexander, 142

Anya (Olga Adamova-Sliozberg memoir), 17, 23–24

Article 7 (measures in public interest), 302

"Article 7:35" (socially dangerous elements), 302, 305

Article 35 (specifying public interest measures), 302

Article 58:8 (terrorism), 25, 64

Article 58:10 (subversion), 128, 302

Article 58:12 (failure to denounce), 64

Article 70 (Criminal Code), 335

Artyomova, Nurse, 183, 186

Ashkenazy, Sonya, 25, 30

Askhab (Olga Adamova-Sliozberg memoir), 46

Averkieva, Nina, 107–108

Babin, Boris, 97, 98, 99–100, 103, 106

Babin, Igor, 97, 100, 108

Babina-Nevskaya, Bertha: Kolyma fellowship of, 98, 336–37, 338; life of, 97–98; photograph of, 96; stay in Butyrki Prison, 104–109; transferred to Butyrki, 99–103. *See also* prisoner memoirs

Balta, Almaza, 237

Bandera, Stepan, 209

Barkova, Anna: life of, 213–14; photograph of, 212; selected poems of, 215–18. *See also* prisoner memoirs

Basya (Olga Adamova-Sliozberg memoir), 54–55

Bauer, Natasha, 105

Belostotsky, Boris, 175

Beria, Lavrenty, 129, 283

Biletov, Nikolai (Uncle Kolya), 331–32

Bird Island, 56, 57

Black Crow (prison van), 16, 26, 99, 119, 129, 320

The Bluebird (play), 151

Bogdanov, Vanechka, 236

CONTRIBUTORS
AND TRANSLATORS ━━━━

SIMEON VILENSKY was arrested as a student in 1948 and sent to Kolyma. On his return he worked as a journalist and writer. He is founder of *Vozvrashchenie*, an organization in Moscow dedicated to preserving and publishing testimonies of Gulag inmates and aiding camp survivors. In 1997 he was made a member of the Presidential Commission for the Victims of Political Repression, headed by Alexander Yakovlev.

ZAYARA VESYOLAYA was arrested in 1949 while studying at a Moscow teacher-training college and sentenced to five years in exile. Released soon after Stalin's death in 1953, she worked as an editor, publishing several books for children and young adults. A member of the Russian Writers' Union, since 1990 she has been editor of the Poet-Prisoners of the Gulag series.

JOHN CROWFOOT is a freelance translator and has lived and worked in Moscow since 1986. From 1992 to 1998 he was coordinator of the Booker Russian Novel Prize. He is translator of *Arrested Voices: Resurrecting the Disappeared Writers of the Soviet Regime* by Vitaly Shentalinsky and *True Stories* by Lev Razgon.

MARJORIE FARQUHARSON, as the representative of Amnesty International in 1991, was the first foreigner to work on human rights in the USSR. She now lives and works in Strasbourg and travels extensively in the Russian Federation.

CATRIONA KELLY is Reader in Russian, University of Oxford, and Fellow of New College. She is author of *A History of Russian Women's Writing, 1820–1992* and *Petrushka: The Russian Carnival Puppet Theatre*; editor of *An Anthology of Russian Women's Writing, 1777–1992*; and coeditor (with David Shepherd) of *Constructing Russian Culture in the Age of Revolution, 1881–1940*.

SALLY LAIRD is a freelance writer, critic, and translator who teaches at the European Film College in Denmark. She was formerly Director of the Central and East European Publishing Project and editor of *Index on Censorship*. Her translations include two works by Ludmila Petrushevskaya, *Immortal Love* and *The Time—Night*.

CATHY PORTER is a translator and literary scholar who lives in London. She is author of *Alexandra Kollontai: A Biography* and translator of *The Diaries of Sophia Tolstoy, The Ship of Widows* by I. Grekova, and *Witch's Tears and Other Stories* by Nina Sadur.